IRISH ARCHAEOLOGY ILLUSTRATED

IRISH ARCHAEOLOGY
ILLUSTRATED

EDITED BY
MICHAEL RYAN

COUNTRY HOUSE
DUBLIN

First published in hardback in 1991 by
Town House and Country House
42 Morehampton Road
Donnybrook
Dublin 4

Paperback edition, 1994

©Country House and the contributors, 1994

British Library Cataloging in Publication Data available

Cover photograph
Funerary pottery of the Earlier Bronze Age in Ireland
(National Museum of Ireland)

Opening photograph, (page 10)
Entrance stone of Newgrange passage tomb, County Meath,
c. 3200 BC

ACKNOWLEDGEMENTS
The publishers and the editor Michael Ryan would like to thank the following for their help during the
preparation of this book: The Director of the National Museum of Ireland, the Director of the Ulster Museum,
the Trustees of the British Museum, the Trustees of the British Library, the Board of Trinity College Dublin, the
President and Council of the Royal Irish Academy, the Office of Public Works, Dublin, and the Ordnance
Survey Office, Dublin.
     Photographs were specially taken for the book by Valerie Dowling. For enormous help in acquiring
photographs we are grateful to Liam Blake, to John Teahan of the National Museum of Ireland, John Scarry and
Con Brogan of the Office of Public Works, and Richard Warner and Sinéad MacCartan of the Ulster Museum.
Thanks also to Clare Foley of the DOENI, Barry Hartwell of Queen's University Belfast, Noel Delaney, Paul
Mullarkey and Judith MacCarthy of the National Museum of Ireland, and Rosemary Evans of the Northern
Ireland Tourist Board. And we thank most sincerely all those contributors who provided their own photographs.
     To Angela Clarke, Desmond Hourihane, Ursula Mattenberger, Sive Modell, Eileen Johnson and Aidan
O'Sullivan for drawings. Our thanks to Gina Johnson and Eithne Boland for picture research, and to Siobhán Ní
Laoire for reading the text at an early stage.
     Lastly we thank the contributors themselves, for their scholarship and for their loyalty to the long-awaited
publication, in particular Raghnall Ó Floinn who read the entire text.

ISBN: 0-946172-33-1

Book editor: Dr Michael Ryan
Managing editor: Treasa Coady
Text editor: Elaine Campion
Design: Ger Garland
Picture research: Gina Johnson and Eithne Boland
Typesetting: Printset & Design Ltd, Dublin
Origination: Kulor Centre, Dublin
Printed in Great Britain by
Butler & Tanner Ltd, Frome and London

CONTENTS

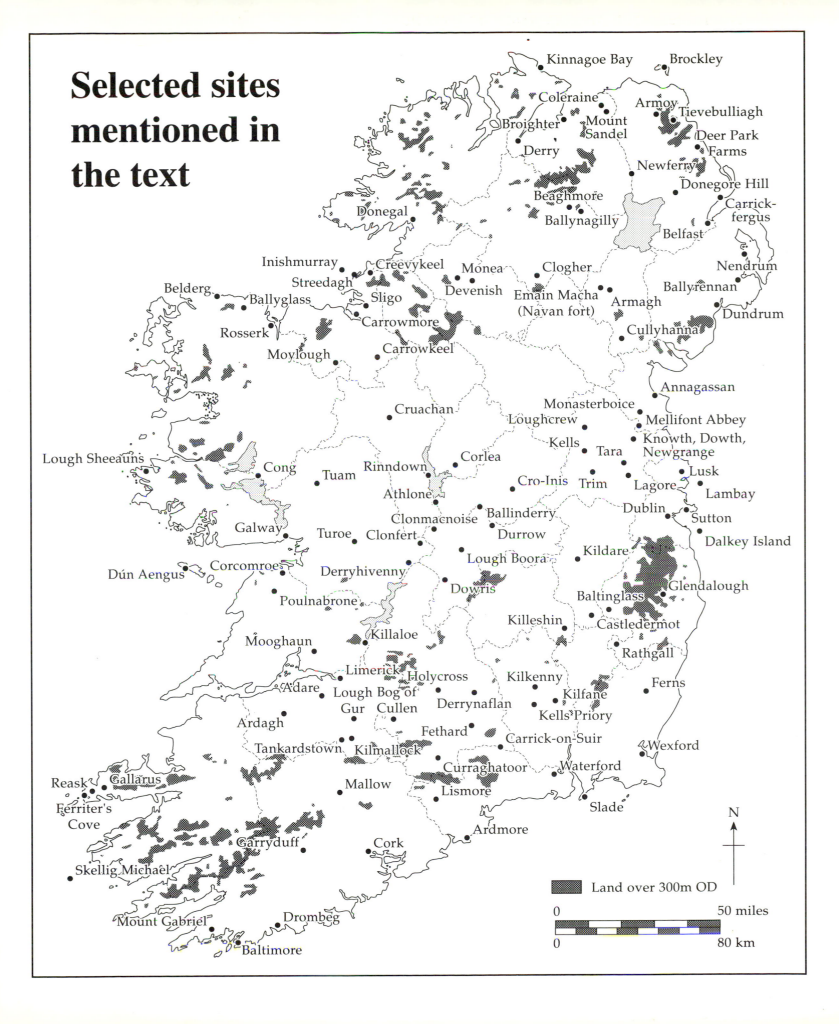

Selected sites mentioned in the text

Kinnagoe Bay
Brockley
Coleraine
Armoy
Tievebulliagh
Broighter
Mount Sandel
Deer Park Farms
Derry
Newferry
Donegore Hill
Beaghmore
Carrick-fergus
Donegal
Ballynagilly
Belfast
Inishmurray
Creevykeel
Monea
Clogher
Nendrum
Streedagh
Devenish
Ballyrennan
Belderg
Sligo
Emain Macha (Navan fort)
Armagh
Ballyglass
Carrowmore
Dundrum
Rosserk
Cullyhanna
Moylough
Carrowkeel
Annagassan
Cruachan
Monasterboice
Loughcrew
Mellifont Abbey
Kells
Knowth, Dowth, Newgrange
Lough Sheeauns
Tara
Lusk
Cong
Rinndown
Corlea
Cro-Inis
Trim
Lagore
Lambay
Tuam
Athlone
Dublin
Sutton
Galway
Clonmacnoise
Ballinderry
Dalkey Island
Turoe
Clonfert
Durrow
Corcomroes
Derryhivenny
Lough Boora
Kildare
Dún Aengus
Dowris
Glendalough
Poulnabrone
Baltinglass
Mooghaun
Killaloe
Killeshin
Castledermot
Rathgall
Limerick
Holycross
Kilkenny
Ferns
Adare
Lough Bog of Gur
Cullen
Derrynaflan
Kilfane
Ardagh
Fethard
Kells Priory
Tankardstown
Kilmallock
Carrick-on-Suir
Wexford
Reask
Gallarus
Curraghatoor
Waterford
Ferriter's Cove
Mallow
Lismore
Slade
Ardmore
Garryduff
Cork
Skellig Michael
N
Mount Gabriel
Drombeg
Baltimore

Land over 300m OD

0   50 miles
0   80 km

NOTES ON THE AUTHORS

ANDERSON, Elizabeth
is based in the Department of Archaeology, University College Cork. Her doctoral research is concerned primarily with Irish Mesolithic flint technology.

BAILLIE, Dr Michael
is Associate Professor in the School of Geosciences at Queen's University, Belfast. His current research interests are in chronological refinement and environmental reconstruction using tree-rings. A particular interest relates to the catastrophic effects of large volcanic dust-veil events on human populations in the past.

BARRY, Dr Terry
is Head of the Department of Medieval History at Trinity College Dublin and a member of the Council of the Society of Antiquaries of London. He is author of *The Archaeology of Medieval Ireland*.

BRADLEY, Dr John, MA
is a lecturer in the Department of Archaeology, University College Dublin. His research interest is Medieval Ireland, particularly its towns.

BRINDLEY, Anna
worked as an archaeologist with the Office of Public Works. She is now working in Holland. Her special interest is Neolithic pottery.

CAHILL, Mary
studied archaeology in University College Cork. She is an Assistant Keeper in the Irish Antiquities Division of the National Museum of Ireland. She has excavated a number of sites and specialises in the study of prehistoric Irish gold. Her book on Irish gold will be published shortly. She is co-author of the exhibition catalogue *Gold aus Irland 1981*.

CHERRY, Stella
studied archaeology in University College Cork, undertaking postgraduate research in Irish prehistory. She worked in the National Museum of Ireland from 1986 to 1992. In addition to Irish archaeology she has researched ethnographical material. In 1990 she prepared a major exhibition of the Museum's important Maori collection and compiled its first modern catalogue *Te Ao Maori*. Her guide to the collection of Sheela-na-Gigs was published in 1992. In that year she also became Curator of the Cork Public Museum.

DOODY, Martin, MA
is Senior Demonstrator in the Department of Archaeology, University College Cork, and Director of a Discovery Programme project. His main research interests are Bronze Age burials and settlements.

DUNLEVY, Mairead
was seconded from her position as Assistant Keeper in charge of glass, ceramics, textiles and postal history in the Art and Industrial Division of The National Museum of Ireland to become Director of the Hunt Museum, Limerick. She specialises in decorative arts of the period from the seventeenth century to modern times. Her publications include *A History of the Irish Post Office, Some Irish Fashions and Fabrics, Ceramics in Ireland, Penrose Glass* and *Dress in Ireland*.

EOGAN, George
is Professor of Archaeology at University College Dublin. His research work includes investigations into the problems of the Later Bronze Age and he has published several studies on aspects of this period. He is a member of the Royal Irish Academy and of many international bodies. He is well known for his large-scale excavations at the passage tomb of Knowth in County Meath.

FLANAGAN, Laurence
joined the Belfast Museum and Art Gallery (later the Ulster Museum) in 1955 as Assistant in the Antiquities Department, becoming Keeper of Antiquities from 1958 until his retirement in 1988. Among his books are *Ulster, Ireland's Armada Legacy* and *A Dictionary of Irish Archaeology*.

GOWEN, Margaret
graduated from University College Cork in 1979 with an MA in Archaeology. Since then she has worked mainly on pre-development archaeological excavations.

GROGAN, Eoin
is a freelance archaeologist specialising in prehistoric settlement patterns and social systems. He completed his MA and PhD at University College Dublin where he is a part-time lecturer. He is Director of a Discovery Programme project.

HURLEY, Maurice
was Senior Archaeologist with Waterford Corporation from 1987 to 1991. He is now City Archaeologist for Cork Corporation.

JACKSON, John
was Keeper of the Natural History Division of the National Museum of Ireland from 1957 to 1968. He lectured in geology in University College Dublin and Trinity College Dublin. He retired from geological consultancy work in 1989. He is the author of numerous articles on prehistoric mining. He died in 1991.

JOHNSON, David Newman, B Arch, MA, BA, Dip TPI
was Inspector of National Monuments for Ireland for the past twenty years. He is currently a consultant with Heritage International Ireland. He is the author of two books on Irish castles and is presently working on a major publication on Irish castles.

KELLY, Eamonn P
studied archaeology in University College Dublin and undertook a number of important excavations before joining the National Museum of Ireland. His research interests include the Later Bronze Age and Iron Age transition. His recent papers include a publication on the Lough Kinale book-shrine and he is the author of *Early Celtic Art in Ireland*. He is active in underwater archaeology and in the campaign to protect the heritage of portable archaeological material, mounted by the Museum's Antiquities Division, of which he is Acting Keeper.

LACEY, Brian
was educated at University College Dublin, where he studied Celtic archaeology and Early Irish history. He directed a series of rescue excavations in Derry in the 1970s and the Donegal archaeological survey in 1980-1. His publications include *Historic Derry* (1988), *The Siege of Derry* (1989) and *Siege City: the Story of Derry and Londonderry* (1990). He currently heads Derry City Council's Museum Service.

LYNCH, Dr Ann
is Senior Archaeologist with the National Monuments Branch of the Office of Public Works. She is currently Programme Manager for the Discovery Programme.

LYNN, Chris, B Sc, PhD
is Senior Inspector in Environment Service, Historic Monuments and Buildings, DOE(NI). His research interests are Iron Age and Early Medieval settlements, as well as timber buildings of all periods.

MEEHAN, Bernard, MA, PhD
studied at Edinburgh University. He is Keeper of Manuscripts at Trinity College Dublin.

Ó CRÓINÍN, Dáibhí
is a lecturer in history in University College Galway. He is best known for his pioneering research into the contexts of early Irish manuscript production, bringing together the evidence of history, art history, palaeography and archaeology.

Ó FLOINN, Raghnall
is Assistant Keeper in the Irish Antiquities Division of the National Museum of Ireland. His interests within Medieval archaeology are wide-ranging. He is the author of numerous papers and has excavated at a number of sites, including Clonmacnoise and Derrynaflan. He is the editor of the *Journal of Irish Archaeology*.

Ó NUALLAIN, Dr Seán
recently retired from his post as Senior Archaeologist at the Ordnance Survey, Phoenix Park, Dublin. He is a member of the Royal Irish Academy. He is co-author with the late Professor Ruadhrí de Valera of the *Survey of the Megalithic Tombs of Ireland* and author of many papers on prehistoric monuments. He is a past President of the Royal Society of Antiquaries of Ireland.

O'BRIEN, Dr William
is a graduate of University College Cork. He is Lecturer in Archaeology at University College Galway. His research interests include the study of early mining and metallurgy in Ireland and its wider Late Neolithic and Bronze Age background.

O'CONNELL, Dr Michael
is a lecturer in the Department of Botany, University College Galway. His main research interest is palaeoecology and, in particular, the reconstruction of prehistoric environments in the west of Ireland.

O'CONNOR, Nessa, MA
is an Assistant Keeper in the Irish Antiquities Division of the National Museum of Ireland. Her research interests are underwater archaeology and early metalworking techniques.

POWER, Denis
is a graduate of the Department of Archaeology, University College Cork. Since 1982 he has been Director of the Cork Archaeological Survey, which produced a Sites and Monuments Record (SMR) for the county in 1988 and in 1992 published the first four volumes of the regional inventory for the county.

RAFTERY, Dr Barry
is Associate Professor of Celtic Archaeology at University College Dublin. He was guest professor in Munich University from 1988 to 1990. He is a Fellow of the Alexander von Humboldt Foundation and a member of the Royal Irish Academy and the German Archaeological Institute.

SHERIDAN, Alison
graduated in 1979 with an honours degree in Archaeology and Anthropology. After completing her doctoral dissertation on production and exchange in Neolithic Ireland, she became a Junior Fellow of the Institute of Irish Studies at Queen's University, Belfast, where she worked on Irish Early Bronze Age pottery. She joined the National Museum of Scotland in 1987, as Assistant Keeper of the Archaeology Department.

STALLEY, Roger
is Professor of History of Art at Trinity College Dublin. His special interests lie in the field of Medieval architecture and sculpture.

SWAN, D Leo, MA, H Dip Ed
is an archaeologist with wide experience in research, excavation and field survey. He has pioneered the use of aerial photography in archaeology, and has lectured extensively both in Ireland and abroad.

SWEETMAN, David, MA, FSA, MRIA
was educated at University College Dublin and the University of Calgary, Canada. He is a member of Chateau Gaillard and Castles Studies Group, and specialises in Medieval archaeology and, in particular, Irish castles. He is currently head of the Archaeological Survey of Ireland.

WADDELL, Professor John
lectures on European prehistory in the Department of Archaeology, University College Galway. His research interests include Earlier Bronze Age burials. He has surveyed the ancient royal site of Rathcroghan and the archaeology of the Aran Islands. His publications include *The Bronze Age Burials of Ireland*.

WALLACE, Dr Patrick F
is Director of the National Museum of Ireland. He studied archaeology and history in University College Galway, where he also undertook postgraduate research. He excavated in Dublin from 1974 to 1981, when he was an Assistant Keeper in the Irish Antiquities Division of the Museum. He has devoted most of his research and publication efforts in recent years to the results of these excavations.

WARNER, Richard
heads the Department of Archaeology and Ethnography at the Ulster Museum. His interests include theoretical archaeology, the Irish Iron Age and Early Medieval periods, and the relationship between archaeological and historical evidence.

WOODMAN, Peter
is a specialist in the early prehistory of Ireland. He is Professor of Archaeology at University College Cork and was formerly on the staff of the Ulster Museum, Belfast.

I
Interpreting the evidence

*H*ow *old is it? What was it used for? When did the Celts come to Ireland? How did they build Newgrange or how did they balance the stone of the dolmen on its uprights? There are more questions than answers, and as an archaeologist I have always thought it would be useful to have a single book such as this to which questioners could go, if not always to find answers, at least to learn what the current best guesses are about the past. Because archaeological knowledge is growing at a faster rate than most of us can keep pace with, such a book is best served by a team effort. That is why there are contributions from thirty-seven authors, all of whom are active in fieldwork and research in Irish archaeology. The topics and pictorial surveys provide a succinct overview of archaeology in Ireland today.*

The nature of archaeology

Michael Ryan

Archaeology is the study of the past through the systematic examination of material remains left by human activity. Most people identify archaeology with excavation, the careful dissection of a site and the recording in detail of the soils, structures, artifacts and environmental evidence. Everything is grist to the excavator's mill: traces of structures; man-made objects (artifacts) of all kinds, complete or fragmentary; food wastes (animal bones, fruit seeds, nutshells); craft or industrial refuse (debris of stone, tool-making materials, slags, ores); environmental evidence (fossil plant, insect or animal remains), and of course human remains from burials. To interpret much of this the archaeologist needs the help of experts from the natural sciences, such as anatomists, engineers, metallurgists, analytical chemists and others. To find sites or assess their potential, the archaeologist uses aerial photography and detailed field survey, or often just plain old-fashioned walking and looking. A range of techniques is used to assess the potential of sites and to plan excavation campaigns, such as soil analysis, or plotting the different electrical resistances of soils that have been disturbed, and even radar, which can be used to 'see' into the ground. If all goes well, then a picture can be built up of the life of the occupants of the site over a period of time.

The sequence of development at a site can be worked out by stratification. The principle is simple; as a general rule, if one thing is found at a lower level than another, then it was deposited at an earlier date. However, pits and foundation trenches can be dug from above, bringing earlier material to the surface or introducing later objects into earlier layers, so the archaeologist must learn to excavate carefully in order to identify later interference with lower deposits. The recording must be of a standard which would enable a later researcher to reassess completely the excavation and, if necessary, overturn the original excavator's interpretation. Because of such practices, Dr Chris Lynn has been able to show that

structures uncovered by excavation at Lagore Crannog in County Meath in the 1930s, were not the flimsy huts of the workmen who had built the artificial island, which was the original interpretation, but the earliest dwellings which had gradually subsided and been built upon. The late Professor Seán P O'Riordáin tested his own theory that raths or ring-forts were Bronze Age in origin, and eventually decided that evidence which he himself had brought to light at Cush, County Limerick, had not been interpreted correctly. Archaeology is not an exact science and so this often happens.

Excavation is not the only way in which archaeologists work; important results can be obtained by field survey of monuments without ever putting a spade into the ground. Field survey has assumed a new significance nowadays with the growing consciousness of the need to develop policies to protect our heritage — these cannot be prepared without knowing where sites are and in what numbers. Many archaeologists happily work on artifacts and rarely, if ever, excavate. The archaeologist will use statistical methods to describe and analyse objects, their find contexts and associations, and attempt to identify significant patterns. Laboratory analysis often produces interesting results. It is particularly useful in shedding light on how materials were used and in assessing the level of technology achieved. Attempts to trace the sources of raw materials by trying to match their unique chemical compositions with known sources have been only partly successful. Metal and stone in particular have been studied in this way. The examination of stone axes has led to the identification of the products of Neolithic axe-factories in Ireland and Britain and has shed light on the patterns of long-distance exchange in that remote period. The study of metal, however, has been less successful; scrap was collected in ancient times, and copper, silver and gold must have been extensively recycled, but in the process they were mixed with metal from different sources, so that clues to the origins of the raw material have been confused.

Studies attempting to arrange objects in sequences of technical or stylistic progression or regression (typology) were once very common. It was assumed that such schemes of development provided a real insight into the past. While we are more cautious nowadays, we need only look at the extent to which motor cars or domestic appliances have changed in the last twenty years to see that improvements in performance and changes in fashion have shaped the appearance of objects profoundly; this must also have happened in the remote past. Human inventiveness can be both a slow process, involving small modifications over a long period, or a swift leap of genius; it is never uniform and varies from place to place, making things difficult for the archaeologist. However, with caution and good supporting evidence, typological studies can still be valuable.

It is important to remember that classifications or period definitions given by archaeologists are simple, often crude methods of describing in a general way what we think might have happened in the past. Older textbooks are often very specific in their conclusions and dogmatic about theoretical events: for example, they might show in detail how Neolithic settlers progressed inland from landing sites by plotting their tombs; they might say exactly when the Celts 'came' to Ireland; they might give an 'accurate' date for a work of art of the Early Medieval period, and so on. We are less sure of ourselves nowadays and we know there are many questions that archaeology simply cannot answer. Our modern theories about the past are just that, theories and not facts.

The people who lived long ago were not aware that they would be part of an archaeologist's scheme. Neolithic farmers in Ireland around 2000 BC were completely unaware that they were being dragged kicking and screaming into the Earlier Bronze Age; the sculptor of a high cross probably had no knowledge of the detailed derivation of many of his patterns, and would most likely have regarded the art historian's complex argument about his work as quite mad. Imagine trying to explain the benefits of Scandinavian cultural contacts to a ninth-century Irish monk.

Some chapters of this book are written by archaeologists who are principally fieldworkers, and others by those who prefer to find their evidence in warm, dry conditions: neither has a monopoly on scientific virtue.

The public sets a high premium on 'discovery', but to the archaeologist it is the follow-up to the discovery that matters — how it is studied and interpreted, and above all, how it is published, so that it can be added to the general pool of knowledge. Discoveries of all kinds, through excavation, by accident through development work, in survey, at the desk or in the laboratory are constantly changing our perception of the past. For example, there has been a revolution in methods of dating in the past forty years — first radiocarbon dating, which is now undergoing a new revolution, and then dendrochronological or tree-ring dating — which has completely changed our perspective by making it clear that many processes in the past were much longer and older than had originally been thought, and things which we had believed contemporary were widely separated in time. The Neolithic period in Ireland was once thought to have lasted for some 500 to 700 years, from about 2500 BC to about 1800 BC. We now know that it began in Ireland about 4000 BC and lasted for at least two thousand years, a space of time as long as from the birth of Christ to our own day. We must now look at the sites and monuments identified with that period against the background of significant environmental change documented for us by palaeobotanists, that is, scientists who study fossil plant remains in order to reconstruct ancient environments. This lengthening of the timescale has shifted archaeologists away from attempting to identify short-term *events* and more towards dealing with the processes by which change came about. Some of the most common questions asked of archaeologists, such as when a Celtic language was first spoken in Ireland, cannot be answered because they demand knowledge of specific events, or assume that such an event — an invasion for example — is the only way in which certain changes could have occurred. Some questions deal with issues which go beyond archaeology — the Celts again, for example, because they have as much to do with linguistic history as with archaeology. A great many questions would have to be answered before we could begin to deal sensibly with the problem. What do we mean by Celts? Can a language be transferred to a new area without a massive transfer of population? If such a transfer did take place, how would we identify it in archaeology? Would a change of fashions in tools be enough, or in burial ritual, or in settlement patterns? Are there any other factors which could account for these changes?

Archaeologists must always work with the knowledge that most of their evidence is missing: sites have been destroyed in every generation, objects of perishable materials have decayed, metals have been recycled constantly. Only a fraction of the original body of evidence survives and this is itself biassed in many ways.

The wedge tomb of Labbacallee, County Cork. The sloping roof-line is characteristic of this class of tomb.

Much is dependent upon the chances of preservation and discovery. Some sites, such as Early Mesolithic habitations, are inherently difficult to find. Some groups, for example, are archaeologically invisible. Because it is easier to discover the substantial remains of prestige dwellings or important ritual monuments — churches or megalithic tombs for example — our evidence of most periods is likely to be heavily biassed towards the better-off members of society. But the poor must also have existed to prop up the lifestyle of the rich and successful. When documentary evidence shows that there was an extensive underclass, we cannot point to convincing archaeological traces of them. Very often the poor would have lived in flimsy dwellings and had few possessions, mostly of perishable materials, which would undoubtedly have disappeared. Yet we only have to reflect that the population of Ireland peaked in 1846 at about eight million. In the 1830s there were two million chronically poor: what archaeological traces of any substance could this huge number of people have left behind? The picturesque abandoned homesteads in the west of Ireland were the houses of the better-off. Perhaps traces of cultivation on marginal lands are attributable to them, but of their houses almost nothing is known.

In the twentieth century our archaeological heritage has come under a great deal of pressure: development projects have gobbled up large areas of farmland and encouraged wholesale quarrying to provide building materials; changes in agriculture have resulted in damage to visible sites and to underground ones reached by deep ploughing for the first time; environmental pollution threatens stone monuments and can have long-term effects on lake sites; peat-cutting removes vast quantities of environmental information annually, and where it is mechanised, it results in the destruction of artifacts and sites. People interested in the past also can pose a threat — the pressure of visitor numbers at sites in Britain and France has forced their closure. Some would argue that all sites should be developed and made accessible in some way to the tourist. Since there are about 150,000 visible sites in Ireland, this is clearly unrealistic and not economically viable. We need to preserve and present not only the best of our archaeological sites, but also those which are representative, so that we can conserve the balance in as near their pristine condition as possible. The sheer value of undeveloped sites is difficult to quantify. The site-based approach is itself misleading, as there are still ancient *landscapes* in parts of Ireland which deserve protection as a whole, for example, the Burren in County Clare, with its extraordinary concentration of megalithic tombs and stone forts; the farming landscapes covered by bog in County Mayo, or the ghosts of field systems and dwellings revealed by aerial photography in almost every county.

The development of archaeology in Ireland

The origins of archaeology in Ireland can be traced to two traditions: native historical scholarship and the curiosity of the people of the eighteenth-century enlightenment. More and more antiquities came to their attention as Ireland developed in the great economic expansion of the ascendancy. Both strands enjoyed a brilliant flowering in the early nineteenth century, when Irish scholars like John O'Donovan and Eugene O'Curry worked with George Petrie in the Placenames Section of the Ordnance Survey of Ireland. The scholarly leadership of the Royal Irish Academy was crucial too and the building up of its collection of antiquities fixed the importance of archaeology in the public mind as never before. Modern methods of study were pioneered by Sir William Wilde, whose catalogues of the Academy's collections brought Irish archaeology to international attention and raised many of the research issues which are still debated today. From 1861, the Academy had the privilege of administering the Crown's right to Treasure Trove (objects of gold and silver concealed with the intention of recovery, but not retrieved by the owner). Aided by a wave of discoveries not matched until the 1980s, an extraordinary collection was built up. This passed into the care of the National Museum in 1891. The Royal Society of Antiquaries of Ireland (founded in 1849 as the Kilkenny Archaeological Society) provided an important focus for archaeological and historical studies and pioneered work on the preservation of monuments *in situ*.

Two important developments occurred in the 1930s in what was then the Irish Free State: the passing of the National Monuments Act to protect both monuments and artifacts, and the beginnings of systematic funding of excavations by the government. In Northern Ireland, Queen's University, Belfast, led the way in excavation, while later the establishment of the Archaeological Survey marked the beginning of the systematic recording of all the monuments of the region. Nowadays, archaeology in Ireland is cared for mainly by the National Museum of Ireland and the Office of Public Works (OPW), both in Dublin, and by the Department of the Environment (DOENI) and the Ulster Museum in Belfast. In general, the OPW and the DOENI take responsibility for field monuments and maintain surveys, while the museums' primary duties are to care for portable artifacts, but in practice both engage in a broad range of operations. Archaeological activities are strictly controlled by law in both jurisdictions, and the state institutions operate the procedures. Archaeology requires a great deal of effort, and many professionals not actually employed in the state institutions contribute by working on advisory committees, in voluntary organisations and on excavations. But the picture is far from rosy. Although Ireland has admirable laws and good intentions, the responsibility of protecting our immense and astonishingly well-preserved heritage is out of all proportion to the scale of the overstretched resources. This can at times be heartbreaking, because the inheritance of the past is an asset which cannot be renewed.

A note about this book

We have chosen to survey the period from the earliest identified settlers down to the seventeenth century AD. The starting point is obvious, the end less so because archaeology does not stop at any particular date. Valuable insights can be learned about the past by studying the material remains of more recent times — industrial archaeologists, students of folklife and the decorative arts can all testify to this. This book brings us to the threshold of the modern world at a time when great and often painful changes were in train. On a less dramatic scale it was at a time when long-distance trade and organised manufactures were beginning to replace the products of the individual artisan and domestic craft. For some it was a time of dispossession. It is also the period when our sources for reconstructing life in Ireland become more plentiful and archaeology declines in relative importance: before the late seventeenth century documentation is often sparse; there is no Irish school of painting which shows life like the Dutch and Flemish schools; few ancient buildings still in use survive, and none with their original contents. Unlike other European countries there are huge gaps in our knowledge and it seems that archaeology alone can fill them. We have attempted to answer the questions which most people regularly ask us, but our ignorance is vast and some questions just cannot be answered now, and perhaps not ever. This book, like any other archaeological book, is simply an interim report on work in progress.

Dating the past

Michael Baillie

Up until the 1960s, the scheme of Irish archaeology was based entirely on relative and stratigraphical dating. For example, it was known that the first farmers, the Neolithic people, had arrived in Ireland before the Bronze Age. Neolithic material on some sites was found stratigraphically below material associated with the Bronze Age, and so had to be older. Neolithic implements could be recognised by comparison with implements from sites across Europe and the Near East. In the Near East, literate civilisations allowed dates for the transition from Stone Age to Bronze Age to be worked out. So, if the transition were at 3000 BC in the Near East then, allowing some time for the new technology to travel across Europe, we could expect that the Bronze Age had begun in Ireland around 2000 BC. There were also some 'fixed points' in the scheme. For example, it was known historically when Christianity arrived in Ireland. It was generally accepted in Europe that ironworking began in the mid first millennium BC, and hence probably arrived in Ireland a few hundred years before Christ.

This sort of logic, carefully applied over a century of study, had allowed quite a good scheme to be developed. Archaeologists could identify material objects from all the main periods — Stone Age, Bronze Age, Iron Age, Medieval — and could subdivide the material into 'early', 'middle' or 'late' within most periods.

However, there were several areas of difficulty. What happens if a site contains a hearth and some post-holes but no artifacts. It could belong to almost any period, and hence it enters a sort of chronological limbo! Some substantial enclosed sites with hearths and huts fell into this category, for example, Cullyhanna hunting lodge, County Armagh. There was also the problem that the first arrival of the Neolithic farmers was undated — the Neolithic period was estimated to have lasted anything from a few hundred to a few thousand years. The problem was even worse in relation to the earliest settlers of all — the Mesolithic hunter-gatherers. Some archaeologists argued that they belonged to a period before the Neolithic, while others believed they were contemporary — farmers who had reverted to hunting and gathering, at least seasonally.

New methods

New scientific dating methods began to make an impact in the 1960s. Two of these — radiocarbon dating and tree-ring dating or dendrochronology — have proved to be very important for our understanding of archaeological chronology in Ireland. The two methods are related because dendrochronology has been used to check and refine the radiocarbon method. Although dendrochronology is more accurate, it only applies in the main to oak timbers. Radiocarbon on the other hand can date any organic material, and so, although it is not as accurate, it is more widely used.

Radiocarbon dating

This dating method was developed in America by Willard Libby, and the logic behind it is extremely elegant. The lead in a pencil is composed of graphite, a pure form of carbon. That carbon is extremely old, having been mined from geological deposits, and is composed of the isotope carbon-12. The carbon in coal, lignite and oil is also carbon-12, so it is a very common and stable isotope. However, in living plants and animals, mixed with the common carbon-12 is a rare radioactive isotope called carbon-14. This radioactive isotope is formed in the upper atmosphere — by the cosmic radiation which constantly bombards the earth — and ends up in a more or less fixed amount in the atmosphere. Plants take up their carbon from the atmosphere while animals derive their carbon from eating plants or eating other animals whose carbon was ultimately derived from plants. So all living things have a fixed ratio of carbon-14 to carbon-12 in their tissues. Libby noted all these facts and deduced the following logic:

1. Living organisms have a fixed proportion of C_{14} to C_{12}.

2. When an organism dies it ceases to take up C_{14}, and the C_{14} present in its tissues begins to decay radioactively.

3. C_{14} decays radioactively at a known rate (half life 5730 years, that is, one half of any given amount of C_{14} will decay radioactively in 5730 years).

4. If an archaeologist digs up an ancient organic sample and a laboratory measures the remaining proportion of $C_{14} : C_{12}$, then, knowing the decay rate, it is possible to work out the time which has elapsed since the sample died.

Libby tested the method on samples of known age from both tree-rings and dated Egyptian tombs, and it worked. He also noted that the method was only useful for samples from the last 40 000 years. Samples older than 40 000 years have so little C_{14} remaining that it is difficult to measure. This also explains why coal, oil and graphite, which are extremely old, contain only C_{12} — all their C_{14} has long since decayed. However, the method is extremely important in Ireland, which has been occupied for much less than 40 000 years.

The impact of radiocarbon dating on Irish archaeology

By 1970, an overall scheme of dates became available for Irish prehistory. The beginning of the Bronze Age produced radiocarbon dates around 4000 BP (before present), very much in line with what had been expected. However, the Neolithic period proved to be longer than anticipated, with dates around 5100 BP for the beginning, and even a few tantalising suggestions that the very earliest agriculturalists might have been in Ireland some five hundred years earlier than that — though this suggestion is still very speculative. What was most surprising was the finding, at more than one site, that the Mesolithic period — previously one of the most ephemeral and argued about periods — began around 9000 BP, thus proving to be longer than either the Neolithic period or the Bronze Age. The dating of the Mesolithic period demonstrates perfectly the power of an independent scientific method like radiocarbon. A cultural period whose extent could only be guessed at is suddenly given real substance by the application of a handful of dates.

Radiocarbon dating quickly became widely used in relation to sites of all periods. For example, a timber from Cullyhanna hunting lodge was dated and immediately the site was assigned to the middle of the Bronze Age. Within a decade of the first serious application of the method, Irish archaeology was fitted with a radiocarbon chronology. At least some features or levels from most sites were radiocarbon dated to allow them to be slotted into the new chronological framework.

Calibration

Irish chronology cannot be separated from happenings in the rest of the archaeological world. During the 1960s it had become clear that there were problems with the radiocarbon method. Radiocarbon dates for samples from Egyptian tombs were consistently younger than the historical date of the tomb. It became clear that radiocarbon dates had to be checked against some standard, that is, they had to be calibrated. The first calibration curve or graph was produced in America, where the radiocarbon activity of wood samples from the bristlecone pine was measured — the bristlecone pine is an immensely long-lived tree which grows at high altitudes in the south-west United States. The results showed that in the prehistoric period radiocarbon dates were too young by hundreds of years. If the curve was applied to Irish dates, for example, it showed that the Neolithic period started shortly after 4000 BC, while the Bronze Age began around 2500 BC. These differences were significant, but they did not alter the order of events in Irish archaeology. In fact, Ireland could work quite happily on a radiocarbon chronology. Calibrated dates were only required if comparisons were

to be made with areas using a historical calendar.

However, the details of the calibration curve did cause international controversy for two reasons. First, there was the question of whether a calibration worked out in America could be used in this side of the world. Second, there were wiggles in the graph which made interpretation of the dates difficult. It was as a result of this controversy that it was decided, around 1970, to build an Irish tree-ring chronology and produce an independent calibration curve.

Dendrochronology

It turned out that Ireland was a near-ideal place to build a tree-ring chronology. Oak timbers were available for all periods — from modern trees, historic buildings, archaeological sites and bogs. Bog oaks formed a major

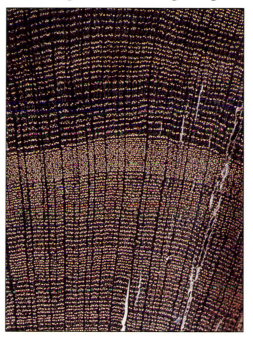

The narrow rings indicate two decades without summer growth, experienced by many bog oaks in Ireland between 1141 and 1159 BC.

natural resource, with specimens available back to beyond 5000 BC.

The chronology, which eventually extended from the present back to 5289 BC, was built in a series of sections. Modern timbers were linked to those from seventeenth and eighteenth-century buildings and back to join with timbers from Viking and Norman Dublin. That chronology covered the last millennium, and the only difficulty proved to be the fourteenth century. It appeared that the Black Death (a deadly bubonic plague, so called because of the black spots which appeared on the skin) and the resultant reduction in population gave rise to a regeneration phase for oak forests. A separate section of chronology, covering the first nine centuries AD, was constructed using timbers principally from crannogs and horizontal mills (the simplest mechanised watermill which uses a wheel in the horizontal plane and hence does not necessitate gearing). That chronology was eventually linked to the sequence of the Dublin timbers via sections from England, because it proved impossible to find Irish oaks which bridged the period from AD 750 to AD 1030. On the basis of the results so far available, there is a missing generation of oak trees from archaeological sites in Ireland. No oaks have been found which started growth between AD 750 and AD 830, while no oaks appear to have been used between AD 930 and AD 1030. Almost certainly some social factors relating to the availability and use of wood are responsible.

While the problems of linking together the AD chronologies were being tackled, a major programme was begun which was aimed at exploiting the large numbers of bog oaks which were becoming available from drainage and construction operations. These oaks originally grew on the surface of raised (valley) bogs. They were frequently blown down and buried by the peat, and have consequently been preserved in excellent condition. The approach was to build site sequences and eventually to link these together into one continuous chronology. This work proceeded smoothly during the 1970s, and by the early 1980s two chronology units were available, spanning the periods *c.* 200 BC to *c.* 950 BC and *c.* 950 BC to *c.* 5200 BC. Again it proved impossible to bridge the remaining 'gaps' in the chronology using Irish material alone. However, by 1982 all the essential links had been made using Roman wood and bog oaks from England. By 1984 the chronology back to 5289 BC had been agreed with workers in Germany. At that

Schematic representation of the principle behind the construction of a tree-ring chronology.

stage the Irish chronology was the second longest continuous tree-ring chronology in the world.

Irish high-precision calibration

The primary purpose of the Irish oak chronology was the production of a new calibration of the radiocarbon timescale. With the tree-ring chronology complete, it was possible to produce blocks of ten or twenty growth rings of known date. These samples were then submitted for measurement of their radiocarbon activity. The research necessary to improve the accuracy and precision of radiocarbon measurement in this new exercise was undertaken by Dr G W Pearson of Queen's University, Belfast. By painstakingly assessing every possible source of inaccuracy in the measurement of radiocarbon activity, he achieved, over a period of years, a system which would allow the production of radiocarbon dates with errors of only $+/-20$ years. The resulting high-precision calibration was then produced between 1975 and 1985 and superseded the original bristlecone-pine calibration. The Belfast calibration now forms the basis for an international standard calibration curve. All radiocarbon dates in the last seven millennia can now be converted to calendrical age ranges using the curve.

The impact of dendrochronology on Irish archaeology

Although the Belfast oak chronology was constructed primarily as a source of wood samples for radiocarbon calibration, it now forms a powerful dating method in its own right. Moreover, the extreme accuracy of the dates produced by the method constantly confronts archaeologists with the need to refine further their existing chronologies. The method appears to 'solve' archaeological 'problems' in a particularly effective manner. For example, horizontal mills had proved particularly difficult to date. The sites where these mills were found, though comparatively common, seldom produced any archaeological dating evidence. Dendrochronology allowed the direct dating of the constructional timbers from the sites and showed that the vast majority of excavated examples belong to the period between AD 630 and AD 930, with two-thirds of all examples being constructed between AD 750 and AD 850. It can be suggested that these mills no longer represent a problem for archaeologists — the 'problems' have now shifted into the realm of the historian.

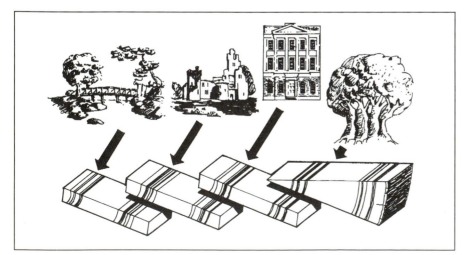

Perhaps the most profound advance has been the production of calendar dates for prehistoric sites. It appears that the act of dating many prehistoric sites — particularly bog trackways — actually makes the sites important. When the felling of the timbers used in the Corlea trackway in County Longford was specified as between 'the autumn of 148 BC and the spring of 147 BC', it suddenly became the 'only known second century BC site in Ireland'. As time goes on and more sites are dated, there is little doubt that the whole archaeological framework will have to be refined as radically as it was by the first widespread use of radiocarbon dating.

Chronology and its offshoots

Radiocarbon and dendrochronology are not the only scientific dating methods available to archaeologists. However, for Ireland they represent the most widely used chronological tools. They also have the advantage that both methods are now in control. The tree-ring chronologies, which provide direct dating of oak structures and which underpin the high-precision calibration, are highly replicated, not only internally but against equivalent oak chronologies from Germany. The calibration itself has been extensively duplicated by other independent high-precision laboratories. It is now a matter of applying both methods to the resolution of long-standing archaeological questions throughout Ireland.

A major bonus of the tree-ring method is based on the fact that dendrochronology 'works' because the trees are responding to some common signal. Some components of that signal must be climatic or environmental. It is now widely recognised that the annual records of tree-growth form a filtered record of past climatic or environmental conditions. As an extreme example of this, it was discovered that Irish bog oaks had been recording major volcanic eruptions in the northern hemisphere. The mechanism appears to be as follows. Major eruptions are responsible for dust-veils which cause cooling. That cooling causes disruption to the circulation patterns in the atmosphere, and one consequence is increased wetness in Ireland and Britain. Increased wetness would have raised the water-tables of the bogs on which the oaks originally grew — as a result the trees suffered stress and developed extremely narrow rings. We can now give exact dates for some of the most significant eruptions of the last 7000 years, and we can suggest that these events may have had important implications for marginal agricultural populations. Hopefully this new information will work through the archaeological system to improve our understanding of the prehistoric past.

The landscape of Ireland

Michael Ryan

Ireland is an island in the eastern North Atlantic. It is part of an archipelago which includes the neighbouring and larger island of Britain, and many smaller islands and islets. At its nearest approach, in the north-east, the two principal islands are very close, and so it is possible to look on Britain as a kind of bridge connecting Ireland with the large landmass of continental Europe. The two islands were physically linked at the end of the last Ice Age, and many of the species which today form the flora and fauna of Ireland migrated from Britain. The Atlantic position has also given Ireland direct access to mainland Europe, and this has often been of importance in prehistory and history.

The shape of Ireland is not — and never has been — static; the processes which we see at work today, erosion and flooding for example, were at work also in the past. In recent geological time, say within the last ten to twelve thousand years, there have been dramatic changes in the level of the sea in relation to the land, caused partly by the fact that huge amounts of water were released by the melting of the great ice-sheets of the last Ice Age, and partly by the removal of the great weight of the glaciers which allowed the land to rise slowly. The change was not a uniform process — there were times when the land was higher than it is today, relative to sea-level, and others when the sea inundated areas which nowadays are high-and-dry. But this is all very recent: the rocks and the skeleton of the landscape were formed over hundreds of millions of years by volcanic activity; by the slow deposition by wind and by water of the soils of now vanished continents on the beds of ancient seas; by dramatic convulsions which heaved these sediments up and folded the land into the mountain ranges we know today; and by slower processes that moved widely separated sections together as landmasses drifted. These ancient events were profoundly significant, resulting in the formation of our most important minerals and much of the basis of our drainage system. Although Ireland's geology presents an astonishing variety in such a small area, it is heavily masked by soils deposited by the glaciers of the great cold periods — the Ice Ages. These, too, affected human history by modifying drainage in certain places or by being inhospitable to early

The Giant's Causeway, County Antrim. (see p212)

agriculture, and in others — for example, the eskers of the midlands — by providing routes through areas later inundated by bog.

The most recent major cold period came to an end about ten thousand years ago. As temperatures gradually rose, plants and animals began to recolonise the land and, it seems, in about 7000 BC, humans also arrived on the scene. It is typical of our species to regard ourselves as the centre of our universe and to look on all that went before as culminating in our arrival. Yet even after the first humans began to settle in Ireland — many thousands and even hundreds of thousands of years later than elsewhere in Europe — the environment continued to change, forcing the people to change their behaviour. Nature had a few surprises to spring.

At a stage when we have reduced our natural biological environment on land to a few precious fragments, we ought to remember that for most of the time that humans have been on earth (and for about a third of the short span we have been in Ireland), we have fitted into niches in nature: we have been controlled to a large extent by the naturally occurring food supply, and have adapted our patterns of life to those of the world about us.

This is not to say that ancient people were somehow morally superior to their modern descendants. From the moment the first people began to make tools, they were attempting to improve the odds in the struggle for survival. In trying to cope with the world around them they were, however falteringly, taking the first steps towards controlling it. Humankind's capacity to modify the natural world has been limited mainly by the technology available. Today we are aware of the fragility of the environment, and its protection is now firmly on the political agenda, but our capacity to alter it unpredictably is now also immense.

Understanding the natural world — the flora, the fauna, the geological structure and the climate — is essential to trying to come to an appreciation of how human society developed and coped with the task of survival. The environment was changing as climate changed, as people modified their surroundings by clearing forests, draining wetlands, promoting soil degradation by wasteful agricultural practices. As the environment changed, so populations changed also, and new social arrangements were worked out — all adding complexity to our study of archaeology.

Rescue archaeology

Margaret Gowen

In the past, archaeological excavations were usually planned and carried out to confirm theories or to fill perceived gaps in the knowledge of the day. When accidental archaeological discoveries were made, they led to the detailed investigation of sites which might otherwise have remained unknown. This ordered and academic approach to archaeological excavation is generally described as research excavation and, where possible, it remains the preferred option.

Since the 1960s, destruction of archaeological sites has increased dramatically, and often in unresearched aspects of the study. The development of farmland, the extensive and mechanised working of bogs, arterial drainage schemes, the building of hydro-electric dams, the development of new forestry plantations, and urban renewal, have led to the discovery, survey and excavation of archaeological sites that would not necessarily have been investigated had these developments not taken place. In the more recent past, the pace of rural and especially urban development has accelerated, and archaeological sites are being threatened and destroyed on an unprecedented scale. As a result, archaeologists are increasingly engaged in what is known as 'rescue' excavation and survey, on sites or areas of archaeological potential threatened by development or discovered during the development process.

Sometimes excavation has to be conducted at great speed. In such instances the term 'salvage excavation' is probably more appropriate, as rescue excavations are generally carried out with the same care and attention to detail as applies in research. It is seldom necessary to salvage archaeological information under severe pressure of time, but occasionally, when a feature is discovered during the actual development process, this is the only course left to the archaeologist.

The increase in recording by survey and excavation prior to development has led to an explosion in the quantity of archaeological data available and artifacts recovered. Rescue excavation has had spectacular results in urban areas and has led to the discovery of numerous rural sites which might not otherwise have appeared in the archaeological record. However, there are drawbacks.

The element of choice in deciding on where and when to excavate is no longer based on purely archaeological considerations, and in a period of limited government funding for archaeology, research excavation often has to take second place.

The agents of destruction are many and varied. 1. In towns and cities redevelopment, in the form of office, shopping and housing complexes, is often carried out in areas which coincidentally form their historic centres. 2. In rural areas farmland is being opened up, reclaimed, drained and developed in an increasingly mechanised way. 3. Our large raised bogs have been massively exploited with highly specialised machinery over the past twenty years. 4. Quarrying for gravels and mineral extraction accounts for a large amount of land removal.

Fishamble Street, Dublin. (see p212)

(left) In November 1983, archaeologists had a brief opportunity to investigate seventeenth-century Belfast. (see p212)

5. Afforestation continues, and the pace of the plantation is increasing. 6. There are countless linear developments such as motorways, roads, and gas and water pipelines.

Excavation of a lintel-grave cemetery at Westereave, County Dublin, during the construction of the North Eastern Gas Pipeline, Phase 2. (see p212)

7. Some sites are threatened by the natural forces of erosion. 8. Many sites in state care require investigation in advance of conservation. 9. Finally, there is the regrettable pillaging of archaeological sites, both on land and under water, aided by the use of metal detectors.

Given the urgency of identifying and recording the surviving monuments in the country, apart from those already in state care, and the need to define historical urban areas of interest, Sites and Monuments Record (SMR) county surveys have been completed in many areas. These are sometimes regarded as rescue surveys because the emphasis is on recording extant monuments quickly, and the time and resources for detailed and expensive archaeological study are not available. The SMR surveys serve as a data base for planners, developers, county councils and urban authorities, helping them to avoid identified archaeological areas of interest where possible. They facilitate the sensitive and indeed sensible planning for the archaeological remains in any proposed development. They have also recorded the incredible rate of destruction of monuments mapped in the 1830s and 40s on the first editions of the Ordnance Survey. A staggering destruction rate of 66 per cent has been noted in the Cork Harbour area, while in other counties surveyed the rate varies from 27 to over 50 per cent. While public ignorance of archaeological monuments and their importance remains widespread, the increased numbers of archaeologists engaged in fieldwork related to these surveys has certainly raised public awareness in recent years. However, the financial incentives for the development of farmland and urban areas often override the archaeological considerations and, where a developer is less than anxious to involve archaeologists at the planning and pre-development stage, legislation is often the only protection left.

Urban renewal and rescue archaeology

Redevelopment of our major cities has led to the discovery of a wealth of Medieval and earlier archaeological information. In Dublin during the sixties and seventies the clearance for redevelopment of large areas around Christ Church cathedral in the heart of the ancient walled town led to the discovery of unusually well preserved archaeological strata, dating from the Viking period. The threatened destruction of some of the richest archaeological deposits in Europe on the Wood Quay site brought rescue archaeology in Ireland to widespread public attention, leading to an unprecedented public outcry in support of the archaeologists engaged in the work. The early excavations in Dublin set a standard in urban archaeology for Ireland, and also alerted developers and local authorities to the necessity for the archaeological investigation of sites within historic towns and cities.

Large-scale urban excavations have been carried out on several sites in Cork since the early seventies, where deep, well-preserved deposits and the remains of structures dating from the twelfth and thirteenth centuries have been thoroughly investigated. In Waterford, a dramatic townscape of the eleventh and twelfth centuries has been brought to light. Major excavations in Armagh, Carrickfergus, Cork, Wexford, Limerick and Galway, have widened our knowledge of urban history. In Wexford, houses and artifacts very similar to the Dublin Viking houses of Fishamble Street have been unearthed. Viking remains have been discovered in Limerick, and Galway provides evidence of a different nature, dating from the thirteenth to the fifteenth century. Countless smaller excavations have also been required in other urban areas all over the country as a prerequisite of planning permission, for example at Drogheda, Coleraine and Derry, and many smaller excavations have taken place in other urban contexts.

Rural developments

Some of the most unexpected and important recent archaeological discoveries have been made during developments in rural areas. While deep ploughing has been responsible, to a very large extent, for the destruction of the low, eroded earthworks of ring-forts, ecclesiastical enclosures, deserted Medieval villages, ring barrows and tumuli, it has also led to the discovery of numerous Bronze Age cist graves, Christian cemeteries, flint scatters, souterrains and other sites which have no surface remains. Housing developments on the outskirts of towns occasionally lead to discoveries, such as at Mount Sandel, County Derry, where an important Mesolithic habitation was found. Quarrying sometimes unearths the remains of Bronze Age burials and souterrains, which can also collapse under the weight of large machines during land clearance or levelling. At Marshes Upper, Dundalk, a total of eight souterrains on five sites, two with enclosure ditches, was revealed and subsequently excavated during development of an advance factory site by the Industrial Development Authority. Land drainage has resulted in the destruction of some sites, such as *fulachtaí fia*, which have not already been levelled by ploughing. The related lowering of levels in lakes has led to the discovery, and occasionally the destruction, of crannogs, such as those investigated at Lough Gara, County Sligo, Moynagh Lough, County Meath, and Newtownlow, County Westmeath. Long, well-preserved 'toghers' or trackways, dating to the Iron Age and Bronze Age, such as those discovered and subsequently excavated at Corlea Bog, County Longford, have been revealed as a result of the exploitation of the bog for milled peat.

Some unusual discoveries of recent years have occurred on Irish Gas pipelines. In 1981 fifteen extensive archaeological sites were excavated, including a unique Bronze Age hut group at Curraghatoor, County Tipperary, and the multi-phase Bronze Age burial site at Ballyveelish, with its mortuary structure. In 1986 spur lines to the main Cork—Dublin route led to the discovery in County Limerick of a well-preserved Neolithic house at Tankardstown, near Kilmallock, a double-ring round house, unique in Ireland and possibly dating to the Iron Age or Early Christian period, and a number of enigmatic Bronze Age ditched sites.

Occasionally the return to a previously excavated site where development is required can lead to totally unexpected discoveries. At Newgrange, County Meath, a return to the monument for the excavation of a proposed visitor centre site led to the spectacular reinterpretation of a unique henge monument of Late Neolithic/Early Bronze Age date.

The future

Our archaeological heritage is unfortunately an ever-diminishing resource, which can never be regenerated. Each archaeological site is unique, and once destroyed a window on the past is closed forever.

The pace of development is unlikely to be stemmed in forthcoming years, and so archaeologists will, by and large, concern themselves with recording those aspects of the threatened heritage which are about to be destroyed. While the resources for research become increasingly diminished, rescue excavation and survey will retain a very important role in Irish archaeology for the foreseeable future.

Underwater archaeology

Nessa O'Connor

Lake and river form a major part of the landscape and topography of Ireland. From earliest times, people have used the waterways for transport and trade, as a source of food, and as a means of protection. Today, a vast and diverse range of remains lies concealed beneath our inland and coastal waters, ranging from shipwrecks, logboats and dwelling places, to ancient causeways, fish weirs, jetties and river crossings.

As a formal discipline, the growth of underwater archaeology in Ireland is very recent. However, significant incidental finds have been made and preserved over a long period of time, particularly by early collectors and antiquaries. Objects were recovered in the nets of fishermen, or revealed because of tidal conditions, falling water levels and, extensively, as a result of drainage work in the Irish midlands. Many of the most important antiquities in the collections of the National Museum of Ireland come from marine or freshwater locations or wetlands. For example, a ceremonial bronze trumpet decorated in the La Tène style of the Iron Age was found in the waters of Loughnashade, County Armagh,

a first century BC bronze sword hilt in human form was found in Ballyshannon Bay, County Donegal; and the gold hoard from Broighter, County Derry, which includes a little sheet-gold boat with mast and oars, may originally have been deposited at the sea as an offering to the gods. Even the Tara brooch was found near the mouth of the River Boyne, County Meath, and one of the most significant finds of the past decade, the Lough Kinale book shrine, was found on a County Longford lake-bed. In the public eye, few of these finds would be regarded as having any connection with underwater archaeology.

Perhaps more than anything else it is the shipwreck, and more specifically the Spanish Armada, which has captured the public imagination and the attention of the media. Underwater archaeology extends far beyond the confines of ship archaeology. It requires much broader definition, to include the study of the archaeological remains of lakes, rivers, wetlands, harbours, associated dryland sites, and the applied technology which enables us to recover information in a scientific manner. Furthermore, many sites are only partially submerged or would originally have been on dry land.

Shipwrecks are perhaps the most valuable because of the glimpses they afford us of the everyday lives of those on board. Every ship has its home port and cultural and political milieu; each crannog must have been supported by social structures and an agricultural hinterland. Therefore, maritime archaeology is inseparable from its dryland counterpart and should be regarded as an integral part of archaeology as a whole. Frequently, its vital role is in extending survey work initiated by the land-based archaeologist.

Modern developments

How has this underwater world become familiar? As early as the Bronze Age, sponge divers carried out lengthy breath-holding dives, and there are stone carvings which depict Assyrians using goat skins to hold an air supply. In Ireland there are records of sixteenth-century attempts to salvage Armada wrecks, while in Scotland in the early years of this century, the intrepid monk Odo Blundell attempted to explore the lake dwellings of Inverness-shire — all using unsuitable bulky equipment and air supplied from the surface. None of these methods was reliable or allowed sufficient time for the diver to carry out any serious work. The

(opposite) Finds from the Armada ship, the Girona *(see p212)*

Artillery equipment, including shot-gauges, powder-scoop and ramrod, from the Spanish Armada ship La Trinidad Valancera. *(see p212)*

A little gold boat from the hoard of Broighter, County Derry. From the Iron Age, first or second century AD. (see p212)

A sixteenth-century sword recovered during an underwater survey just south of Ballinasloe, County Galway, in 1991. (see p212)

*(right)
Examination of
the body of a
young woman of
the sixteenth
century AD,
found wrapped in
a cloak in a bog
at Meenybradden,
near Ardara,
County Donegal.*

development of the aqualung in 1947, by Emile Gagnan and Jacques Cousteau, revolutionised underwater exploration. In time, it allowed the diver to reach depths in excess of 40m (130ft), and to remain in shallower water for periods sufficient to permit methodical investigation and recording.

However, modern technological developments have brought with them new problems as well as advantages. Dryland survey and excavation equipment is often only marginally adapted for underwater conditions, and there is the added difficulty of working in a foreign environment, which tends to reduce productivity and efficiency. The diver is confronted with the need to maintain neutral buoyancy and to achieve a working position which will not disturb the remains that are being examined. The diver must remain constantly aware of safety factors in an environment which can be unforgiving of human error. In lakes and rivers, peat particles and silt in suspension can greatly reduce visibility.

Apart from practical difficulties, the ready availability of sub-aqua equipment facilitates not only the scientist and researcher, but also the treasure hunter and commercial salvor. Countless important sites have been damaged or destroyed because of pillaging, both in Ireland and elsewhere. The raising of material from the sea is controlled by the Merchant Shipping Act and the National Monuments Acts, and anything lifted must be reported to the local receiver of wrecks. Licences are now required to dive, survey or excavate any wreck-site more than 100 years old. This system is designed to give the state control over the rate at which underwater sites are to be exploited. The unsolicited raising of material has put an intolerable burden on limited conservation facilities. Emphasis is now placed on the importance of survey and recording. There is, in any case, a necessity for the detailed recording of all sites in advance of any excavation, and often, better results can be achieved for the part-time worker, with less time expended.

The Spanish Armada

For many, the wrecks of the Spanish Armada — sent by Philip II of Spain to attack England in 1588 — are the epitome of Irish underwater archaeology. The earliest formal investigations under water in Ireland took place on the sites of Armada wrecks at Blasket Sound, County Kerry, Kinnagoe Bay, County Donegal, and Lacada

Point, County Antrim. These sunken ships, located here in the sixties and early seventies, the *Santa Maria de la Rosa*, *La Trinidad Valencera* and the *Girona*, contributed in a major way to Armada research and provided a remarkable range of artifacts associated with shipping, navigation, ordnance and personal effects. In the 1980s, further discoveries were made at Streedagh, County Sligo, and at Kinnagoe Bay.

Licensed survey work is continuing at these sites. The pioneers of this work off the west coast of Ireland were often subjected to the same treacherous and inclement conditions experienced by the Spanish sailors of 400 years ago. Some of the Armada remains lie in as much as 40m (130ft) of water, ripped by ferocious currents. Apart from other difficulties, the threat to personal safety in investigating these wrecks remains an overriding factor in the planning of projects. Another major consideration is the availability of suitably trained divers. Many sports divers affiliated to CFT (The Irish Underwater Council) have become involved in survey work, and their contribution has proved invaluable. Basic training in archaeological techniques and surveying is now regularly available, and many divers have become involved in practical fieldwork. Amateur divers have begun to survey waters in their own localities, and are thus helping to record hitherto unknown remains such as shipwrecks, crannogs and logboats.

Other studies

The study of boats and ships is of course a significant element in underwater archaeology. Many isolated finds of logboats or dug-out canoes have been recorded. These frequently come to light during dry summers, on newly exposed stretches of lake and river shore. A recently commenced systematic study of midland lakes and rivers has allowed for a more complete study of boats and other artifacts, such as weaponry and personal ornaments, in an established context of site and environment. Working on Loughs Ennel and Lene in County Westmeath, the National Museum, in conjunction with Cornell University and CFT, is recording sections of crannogs and related sites which are inaccessible to land-based archaeologists. The project is also attempting to establish the context of artifacts long known about.

In the archaeology of shipwrecks and inland waterways, a high level of scientific technology is being applied in recording, dating and conservation. This includes sophisticated electronic surveying equipment, magnetometers for surveying wreck sites, computers, underwater photographic equipment and the use of dendrochronological dating. Though equipment can be costly, it is essential for increased efficiency and labour reduction.

The scope and diversity of underwater archaeology in Ireland is very great, ranging as it does from prehistoric river crossings and hunter-fisher lakeside settlements, through the crannogs of the Early Medieval period, to the shipwrecks of the past couple of hundred years. The latter includes recently investigated ships, such as the *Aid* off Wicklow Head and the early steamer, the *Victoria*, off the Baily, County Dublin. It spans all periods and practically every aspect of man's material remains.

Wetland archaeology

Ann Lynch

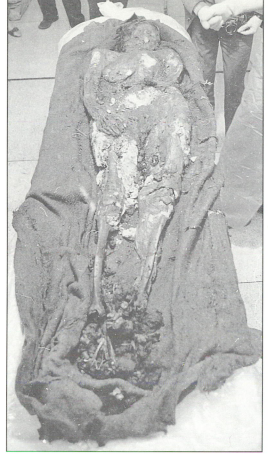

Our wetlands or peatlands have inspired poets and painters, and yet are regarded by many as bleak and soggy wastelands, associated with poverty and hardship. In recent years a strong conservation lobby has emerged, whose aim is to preserve a representative sample of our rapidly disappearing peatlands. People are finally beginning to realise that our bogs are special places for flora and fauna, and because of massive exploitation elsewhere, are now almost unique in Europe. Less well understood, perhaps, is the fact that our peatlands are also rich repositories of information about our past, and as such should be regarded as a vital archaeological resource.

Formation and composition

Peat consists of the remains of plants which have slowly accumulated in waterlogged areas over thousands of years. The layers of peat which have gradually built up may be likened to the pages of a book, with the surface of the bog representing the most recent (in some cases the final) page.

There are three different types of peatland in Ireland, classified on the basis of plant composition and water source; these are fens, raised bogs and blanket bogs. Fens have suffered greatly as a result of land reclamation, and the few surviving examples are to be found in lowland areas of western counties. Raised bogs are the deepest of the peatlands, many over 10m (33ft) deep, and are found in the midland counties. Blanket bog is usually shallower, ranging from 2m to 8m (6½ to 26ft) in depth, and carpets large areas of hillside and flatland, where the average annual rainfall is greater than 1200 millimetres or, in the case of mountain blanket bog, occurs above an elevation of 200m (656ft).

Peatlands in general began to form at the end of the last glaciation — some ten thousand years ago — but in the case of blanket bog, some areas were not engulfed until much later. No one date may be assigned countrywide to the formation of peat, since local topography and climatic variation play a large part in peat initiation. Structures and artifacts of all periods may therefore be found trapped within our bogs.

Hidden wealth

Dryland sites produce the bones of archaeology, but

The clothes of a later seventeenth-century, middle-aged man found in a bog at Tawnamore, County Sligo. (see p212)

Leather shoe from Ballindoolin Bog, County Kildare.

Woman's gown, of woollen twill, from Shinrone, County Tipperary. (see p212)

Hand-cutting of turf in a bog near Maam Cross, Connemara, County Galway. (see p212)

wetland archaeology puts the flesh on those bones. It is their exceptional powers of preservation which make wetlands a unique archaeological resource. The oxygen-free conditions prevailing in the waterlogged peat mean poor microbial activity, which in turn allows for almost complete preservation of organic materials.

Traces of Ireland's earliest settlers — the hunters and gatherers of the Mesolithic period — have been revealed under the raised bog at Lough Boora in County Offaly. Discarded artifacts of chert and ground-pebble axes, burnt mammal, fish and bird bones, and charred hazelnuts, all bear testimony to a temporary campsite on the shores of an ancient lake sometime around 7000 BC. Evidence of how Ireland's first farmers organised their properties lies hidden under many of our bogs. At Behy and Glenulra in County Mayo, a field system, last used about four thousand years ago and now buried under 4m (13ft) of blanket bog, has been located and surveyed. The organised layout of the walls suggests a sizable community acting to an agreed plan, and the total area enclosed suggests that these fields were used for pasture. Megalithic monuments of the Later Neolithic or Bronze Age periods have also been engulfed by blanket bog in mountainous areas. These are often uncovered during turf-cutting, as was the intriguing collection of circles, cairns and alignments at Beaghmore, County Tyrone.

A simple mound in a bog may well conceal the remains of a crannog or lake dwelling. Crannogs are artificially constructed islands sited in marshes or lakes, which were built as defended homesteads and were primarily a feature of the Early Medieval period. Many of the marshes or lakes have since been transformed into fens or peatlands, with consequent preservation of their crannogs. The building materials used included timbers, brushwood, wickerwork, straw and bracken, which can emerge as new from the waterlogged conditions in the bog.

Entombed between the peaty pages of each bog are structures and artifacts abandoned or lost throughout the ages. Our raised bogs must have been major obstacles to transport since Neolithic and Bronze Age times; trackways or 'toghers', which would have served both pedestrian and wheeled traffic, are commonly found at various levels in the bogs. Construction techniques included large oak sleepers on long runners or bunches of brushwood, sometimes incorporating woven hurdles. Layers of gravel have also been recorded from toghers in County Offaly. Excavations of Bronze Age and Iron Age trackways in County Longford throw light on the woodworking techniques of those periods and on the location of the population centres served by such routeways.

Artifacts of all types and all periods have been found during turf-cutting, and they now form unique collections in the National Museum of Ireland in Dublin and in the Ulster Museum, Belfast. These range from stone and bronze axeheads, bronze cauldrons, bronze weapons, amber and jet beads, to hoards of gold ornaments. The preservation of organic materials provides an extra dimension: axeheads or arrowheads may be found with their wooden handles intact; iron-shod wooden spades have been recorded; and articles of clothing, such as woollen caps and cloaks, have survived.

Human burials

A more macabre aspect of wetland archaeology is the eighty or so human bodies recovered from boglands throughout the country over the past two centuries. Many of these were never fully documented and have not survived. Those whose remains are in the possession of the National Museum are currently being researched. The study of bog bodies can tell us far more about the physical appearance and lifestyle of early people than the analysis of bones from dryland sites. The colour and type of hair can often still be seen, the clothing in which they were buried has usually survived, and in instances of

exceptional preservation, analysis of stomach contents can throw some light on the ingredients of the last meal! It seems likely that the majority of Irish bog bodies date to Late Medieval or modern times, although further radiocarbon dating is indicating prehistoric examples. Generally speaking, burial appears to have been accidental (for example, as a result of bog slides or simply falling into a bog hole), but in the case of an Iron Age burial from Gallagh, County Galway, deliberate burial, possibly after strangulation, has been suggested.

It is an unfortunate fact that commercial exploitation and other land-use patterns mean that our wetlands, together with their archaeological, botanical and zoological treasures, are rapidly disappearing. Evidence suggests that if present rates of destruction continue, all raised bogs of scientific interest will have disappeared before the end of this century, while blanket bog will not survive for more than a hundred years.

A gold dress-fastener of the Later Bronze Age found at Killymoon Demesne, County Tyrone, in the early nineteenth century. (see p212)

Eighth-century reliquary containing a leather belt, found during turf-cutting at Moylough, County Sligo.

II
The Stone Age

As far as we can tell, the first human communities were settled in Ireland about 7000 BC. These people belonged to what European archaelogists call the Mesolithic period or Middle Stone Age, but we cannot say definitely that there was no colonisation before then. If people had reached Ireland in even earlier times, then the evidence of their habitation has been destroyed or buried so deep by the glaciers of the Ice Ages that we cannot now find it. Only in the south, where large parts of Munster were not covered by ice, have we a reasonable chance of finding Palaeolithic (Old Stone Age) sites or artifacts preserved in position. The higher slopes of the valleys of the Munster Blackwater and its tributary the Bride, safe from the scouring floods, or other places south of the limit of the main ice sheet and free of local glaciers, are likely places to look. No significant attempt has been made in modern times to discover who first inhabited the island. In the various warmer stages during the last great cold period, Palaeolithic bands hunted across Britain, and it is most unlikely that Ireland remained unvisited.

This is speculation, and we can only deal with the evidence which we have. The earliest Mesolithic hunters entered an island which was heavily forested. The climate was slowly becoming warmer. The rivers were full of fish, the woodlands were teeming with game. Salmon and eels, deer, pig and smaller mammals and game birds were all abundant, although the range of species in Ireland was then — as it is today — smaller than in Britain. We do not know how these first settlers arrived, but they must have come by boat because any land connection between Ireland and Britain would have been broken by 7000 BC. Because the coastline has changed dramatically since then, the earliest sites have been covered by the sea for thousands of years.

We cannot think of the first settlement as an invasion: it was probably a process involving many groups from different parts of what was then the western coast of Britain. Whether the movement of a given group began as seasonal visits to exploit the resources of the virgin land, thus avoiding competition with neighbouring bands, we have no way of knowing, but it is a strong possibility. It would be logical to assume that the crossing of the sea by any band, either a family or group of families, was prepared carefully, but the surviving evidence is so thin that we must use our imagination to flesh out the picture.

Even treated soberly as it must be by scientists, it is impossible to drain the drama from that first arrival of colonists. Dependent entirely on hunting and gathering edible plants and shellfish, they had entered a land where they had first pick of the natural resources. There can be little doubt that they made a significant contribution to the genetic inheritance of the people who live in Ireland today: their presence throughout the land in however small numbers must have had a profound effect on the peoples of the following Neolithic period. By their adaptation to the island environment, the Mesolithic peoples forged the first distinctive Irish identity.

(left)
The burial chamber of the passage tomb of Fourknocks, County Meath.

Early environments and the first settlers

Michael O'Connell

The importance of the environment is now understood: it provides a backdrop to living which can never be substituted for by advances in modern technology. For prehistoric peoples, the environment had even greater immediacy and relevance. It determined not only the quality of life, but survival itself. From the immediate surroundings of the settlement, the daily food supply as well as fuel, clothing and shelter had to be won: the ability to cope with and exploit the environment was the key to survival and development.

About eleven thousand years ago, as the last Ice Age came to an end and temperatures rose, Ireland was still part of the main European landmass and, as a result, migration of plants and animals from the warmer south could take place largely unhindered. The bare soil was quickly colonised by herbaceous species including grasses, dock and meadowsweet. These, in turn, were invaded by various shrubs, such as juniper, willow, birch and finally hazel.

About ten thousand years ago, shortly before the Mesolithic or first known inhabitants arrived, the Irish landscape had a very different appearance. Hazel scrub, similar to that which can be seen in the central Burren, County Clare, was the dominant vegetation. Pine, oak, elm and ash had arrived and would later overshadow hazel and form tall canopy woodland. The area under grassland and bog was extremely limited. Lakes were the only extensive open features. In the midlands and in the flood plains of the Shannon there were large bodies of shallow open water. Here, accumulation of aquatic plant and algal remains quickly led to sediment accumulation in the lake basins; reed swamp developed, and eventually this was replaced by raised bog in areas where Sphagnum, or bog mosses, dominated.

The Mesolithic peoples chose river banks, such as the Lower Bann, lake margins and islands, as at Lough Boora, County Offaly, and coastal situations for their settlement sites. These areas provided a ready supply of food for people who depended on hunting, fishing and the gathering of wild fruits and berries.

In Ireland at this time there were very few large animals. The giant Irish deer, with its antler span of up to three metres, had become extinct at the onset of the short but severe cold spell that immediately preceded the end of the Ice Age. Aurochs (the wild ox of Europe which became extinct in Poland in the seventeenth century), although present in Britain at this time, has not been recorded in Ireland. It has long been thought

The base of the high cross at Moone, County Kildare, which is made of local stone. (see p212)

Flint nodules in beds of chalk. County Antrim.

that the same is true for the elk, but recent evidence suggests that this deer-like animal was present in early Ireland. On the other hand, the red deer was certainly represented in the early Irish fauna, but the available evidence points to the wild pig as the main quarry of the Mesolithic hunter. Woodlands provided the habitat for this important meat source, but they were also a source of game birds, such as woodpigeon, woodcock, goshawk and capercaillie. The abundant hazelnut was a very important part of the diet and, since it could be readily stored, it probably served as a reserve food for the winter and early spring, before the salmon run began in the rivers.

Did these people modify the environment? In upland Mesolithic settlements in Britain, for example, it has been suggested that they cleared the thin woodland cover by fire, in the knowledge that herbivores are attracted to such areas, where they are also an easier quarry. At Newferry, County Antrim, in the middle reaches of the Lower Bann river, charcoal layers and an increase in the pollen of herbaceous plants in Mesolithic settlement layers, dating to approximately 6000 BC, point to forest clearance. However, by and large, Mesolithic peoples, while being efficient at exploiting the surplus produce of their natural environment, probably did not seriously interfere with natural woodland or soil development. But this was to change dramatically with the beginning of the Neolithic period.

The geology and raw materials of the Stone Age

John Jackson

Of all the materials used from earliest times for fashioning domestic utensils, weapons for hunting or war, agricultural tools and objects of adornment, stone is the most enduring; it has survived from the world's earliest habitation sites and has given its name to the earliest cultures. The base

metals are prey to rust and organic materials to decay. However, because archaeologists speak of a 'Stone Age' and 'Bronze' and 'Iron' ages, we must remember that stone as a cheap, durable and easily formed material, remained in use for many practical purposes long after new technologies appeared.

The early inhabitants of Ireland developed remarkable expertise in selecting stone which possessed particular characteristics for specific purposes. *Flint*, from chalk deposits, and *chert*, found in Carboniferous limestone, are almost universal on Stone Age sites in Ireland, used for edged tools and projectile points. Hard, tenacious stone, capable of being ground and polished, resistant to fracturing, of relatively high density and suitable for polished stone axes, was prized. A celebrated example was the *porcellanite* from the basalt volcanic vent at Tievebulliagh, County Antrim, and Brockley on Rathlin Island. This proved so successful that stone axe 'factories' were established at both these sites and their products were distributed over the greater part of Ireland, the Central Valley and the Southern Uplands of Scotland, and down the west of England as far south as Wiltshire. It was Ireland's first export trade. The substantial number of stone axes made from *Lambay porphyry* recovered from the east of Ireland suggests that an axe 'factory' may have been located on this distinctive rock near Portrane, County Dublin, or on Lambay Island.

Tabular, thinly bedded, hardened *mudstones, siltstones*

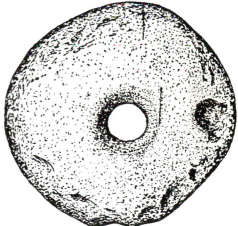

Three bracers (archer's wristguards) from County Antrim. (see p212)

A decorated rotary quernstone for grinding corn, from Inishkeen Glebe, County Monaghan. It is made of local gritstone.

and bedded *sideritic ironstone* make a characteristic and readily recognisable type of stone axe; the original stones are typically rectangular, bounded by joint planes on four sides and by bedding planes above and below. One of the shorter joint planes was ground down to make a sharp cutting edge, whilst the opposite face, the butt end,

is frequently unmodified. The sides, corresponding to the longer joint planes, are very slightly modified to produce a slight taper at either end. Such implements can be described as ground slab axes. A number of them came from the Mesolithic site at Lough Boora, County Offaly. They are common on the River Shannon below Killaloe, on the Barrow at Rheban, upstream of Athy, and at other river crossings; hence the name once applied to them, 'River Ford axes'. The source of the material is typically local.

The range of stone used in the manufacture of Irish polished-stone axes is diverse and includes such igneous rocks as *felsite, andesite, porphyry, trachyte, basalt, gabbro*; metamorphic rocks like *quartzite, porcellanite, micaschist, metadolerite*; sedimentary rocks like *conglomerate, sandstone, arkosic sandstone, greywacke, siltstone, bedded black chert, flint*, and pyroclastic rocks such as *fine volcanic ash* (tuff) and *coarse volcanic ash* (agglomerate), and many other rock-types.

Hones and whetstones require an abrasive material — *sandstone* for preliminary sharpening and *siltstone* for giving a final edge — and continuity with these ancient skills can be seen today in scythe-stones, made until a few years ago from local Millstone Grit sandstone at Eshbralley, County Fermanagh, and at Killyclogher, County Leitrim. Quern-stones require a coarse abrasive material for crushing and grinding grain. There are two rock-types particularly associated with querns: saddle-querns in south-east Ireland are typically of local *granite*, and of the many examples found at Glendalough, some may have been used for crushing the local lead ore for the extraction of silver. Rotary querns are frequently made of a very pure, coarse-textured *white sandstone* — almost entirely of quartz grains — which comes from the junction beds separating the top of the Old Red Sandstone from the base of the overlying Carboniferous System. At Ardagh Hill, County Longford, this beautiful sandstone contains *sphalerite* (zinc sulphide), and many local querns include this mineral in their composition, indicating a local source. If extremely tough tenacious material were required for such critical items as archers' wrist-bracers, then an exceptionally fine-grained stone such as *flint* or *jasper* (related to flint) was chosen. If thin slabby stone, not necessarily hard but which could be easily cut into discs and perforated for use as spindle-

whorls, loom-weights or line-sinkers were required, then thinly bedded *shale, soapstone*, cleaved *slate* or fissile material such as *micaschist* was selected.

Steatite, talc or *soapstone* was used for making casting moulds in the Bronze Age, and for stone lamps, stone beads and spindle-whorls; in later times it was used in the making of quite large stone bowls. Steatite occurs in Inishbofin and Inishark, and a very large deposit, recently discovered, is located to the south-east of Westport. Smaller deposits occur in County Donegal, notably at Croghy Head. Many of the soapstone artifacts are of native material, though imports also occur.

Lignite and *jet* were used for making bracelets. Both were almost certainly imported, although extensive deposits of lignite occur around Lough Neagh and at several other localities in northern Ireland, including Armoy, County Antrim.

Building stone

Excepting small portable items, polished stone axes, querns, domestic, agricultural and hunting implements, Ireland's early inhabitants did not transport ponderous blocks of stone for great distances. Transport was very difficult and confined to pack-animals and primitive vehicles and boats. In the megalithic tombs of the Neolithic period, the stone used was invariably local: the Lower Palaeozoic *greywackes* and fracture-cleaved *sandstones* of the passage graves of the Boyne Valley and Slieve na Caillighe or Loughcrew Hills; the Carboniferous cherty limestone of Carrowkeel, Carrowmore and Knocknarea in County Sligo; and the granite of the portal tombs on the flanks of the Dublin and Wicklow Mountains, are all of local provenance. The Turoe stone, County Galway, was transported in a different way. This great boulder of pink felsparred Galway granite, beautifully decorated with La Tène motifs, was ice-embedded as a glacial erratic and thus transported by an east-flowing ice sheet from its east Connemara source some 40km (25 miles) to the Loughrea area, where it was later carved and erected. Similarly in the Christian period the Old Red Sandstone of the Ahenny high crosses; the granite of the high crosses of Old Kilcullen, Moone and Castledermot; the Carboniferous limestone of the high crosses of Dysert O'Dea and Kilfenora, are again of immediate local origin. The transport of substantial blocks of stone by sea had to await the coming of the Normans, who brought

Whetstone from a crannog at Newtownlow, County Meath. (see p212)

oolitic limestone from Caen in Normandy and from Dundry Hill in Somersetshire for Norman stonemasons to carve and letter and build into the fabric of their monasteries, friaries, abbeys, priories and cathedrals, where it coexists in harmony with the local building stone. The great importation of building stone dates to as late as the eighteenth century, when Portland stone was brought from the south of England for public buildings in Dublin and elsewhere; for Georgian country houses and churches; for colleges and a host of other buildings.

Flint and chert

Flint is a siliceous rock which was deposited in the form of nodules. These are concentrated in discrete layers within chalk, and were mined underground by early peoples. One of these flint-mining areas, Grimes Graves in Norfolk, is pitted by the infilled mine shafts, resembling a shell-pitted battlefield. A remarkably similar surface occurs at Tievebulliagh in County Antrim, but is regarded as the result of eighteenth-century diggings.

Flint *in situ* was thought to be confined in Ireland to the chalk of the north-east, but some years ago small outcrops of chalk with flint nodules were recognised in Kerry, particularly to the north of Killarney, and recent offshore drilling for oil and gas has found great thicknesses of Cretaceous chalk with flint in the Irish Sea, the Celtic Sea and in the Atlantic off the west coast.

During the great Ice Age, Scottish ice filled the Irish Sea basin and ploughed out marine sediments and rock from the sea-floor, including flint nodules, spreading them on the land intermixed with boulder clay. Subsequent erosion has released these nodules into the beach sands and shingle. They are therefore glacial erratics from relatively close submarine sources, and not far-travelled from remote outcrops as previously thought. They are particularly abundant in the beach sands at Lady's Island Lake and Tacumshin in south-east Wexford, but are common in virtually all beach sands on our east coast.

Chert is also a chalcedonic form of silica, and physically and chemically is indistinguishable from flint. The differences between the two are essentially stratigraphic, in that flint is often honey-coloured and occurs in the Cretaceous chalk, whereas chert is typically black and occurs in limestone of Lower Carboniferous age. But chert can also be white, as in a well-defined belt from Leitrim and north Cavan to Monaghan and north Meath, and it then closely resembles flint. The two can best be differentiated from each other by their chemistry microscopically by identifying the quite different microfossils which characterise each of them. The mutual substitution of flint and chert is clearly seen in the microliths fashioned by Early Mesolithic peoples in Ireland. At Mount Sandel on the north coast and close to Cretaceous outcrops and readily available flint, the microliths are of flint, whereas at Lough Boora in Offaly, resting on Carboniferous limestone of the Irish midlands, they are of chert.

Festoon chert is a variety of chert in which dark narrow bands form a distinctive soap-bubble pattern. It was first recognised at Lough Derravarragh in Westmeath, and a Mesolithic flake industry on the lake shore exploited this type of local chert. Festoon chert occurs in a broad belt stretching from Westmeath, Longford and Cavan eastwards to Meath and south Monaghan.

Flint and stone tools

Elizabeth Anderson

Wherever flint was available, Stone Age people used it to make tools. In Ireland, the most prolific source of flint is in County Antrim, although it is also to be found throughout the country. Flint breaks like glass, and while very hard can be chipped quite easily, giving a fractured, razor-sharp edge. In the Mesolithic period, flint was obtained mainly from the banks and beds of rivers or from the sea-shore. Neolithic people were more selective, obtaining flint direct from the source where possible. Large flint mines of this period are known in southern England and north-eastern France and Belgium. Yet prehistoric communities were not necessarily dependent on flint, and in areas where it was not readily available, alternative raw materials were used; these included quartz, quartzite, chert, rhyolites, siltstones and sandstones. In modern times, Australian aborigines discovered that bottle-glass and porcelain telegraph insulators served as good materials for making spearheads.

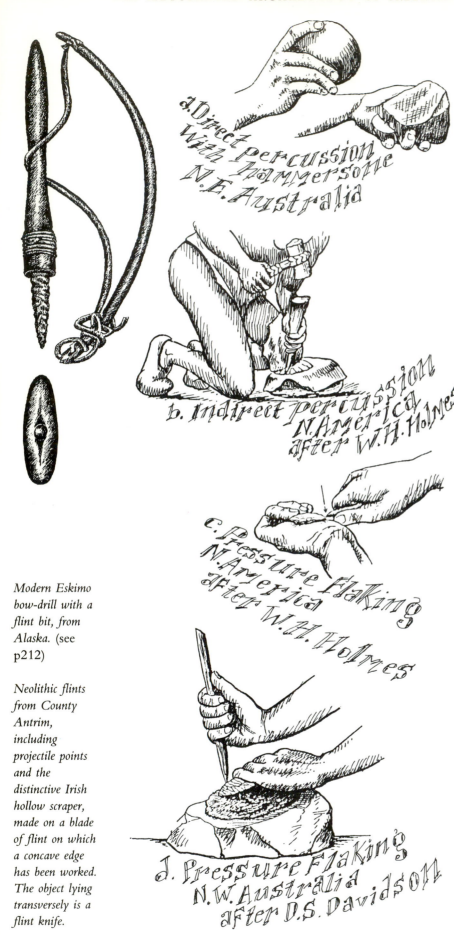

a. Direct percussion with hammerstone N.E. Australia

b. Indirect percussion N. America after W.H. Holmes

c. Pressure Flaking N. America after W.H. Holmes

d. Pressure Flaking N.W. Australia after D.S. Davidson

Modern Eskimo bow-drill with a flint bit, from Alaska. (see p212)

Neolithic flints from County Antrim, including projectile points and the distinctive Irish hollow scraper, made on a blade of flint on which a concave edge has been worked. The object lying transversely is a flint knife.

Production techniques

Skill and experience are essential to the flint worker, or 'knapper', both in the selection of suitable stone and in the application of different flaking techniques. The competent knapper will take great care in the preparation of the flint core and can produce very consistent results.

In its simplest form, a stone tool that will cut may be produced by breaking a nodule of flint in half and using the resulting sharp edge. Specialised tools can be made by employing different flaking techniques. There are several methods of flaking stone, each probably used at some stage in prehistory. The flint worker can either apply force (percussion) by directly or indirectly hammering the flint nodule with a stone or an antler *bâton*, or alternatively flakes can be removed from the core by applying pressure, for which an antler *bâton* is well suited.

While the blades and flakes removed from a core usually have sharp, useful edges, the flint knapper may modify the tool by removing small flakes from the edge;

this technique, known as retouching, can either strengthen, sharpen, smoothen or entirely alter the shape of a tool, and can be achieved either by percussion or pressure.

Tool types

While the methods of flaking and the shape of tools changed throughout prehistory, the need for tool types that could perform certain tasks remained constant. Tools for hunting and fishing were used throughout the Stone Age. During the Early Mesolithic period, small retouched blades or microliths, set in rows in wooden handles or shafts, were used for cutting or sawing, or as hunting and fishing spears. Large numbers of flint microliths have been found at Mount Sandel in County Derry, while chert microliths were used by the hunter-gatherers at Lough Boora, County Offaly.

In the Later Mesolithic period a new method of flaking was used to produce larger blades and flakes which had long cutting-edges. These large blades were probably set in handles and used for cutting and whittling, while some may have been used as projectile heads. Flint blades such as these have been found at sites like Newferry, County Antrim and Dalkey Island, County Dublin, while at Ferriter's Cove, County Kerry, where flint was scarce, the occupants chose to use green rhyolites and siltstones to produce similar tools.

In Neolithic times, pressure-flaking, a technique previously unknown in Ireland, was introduced. This method allowed for the production of finely crafted tools, in particular the piercing arrowhead. Leaf- and lozenge-shaped arrowheads and javelin or spearheads are typical tools of this period. These arrowheads could have been used both for hunting and warfare. Similar types of arrowhead have been found embedded in human vertebrae at the Neolithic site of Hambledon Hill in England. Plano-convex knives — that is, with blades which are D-shaped in cross-section — were also used during this period. Even with the introduction of metal during the Bronze Age, this flaking technique continued to be used to make barbed and tanged arrowheads for hunting and warfare.

Scraping tools, used in the processing of animal hides for clothing, containers or tent coverings, were employed in varying degrees throughout the prehistoric period. Scrapers were tools which had been retouched to such a degree that, while sufficiently sharp to remove excess fat and tissue from a hide, they remained blunt enough to avoid cutting through animal skin. Curing agents like ochre, grit, urine, and in some cases brains, would have been added during the preparation of the hide, helping to keep vermin in check and to make the hide more supple. Scrapers are rare for the Mesolithic period in Ireland, but become more common in Neolithic times, perhaps reflecting an increased dependence on domesticated animals. The Neolithic period also saw the appearance of a new form of scraper, the hollow scraper, which is virtually confined to Ireland, with some examples from the Isle of Man. Though the function of these scrapers is still unknown, their distinctive shape has led some people to suggest that they may have been used as arrow-shaft straighteners or as reaping tools. Speculations like these serve to illustrate the difficulty in interpreting the use of stone tools. With the application of high-powered microscopy, it is possible to determine the use of certain tool-types, for example those that were used for wood-working, hide processing and cereal harvesting. Perhaps the smallest of these tool-types is the thumb-nail scraper, which is considered characteristic of the Earlier Bronze Age.

Axes for wood-working were common throughout prehistory. Flint axes that had been flaked into shape were used during the Early Mesolithic period. Experiments carried out in Denmark using similar types of axes have shown them to be extremely effective in felling trees. However, the need for more durable tools for wood-working on a larger scale led to the manufacture of polished-stone axeheads. A polished edge is less susceptible to damage than a flaked edge. The earliest of these axeheads in Ireland are simply elongated pebbles on which a cutting edge has been ground. Over forty-five polished-stone axeheads were found at the Later Mesolithic riverside site at Newferry, County Antrim. In Neolithic times, extensive forest clearance for cultivation and wood requirements for house construction saw the need for axes of a much higher quality. One rock used in the production of these axes was porcellanite. The best known sources of porcellanite are at Tievebulliagh, County Antrim and Brockley on Rathlin Island. These porcellanite axes were first flaked into shape to produce a rough-out. The cutting edge or the whole surface of the rough-out was then ground down by rubbing on a wetted sandstone; quartz sand may have been added to provide more friction. The axe may then have been finished off by burnishing, perhaps with a soft leather cloth, giving the surface a finer gloss.

While most flint and stone tools may have been used in domestic activities, others would seem to have had a more prestigious significance. Flint and stone tools are sometimes included in different types of grave deposit, symbolising some ritual importance, either for the living or the dead. The elaborately decorated flint mace-head from the chambered tomb at Knowth, County Meath, could be seen as a symbol of power or status and was probably never intended for use. Three Bronze Age barbed and tanged arrowheads were included in a grave deposit at Fenagh, County Antrim, while stone battle-axes were found in Bronze Age graves at Laheen, County Donegal, Tara, County Meath, and Ballintubbrid, County Wexford. It has also been suggested that the use of orange-coloured flint for some Bronze Age arrowheads may have reflected a desire to imitate the use of copper or bronze.

Even as metal grew in popularity, the use of stone tools continued. Stone mauls were used in the extraction of copper ore during the Bronze Age. Scrapers made from flint, chert and quartz are a relatively common occurrence on Early Christian sites, as are strike-a-lights for making fire. Gun-flints, made to fit the striker in flint-lock guns and pistols, were still being produced in England until quite recently.

Flint and stone tools are sometimes considered 'primitive' objects, used by people who had yet to realise the advantages of metal tools. Yet the skill of making and using stone tools, a technique which is virtually lost to us today, should never be underestimated. Their continued use long after the introduction of metal is testimony both to their effectiveness and to the importance attached to them by prehistoric peoples.

FIG. 1—Detail of the Upper Portion of the Deposits.

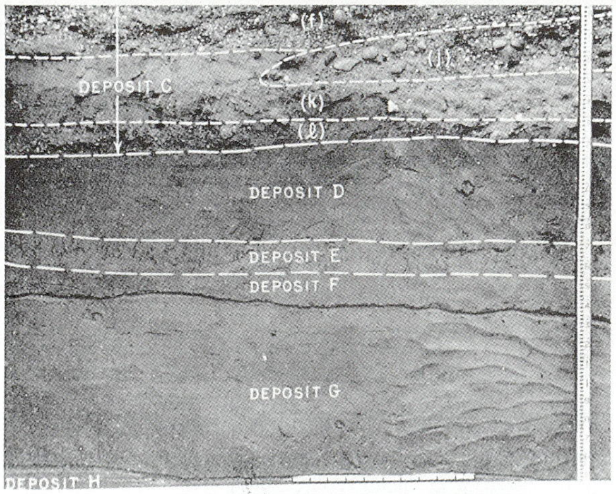

FIG. 2—Detail of the Lower Portion of the Deposits.

The Mesolithic period

Peter C Woodman

Ireland, Norway and Finland all claim a human history of less than ten thousand years. There is no evidence so far that these peripheral parts of Europe were occupied by human societies during the Pleistocene or Ice Age, as it is sometimes called. Norway was mostly covered by ice, while Finland was covered by a combination of ice and sea, yet bands of hunters moved in rapidly as the ice began to retreat. In contrast, a significant portion of Ireland remained free of glaciers for the last fifty thousand years, and by the time of our earliest known human settlement of Mesolithic or Middle Stone Age peoples, Ireland had been effectively ice-free for at least four thousand years. This apparent time lag is made even more incongruous by the fact that at various times within the last hundred thousand years, Ireland was populated by animals such as mammoth, giant deer and reindeer, which, in turn, were scavenged upon by hyenas, wolves and arctic foxes. Although we have found no evidence that these creatures were preyed upon by bands of hunters, it is possible that one day evidence of a much older human colonisation of Ireland will emerge.

The Early Mesolithic peoples

The Mesolithic people were the stone age hunters, fishers and gatherers who lived in Europe after the end of the Pleistocene, that is, less than ten thousand years ago, and before the appearance of farming. Where did these people come from? Although the level of water in the world's oceans was lower then than it is today, it is likely that a stretch of open water existed between Ireland and the rest of Europe, and that any bands of hunter-gatherers coming to Ireland would have had to cross by boat or raft. This would, of course, have limited the numbers who could travel at any one time, and it would have perhaps minimised continued contact with kinship groups elsewhere. But so little is known about both the Irish Mesolithic inhabitants and the Mesolithic peoples of regions adjacent to Ireland that it is impossible to give a definitive answer. We cannot merely look at a map and point to the shortest route. It would seem most probable that the earliest Mesolithic settlement was somewhere on the east coast of Ireland, probably the northern half, but one single find could change that picture.

Mount Sandel

It is difficult to establish a detailed picture of the lifestyle of these Mesolithic hunters. There are no monuments associated with the Mesolithic, therefore their settlement sites can be quite difficult to find. Because so much of the soil in Ireland is acidic, virtually all the tools made from organic matter have rotted away, and frequently the only indication of their presence is a scatter of stone tools and fragments in a ploughed field, river bank or seashore. Yet we have managed to glean some information about the way of life of these hunter-gatherers. Much of this is based on excavations at Mount Sandel, County Derry, where microliths and other distinctive forms of Mesolithic tool had been ploughed up for nearly a hundred years. This is a group of fields centred on Mount Sandel fort, about 30m (98ft) above sea-level, at the edge of an escarpment overlooking the estuary of the Lower Bann. Excavation on Mount Sandel revealed an extensive Early Mesolithic settlement. The site has produced radiocarbon dates ranging from 7040 ± 80 BC to 5935 ± 120 BC, but they are mostly concentrated between 7000 BC and 6650 BC. This site represents the earliest known certain occupation of Ireland.

In spite of destruction caused by ploughing, traces of some dwellings survived — a series of post-holes were particularly common in one part of the site where they had been protected in a slight hollow. These arcs of post-holes centred on scooped-out hollows, about 1m (3ft) across and 20cm (8in) deep. These were the central fireplaces of huts. The huts were about 6m (19½ft) across, and nearly circular. They had been built by placing a series of saplings in the ground. These were often set close to 30cm (11½in) into the subsoil and at an angle. They may sometimes have been woven together to make an inverted basket shape or tied together to make a rather taller tepee-like structure. It is impossible to say how the Mount Sandel huts were roofed, with skins or reeds, or perhaps the walls were covered with earth or sods to make an earth lodge.

It is apparent that Mount Sandel was a popular location, and there is evidence of a multiplicity of post-holes, pits and hearths from the numerous re-occupations there. It would seem, however, that at any one time there was probably no more than one large hut, and adjacent to it an area for manufacturing stone tools and dumping the left-over debris. Perhaps there were other specialist areas, for example for skin cleaning. The occasional large deep pit found on the site could have been used for storage.

Hunter-gatherers are usually thought of as highly mobile groups, at the prey of every minor seasonal change and, therefore, living in very light shelters which could be erected quite quickly, but the occurrence of such large dwellings at Mount Sandel suggests a more settled lifestyle. This is confirmed by the other information which was obtained from the excavation.

Mount Sandel lies in an area of acidic soils where animal bones do not survive long. Fortunately, however, the inhabitants threw quantities of bones onto their fires. These burnt fragments survived and give us one of our best pictures of the lifestyle of the Mesolithic community. Although over three hundred mammal bones were found, only three animals were represented. One bone was from a domesticated dog, three were from Irish hare, and the remainder were from wild pig. Those identified were usually foot bones, as most of the others had been

Deposits excavated in 1935 at Curran Point, Larne, County Antrim.
(see p212)

twisted and shattered by the heat of the fire. These fragments had to be picked from many thousands of tiny unidentifiable pieces. Some bird bones were recovered, including thrush, pigeon, and even the occasional bone of the capercaillie or black goose. A few bones of eel and sea-fish were also found. The vast majority of fish bones were those of salmon and trout, which were probably caught during the summer months. Even today, there is a commercial salmon fishery on this part of the River Bann.

Evidence of plant foods is extremely difficult to find, but besides substantial concentrations of burnt hazelnut shells, some carbonised water lily and what may be apple seeds have also turned up.

It would appear that the inhabitants of the Bann Estuary could live for most of the year on food from the surrounding area. The spring and summer saw runs of salmon in the estuary, while in the autumn a rich array of nuts, berries and fruit, and eels running downstream, would have been available. During the winter, stored supplies of food and wild pig would have been the main sources of nourishment. We must imagine these people as capable of planning ahead and deciding where exactly to live — in particular, where they could maximise the returns from their environment.

Lough Boora

At one stage it was felt that the availability of raw materials for the manufacture of stone tools was a factor which inhibited Mesolithic settlement in Ireland. In particular, the concentration of sites in north-east Ireland and the plentiful sources of flint were presumed to be related. Yet flint was only one of the range of materials which could be used, and so it is not surprising that in the mid-seventies, a series of encampments was discovered on the shore of an ancient lake, now the site of the modern Lough Boora in County Offaly. These seem to date to about 8500 years ago, although one date might just suggest earlier occupation. Lough Boora has produced many of the same types of implement as found at Mount Sandel, but mainly of chert rather than flint.

Lough Boora shows not only early settlement in the centre of Ireland, but it is also an example of what may be a little summer shoreline camp, where salmon and eels could be caught and pigs hunted in the surrounding forests. As at Mount Sandel, few traces of other large mammals have been found, and in particular no red deer bones have been discovered at either site.

We can now be reasonably certain that these early colonists spread very rapidly throughout the whole island. Not only can they be found in the centre of Ireland, where most of their campsites have been masked by the growth of raised bogs, but in recent years an increasing number of locations have been identified in Munster, producing the same range of microliths. These are usually found on areas of high ground overlooking rivers such as the Cork Blackwater.

The Later Mesolithic period

So far, sites which have produced microliths have always produced radiocarbon dates more than eight thousand years old. One of the unexplained problems associated with the Irish Mesolithic period is that apparently sometime after 6000 BC, Mesolithic communities changed their whole stone-working technology, replacing composite tools set with microliths with much larger single-piece artifacts. The most common forms are large, sometimes leaf-shaped flakes of flint which have been constricted at the butt end. Because they have been found in such profusion in the Bann Valley, they are frequently called Bann Flakes. These tools and related forms have now been found throughout Ireland, made from flint in the north-east, chert in the midlands, and even rhyolites and sandstone in the south-west.

Why this change took place is unknown. The stages of the changeover from one technology to another cannot be identified as there is a gap of nearly eight hundred years in which there are no good substantial Mesolithic sites. Therefore at Newferry, County Antrim, we can see the end-product of the change just over seven thousand years ago, without being able to understand the process. There are, however, enough small sites present to show that Ireland was not abandoned and then re-populated.

A number of other changes were taking place at the same time. The climate had become more Atlantic, that is, wetter and warmer, the vegetation had changed to one dominated by oak and elm, with an increasing proportion of alder in damper locations. Sea levels were rising and flooding river valleys, while raised bogs were beginning to grow on many of the smaller lakes in the midlands. At the same time, perhaps, the population of

Ireland was steadily increasing.

Did any or all of these factors lead to the dramatic technological changes which took place? We cannot decide whether any of them contributed, but the end-product was a range of tools which made the Irish Later Mesolithic period distinctive in Europe. Research is now beginning to suggest that one major factor may be increased wood-working during this period, and it is of interest that ground-stone axes became quite common — it is thought that these implements were especially adapted for felling and trimming trees.

Apart from a site at Sutton, County Dublin, there are no large Late Mesolithic campsites such as Mount Sandel. Those in the Bann Valley are situated in the floor of the flood plain. A classic example is Newferry, where interleaved with the river deposits is evidence of intermittent occupation for a period of two thousand years. Could all that wood-working equipment have been used for building fish traps?

While none of the Later Mesolithic campsites were long-term, it is only at this later period, when sea and land levels had stabilised, that we can get a glimpse of how these communities exploited the sea. Ferriter's Cove in County Kerry is choked with sand dunes, but below them are the traces of small temporary campsites. These may have been occupied for, at the most, a few days. Excavations here have shown that the inhabitants scavenged on the beach for flint, rhyolite, siltstones and other rocks as raw materials for their tools. The beach was also carefully combed for shellfish. Very often little heaps of only a few hundred of one species of a particular size have been discovered, indicating a surprising degree of selectivity. Numerous large fish, such as tope, were caught in the open sea, while rock-fish, such as ballan wrasse, were also taken. Of food from the land, pig bones were the most frequently recovered. In general, even though settlement was very transitory, these early settlers displayed a remarkable knowledge of the environment and a confidence in their ability to exploit it.

The various means by which these hunter-gatherers adapted to a distinct island environment and their unique development points to the fact that they had become the first indigenous Irish community.

Flint artifacts, including microliths, from Mount Sandel, County Derry.

Excavations in progress at the Late Mesolithic site of Ferriter's Cove, County Kerry. (see p212)

The Neolithic period

People's dependence on the environment for what they could hunt, trap or collect for their survival was very limiting. A revolution in their prospects began with the slow development of food-producing in the Near East from about 10 000 BC onwards. The harvesting of the wild grasses, ancestral to our modern cereals, and the realisation that animals such as the ox, goat and pig could be controlled and even modified by selective breeding, led to the appearance of fully agricultural communities and, by about eight thousand years ago, to the emergence of town life. The revolutionary benefits of controlling the food supply were many: groups could produce surpluses which would feed them in the leaner months of the year; they could settle more permanently and not be preoccupied by the overwhelming need to seek food; they could develop specialised crafts. The new way of life spread rapidly throughout western Asia and Europe.

Where did the first Irish farmers come from? It seems reasonable to look to the shortest sea-crossings from Britain as being significant, and there are many close resemblances between the cultures of Ireland and Britain at this time. There are also hints of contact with continental groups. The archaeological evidence is varied — house-plans (usually only found by chance), great stone tombs (megalithic tombs), stone tools, pottery fragments,

plant pollen — and the time-scale so vast (we now know that the Neolithic period lasted in Ireland for more than two thousand years) that we must begin to think of this period in new ways. It was a time of great changes — the first great modification of the environment by people, the appearance of the first monumental architecture and the complex social organisation needed to achieve it. We can only dimly guess at the needs that great tomb architecture such as Newgrange or Creevykeel were intended to fulfil, but it is likely that it went far beyond the mere disposal of the dead. The Neolithic period also saw an increasing complexity in the economy — in addition to a large increase in the tool-kit and domestic equipment, specialised production of tools such as axeheads and long-distance exchange of goods began. During this period, Ireland was not a backwater, and contact with the wider world was frequent. There is growing evidence of settlement by new groups during the later Neolithic period.

With the introduction of farming, things could never be the same again. By the end of the Neolithic period, extensive forest clearance had taken place, parts of the land had been divided into fields, settled — or nearly settled — communities had occupied the whole island, and Ireland had been opened up to regular contact with peoples overseas.

(opposite page) Newgrange, County Meath. At sunrise on the winter solstice, the shaft of sunlight strikes through the roof box and illuminates the rear of the burial chamber.

The Neolithic environment

Michael O'Connell

In the period prior to 4000 BC, the climate was warm and wet, but stable. Dense woodland covered the landscape, and an equilibrium had been reached between vegetation, environment and the Mesolithic peoples, whose impact was largely confined to the immediate vicinity of their settlements. In western Ireland, pine and oak were dominant, and the expansion of blanket bog, which today typifies so much of the landscape of the western seaboard counties, had not yet taken place. In north-eastern and south-eastern Ireland, oak was more important than pine, while in the fertile midlands, oak and, above all, elm flourished, and hazel was important in the understory of the woodlands.

(opposite)
Fig 1. Pollen diagram, Scragh Bog. (see p212)

Fig 2. Pollen diagram, Lough Sheeauns.

Bark of an elm, showing the disease which killed many hundreds of thousands of trees in the 1980s. (see p212)

Woodland clearance

The introduction of agriculture had important and far-reaching consequences. Crop production especially required at least some open landscape, more or less devoid of trees. Woodland clearance was, therefore, necessary for the expansion of Neolithic cultures. Pollen diagrams from two contrasting sites — Scragh bog, County Westmeath and Lough Sheeauns, north-west of Connemara — provide good evidence for the large-scale changes in vegetation brought about by the Early Neolithic peoples.

Pollen analysis

To reconstruct prehistoric landscapes and environments, we must rely on various forms of evidence, especially pollen diagrams. A pollen diagram simply shows the changing proportion of different pollen types in a vertical core of lake sediment or in a long sod taken from a peat-bank face. The sediment or peat has accumulated gradually, so that a time sequence is represented which may extend from the end of the last glaciation, normally the base of the core, to the present day, which will be represented by the uppermost sediments. The proportion or percentage of different pollen types at a particular depth in the core may be taken as a guide to the importance of the various species in the landscape at the time when that sediment was laid down. The technique provides a detailed record which is free of human bias.

Scragh Bog

Fig. 1 shows a pollen diagram from Scragh Bog, near Lough Owel, County Westmeath. This basin, which was a lake until the beginning of the Christian period, is surrounded by some of the most fertile land in Ireland. A core from it provided a record of the vegetational history of the area since the end of the Ice Age. At the base of Fig. 1, which relates to the period immediately prior to the advent of Neolithic peoples, the pollen is overwhelmingly that of trees, indicating the dominance of woodland at that time. Also noteworthy is the prominence of elm, the pollen of which constitutes 30 per cent of the total. Then, suddenly, the elm pollen drops to a few per cent, and hazel pollen and also the pollen count for grasses and ribwort plantain (a weed of cultivation) expand. Most significantly, *cereal* pollen is recorded in the sediment as the elm begins to decline and before the expansion of grass and plantain pollen. This suggests that arable farming was initially important and that later, as more open areas were created, the grazing of animals increased in importance. The dramatic decline in the amount of elm pollen in this Early Neolithic period has usually been interpreted as indicating widespread clearance of elm-dominated woodlands to make way for farming land, but there are other possible explanations (see below). After some time the woodlands recovered, this recovery being followed by another clearance episode, which may date to the Later Neolithic period.

The decline in the amount of elm pollen, coinciding with the first arrival of the Neolithic peoples, is seen in most pollen diagrams, not only from Ireland, but also from north-west Europe. This raises the question of how people with only stone tools could have produced such a dramatic change over a wide area, within a period of a few centuries at most. Perhaps the human factor may not have been the primary cause of the so-called Elm Decline. A recently constructed pollen diagram relating to the same period from western Ireland provides some interesting clues.

Lough Sheeauns

Lough Sheeauns lies east of Cleggan in north-west Connemara. This small lake, of about 100m (328ft) diameter, lies in the centre of a dense concentration of megalithic tombs. Within a radius of less than one kilometre, five tombs have been recorded, one of which is a portal tomb 50m (164ft) from the edge of the lake. Because of the proximity of Neolithic activity to the lake, it was assumed that the lake sediment would contain a good record of the early land use. A detailed study of the sediment has provided important new evidence as to the nature, age and duration of the Neolithic farming, and its impact on the natural vegetation and soils.

The pollen diagram presented in Fig. 2 has a number of noteworthy features, the most pronounced being the major expansion of grasses, plantain, bracken, dandelion, daisy, dock and buttercup, which can be seen in the lower part of the diagram. Corresponding with this expansion, a decline occurs in the amount of tree pollen, especially oak, elm and hazel. An occasional cereal pollen is recorded. The time scale, which is based on a series of radiocarbon dates from the sediment, indicates that this part of the diagram dates to the Early Neolithic period.

The Neolithic population at Lough Sheeauns had a major impact on the local environment. Woodland, at least in the vicinity of the lake, was almost completely cleared (the tree pollen which remains was probably blown in from woodlands elsewhere in Connemara) and pastoral farming was pursued. Few cereal pollens are recorded, suggesting that cereal production played only a minor role in the farming economy. We must,

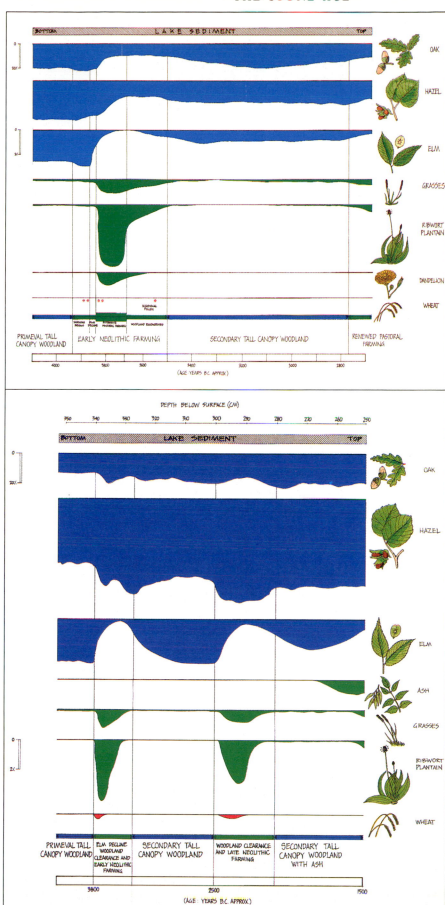

however, be cautious here because cereal pollens do not disperse well and are therefore under-represented in the fossil record. It is also of interest that charcoal particles or soot were not common in the sediment, which would suggest that woodland clearance was carried out not by fire, but presumably by means of stone axes. This, in turn, points to the presence of a sizeable population, which one might suspect anyhow from the number of megalithic tombs, the construction of which called for considerable amounts of labour.

It is interesting to speculate as to the relative importance of the axe as distinct from fire for woodland clearance during the Neolithic period. At present we do not have the necessary detailed information from a sufficient number of sites to draw general conclusions with any confidence. However, at Ballynagilly, County Tyrone, investigations have revealed pine charcoal stratified in peat which dates to the earliest major Neolithic clearance phase, indicating that fire certainly played a role there.

It is usually assumed that soil deterioration was a normal consequence of Early Neolithic woodland clearance and that, in response to this, a nomadic style of farming was adopted, with cleared areas being abandoned and new patches of virgin woodland being opened up so that crop production levels could be maintained. At Lough Sheeauns, however, soil deterioration does not appear to have taken place. The heathers and the sedges — usual signs of such deterioration — do not expand greatly in the pollen record, and the chemical characteristics of the lake sediment, which have also been studied at this site, show no evidence that the soils in the catchment were

degraded. It is, therefore, all the more enigmatic that the intensive farming period lasted only about a hundred and fifty years, and within another two hundred years woodland had fully regenerated. After woodland regeneration is complete, there is a gap of 670 years before human activity again registers in the lake sediment (Fig. 2). This, of course, does not mean that there was no human presence in the region as a whole during mid-Neolithic times; it does indicate, however, that there was no interference with the woodland within a radius of up to a kilometre about the lake.

The Elm Decline

Even though elm is poorly represented at Lough Sheeauns, a distinct Elm Decline is registered before the major clearance phase (Fig. 2). As in many other pollen diagrams, the elm alone is initially affected, while the representation of the other trees remains unchanged. Analysis of the sediment before the Elm Decline revealed evidence for farming in the form of cereal pollen and ribwort plantain. In other words, prior to the Elm Decline there was a Neolithic presence which was probably limited to small clearings in the oak-dominated woodlands. This discovery is important as it shows that the Elm Decline and the introduction of farming are not contemporaneous at this site, and the connection between the Elm Decline and the advent of Neolithic peoples, so often made in the past, may not be tenable. Many scientists now believe that a disease similar to the present-day Dutch Elm disease affected the elm population at about 4000 BC, and that the disease may have been unintentionally spread as early farming expanded into north-west Europe. If this is so, we must then assume

(below left) Basket found about 3.5m (11½ft) deep in a bog at Twyford, County Westmeath. (see p212)

(below right) The Early Neolithic site of Donegore Hill, County Antrim, discovered through aerial photography by Barrie Hartwell of Queen's University, Belfast. (see p212)

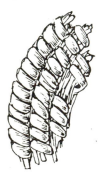

that the major changes in the elm values recorded at Scragh Bog may only partially reflect woodland clearances by the Early Neolithic settlers. It is obviously a challenge for future research to resolve satisfactorily the role played by disease, human activity and possibly climatic change in bringing about the vegetational variations which are recorded in the pollen in our lakes and bogs.

The first farmers

Alison Sheridan

The first certain evidence for farming in Ireland dates to around 4000 BC. We can be sure that the domesticated animals and plants involved in agriculture were imported to the island, since the wild progenitors of most of the species are not found here, and in the case of pigs — where their wild ancestors were native — there is no evidence for the slow process of domestication. The associated archaeological evidence suggests that the people who sailed over with these animals were probably not the Mesolithic inhabitants of Ireland, but small groups of pioneering farmers. Similarities in material culture and burial traditions between the earliest farmers in Ireland and those in northern and eastern Britain suggest links between these areas, but the ultimate origin of these agricultural communities remains a matter for debate.

It used to be thought that these earliest farming communities landed in one part of Ireland (either in the north-east or in the west), then spread westwards or eastwards from there. However, recent evidence suggests that they may have arrived at various points around the coast. The date of around 4000 BC for the newly discovered rectangular house at Tankardstown, County Limerick, demonstrates that this early settlement was not limited to the northern third of the island, as some had previously thought.

Early agriculture: resources and tools

The domesticated animals and plants which are known to have been introduced by the first farmers were cattle, sheep/goats (the skeletal evidence of both is very similar), pigs, wheat and barley. The species of cereal are represented by primitive varieties, such as emmer and einkorn wheat; the cattle and pigs are larger than those found on later prehistoric sites, and the sheep/goats were probably of a type ancestral to the Soay breed. The early farming communities also made use of Ireland's abundant wild resources, such as fish, deer, wildfowl, nuts and berries. At Tankardstown, archaeologists found traces of crab-apples, which may have been hung around the walls of the house to dry — a practice which is carried on to this day by peasant communities in south-east Europe.

Along with the novel domesticated species, the farmers introduced the technology needed to exploit them. Although not a new implement, the ground-stone axe gained prominence as a tool for clearing woodland, both for grazing and cultivation, and for providing the raw materials for houses and miscellaneous timberwork. Simple ards (scratch ploughs) and spades were used to cultivate the land, various flint and stone tools to harvest the crops, and stone saddle-querns to grind the grain. The processing of animal carcasses would have been carried out with the aid of tools such as scrapers (one variety of which — the so-called 'end scraper' — had already been in use in Mesolithic Ireland); and we may be sure that the farmers' tool-kit would have included many implements of perishable material such as wood, bone and twine.

Consequences of the new lifestyle

The implications of producing one's own staple diet, rather than relying entirely on food garnered from nature, were far-reaching. Firstly, the fact that crops had to be tended and harvested meant that communities were more likely to remain in one place than to move around *en masse* to take advantage of seasonal resources. The robust nature of Neolithic timber houses, contrasting as it does with what we know of Mesolithic habitations, suggests the existence of permanent settlements. Part of the community may have spent periods away from home, engaged in hunting, fishing, trading or accompanying cattle to summer pastures. However, the prevailing impression of the Neolithic settlement pattern is that of scattered individual farmsteads, each containing

Ritual stone object found in a depression outside the entrance to the western tomb in the great passage tomb mound of Knowth, County Meath. (see p212)

47

perhaps one extended family. The exception is the small 'hamlet' site of Lough Gur in County Limerick, where several houses cluster round a lake; this may represent a particular local development from the original basic pattern.

Secondly, this change in subsistence strategy appears to have caused a long-term increase in population. Previously, groups of hunter-gatherer-fishers would almost certainly have kept their numbers down to a level which the natural environment could sustain. The introduction of agriculture and stock-keeping would have appeared to provide a more secure food supply, whilst at the same time requiring more people to do the necessary work. Some idea of the consequences of this population growth is given in two widely separated parts of Ireland. In County Antrim, the enclosed hilltop site of Donegore Hill, with its deep ditches cut from the living rock and a timber stockade, hints at the emergence of local hostilities around 3500 BC, perhaps as a result of land shortages in the area. In County Mayo, there is

growing evidence for a major reorganisation of the landscape around 3100 BC. Field systems running for several kilometres, straddling neighbouring hillsides, were laid out in what is thought to have been a major cattle-rearing area. It has been calculated that this arrangement would have accommodated a high density of both cattle and people. Thus the field systems may represent a solution to the problem of increasing population density.

Thirdly, the introduction of agriculture seems to have heralded the end of the old hunting-gathering-fishing way of life of the native population. The available evidence suggests that this traditional lifestyle did not continue for more than a few centuries after the appearance of farming. One possible reason for this is that the indigenous communities gradually took advantage of the opportunities offered by agriculture to enjoy what seemed to be a more secure resource base. There would have been plenty of scope for contact between the farmers and the native population, based as it was in coastal, riverine and lakeside areas — major transport routes in a largely forested environment.

Pottery

Pottery makes its first appearance in Ireland at this point, being used alongside containers of wood, leather and other perishable material which had probably served the purpose in the past. The earliest pottery consists of undecorated bowls of various sizes, many with a 'shoulder' distinguishing the belly from the neck. Many are fine, well-fired, thin-walled vessels, and some show evidence of having been polished prior to firing. Although many such pots are of a deep, rich brown colour, a variety of other colours are found, and these relate both to variations in the clay used for their manufacture and to firing conditions. Pottery manufacture is likely to have been a small-scale, localised activity, with most communities having easy access to the raw materials. The pots were made by hand, using rings of clay, and after drying were fired in above-ground bonfires or in firing pits, at temperatures of around 800 degrees centigrade.

A few centuries after the introduction of this plain pottery, local and regional variations in its style can be discerned, and quality shouldered bowls with all-over external decoration can be seen around 3700 to 3400 BC, with examples turning up in burial and occupation sites

as far apart as Cork and Antrim. A variety of other decorated pottery types came into use during the third millennium BC; one type, known as Carrowkeel ware, is closely associated with the use of a particular type of burial monument known as a passage tomb.

Weapons

Although spears and perhaps bows and arrows had been in use in Ireland since the beginning of the Mesolithic period, new types of projectile point appear with the arrival of the first farmers. These are leaf- and lozenge-shaped arrowheads and javelinheads, which differ from their Early Mesolithic precursors in forming a single-piece projectile point, rather than a composite one (that is, comprised of several tiny blades set into a shaft). As rare intact specimens demonstrate, these points were affixed to their shafts using resin, sometimes reinforced by twine. A particular type of scraper — the 'hollow scraper', which became more popular in Ireland than in Britain — may have been used for stripping and whittling the rods for the shafts. Although no wooden bow of Neolithic date has yet been found in Ireland, a remarkably well-preserved specimen of a long bow was recovered from a Neolithic wooden trackway, the Sweet Track, in Somersetshire in England.

It is likely that these arrows and javelins were used as weapons as well as for hunting. In Britain over a dozen Neolithic bodies have been found with arrowheads embedded in them; and in Ireland it may be that some of the arrowheads which are found in burial monuments entered the tombs in — rather than alongside — the human remains.

Jewellery

Although little work has yet been done on Neolithic beads and pendants in Ireland and Britain, there are remarkable collections, for example, those from Lough Gur (including a necklace associated with a child's burial), and a spectacular necklace of 112 beads from a tomb at Creggandevesky, County Tyrone. No beads or pendants are known from pre-Neolithic contexts in Ireland, and it is assumed that the idea of wearing them came with the first farmers, but this is uncertain.

Most Neolithic Irish beads and pendants are made of stone; the remainder are of bone, with one example of a bear's tooth pendant from a tomb at Annaghmare, County Armagh. Wooden specimens are unlikely to have

(opposite page)
(left)
Stages in the manufacture of Neolithic pottery.

(top)
A hoard of polished stone axeheads, made of porcellanite, found at Malone, Belfast. (see p212)

(bottom)
Neolithic pottery from court tombs: decorated vessel, Ballymackald-rack, County Antrim; large shouldered bowl, Ballintaggart, County Armagh; smaller bowl, Audleystown, County Down.

survived, and there are no examples of amber or jet beads of this antiquity in Ireland. Interestingly, many of the stone beads and pendants are made from serpentine, and it may well be that ornaments of this material were traded around.

Communications networks

The first farmers established networks of contacts, both within and outside Ireland, which would have been used not only for social purposes but also for the exchange of raw materials, artifacts, and people. The high-quality flint of north-east Ireland was highly prized for the manufacture of tools such as arrowheads, knives and scrapers. Also in the north-east, at Tievebulliagh, County Antrim, and on Rathlin Island, are sources of a dark, blue-grey, speckled porcellanite, which was ideal for the manufacture of axes, adzes and chisels. Adzes are mounted like axes but with the cutting-edge at right angles to the handle. They are specialised woodworking tools used for purposes such as trimming boards. Both flint and porcellanite were exported to great distances from their source areas. Porcellanite axes, which are known to have been produced from around 3700 BC, turn up as far away as Cork, Kent and the Northern Isles of Scotland. It may be that many of the inhabitants of north-east Ireland, south-west Scotland and the western isles of Scotland obtained their supplies of porcellanite by visiting the source areas themselves; others, at greater distances, probably relied on contacts in the exchange network.

Rare examples of definite imports to Ireland include a few pieces of Arran pitchstone (a greenish, blackish volcanic glass like obsidian), which have turned up on three coastal sites in County Antrim; occasional stone axes from Cumbria and south-west Wales, found in north-east Ireland; and a flint axe and adze of Scandinavian type, found in a rabbit burrow at Doonooney, County Wexford. We can only speculate about the chain of exchanges which brought these exotic objects to south-eastern Ireland, but it should be noted that other similar artifacts have been discovered in southern Britain and Wales.

Burial monuments

The most noticeable innovation introduced by the first farmers was the burial monument. There is no evidence to show how bodies were disposed of in Ireland prior to the appearance of agriculture, but after 4000 BC a remarkable series of funerary monuments was built. These served not only as repositories of human remains and as durable monuments to the ancestors, but also, arguably, as territorial markers and — in some cases — as symbols of power.

Three basic varieties of megalithic tomb (made using massive stones) have been identified: the court tomb, the portal tomb and the passage tomb. A fourth type of burial monument — the so-called Linkardstown-type cist — has recently been shown to date from around 3500 BC.

Linkardstown-type cists differ from the other tombs in several respects. Firstly, they consist of a large, box-like stone cist set in the centre of a round mound. This mound is sometimes kerbed, and it generally consists of a stone core covered with layers of sods and earth, capped in one case by a clay mantle. Secondly, their use is often restricted to the interment of small numbers, and, occasionally, single individuals. Adult males are most commonly found in them. Thirdly, their distribution is confined to the southern half of the island, with most of the eight known examples running in a north-east/south-west line from County Kilkenny to County Dublin, and one in County Tipperary. The sparse grave goods accompanying the burials suggest links with the users of court and portal tombs, and it may well be that these tombs represent a specific regional development amongst the descendants of the earliest farming communities. The fact that in many instances only a few adult males were buried in this way suggests that perhaps these were local leaders, who chose to underline their status through their funerary monuments.

Court and portal tombs can be regarded as two variants of the same basic funerary tradition, closely associated with the early farming communities. It is possible that both types evolved from a non-megalithic prototype, consisting of a linear timber structure fronted by a timber facade, and eventually covered by an earthen mound. Traces of such a monument can be seen in the first phases of construction of the court tomb at Ballymacaldrack, County Antrim; and several examples of this type of funerary monument are known from northern and eastern Britain. In Ireland, the transition to constructing these monuments in stone may have occurred some time after the initial agricultural settlement.

Passage tombs appear to represent a separate tradition of tomb building and use. It may be that the builders of the earliest passage tombs — the small simple structures as seen, for example, in the cemetery at Carrowmore, County Sligo — belonged to a different set of immigrant farming communities. Again, the evidence relating to their origins is tantalisingly sketchy, but there is a tradition of building simple, often passageless 'passage tombs' along the Atlantic coast during the fifth and early fourth millennia BC; and wherever there are signs that the later builders of Irish passage tombs were in contact with the outside world, it is with areas along the Atlantic seaboard such as western Iberia, Brittany, Wales and the Orkney Islands. Striking evidence for such contacts includes the carved sandstone 'idol' from the entrance to the western tomb at Knowth (site 1), which has its only parallels amongst material from passage tombs in the Lisbon area; a carved pebble from the main tomb at Newgrange, closely resembling items from north-west Iberia; and the stunning spiral-decorated flint macehead from the eastern tomb at Knowth (site 1), which is of a type known from several British findspots.

Social organisation

The nature of society in Neolithic Ireland has long been a contentious subject, but one view which became popular in the 1970s held that the farming communities who buried their dead in the court and portal tombs were basically egalitarian, whilst the builders of passage tombs were members of a stratified society. Developments in Irish archaeology over the last decade have shown, however, that the true story is probably far more complex than that.

There is no reason to suggest that the farming communities of the first few centuries of the Neolithic period (say from 4000 to 3500 BC) were anything but egalitarian. In areas where court and portal tombs were erected, such monuments can be regarded as the communal (and not necessarily permanent) repositories of the human remains of a basically classless society. The same may well be true of the first passage tombs, whose builders seem to have been present around this time as well. If one interprets these tombs as monuments to the ancestors, one can see from recent ethnographic parallels that the ancestors (and, by extension, the elders of a community) could have been treated as the seat of power

and authority. In the case of court and portal tombs, which appear to be scattered amongst the agricultural settlements, the monuments themselves could have been used to settle disputes over land. A community could justify its claim to a piece of land, for example, by arguing that its ancestors were buried there.

However, certain changes in social organisation can be detected in different parts of Ireland around 3500 BC. The fortification and re-fortification of the hilltop at Donegore Hill, County Antrim, indicates a period of unrest, perhaps precipitated by increasing population density and its attendant stress on agricultural land. The presence inside these defences of a unique, large, round timber structure (a house?) could be interpreted as evidence for a local 'tribal' leader; certainly some degree of organisation would have been necessary to manage the large workforce needed to construct the defences. All this suggests that the local farming communities were losing their former autonomy. In the south, the Linkardstown-type cists provide a different kind of evidence for emergent social stratification. However, given that very little else is known about the communities responsible for the building of these mounds, we must await the results of further research before speculating any more.

Later developments in the north-west, featuring the laying out of extensive field systems around 3100 BC, have already been mentioned. Apparently contemporary with this was the construction of several large or elaborate court tombs, such as the examples from Ballyglass, County Mayo. The significance of such tombs is debatable: are they the status symbols of local dominant groups who masterminded the reorganisation of the agricultural landscape? Or was the building of the field walls the action of egalitarian communities, co-operating in this large venture and symbolising their unity by building these new tombs? This issue is likely to remain contentious.

The evidence of passage tombs clearly points to a major process of social stratification over the period 3800 to 3000 BC, in which the tombs themselves are used as tools in a strategy of social aggrandisement. Although dating evidence is scarce there is enough to suggest that the small, simple forms, as seen in the Carrowmore cemetery, may be earlier than the massive, elaborate tombs such as the main monuments at Newgrange, Knowth and Dowth. The latter are undoubtedly the product of a highly stratified society, and one can argue that the construction and use of these tombs was a major means of maintaining control over the local population. In these tombs we see a sophisticated fusion of the concepts of ancestral power, celestial power and everyday power; and those groups who were able to manipulate these concepts to their own advantage had a formidable tool at their disposal.

The Later Neolithic period

Anna Brindley

The farming communities of the Later Neolithic period probably differed little in their daily activities from their ancestors, the first farmers. As far as we know, farming practices did not alter to any great degree. Stone axes were still used to clear woodland, crops of wheat and barley were sown and harvested in the cleared areas, and pigs, cattle, sheep and goats were reared. Smaller flint and stone implements, including, in particular, hollow scrapers and, later, triangular knives, were the most popular small cutting and scraping tools in daily use.

Fragments of what were once extensive field systems still exist under the blanket bogs along the Atlantic coast, stretching from Kerry up to North Mayo and probably beyond, and on the uplands of Tyrone and Antrim. Along the north-east coast, at Dundrum and Murlough Bay, on the river margins of the Bann, on islands and on lakesides, as at Island MacHugh, Garoid Island, Rathlin Island and Dalkey Island, traces of the settlements of this period have been found. These locations provided a variety of food resources such as game, fowl, fish and shellfish, while lighter woodland coverage would have meant easier management, and the rivers and sea would have allowed relatively easy passage.

Few details of the settlements themselves survive at these sites. Even with careful excavation, usually little more than a few hearths, sherds of pottery and some stone tools are all that remain. Bone, wood and hide, which formed the raw material of almost everything on these sites, from the houses themselves, to utensils, implements, clothes and food, have not survived. What we know of day-to-day life is gleaned chiefly from the

Ceremonial macehead of polished flint from the eastern tomb of Knowth tumulus, County Meath. (see p212)

A hoard of seventeen flint scrapers found in a bog at Beggarstown, County Antrim.

sherds of fragile pottery which survive, and the ritual and funerary monuments which are scattered through the landscape. Indeed, it is only the scale of some of the architectural achievements, such as the passage tombs at Newgrange, Knowth and Dowth in County Meath, that give any impression of the confidence which these communities had developed after the centuries spent establishing themselves were over.

Pottery

Most of the pottery of this period is round-bottomed, with flat-based pottery being introduced only at the end. One type consists of hemispherical bowls, often decorated all over the outer surface with shell and cord impressions, or lines executed in a technique known as stab-and-drag, where a pointed or flat-tipped implement was dragged irregularly over the surface of the unbaked pot. Pots with this latter decoration are usually called Carrowkeel bowls, and are found not only on settlements sites, but also in graves — mostly in or near passage tombs.

A second type of pottery, known as Grooved Ware, occurs at the end of the Later Neolithic period. It is the earliest flat-based pottery in this country, and is related to the Grooved Ware found in England and Scotland. These pots have straight or very slightly curved walls, and the decoration is usually made up of straight, evenly grooved lines, sometimes with a few lines of impressed cord. Only a little of this pottery has been found in Ireland so far, but it seems likely that it was used both for domestic and religious purposes. In England and Scotland, Grooved Ware is often found at henge monuments. Similar monuments occur in Ireland, although very little is known about them and none have been excavated; it is likely that one day this pottery will be found in them too.

Religious and ritual monuments

The Later Neolithic was a period of maturity, when the religious and social side of life caught up with, took advantage of and went beyond the economic developments of the preceding thousand years. The religious centres of Knowth and Newgrange, and the earthen enclosures of Ballynahatty and Dowth, were designed and constructed during this time, both to impress and to be used by large numbers of people. They show not only great engineering and architectural expertise, and the ability to marshal vast resources, but they also throw light on the social organisation of these people and the strength of their economy. By contrast, it is often difficult to appreciate the relative wealth of communities at this time from the meagre remains of the domestic sites.

The people who used Carrowkeel pottery are best known for the passage tombs which they built in the northern half of the country, in Leinster and in a small area on the Limerick/Tipperary border. These tombs were often built in groups — as in the Boyne Valley. Such concentrations may indicate that these areas were densely populated; indeed the Boyne Valley with its rich natural resources could have supported a large population. Other concentrations or cemeteries of tombs occur in less obviously attractive areas, such as on the summits of the Lough Crew Hills (± 800ft OD) and other elevated locations. These large cemeteries may have attracted more settled communities from a much wider area who shared a communal religious centre.

The smaller and often simple passage tombs fulfilled the same functions as the earlier court tombs within small communities. Many were built in locations suitable for and probably close to settlement, as at Townleyhall, County Louth, Bremore, County Meath, Rush on the Dublin coast, and Magheracar on the Donegal coast.

The construction of the largest passage tombs required considerable co-operation to plan and build. Members

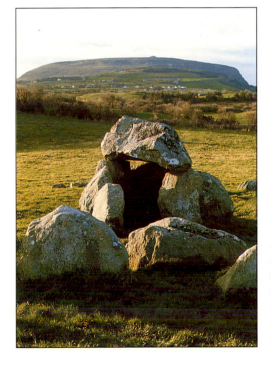

Small dolmen, of a type associated with passage tombs, at Carrowmore, County Sligo. (see p212)

of the community had the architectural experience and the authority to devote resources to large-scale projects. The ability to marshal such resources for a single purpose suggests the emergence of those who were not only individually powerful, but could be seen to be so, and who could extend their power and influence over large areas and communities. These very large tombs also indicate an economy which was able to create a surplus in order to maintain the confidence needed to undertake building on such a scale, but the economic evidence uncovered so far is meagre.

It is not easy to understand the religious or ritual requirements which lay behind these monuments, which must have been enormously costly. Some were probably used purely for burial purposes and whatever rituals were involved in that activity. However, the specific location of some, in situations which are removed from the immediate vicinity of settlements, suggests an interest in the sky which is new to the religious beliefs of these people, at least as far as we can see. Knowledge of the sky and the natural calendar is a prerequisite to any community which is reliant on agriculture for its survival and, perhaps, is interested in sea travel. This knowledge is evident both from the trouble taken to build at high altitudes, which would have allowed a clear line of sight over the abundant tree-cover of the period, and in the details, such as the care which was taken at Newgrange to ensure that the light box was constructed to correct the natural slope on which this unusually long passage tomb was built, thereby enabling the mid-winter sun to illuminate the chamber. It would not have been necessary for simpler passage tombs to have such an elaborate arrangement in order to ensure that light penetrated the chamber at any chosen time of the year; it would have been sufficient to build shorter passages on more level ground and orientate them correctly.

Communications

Perhaps the most influential development which occurred towards the end of the Later Neolithic period was the extent to which contacts were made with communities outside Ireland. This might well be connected with the generation of surplus wealth and the development of structured power. While seasonal and climatic information would have been necessary both for farming and local fishing, a greater understanding of the movements of the sun and the stars would have allowed for more confident navigation further afield, and this chimes with what we know of the orientation and siting of tombs. From around 3000 BC there is evidence along the east coast to suggest fairly regular traffic between the Orkneys, Wales and Brittany, pointing to an interest in navigation and perhaps boat building, which had not been seen since the days when the pioneering farmers first arrived. Several passage tombs were built in Wales, two of which have decorated stones similar to the Irish series. Longer and more spectacular journeys were made to the Orkneys, where a small group of tombs, known as the Maes Howe Group, was constructed. Several large pieces of passage tomb art have also been found in that area. These tombs, built of local stone, resemble to a remarkable degree some of the Irish passage tombs. More spectacular evidence of these journeys was recently found at Knowth, where a very beautifully decorated flint macehead was discovered in the eastern chamber of the large passage tomb. It was imported from northern Britain, where the motifs, raw material and consummate skill required to fashion it existed.

Most of the changes which occur at the end of the Neolithic period are related to these journeys. Evidence for their continuation can be seen in the changes and developments which took place in religious practices, the adoption of the first flat-based pottery and the construction and use of enormous circular earthen-banked enclosures, similar to the large henge monuments which were widespread in Britain. In Ireland these monuments are to be found particularly in the eastern part of the country, and it has been suggested that they were used for astronomical purposes, just as some of the passage tombs were. They are known to occur in the neighbourhood of, and sometimes even to surround, passage tombs. They also occur in the Orkneys, where they have a similar relationship with passage tombs. An enormous circle of pits and stake-holes lies some metres immediately east of the main passage tomb at Newgrange, surrounding a small passage tomb. Recent investigations have shown the pits to contain burnt animal bone, and radiocarbon dates indicate that this monument is contemporary with the construction and use of the large, earthen-banked enclosures. Its location indicates the continuing importance of Newgrange, even after the religious or ritual use of the passage tomb itself had ceased.

The megalithic tomb builders

Seán Ó Nualláin

The spread of the Neolithic way of life throughout Atlantic Europe brought with it the custom of communal burial in great stone structures known as megalithic tombs (from Greek: *megas*, great; *lithos*, stone). As the name indicates, these monuments were usually built with very large stones, often weighing tens of tonnes, and it is clear that considerable engineering skills were required to assemble and erect them. We can only speculate as to the manner of construction. The stones were likely to have been transported on timber sledges, dragged over rollers fashioned from tree-trunks, and then set upright in prepared sockets by means of levers, counter-weights and traction. Roofing stones may have been dragged up ramps and then eased into position above the upright stones which formed the sides of the burial chambers. The chambers were then incorporated in mounds of stones (cairns) or earth (barrows), which helped to stabilise the structure.

We know little about the dwellings or social organisation of the tomb-builders. The cemetery arrangements and the great size of some of the monuments imply settled and well-organised communities of considerable size. The great mound at Newgrange, County Meath, alone has been calculated to contain about two hundred thousand tonnes of stones, and it has been estimated that it could have taken four hundred individuals perhaps some three decades to gather and transport the material and to construct the mound.

In Ireland, the tombs are popularly known by a variety of names, with terms such as 'Giant's Grave', 'Dolmen', 'Cromlech' and 'Dermot and Grania's Bed' being among the commonest forms. Fifteen hundred megalithic tombs have been identified in Ireland, and of these, the major monuments in the Boyne Valley, County Meath, rank with the tomb-builders' finest achievements in western Europe. Many of the Irish tombs are not as well preserved as these world-famous examples, and others have been destroyed, leaving no surface trace whatever.

The surviving tombs can be divided into four classes which are named after their principal characteristic architectural features: court tombs, portal tombs, passage tombs and wedge tombs. These groups are further distinguished by their differing distribution patterns and by the artifacts found in excavated examples.

Court tombs

The court tombs were probably the earliest megalithic monuments to have been built in Ireland, and are part of a north European, long-cairn tradition of tomb-building, extending from Poland in the east to Britain and Ireland in the west. Almost four hundred are known in Ireland, and these, with a few exceptions, are confined to the northern half of the country. Their most distinctive feature is a roofless oval or U-shaped courtyard, set in front of a covered gallery (the burial vault) which is divided by protruding stones, like door jambs, into two, three or four chambers. The court usually occupies the broad eastern end of a long trapeze-shaped cairn. Sometimes the galleries are placed back to back, with the courts at either end of the cairn; occasionally an oval court is centrally placed, and the galleries open off both ends. These monuments, then, can be seen to accommodate two functions, the galleries serving as sepulchres while the courts would seem to have been reserved for long-forgotten rituals associated with the dead.

The burial chamber of the passage tomb of Fourknocks, County Meath. This great chamber, measuring 5.5m (18ft) in maximum diameter, is almost twice the width of Newgrange. (see p212)

Cremation appears to have been the predominant burial rite, though unburnt remains were found at a small number of sites. Preservation is often poor, but a total of thirty-four individuals, both cremated and unburnt, is attested at a tomb at Audleystown in County Down. The burials are usually accompanied by unglazed pottery vessels and stone implements made from flint or chert.

(right)
The chamber of the passage tomb at Newgrange, County Meath, showing the massive uprights from which the corbelled roof springs. (see p212)

(opposite page, bottom left)
Reconstruction drawing of the

wedge tomb of Island, County Cork.

(opposite page, top)
The portal tomb at Kernanstown ('Browneshill'), County Carlow. Its capstone, weighing about 100 tonnes, is thought to be the heaviest Irish megalith.

The pottery includes both elegant round-bottomed bowls, decorated or plain, which may have been ritual deposits, and flat-bottomed coarse wares, perhaps representing domestic vessels. Characteristic stone artifacts include leaf- and lozenge-shaped arrowheads, javelinheads, scrapers, knives, polished stone axeheads and beads. In some cases the artifacts have been burnt, and it has been suggested that these may have been prized possessions of the deceased which were placed on the funeral pyre. Bones of ox, sheep or goat and pig found at a few sites may represent the remains of funeral feasts and indicate that pastoralism formed part of the tomb-builders' way of life. Grain impressions on a few pottery vessels show that cereal growing also had its place in the economy.

The court tomb at Behy, County Mayo, and a nearby habitation enclosure stand within a great complex of pre-bog Neolithic field walls above the sea cliffs at Céide. The size of these fields suggests that they were used to grow grass crops for animal husbandry. The excavation of a centre-court tomb at Ballyglass, County Mayo, uncovered the foundations of a substantial timber house beneath one end of the cairn. The house was rectangular

in plan and measured 13m by 6m (42½ft by 19½ft). These dimensions roughly correspond with those of the houses of small farmers now living nearby. Radiocarbon determinations indicate a date of about 2620 BC for the construction of this house. The tomb is clearly later in date than the house, which may have been deliberately demolished to make way for it. Determinations from other court tombs suggest that the building of such monuments may have begun during the fourth millennium BC and continued into the greater part of the succeeding millennium.

Portal tombs

Portal tombs, though relatively simple structures, are most impressive monuments, and spectacular examples can be seen at Poulnabrone on the Burren in County Clare and Kilclooney near Ardara in County Donegal. There are over one hundred and seventy portal tomb sites in Ireland. These are largely concentrated in the northern half of the country but there is a notable spread of sites in the south-east, between Dublin and Waterford, and a smaller scatter in the Clare—south Galway region. The distribution extends across the Irish Sea to Wales and

Cornwall, where a total of about fifty examples is known.

The standard tombs are based on a tripod design. Two tall portal stones and a lower backstone support a large roofstone poised with its heavier end above the entrance. Massive roofstones are a characteristic feature. Examples weighing up to forty tonnes are relatively common, and the largest, at Kernanstown in County Carlow, has been estimated to weigh one hundred tonnes. Single slabs, resting against the portals and backstone, form the chamber sides. An upright slab placed between the portal stones hinders access or, in some cases, fully seals the entrance to the chamber. A variant form of tomb has a second smaller roofstone resting on the chamber sidestones, and this in turn supports the lower end of the principal roofstone. Some portal tombs are set at the ends of long cairns. One, at Ticloy, County Antrim, has a shallow concave court adjoining the portal jambs. A few others have stones flanking the jambs and these may be the remnants of courts. Some have small subsidiary burial chambers opening off the sides of the cairns. These features provide close links with the court tombs and this connection is strengthened by the occurrence of similar pottery and stone artifacts in both series.

The builders of portal tombs and court tombs had a preference for lowland siting, possibly signifying similar mixed farming economies. Many portal tombs are situated in valleys or on hillsides, and this is particularly apparent in the south-east, where the tombs occur close to the major rivers or their tributaries.

Passage tombs

Passage tombs form a major element of the spread of megalithic monuments throughout Atlantic Europe.

(centre)
Stone beads and pendants from the Carrowkeel cemetery.
(see p212)

(bottom right)
A well-preserved court tomb in its characteristic trapeze-shaped cairn, 18m (59ft) long, uncovered during land reclamation at Creggandevesky, County Tyrone.
(see p212)

Unlike other Irish tomb types, they are often situated on hilltops or ridges, and are generally grouped together in cemeteries, as at Knowth in the Boyne Valley. Over two hundred examples have been identified in Ireland, and others are known to have been destroyed. Their distribution is largely concentrated in the north and east of the country but several examples are known in the south. There are further examples across the Irish Sea in Anglesey, and a few others along the Welsh coast.

The classic form of passage tomb consists of a round mound delimited by a ring or kerb of large stones enclosing a burial chamber, approached by a low narrow passage. The chambers may be round, oval or rectangular in shape. In Ireland tombs with a cruciform plan are common but more complex forms are also found. The passages are roofed with horizontal stones while the chambers are often surmounted by overlapping slabs to form high corbelled vaults.

Visitors to the Boyne Valley tombs may be surprised by the appearance of the great monument at Newgrange. The reconstituted mound there now rises from behind a high concrete retaining wall, faced with white quartz and small dark boulders recovered from the front of the tomb during excavation. This was considered to give a fair representation of the original appearance of the monument, though not everyone would agree that verisimilitude has been achieved. The wall curves inwards towards a structure, so far unique, called the roof-box. This reconstructed feature now permits the rays of the rising sun to shine directly into the back chamber of the cruciform tomb for a few days at the time of the mid-winter solstice (21 December).

An outstanding feature of a number of the Irish tombs and of their antecedents in Brittany is the presence of carved or picked designs on the stones of the tomb or its kerb. Irish passage tomb art is abstract in form, with circles, spirals, arcs, serpentiform lines, lozenges and triangles being the more common elements employed. Though these devices sometimes appear to be scattered at random on the stones, they are often combined in an harmonious composition, ingeniously adapted to the shape of the stones. Certain motifs seem to be favoured at particular tombs or cemeteries; spirals at Newgrange, concentric rectangles at Knowth and rayed circles at Dowth in the Boyne Valley and in the Loughcrew cemetery, County Meath. The meaning of this art is

unknown, but since it is associated with burial monuments it is reasonable to infer that it had a funerary significance. The similarities with the art on the Breton tombs are such that there can be little doubt that the two are related, which, together with certain shared affinities in architecture and artifacts, points to a close correspondence between these two regions. It has been suggested that the area of Brittany around the Gulf of the Morbihan is the likely place of origin of the Irish passage tomb series.

Finds from the Irish passage tombs are remarkably consistent. The characteristic pottery, called Carrowkeel Ware, is named after a cemetery in County Sligo. This consists of coarse, round-bottomed bowls, crudely decorated with looped arcs. Large mushroom-headed pins of bone or antler, stone beads and pendants are common and indicate that personal ornaments were interred with the dead. Small stone or chalk balls found at many sites have been interpreted as fertility symbols. One of the finest artifacts to have been discovered in an Irish passage tomb is the ceremonial macehead from the eastern tomb in the huge central mound of the Knowth cemetery. This is of polished flint and is decorated with elegant spiral designs carved in relief and combined with sunken lozenge-shaped facets. It is clearly a prestige object and is one of the most remarkable examples of prehistoric art and craftsmanship. Large stone basins are a characteristic feature of Irish passage tombs. A superbly decorated example was found in the western tomb at Knowth. Cremation was the normal burial practice, and some tombs were found to contain large numbers of burials. The great quantity of cremated bone from the small tomb at Tara, County Meath, is reputed to represent a hundred or more people.

The few radiocarbon dates available indicate that the main period of passage tomb building was in the centuries around 3000 BC, but some examples may be earlier.

Wedge tombs

The largest group of megalithic tombs in Ireland are the wedge tombs, so named because of their simple, distinctive shape. Over four hundred and sixty of these have been identified and are almost wholly found west of a line extending from north-east Antrim to Cork Harbour. None are known in Great Britain, but tombs quite like the Irish ones exist in Brittany, where they are known as *allées couvertes* (covered passages).

The normal wedge tomb consists of a long narrow burial gallery, which is generally broader and higher at the entrance and tapers in height and width towards the rear. As a general rule the entrance faces in a south-westerly direction. Frequently an antechamber or portico precedes the main chamber, and may be separated from it either by a slab reaching to roof height or by a pair of jamb-like stones. One group, found mainly in north County Clare, lacks the normal antechamber but has two overlapping stones at the front, one of which appears to serve as a moveable doorstone. The roof is formed of stones laid directly on side walls. The gallery is flanked by one or more extra lines of walling, the outermost of which delimits the short wedge- or U-shaped cairn which encloses the gallery. The front of the cairn is marked by short lines of walling linking the front of the antechamber to the sides of the cairn.

The wedge tombs, in general, are found on light, well-drained soils rather than on the lowland drift-covered regions, and unlike the court and portal tombs are evenly spread on land up to nine hundred feet above sea-level. This apparent preference for lighter soils and upland siting may well indicate a greater adaptability to local conditions and an exploitation of the higher lands for stock raising. The great concentration of tombs on the limestone plateau of north-west County Clare shows a remarkable coincidence with the best winter grazing in the region, and similar though smaller occupations of good winterage lands have been noted in other regions. Wedge tombs are located in quite a few areas where copper ore outcrops or primitive mines have been identified, and it may well be that exploitation of these ores was another aspect of some tomb-builders' economy.

The scant evidence available from excavated tombs indicates that collective burial was still practised by the wedge tomb builders, and both cremated and unburnt burials are attested. Artifacts recovered include some Neolithic pottery, flint arrowheads and pots of Bronze Age type, some scraps of bronze, and parts of moulds for spearheads, which would seem to indicate that the tombs were used over a considerable period. A radiocarbon date obtained from human bone found in the large wedge tomb at Labbacallee, County Cork, indicates that the monument was in use in the late third millennium BC.

Neolithic settlements

Eoin Grogan

The study of habitations is one of the most important aspects of Neolithic archaeology, providing an understanding of domestic architecture, social organisation, settlement layout and population distribution. The associated domestic refuse, food debris, discarded or mislaid implements and broken pottery, contributes one of the vital aspects of archaeological research — the rubbish of prehistoric communities!

The principal difficulty in the study of settlements is their discovery, since the main building material used in the Neolithic period and throughout prehistory was timber, which usually leaves traces only in the harder subsoil, and is not discernible above ground. Only in exceptional cases, as at Lough Gur, County Limerick, are the outlines of houses visible above the surface, due to a combination of circumstances such as the use of stones in the construction of the foundations and the undisturbed nature of the landscape in the immediate vicinity of the sites. In most other cases Neolithic houses have been discovered by accident during the excavation of other archaeological material, like the much more visible burial monuments which occasionally have been erected over the domestic sites.

Settlement location

While the identification of settlements is difficult, there are a number of persistent features in the types of location chosen by Neolithic communities. In deciding on a particular siting, these groups took into consideration access to five major resources — water, arable land, grazing land, fuel and building materials. Observation of a wide range of habitation sites has also shown a concern with naturally sheltered positions and a favourable, usually southern, aspect. Many sites are located overlooking a large body of water, usually a lake or a river. Although less clear cut, it also seems that proximity to neighbouring communities was taken into account.

Aerial view of the reconstructed Neolithic houses at Lough Gur, County Limerick.

Site distribution

The pattern of population dispersal in the landscape reflects the quantity of land required by each family or community to support themselves as virtually self-sufficient units. For a single family in the Neolithic period, an area within a kilometre of the farmstead would appear to have been more than adequate for this purpose, and the habitation site is generally located centrally within the farmland. In areas where there is evidence for several families or larger groups, the habitations are frequently spaced about 2km (1 mile) apart, although the quality of the local soils, the nature of the terrain and the availability of other resources appear to have a bearing on site distribution, and so the pattern varies considerably. This desire to remain in close communication with other groups reflects a natural human requirement, and we may expect that within a given area the families formed closely related communities. In some parts of the country larger settlements have been recorded, with several families or kinship groups living on the same site and probably carrying out a form of collective or cooperative agriculture. In these cases, such as Lough Gur (above), the territory exploited by the group is considerably larger and may be up to five kilometres (3 miles) in radius.

The permanent habitation sites form one of the components of an integrated settlement pattern which included burial monuments and seasonal camps that were used as occasional centres of activity (for example, hunting, fishing, grazing). Several seasonal sites have been excavated and these occur within the wider landscape exploited by the farming communities. At Townleyhall 2, County Louth, several hut or tent frames were represented by stake-holes and fireplaces; the site had been visited on several occasions and may have been a fishing camp used by groups living closer to the passage tomb cemeteries in the Boyne Valley, less than five kilometres away. More elaborate structures were found at Carrowmore, County Sligo, high up on the hillsides. Temporary camps, like Carrowmore, possibly associated with summer grazing, are widespread, and a group of these has been studied in the Glencloy area of Antrim; several of them have produced evidence for extensive flint-working, especially the production of finished artifacts. The main function of the site at Goodland, County Antrim, was the extraction of flint nodules and the working of these into portable blocks. A ritual aspect of this activity is suggested by the careful replacement in pits of some of the re-assembled nodules, and their occasional accompaniment by pot sherds.

The frequent occurrence of habitation evidence, including houses, beneath megalithic tombs suggests that there was a close spatial relationship between these two components in the settlement pattern. Therefore the tombs, with their greater visibility in the modern landscape, can act as accurate markers for the location of the settlements.

Houses and habitation sites

In Ireland we are fortunate that several well-preserved habitations belonging to various stages of the Neolithic period have been excavated and have provided a wide range of domestic features. Despite considerable variations in layout, several have produced evidence for a house and associated features such as rubbish pits, external working areas and, occasionally, ancillary buildings used as work huts or for storage. A Neolithic house, while having a variety of functions, would not have been the all-purpose building of modern type; it was principally a place of rest and shelter. Cooking and eating would frequently — but not always — have taken place within the house. Many tasks, such as the finishing of tools and the manufacture of pottery, would have required more light than would be normal inside the house. The size of the buildings need not have been directly related to the number of occupants; many houses may have been no larger than was necessary to provide the family with comfortable sleeping quarters. Whatever its size, each acted as the main focus for the family unit and was the most important feature of the habitation site; the houses were of appropriate size for a single nuclear family or a slightly extended one, that is, a group of between four and ten individuals. Internal features usually consist of a fireplace and refuse pits; simple smoke holes positioned over the fire would have provided ventilation. The refuse pits are occasionally quite large and these may have had wooden covers. At Site C, Lough Gur, County Limerick, small closely spaced stakes set around the fire suggest the presence of a pot hanger or spit. The floors were of packed earth, but small areas of paving do occur; it is probable that straw, reeds or possibly animal skins were used as floor coverings. The height of the walls would have allowed an adult to stand upright at the sides of the houses.

A range of building materials was used, but in most cases the structural timbers were of oak. Hazel or willow saplings were probably used for the wattle screens, and the evidence suggests that these were produced from coppiced trees. Stone is not a feature of Irish Neolithic houses and its use was largely confined to packing post-holes or bedding trenches. The roofs appear to have been thatched, and straw is the most probable material; where available, rushes or reeds may have been used. Although

entirely a matter for conjecture, the doors may have been constructed of light timber frames with hides stretched over them. One building technique used planks, and all known structures of this type were rectangular. At Tankardstown, County Limerick, two houses set within 20m (65½ft) of each other have been excavated. While these appear to have been occupied at the same time, the size and structure of the two buildings vary somewhat. The southern house consists of a single room measuring 6.5m by 5m (21ft by 16½ft), with access through a simple doorway at the south-eastern corner. The walls were made of upright split-oak planks, set edge to edge in a bedding or foundation trench, and were held in position by earth and stones of various sizes. The joints between the planks were probably sealed with a mixture of clay, dung and straw. A line of posts across the central span of the house helped to support the gabled roof, which was erected at an angle of about 45 degrees, giving it a maximum height of around 3.5–4.5m (11½–14½ft). Within the house there was a single central fireplace and some small pits for refuse. Immediately outside the house, on the western side, there was a large earth-cut pit used for storing grain. The northern house is considerably larger, 15m by 7.5m (49ft by 24½ft) and contains three rooms. The central room, although bigger, has similar proportions to the other building and measures 10m by 6.5m (33ft by 21ft). At either end there is a long narrow room set through the short axis of the house and

(below top right) Reconstruction of a Lough Gur Neolithic house at the Ulster History Park, Omagh, County Tyrone.

(below bottom right) Reconstruction of the Neolithic house excavated at Ballyglass, County Mayo, in the Ulster History Park, Omagh, County Tyrone.

(below bottom left) Reconstruction of a Neolithic settlement based on evidence from various sites.

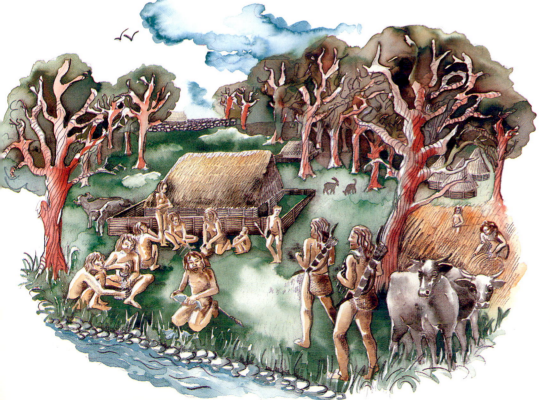

Polished javelin-heads from tomb finds at Ballyglass, County Mayo.

partitioned off from the central area. The entrance appears to have been at the north-west corner, and the room at this end probably functioned as a hall or annexe. There are good parallels for both houses in Ireland.

At Ballynagilly, County Tyrone, a single-roomed structure measuring 7m by 5.5m (23ft by 18ft) occurred at the centre of a wide range of domestic features on a low hill overlooking a small lake. The building style of the house was very similar to that of the smaller structure at Tankardstown. The north Mayo house at Ballyglass was three-roomed and measured 13m by 6m (42½ft by 19½ft). It seems to have been demolished to allow the construction of a court tomb at the same location. Again a feature of this structure was a large central compartment partitioned from two narrow rooms at either end. Several post-holes in the entrance room are additional to the requirement of roof support, and suggest a second floor, possibly used for the storage of grain. The proportions and internal layout of the house are similar to a large number of houses in west-central Europe, typical of the Early Neolithic period.

At Lough Gur, several houses, forming a hamlet or small village, have been excavated on the south-facing slopes of the Knockadoon peninsula, which extends out into the lake. Both circular and rectangular buildings occur, and all are post-framed. The largest rectangular house, Site A, measures 12.2m by 7.6m (40ft by 25ft) externally, but only 9.2m by 5m (30ft by 16½ft) inside. The wall was formed by rows of posts set on the inner and outer line of the wall in opposed pairs 1m apart. These supported the hipped roof and the wattle screens which made up the remainder of the wall structure. Daub, a mixture of clay, dung and straw, was smeared on the screens to provide a water- and draught-proof finish. Between the wall facings, the cavity had a damp-proof course consisting of a foundation of loose stones up to 30cm (12in) high. On this was set the wall insulation of straw, reeds or possibly sods. The entrance was in the south-western corner of the house, which was erected on a gently sloping natural platform that provided a natural drainage feature. Other rectangular houses at Site B and Circle K were of similar style.

Several circular or oval buildings, including three each at Site C and Circle L and two at Site D, occur within the Lough Gur settlement. Some of these, including houses 1 and 2 at Site C, were otherwise structurally identical to the rectangular buildings, suggesting a local building style. Two circular houses have also been discovered at Slieve Breagh, County Meath, and while the comparative dating of the structures from the various habitation sites is insecure, it may be that the circular form is generally later than the rectangular style.

Other structures

Other buildings which may have served a variety of functions occur at several sites. These huts are smaller than the houses and do not usually contain evidence for fireplaces or internal pits. At Lough Gur they are represented at Sites G, H and I; the latter is a small rectangular building measuring 3m by 2m (10ft by 6½ft) internally, and is set beside a small field. It may have been associated with the immediate care of herds or flocks, perhaps even ewes at lambing time. At Ballyglass, two small buildings were discovered beneath a second court tomb about 275m (902ft) to the south of the main house site. While the three structures are not contemporary, their variety indicates the range of structures in use during the period.

Wood-working techniques

Little of the actual buildings survives from the Neolithic period, but occasionally burnt timbers give an insight into the details of the structural techniques employed. At Tankardstown the stumps of the radially split planks were found in the base of the foundation trench, while part of a wall plate occurred at Ballynagilly. The range of wood-working tools, and especially the variety of stone axes and chisels, suggest that quite sophisticated carpentry, including basic mortice-and-tenon joints, could be achieved, and this is confirmed by the discovery of timbers preserved in Neolithic trackways in Somerset, England. In house construction, however, the difficulty of placing and securing large structural timbers would have made such joints impractical, and the timbers would have been tied or pegged.

Enclosed habitation and burial sites

During the Late Neolithic period, after around 3200 BC, some of the Lough Gur houses were set within enclosures consisting of two low, closely spaced walls formed of large boulders, within which earthen banks were raised. At Circle K the entrance contained two stout gates, one along the line of the inner wall and the other at the outer side. Outside, a passage made of boulders extended from the entrance. Most of the enclosures, of which about twenty-five have been identified, are circular, and the largest examples are over 30m (98½ft) in diameter. In some cases, however, the walls are erected around natural platforms on the sloping sides of the peninsula, and larger areas of limestone outcrop were often incorporated to form part of the perimeters. While the enclosures may have been intended to exclude grazing animals from the immediate vicinity of the domestic buildings, several houses of this period are not enclosed. The excavated enclosures have produced a greater quantity of pottery, tools and items of personal adornment, and the overall evidence suggests that these sites were occupied by an elite within the local community.

Single burials occur within several habitation sites including Lough Gur, Townleyhall 2 and Dalkey Island. The bodies were placed in pits, usually at a slight distance from the houses, but occasionally they were interred in abandoned structures. The practice of placing burials on settlements is a widespread feature of the Neolithic period in Europe.

Defences

Only two settlements with apparently defensive features are known — Knowth, County Meath, and Donegore Hill, County Antrim — but this may have been a more widespread phenomenon. At Donegore Hill, a hilltop habitation was enclosed within a massive defensive earthwork and a timber stockade. At Knowth, the earliest house was succeeded by a phase during which a palisade 2m (6½ft) in height was erected on the low hill overlooking the River Boyne. Later tillage in the area has removed much of the evidence, but the enclosure may have been up to 85m (279ft) in diameter. A pebbled area, about 3m (10ft) wide, may represent an entrance. A second, outer trench suggests the addition of another palisade. Although there are no domestic buildings surviving, a cobbled yard, probably associated with animal husbandry, occurred within the defences, and there were several concentrations of evidence, including pits, fireplaces and an area of flint-working. While it can be argued that the construction of the great Boyne Valley passage tombs around 3200 BC may be associated with increasing stratification in society and the resolution of stress within the local communities, it is interesting that

Aerial view of the excavation of the central court tomb and rectangular Neolithic house of Ballyglass, County Mayo. (see p212)

the domestic phase at Knowth, and the construction of the palisade defences, appear to predate the cemetery and suggest the emergence of these stresses before 3500 BC.

Other extensive hilltop settlements, at Feltrim Hill, County Dublin, and Lyles Hill, County Antrim, may also have been located with an element of defence in mind; while there was no evidence for artificial defences at Feltrim, part of a possible palisade has been identified at Lyles Hill.

At Mullaghfarna, County Sligo, a large settlement consisting of about one hundred enclosures is located on a level ridge below the passage tomb cemetery of Carrowkeel. While there is no direct evidence to associate the two complexes, some of the enclosures, which are very similar to those at Lough Gur, are covered by the same development of peat which has engulfed the base of the cairns. The idea that the passage tomb builders, and particularly those who constructed large clusters of monuments, lived in large communities, forming villages, has always been an attractive one, and the circumstantial evidence at Mullaghfarna offers just such an intriguing possibility. While habitation sites associated with objects of the type found in these tombs are virtually unknown, and we have no clear idea of the location and layout of their settlements, a group of round houses associated with passage tomb material occurs at Knowth. It has been argued, with some justification, that the domestic sites of these communities will produce the same range of artifacts, including the plain, round-bottomed pottery and implement types, as those of the groups who built court or portal tombs, or indeed those who, as in the Lough Gur area, built no tombs and buried their dead in flat graves.

III
The Bronze Age

The introduction of new technologies and raw materials can bring about radical changes in a society. We have seen dramatic innovations in modern times with the development of mechanised manufacturing, electronics, plastics, bio-engineering, all giving rise to revolutionary economic and social developments. In prehistoric Europe the pace of change may have been much slower, but that which brought about the introduction of metallurgy was nevertheless very significant.

Some of the earliest metal tools may have been imported. If so, they may originally have been valued as curiosities rather than as an advanced addition to the tool kit. The first metal tools are predominantly of copper, some of which is fortuitously hardened by naturally occurring impurities such as arsenic. The date of the appearance of copper-working in Ireland is only approximately known. The appearance of true bronze (a hard artificial alloy of copper and tin) belongs to a later time. At what point native sources of copper ore began to be mined is uncertain, but it seems to have been early, because characteristically Irish metal occurs in objects of the earliest types. The skills of metallurgy — prospecting, mining, smelting and casting — were unknown in Neolithic Ireland, with the exception of extracting flint from chalk deposits in County Antrim and suitable rock from outcrops for axeheads. We can probably assume that some new groups who possessed the required knowledge did enter the country. What impact these immigrants had on the native population is difficult to assess but the Earlier Bronze Age is a period of great variety in burial customs and regional preferences in tool-types. The application of radiocarbon dating in a coherent programme is beginning to sort these into order in time and space. Studies of mining and industrial practices are now showing a sophisticated system of exchange of finished products; they also reveal that production centres were not necessarily located in mining areas but were probably nearer to customers living on good land.

We cannot think of the population in Earlier Bronze Age Ireland as living a uniform, egalitarian existence; they were highly organised and there was probably a social hierarchy, but what this was is unknown. Agriculture was the mainstay of the economy. Stock raising was important — the bones from the habitation at Newgrange show this clearly. Pollen studies show local changes as agricultural clearances were succeeded by regrowths of forest.

Funerary pottery of the Earlier Bronze Age in Ireland.

The environment and human activity in Bronze Age Ireland

Michael O'Connell

During the Neolithic period, when agriculture was first introduced, there was fluctuating and, at times, substantial human impact on vegetation and soils. This was followed in the Bronze and Iron Ages by major changes in the environment, which were to have a profound impact on daily life.

During the cycles of woodland clearance and regeneration, which are recorded in the pollen record from many parts of the country throughout the Neolithic period and the Bronze Age, the relative importance of various trees changed radically. Ash, for instance, expanded and partly replaced elm (see pollen diagram from Scragh Bog, p 45), and pine declined and finally became extinct in its last refuges in western Ireland through woodland clearance at about the time of Christ.

Expansion of yew woodland

The importance of yew is only now being appreciated, as new investigations reveal that, in many parts of western Ireland, it expanded at various times during prehistory and was finally decimated by the woodland clearances that characterised the Early Medieval period. This expansion must have had profound implications for the agricultural economies of the affected areas; its abundance may have spelled disaster because cattle readily graze its leaves, which are poisonous if eaten in large quantities. But the tree is also a source of valuable timber and its wood has been found in a variety of prehistoric artifacts, including spearshafts and knife handles, and in Early Medieval times, reliquaries. Because of its elasticity and durability, the wood was used for specialised purposes, such as the dowels in cart-wheels, examples of which were recovered from a bog in Doogarymore, County Roscommon, and in the Middle Ages its timber was specially prized for bow-making.

Spread of blanket bog

An even more profound landscape change — not least because it was irreversible — was the spread of blanket bog in many parts of western Ireland during the Bronze Age. Extensive areas which had supported substantial farming populations during the Neolithic period, were now rendered largely useless for agriculture. While it is generally agreed that there was a downturn in climate, with a trend towards cooler and wetter conditions during the Bronze Age, the spread of blanket bog should not be ascribed to climatic change, but rather to the substantial impact of farming on vegetation and soils over a long period. Tree regeneration was hindered by the intensive farming pressure and, in the absence of trees, soils became wetter and drainage disimproved. As a result, plant remains began to accumulate on the soil surface and the establishment of bog species such as ling, sedges and *Sphagnum* or bog mosses was facilitated. In this way, large expanses of countryside were lost to productive farming. On the positive side, however, the bog, by forming a protective covering, has preserved in a unique way ancient landscapes and the monuments and artifacts which they contain.

Early settlement and environmental change in the Burren, County Clare

While blanket bog developed over acidic rocks such as granite, sandstone and schists, profound changes were also taking place in the Burren, the karstic limestone area in north-west County Clare. Pollen diagrams show that the Burren once carried woodland of pine, oak, yew and hazel, and excavations at Poulnabrone dolmen, in the central Burren, have provided some evidence for soil cover during the Neolithic period. The densest concentration of wedge tombs is to be found in the uplands of the Burren, suggesting a substantial population at the end of the Neolithic period and the beginning of the Bronze Age. The pollen and the archaeological evidence would appear to suggest that the large expanses of karstic landscape may be a relatively recent development. Just as happens today in the tropical forests, woodland clearance to facilitate farming probably led to severe soil erosion, the soil disappearing without trace through the fissured limestone bedrock.

Farming in later prehistory

There is little evidence that the major technological

advances, which stemmed from the use of metal, found expression in agricultural practices. Well laid out field systems were in use during the Neolithic period. So also was the simple wooden plough known as the ard, which probably had a pointed stone on the tip to penetrate the soil and prolong its lifespan. The marks left by such a plough, recorded at Belderg, County Mayo, in soils dating to the Neolithic period, represent the earliest evidence for the use of the ard in these islands. These crude ploughs and the spade, remained the main implements of cultivation until well into the Iron Age, when ploughs fitted with coulters (a more or less vertically held knife which cut the sod) were introduced, and in Early Medieval times mouldboards (which turned the cut sod upside down) were brought from mainland Europe either directly or via Britain.

There were no major changes in the crops sown until quite late in prehistory. Wheat and barley continued to be the principal grain crops, with oats and rye being cultivated in the Iron Age, though rye assumed importance only from the Early Medieval period onwards. Flax was also grown early in prehistory, as a source of fibre and also for the rich oil supply contained in its seed.

The relative importance of arable and pastoral farming in the country as a whole during the prehistoric period is difficult to assess. Apart from fossil pollen, the evidence at our disposal consists of a very limited number of finds of carbonised (partially burned) cereal remains and the imprint of cereal grains on pieces of pottery recovered during excavations or as stray finds. It is insufficient for a reliable assessment, but we can probably assume that pastoral farming, then as now, was the more important.

The scale of arable farming carried out by individual farmers or communities cannot be thought of in terms of modern-day agriculture, with its extensive fields of cereals maintained weed-free by the use of herbicides. The best modern analogy is possibly the arable plots associated with small farmsteads in the west of Ireland, where cultivation ridges carry potatoes and, in the recent past, oats and rye.

While we can only surmise that individual areas under crops were quite limited, a unique insight into past methods of cultivation is provided by an enclosure and cultivation ridges dating to the Later Bronze Age/Early Iron Age which were discovered in the late sixties preserved beneath blanket bog at both Belderg and Carrownaglogh, east of Bunnyconnellan, County Mayo. The ridges at both sites, but especially those recorded on the sides of the sloping knoll at Carrownaglogh, are indistinguishable in shape and dimensions from those which cover many a hillside in western Ireland today. Like their more recent counterparts, these ridges were probably formed by the spade. Investigations at Carrownaglogh show that during the Iron Age (at about 600 BC), the ridges carried weed-infested crops of wheat and barley. Indeed, the corn spurrey, which was the main weed, may have been as important as the cereals, and we may speculate that the farmers harvested the seed-rich capsules of this plant as well as the cereal crop itself. In other words, what today is regarded as a weed may have been a food crop for our prehistoric ancestors.

A sectional view of the ridges at Carrownaglogh also shows an interesting feature. A solid iron pan underlies the mineral soil/peat interface at a depth of about 8cm (2in). Drainage water cannot pass through this layer, so that even if the peat were not present, the soil today would be unsuitable for arable farming. In the past, waterlogging was certainly not a problem: the ridges were laid out so that they contour the hillside, in contrast to present-day cultivation ridges which invariably run with the slope to facilitate drainage. Iron pan formation occurred after cultivation had ceased, and most likely after the site was abandoned, leading to waterlogging and peat growth, which preserved and concealed the site.

A site such as that at Carrownaglogh has added significance when viewed against the broader canvas of our knowledge of the period. The final stage of the Later Bronze Age was one of considerable wealth and probably also of high population levels. Upland marginal land, such as that at Carrownaglogh, may have been somewhat more fertile in the past, but hardly represented an attractive location, especially for arable farming. It is likely that population pressures were such that, just as in the early nineteenth century, people were forced to bring poor upland soil under the spade. Not only did they cultivate mineral soils, but layers of sand and grit in the peat and stone walls erected on peat nearby show that they extended their farming activities, presumably in the form of grazing animals, onto the bog surfaces. Fluctuations in population levels and in economic activity were probably every bit as much a feature of prehistoric as historical times, though naturally we are more aware of the latter.

The karst landscape of the Burren, County Clare. Recent research suggests that its bare appearance is the result of farming by prehistoric peoples.

Schematic drawing of a section cut through a cultivation ridge at Carrownaglogh, County Mayo. (see p213)

Weeds in a modern oatfield near Carrownaglogh give a good idea of conditions in arable fields in late prehistoric times. (see p213)

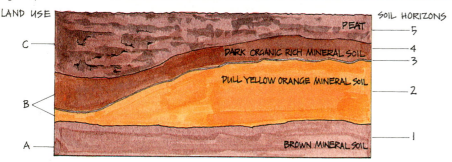

The Earlier Bronze Age

John Waddell

Our knowledge of any prehistoric period is dependent to a great extent on the twin accidents of survival and discovery. The bulk of the evidence of the Earlier Bronze Age consists of a large quantity of finds of metalwork on the one hand, and on the other a great number of graves and the bones and pottery they contain. We know comparatively little about the settlements and the economy of the period, though the picture is gradually improving.

There were several significant innovations in the period 2500–2000 BC, and one of the most interesting was the development of the craft of metal-working. The earliest metals employed were copper and gold, and then an alloy, bronze. Along with this new technology, novel forms of pottery and new fashions in burial and other ritual practices are very much in evidence. Older customs were not entirely abandoned, however, and a few passage and court tombs were still considered to be sacred sites and were re-used as burial places. Many wedge tombs were used and possibly even built at this time, and some communities evidently still favoured the traditional large stone tomb. The use of stone implements, such as flint scrapers and knives, as well as axes of polished stone, continued, and their replacement by metal tools was probably a long and gradual process. Indeed, throughout much of the Bronze Age, copper and tin, the two alloys which constitute bronze, may have been highly prized and costly commodities, perhaps confined to certain levels of society. One of the noteworthy features of this period is the increasing preoccupation with some pottery types or metal objects which, for their owners, must have been symbols of status and rank.

Beaker pottery

The builders of some wedge tombs continued a tradition of megalithic tomb building over fifteen hundred years old, and like those earlier peoples who raised court or passage tombs to contain communal burials, they too were concerned to provide monumental stone containers for the bones of their ancestors. A new departure, however, is the appearance in a number of these tombs of fragments of Beaker pottery. This pottery is exceptionally interesting, not least because in certain parts of Western Europe its appearance coincides with some of the earliest metal objects. Beakers are often elegant hand-made pots with shapes which suggest that they were specially made as drinking vessels. Some sherds from a wedge tomb at Moytirra, just east of Lough Arrow, County Sligo, are decorated with the typical 'comb-impressed' ornament, where numerous small dots made with a toothed piece of bone form a geometric pattern on the exterior. The finest beakers must have taken many hours to make and decorate, they were probably highly prized and their value may have been considerably enhanced by the alcoholic liquid they probably contained. Indeed, traces of a mead-like drink have been identified in a Scottish example. These vessels were once believed to be the characteristic pottery of a distinctive 'Beaker Folk' who migrated over much of Europe, bringing with them the knowledge of copper-working wherever they went. Today it is generally thought that the wide distribution of this pottery type is due mainly to the fact that these pots were prestigious vessels (maybe even part of some cult), much sought after by certain elements of society (the 'Beaker users'), and thus exchanged and widely copied. Beaker pottery does not seem to be as common in Ireland as it is in Britain, for example, and its role as a prestigious item was probably supplanted to some extent by a series of highly decorated bowls and by the well-known gold collars or lunulae, both of which include Beaker decorative motifs in their repertoire of ornament.

The range of copper objects manufactured by these early 'Beaker users' was small and is well illustrated by a hoard found in the last century in a bog at Knocknagur, near Tuam, County Galway. This collection, perhaps left in a watery place as some ritual offering, is comprised of three copper awls, three copper axes and a small copper dagger. These are among the earliest types of metal object ever made in Ireland. It is unlikely that copper axes of this sort would have been all that more efficient for wood-cutting than axes of polished stone, and their real value, initially at least, may have been more magical and symbolic. This special value may well be a part, though only a part, of the explanation for the very

The stone circle of Drombeg, County Cork.

Standing stone, near Eyries, County Cork.

A bone needle and button from a double-compartmented cist grave at Kinkit, near Strabane, County Tyrone.

Bronze weapon of rapier type, found in the River Shannon.

Inchnagree, County Cork. Two halves of a mound for casting, small blades and other implements. (see p213)

vigorous production of thousands of axes of both copper and bronze in the Earlier Bronze Age.

The classic Beaker assemblage, those objects consistently found singly or in varying combinations in Beaker graves in several areas of Western and Central Europe, included a tanged copper dagger, a stone wrist-guard, barbed and tanged flint arrowheads, and V-perforated buttons. They all occur in Ireland but not, as elsewhere, in Beaker graves with crouched burials. Many of the Irish examples are stray finds. A number of stone wrist-guards have been found in bogs, for instance. These are often finely polished and made from a variety of stones, frequently of a reddish colour, including jasper and porphyrite as well as sandstone and slate. The finest examples, like the copper daggers, must have been highly prized possessions. Given the presence of these Beaker-associated items, the absence of classic Beaker burials is a puzzle. Fragments of an undecorated beaker were found with the cremated bones of an adult and a child in the passage of one of the satellite tombs at Knowth, County Meath. Here, as in the Moytirra and other wedge tombs, Beaker users favoured a megalithic monument. It was left to the pottery makers of the Bowl Tradition to practise the classic Beaker single-burial rite, in which the pot was placed in the grave beside a crouched unburnt corpse.

In addition to the fragmentary Beaker pottery from settlement sites such as Newgrange and Knowth, sherds have also been recovered from the Grange stone circle at Lough Gur, County Limerick and from other ritual sites such as the Newgrange timber circle. The ceremonial circle, like the megalithic tomb, had a considerable indigenous history, and Beaker pottery should probably be considered a later accretion.

Tools and weapons

Whether the knowledge of metal-working has a pre-Beaker history is uncertain. Some of the earliest copper objects found in Ireland, the tanged knives and the simple axeheads, may well have been acquired along with some of the earlier Beaker pots. It is possible that the knowledge of copper-working itself may have been introduced by the same acquisitive process and through long-established exchange systems.

Whatever its origins (which are debated), the new metal technology proved to be a remarkably vigorous industry. Whether due to the extent of production or to the scale of discovery, five times as many early axeheads have been found in Ireland compared to Scotland and northern England. These implements appear to be a good example of a typological sequence in which considerations of fashion or function demanded changes in shape and design as time went by. The most primitive copper type, which may be of Beaker or even pre-Beaker date, has a thick butt and almost straight sides splaying only sightly to its cutting edge. It may have been mounted in a wooden club-like haft: in form it resembles the earliest continental axes and was relatively simple to cast. An insular preference for axes with splaying, concave sides, soon developed however, and longer, more slender types appear. Some of these may have been mounted in hatchet fashion in split wooden hafts, but the appearance of raised edges and a raised transverse rib, a so-called stop-ridge, indicate new hafting methods in a split knee-haft. In time fine decorated bronze axeheads became fashionable, and eventually the raised edges or flanges are cast in a more complicated process. The decorated axes were presumably valuable objects, and one, at least, found in a bog at Brockagh, County Kildare, clearly demonstrates this. It was not mounted in a wooden haft as many of these objects evidently were, but was carefully contained in a leather pouch made specially for it. While some of these axes were undoubtedly functional and perhaps even used as weapons, the special nature of others is reflected in the occasional practice of depositing them in hoards containing axeheads alone. Some three dozen hoards with axes are recorded and about 75 per cent of these contained no other type of implement. While these could be the buried and misplaced stock-in-trade of axe-makers, the deliberate ceremonial deposition of axes alone is also a possible explanation.

Hoards comprising of a range of objects (like Knocknagur) are few. One other such mixed find, of several copper axeheads, a dagger and a halberd, was discovered deep in a bog at Frankford, near Birr, County Offaly. The halberd is a broad dagger-like blade, usually with stout midrib and rivets, which was originally mounted at right angles in a wooden haft. Many are of copper but some are of bronze. These are puzzling implements, few show any clear signs of wear and it is generally thought that they would have been clumsy and inefficient weapons. They were fashionable in various parts of Europe, in Iberia, in Italy and in Central Europe where fine specimens with cast bronze hafts are known. These latter examples were certainly ceremonial pieces, perhaps insignia of rank, a function also suggested by some rock-carvings in northern Italy. Some Irish halberds were probably used in a similar way and, like the occasional Neolithic stone mace-head or Bronze Age 'battle-axe' had some symbolic role. If possible evidence for ritual practices seems to be unduly abundant, this is probably because the evidence for the more material aspects of everyday economy and settlement is so scarce. There is a tendency in archaeology to label many an unexplained phenomenon as the product of some ritual process. Prudence is required, but there is much to suggest that Bronze Age and earlier peoples generally, like many recent primitive societies, lived in a world which for them was charged with magic and symbolic meaning.

One obvious reason for the development of the bronze axe was its importance in wood-working. Experiment has shown that the flat bronze axe is about twice as efficient as the stone axe for tree felling, and it is also better for wood-working. The availability of bronze certainly advanced the carpenter's craft and, in time, implements such as tanged chisels were developed. Little or nothing has survived of the timber work and other organic materials that were used, but wood, woven textiles and leather must have been important everyday commodities. Surprisingly, perhaps, a few of the pottery vessels of the period serve as reminders of how widespread the use of wooden and other sorts of organic containers must have been. For instance, among the fragments of Beaker pottery found on the settlement site beside the great Newgrange passage tomb, there were sherds of one or more small plain polypod bowls, a type of vessel with several feet. This could well be a pottery copy of a wooden form, and indeed a larger five-legged wooden bowl found deep in a Monaghan bog is probably of prehistoric date, though not necessarily of the Earlier Bronze Age. It has long been recognised that the impressed triangular decoration commonly found on a series of Bronze Age bowls is an echo in pottery of a wood carver's decorative technique, which involved the cutting out of small triangles from the surface of a piece of timber. Such impressed triangles form a minor element of the decoration on a bowl from Knockast, County Westmeath, which in its horizontal grooving and — perhaps more significantly — in the concentric rings

impressed on its base, may reflect a knowledge of lathe-turning in wood. A large urn from a burial at Labbamolaga, County Cork, bears applied ornament which seems to be a pottery rendering of the appearance of a plaited or wickerwork basket, and the applied ornament on a number of other urns serves to echo the practice of carrying or suspending containers in net or rope holders.

If the use to which some axeheads and halberds were put is debatable, there is little doubt that other implements were intended to be used as weapons. This is true of the more developed daggers and particularly of the spearheads. Simple flat bronze knives only a few inches long might be more suited to domestic chores than to bloodier tasks, but longer daggers with thickened midribs to strengthen the blade were intended as stabbing weapons. As time went by they were made even longer, becoming elegant slender rapiers 30cm (12in) or more in length. Ireland shared in a vigorous way in the manufacture of these long, thrusting, stabbing weapons, and they continued to be popular until they were superseded by the bronze sword, sometime around the end of the second millennium BC. The fact that short dagger-like blades (commonly called dirks) and longer rapiers were in contemporary use has led to the suggestion that, towards the end of the Earlier Bronze Age, two-handed combat was practised with dirk in one hand and rapier in the other. Despite these belligerent possibilities, a ritual element is still present. Rapier hoards are unknown in Ireland but where circumstances of discovery are recorded, it seems as if they have almost all been recovered from watery contexts, in rivers, lakes or bogs. So consistent is this pattern of deposition that some sort of water ritual must have been involved.

Improvements in the design of the bronze spearhead also illustrate another advancement in fighting methods. The earliest spearheads were flat dagger-like blades with a tang, which were inefficiently mounted in a wooden shaft. Socketed forms (with loops to help fasten them to the shaft) were quickly developed, and improved techniques of hollow casting soon allowed the hollow socket to extend into and thus give extra strength to the blade. The discovery of the points of the blades of two spearheads embedded in the spine and pelvis of a skeleton in Gloucestershire is evocative testimony of the lethal possibilities of weapons such as these.

The geology and raw materials of the Bronze Age

John Jackson

In the Bronze Age, woodland and scrubland were more extensive than today, although even by that time Neolithic and Earlier Bronze Age farmers had already cleared significant areas for agriculture. In areas bare of boulder clay or accumulated scree, outcropping bedrock was clearly visible, whether on open ground or on the floor of hazel scrub or mixed woodland. Evidence of the various minerals of copper in such outcrops was manifest in the dull greens of malachite or in the bright blues of azurite, both carbonates of copper, oxidised in the weathered zone of the underlying ore bodies. They were strident indicators which emphatically directed early prospectors to copper mineralisation. It was only later, when the exploitation of the land by Neolithic and Bronze Age farmers led to leaching of minerals in the soil and to the formation of an impermeable hard-pan, causing inevitable water-logging and degradation of the soil, that blanket bogs became widespread. These accumulated on low ground and on hillsides and mountain tops, often covering and concealing the multi-coloured evidence of the underlying copper ore and also the modest drivings of the first metal miners.

Copper is limited in distribution in Ireland, with concentrations in the west Cork/southwest Kerry area, south Waterford, the Avoca area of County Wicklow, the Silvermines/Rearcross area of County Tipperary and in Connemara, County Galway. There is a vast area of the midlands and the north of the country which is either poor in copper or virtually devoid of the metal. The ore used initially by Earlier Bronze Age peoples was native copper; as it was already metallic copper, it required no smelting, and because it was extremely malleable it could be hammered into axes or any other shape required. Native copper is now very rare in Ireland, and it was probably never a significant ore in the Irish Bronze Age.

Gold disc, one of a pair found at Tedavnet, County Monaghan. The Earlier Bronze Age is noteworthy for the number of gold ornaments produced.

(opposite) Bronze Age metalwork. (see p213)

Subsequently, when smelting technology was developed, the oxides of copper occurring in the zone of oxidation of the ore body were used; these occurred at or close to the surface of the ground, could be smelted directly without roasting, and were probably the first ores to be exploited in Ireland during the Earlier Bronze Age. Eventually, when the ores in the zone of oxidation were exhausted, attention had necessarily to be directed to the underlying sulphide ores. These involved quite sophisticated metallurgical treatment and had first to be roasted in order to drive off the combined sulphur, producing a matte which could then be smelted.

In roasting, smelting and melting copper and bronze, the fuel used was charcoal which, when ignited and subjected to a forced draught, becomes incandescent, reaching very high temperatures. Although roasting can be accomplished at relatively low temperatures of 600°

and alloys, copper and bronze. In Earlier Bronze Age halberds, for example, iron never exceeds 'trace' amounts (see Table 1). This is characteristic of a primitive smelting technology in which, by meticulous cobbing — breaking up the ore and selecting the richest parts — the unwanted elements (gangue) in the broken ore, quartz and fragments of the host rock, which often contained iron, were removed by hand, resulting in a smelter-feed which was almost exclusively copper ore. Slag would have been minimal, even in areas associated with protracted smelting activity. In contrast to this, a more advanced smelting technology was employed during the full Bronze Age of the Middle East and throughout the Mediterranean. Here the ore was broken but not meticulously cobbed and, in order to correct an inevitably high iron content of the smelter feed, silica was added as a flux or, if the silica was excessive, an iron

TABLE 1	Locality	Selective partial analysis (Percentages)					
		Copper	Tin	Arsenic	Antimony	Silver	Iron
Chemical analysis of some halberds (Earlier Bronze Age)	Tullamore	96.3	n.d.	2.23	0.81	0.57	Tr
	Ireland	96.2	n.d.	2.54	0.86	0.35	Tr
	Ireland	94.87	0.02	2.90	0.89	0.48	—
	North of Ireland	95.19	<0.01	2.64	0.82	0.30	—
	Norfolk, England	96.9	0.01	2.10	0.30	0.20	—
	Ireland	95.8	n.d.	2.35	1.50	0.28	Tr
	Ireland	96.4	n.d.	2.02	1.03	0.44	Tr
	Ireland	96.4	<0.01	2.50	0.56	0.44	Tr
	Ireland	95.9	0.01	2.39	1.07	0.55	Tr
	Limavady District, Derry	88.5	10.0	1.01	0.13	0.28	Tr
	River Suck	96.2	n.d.	2.57	0.66	0.43	Tr
	Derrycassan L., Cavan	98.2	n.d.	0.90	0.52	0.28	Tr
	Ireland	96.7	n.d.	2.32	0.44	0.30	Tr

n.d. *Not detected.* Tr *Trace.* < *less than.*

to 800°C, copper metal melts at 1080°C, and 'green' timber because of the cooling effect of steam from its sap could only with difficulty reach the temperatures required.

It is unfortunate that no Bronze Age smelting pit has been found in Ireland, and it is therefore difficult to establish the precise pyrotechnology and metallurgy practised by Irish Bronze Age metallurgists or to determine the efficiency of their methods from the analyses of their slags. However, we can deduce something from the analyses of the early smelted metals

flux was added. In either case the iron and silica combined as iron silicate to form a liquid slag which could be tapped and drained from the furnace during the smelting operation, resulting in vast quantities of slag which often dominated the immediate landscape. Copper produced in this way has a substantially higher iron content.

Table 1 also demonstrates that the metal used in the halberds listed was, with one exception, copper and not bronze, with a tin content never exceeding 0.02 per cent and, in the majority of cases, so low as not to be detected during analyses (n.d.). The earliest metal-using period in Ireland was principally a copper-using phase. Subsequently the technology of alloying the copper with a substantial amount of tin, about 10 per cent, to produce bronze was introduced. In Table 1 only the Limavady halberd is a true bronze.

The copper ores exploited by the Earlier Bronze Age miners in Ireland, and particularly in the south-west, are characterised in analyses by a 'trinity' of elements — arsenic, antimony and silver, and this analytical 'fingerprint' identifies Irish coppers and bronzes which were exported to Britain in the Earlier Bronze Age, either as ingots or as finished artifacts. The halberd from Norfolk in Table 1, for example, was cast from a copper with a typically Irish analytical 'fingerprint'.

Tin

Tin in the form of abraded crystals of cassiterite, occurs in quite substantial quantities in the Gold Mines River in County Wicklow, and probably occurred in the oxidised levels of the zone of secondary enrichment at Avoca: it could have been used during the Earlier Bronze Age in Ireland in the production of bronze. Ireland is unlikely to have produced sufficient tin to satisfy the demand of the Later Bronze Age industries, which probably relied on imports from Cornwall. Copper could have been exchanged for it.

Gold

Gold occurs at some 130 localities in Ireland. These include the Delphi Valley and the flanks of Croagh-patrick in County Mayo. The localities also include Curraghinalt in County Tyrone, where conservative estimates of reserves of some 300,000 oz of gold have been established by drilling. At these localities, however, the gold occurs in bedrock, and was probably unavailable to the Bronze Age metal-worker. Gold won during the Bronze Age would have come from placer deposits, as nuggets and flakes in the sands and gravels of the streams and rivers of the country. Many of these are known; two of the most prolific areas are the Gold Mines River and the other rivers draining Croghan Kinsella in south County Wicklow, and the river system of the Sperrin Mountains in County Tyrone. Since gold occurs as a native metal it does not require smelting, but merely melting in crucibles prior to pouring into moulds. Alternatively, as gold is extremely soft and malleable, it can be worked into artifacts by hammering or beating.

Copper mining in south-west Ireland

William F O'Brien

The discovery of numerous copper and bronze objects from the Cork—Kerry region, dating to all periods of the Bronze Age, indicates its importance in the period. These south Munster metal industries reflect significant settlement expansion between 2500 and 500 BC, indicated by the construction of numerous megalithic tombs, stone circles and associated monuments. One factor which contributed to this intensified settlement was the availability of readily exploitable copper ore sources in the south-western peninsulas. Scientific analysis of early copper axes from this region confirms that the earliest metal used during the Later Neolithic period came from rich local quartz vein deposits. The appearance of the earliest bronze industries *c.* 2000—1500 BC coincided with the exploitation of a second ore resource in the form of sedimentary copper-beds. While considerably poorer in metal content than the quartz vein deposits, copper-bed outcrops are far more numerous, with heavy concentrations along the south Cork coastline from Clonakilty to Mizen Head. This type of ore resource was particularly amenable to the primitive technology used in early mines of the region.

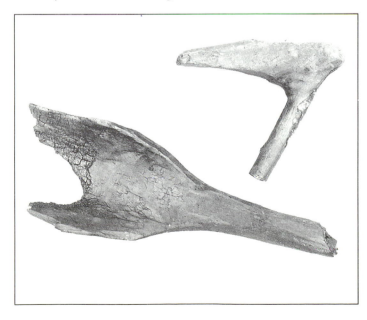

Wooden shovel and pick from mine 3, Mount Gabriel.
(see p213)

Mount Gabriel

Mount Gabriel — a mass of Old Red Sandstone rising to 408m (1339ft) — is the highest mountain of the Mizen Peninsula in south-west Cork. Here, there was extensive mining of surface copper-beds during the Earlier Bronze Age. The thirty-two workings located on its eastern slopes, together with a number of similar sites elsewhere in this region, represent one of the most important early mine-groups in Europe. Recent radiocarbon dating of wood and charcoal from these sites confirms that the main period of mining activity on Mount Gabriel was between 1700 and 1500 BC, making these the oldest copper mines currently known in north-west Europe. Not only are the sites old, but they are uniquely well preserved by the upland blanket-bog which spared them destruction by more recent mining activity. While few comparisons of scale or productivity can be made with modern copper mines, the Mount Gabriel mines nonetheless represent a significant landmark in the history of metallurgy.

The mine-workings on Mount Gabriel follow inclined copper-bearing deposits in the Old Red Sandstone. The early prospectors relied totally on surface exposure and did not possess the technology to extract ore at depths exceeding ten to fifteen metres. The majority of known copper-rich outcrops in this region occur in the hilly interior and wave-scoured coastline, which provided an ideal setting for the development of this early mining industry. The distribution of mine-workings on Mount Gabriel suggests a careful and systematic search for ore and shows that it had become possible to recognise the rock formations which were most likely to contain copper.

Two principal areas can be identified in the organisation of a Mount Gabriel mining camp, namely the mine-working from where the ore was extracted, and the spoil dump where primary crushing and hand-sorting was undertaken. Further activity occurred on the site periphery, where ore concentrates were washed and sorted, and where mining equipment was prepared for use. Given the limited scope of modern archaeological dating methods, it is uncertain whether the Mount Gabriel mines were operated continuously or intermittently. There are several reasons why the miners may have worked seasonally to extract ore, among them the problems of food supply and of mining in periods of poor weather. To avoid the difficulties caused by flooding, it is likely that individual mines were started and finished within a relatively short period, perhaps with day- and night-working. Mining may have overlapped at adjacent sites to provide for continuous ore production during the season. The labour force was probably divided into those who extracted and processed the copper ore, and those involved in activities such as fuel collection and gathering beach cobbles for use as hammers. The ore was taken elsewhere for final reduction to metal.

The mine-workings consist of shallow inclined openings, technically termed drift-mines, where the ore was followed away from the surface of the ground. In one area no fewer than fourteen openings have been identified over a 200m long (656ft) mineralised exposure. Within this group there is a progression from shallow surface openings less than 1m in depth, to underground mines reaching inclined depths of up to 11m (36ft) and possibly more. The occurrence of the ore influenced the range of extraction techniques employed and the eventual form of the workings. The depth of the mine depended on the richness of ore present and the problems posed by deep underground working. The shallow profile of these mines suggests an economy of effort to remove only the grey-green sediments containing copper ore. Accordingly, these mines generally narrow from the entrance inward, with the confined interiors allowing for one or two workers at the mine face.

The interior walls of these mines show no trace of the use of metal tools, and instead have the smooth domed profile, often with traces of smoke staining, characteristic of fire-setting, a technique used in primitive mines all over the world. Bonfires were set against the rock face for several hours, causing it to fracture. As well as directly removing fragments of rock, this heat treatment loosened the structure of the mine face. This was followed by heavy pounding, using stone cobble hammers and wooden wedges to prise out rock from the heat-shattered surface. Mining would have required a great deal of fuel. Wood would also have been needed for the production of equipment and the construction of temporary shelters. Recent excavation of Mine 3 on Mount Gabriel uncovered large quantities of oak, hazel, ash and willow roundwood, indicating a mixed deciduous woodland source, presumably in the immediate vicinity of the mines. The investigation of a Mount Gabriel-type mine

Stone alignment near Waterville, County Kerry.

Entrance to a mine, Mount Gabriel, County Cork.

near Goleen, County Cork, in 1854 uncovered a cache of polished-stone axes which could have been used in the collection of fire-setting fuel. No such discovery has been made on Mount Gabriel, partly because tooling features on preserved roundwood suggest the use of bronze axes, which would not have been readily discarded in the mining camp.

On Mount Gabriel, workings of less than 2m (6½ft) in depth were essentially surface operations, with rock being passed directly from the working face for treatment in the area outside. While the entrances of larger workings were usually low and confined, access was comparatively easy, if at times awkward, and was often facilitated by the use of foot-notches and possibly entry-ropes. The haulage of wood-fuel and equipment into the mine and the removal of rock extract was accomplished by relay teams of two to six individuals. The bulk of this material would have been moved by hand, and though no evidence of the containers has been found, it is likely that leather-skin sacks or wooden trays were used. A short-handled wooden shovel of alder was recently found in Mine 3. Similar shovels have been found in Austrian Earlier Bronze Age mines.

Some form of artificial lighting was necessary in the larger mines. Large quantities of resinous pine chips and brushwood were discovered in Mine 3, which would have served as torches to illuminate the mines and to ignite the underground bonfires. Water seepage was one of the most serious problems in the workings. This would have hindered fire-setting and often caused the premature abandonment of operations. Simple hand-bailing by relay teams may have been employed, however it is more likely that the miners would have

worked rapidly to avoid flooding, abandoning operations when they became uneconomic.

The most visible surface features of these sites today are the large mounds of rock debris frequently located outside the mine entrances, which accumulated as a result of continuous ore treatment. These loosely compacted dumps have a high charcoal content and are littered with broken stone tools. On removal from the mine, it was necessary to process the mineralised rock so as to separate the valuable copper minerals from unwanted waste. In the Mount Gabriel operations, this involved the crushing of rock extract using stone cobble hammers, a process that was greatly facilitated by the fire-setting which had already reduced much of the rock to thin splintery fragments. This size reduction was accompanied by hand-sorting of visibly mineralised rock, which bore the characteristic green coloration of the oxidised copper ore. Simple cobble hammers like those from Mount Gabriel seem to have been universal in primitive metal mines before the advent of tempered iron implements. Because of their relatively brief use-life, thousands of these tools were employed in the Mount Gabriel mines. The cobbles came from storm beaches about 5km away. Most were hand-held, but some were fitted with wooden handles as multi-purpose rock-breaking implements.

The various treatment processes in the mining camp would have succeeded in removing much of the rock waste from the copper ore, producing a high-grade concentrate for further refining by smelting. There is no evidence that this final reduction to metal took place in the mine area and it is possible that the ore was removed to lowland settlement bases for treatment. There is very little evidence in the archaeological record today of the location and organisation of these settlements or the smelting sites. The discovery of a bronze axe and two fragments of raw copper outside the entrance to a wedge tomb in Tourmore townland, 9km (5½ miles) south-west of Mount Gabriel, confirms local metal production in this period. This is further supported by a contemporary stone mould for casting bronze axes from Doonour near Bantry, County Cork. Recent studies of fossil pollen in peat bogs have confirmed that the main period of mining on Mount Gabriel was broadly contemporary with expanded human settlement in south-west Ireland. Related to this intensified settlement is the emergence of the important Stone Circle Complex in this region during the mid to late second millennium BC. This group of burial/ritual monuments, which includes stone circles, alignments, monoliths, cairns and possibly simple rock scribings of cup-and-ring type, emphasises the importance of this region during the later stages of the Earlier Bronze Age. The ore sources of south-west Ireland constituted a critical resource during this period, contributing to the emergence of controlling elites who had an important managerial role in the production and distribution of metal.

Metal production

Laurence Flanagan

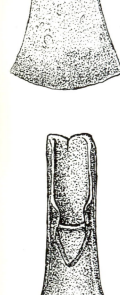

Pair of bronze palstaves from near Kilalloe, County Clare.

If native copper (copper existing naturally in its metallic form) had been commonplace and widespread in Ireland, instead of existing sporadically and in small quantities, life would have been considerably easier for the prehistoric metal-worker. Unfortunately nature was not so beneficent, and the prehistoric metal-worker was faced with the problem of extracting his metal from ores, where the metal being sought was combined, both chemically and physically, with a lot of material in which he had no economic interest.

This extraction process required energy, in surprising quantities. To deploy this energy efficiently required skills, both technical and organisational. The energy sources available to the Bronze Age craftsman were of two kinds: animal-power (mainly, it would seem, in the form of human labour) and heat, obtained almost inevitably from vegetable sources, mainly, if not solely, in the form of wood from the extensive forests of oak, ash and elm that were widespread.

The production process

Our lowest estimates of the original production of the earliest copper axes of Lough Ravel type would have required about 20kg (44lb) of metal annually. If we assume a copper concentration of 2 per cent from normal Irish ores, to start the production process would necessitate one tonne of sorted and comminuted ore at the minehead, that is, ore of good consistency, with all the unproductive parent rock removed and the ore itself reduced to a suitable size for smelting. We shall assume that two men could carry out this initial process in two days, to produce the required one tonne of prepared ore. This tonne has then to be carried to the smelting site, at an assumed distance of 3km (2 miles) from the minehead, where abundant supplies of fuel are conveniently located. We shall assume that two men, working for a further two days, could cope with this transportation. Meanwhile, at the smelting site, other men, amounting in total (we again assume) to 100, each working for a full week, have assembled the quite incredible amount of fuel required to smelt one tonne of ore, a total of 2500 tonnes of dry fuel — the equivalent of 100 mature forest oaks, felled, logged up and converted to charcoal, ready to be used. Ideally this fuel preparation would have been carried out well in advance, to give the wood adequate time to dry. It becomes immediately obvious why the ore was transported to the smelting site.

Now, and only now, are we ready for the actual smelting operation, in which a heat of at least 1200°C is required; by a combination of heating and poling with a green wooden rod, the sulphurs combined chemically with the copper ore are driven off (most of the demonstrably worked Irish ores being sulphide ores) and the metallic copper allowed to run from the non-productive waste. The metallic copper is then formed into ingots or 'copper cakes', known to archaeology from such hoards as those from Monastery, County Wicklow and Carrickshedoge, County Wexford, some twenty in number, at an average, roughly standard weight of 1kg

(2lb). We will assume that two men, each working for a week, setting the fire (or primitive furnace) and supervising and tending the operation, would be required to carry out the actual smelting and ingot-forming process.

It is only now, after this lengthy and energy-consuming operation, that we are able to contemplate the final stage of the production process — the actual manufacture of implements. For this process again, fuel is required, though, in view of the vastly reduced quantities of raw material involved, we can proportionally reduce the amount of fuel required to a mere two mature forest oaks, yielding some fifty tonnes of dry wood. Again the labour of two men, each working for a week, can be assumed. In addition, crucibles in which to melt the metal are required (though no example has survived), as are moulds into which the molten metal is poured. The earliest moulds are single-piece and would have required a simple lid or covering slab to prevent excessive oxidation. The opening at one end would have served as a 'gate' for pouring the molten metal, while the opening at the other would have served as a 'riser' to permit the escape of air and fumes. The copper in the cakes would need to be broken up to facilitate melting in the crucible, at a heat of some 1000°C, in order to be poured into the waiting and preheated mould. If alloying tin, whether imported or produced in Ireland, were to be added to the copper, an ideal 10 per cent, that is, some 2kg (4½lb) of this (produced from its ores in much the same way as the copper), would be added at this stage; if, on the other hand, the metal-worker was relying on arsenic to harden the copper, most Irish ores contained sufficient quantities to make the deliberate production of this element unnecessary. For this stage we can assume that two men, each working for two days, tending the fire, charging the crucibles and preparing and filling the moulds, would have been sufficient. The end-product would have been the equivalent of forty axes of Lough Ravel type, having an average weight of around 500g (17½oz). These, of course, would have been crude unfinished castings, requiring cleaning up and further post-casting treatment, including, in many cases, decoration.

The relatively small volume of metallurgical evidence that exists suggests that the post-casting treatment which was carried out, mainly to harden and strengthen the implements, included cold-working, heating, or heating with cold-hammering, forging, and heat-treatment carried out as an annealing operation to facilitate forging. For these operations — also labour intensive — we can assume that our two metal-workers could devote another two days of their time, and more if they went on to decorate the axes with extensive engraving.

In the above account we have assumed that the entire production process was carried out at, or near, the smelting site, as a sort of semi-industrial production. This need not have been the case; indeed the available evidence possibly suggests that it was not, at least from the stage where the ingots or copper cakes were produced. The presence of such copper in relatively small hoards of Earlier Bronze Age implements (albeit not accompanied by suitable moulds) could be construed as evidence of implement production by itinerant smiths working on a very small scale.

Developments in metallurgy

As the Bronze Age progressed, so too did the skills and repertoire of the metal-workers, with, apparently, an advancement of their knowledge of the properties of metals: there is some evidence of their ability to choose different alloys for different purposes, for example, an alloy of a more malleable nature for rivets, from that used for the body or blade of an implement or weapon. Instead of producing what were essentially two-dimensional objects such as 'flat' axes, cast in open moulds, they went on to produce increasingly ambitious objects, cast not merely in two-piece moulds, but in two-piece moulds carrying a central core to produce implements and

Stone mould from Ballynahinch, County Down, with an axe from Culfeightrin, County Antrim, which had been cast in it.

(above)
Detail of the terminal of the gold collar from Gleninsheen, County Clare. Later Bronze Age, eighth century BC.

(below)
Massive gold dress-fastener, from Clones, County Monaghan.
(see p213)

(right)
Gold collar of a type often called a gorget, found in a hoard of personal ornaments at Gorteenreagh, County Clare.

Two gold armlets from a hoard of ornaments found in a bog at Derrinboy, County Offaly. Later Bronze Age, about 1200 to 1000 BC.

(opposite)
Torc made from a twisted ribbon of gold. Found near Belfast. Later Bronze Age, 1200 to 1000 BC.

weapons with hollow sockets, such as spearheads, for which actual moulds have also survived. Moulds for such hollow-socketed implements are generally provided with tiny slots to hold the pins that would have helped support the clay core. For the production of these more elaborate moulds, with a greater array of surface features, such as delicate ribs on the blades of spearheads, the sandstone of the earlier moulds was gradually replaced by the more finely carvable talc-schist or steatite, available in many locations in the west of Ireland.

It was only in the Later Bronze Age that the transition to moulds of clay, with a particularly smooth lining on the inner surface and requiring longitudinal strengtheners in the form of wooden rods until fired, began to replace the earlier carved stone moulds. This plastic material was ideal for repetitious casting of existing models, whether in the form of actual implements which it was desired to copy, or, in the lack of them, of models carved from wood. A further increase in the knowledge of the casting properties of metals on the part of Later Bronze Age craftsmen is reflected in the use of lead as an extra additive to create an alloy more suitable for very fine castings, such as the fine chape — the metal terminal protecting the end of a sheath or scabbard. From the evidence of excavated sites of the Later Bronze Age, such as Lough Eskragh, County Tyrone or Rathgall, County Wicklow, it would seem more likely that established centres of metal-working replaced, or augmented, the production capacity of itinerant metal-workers. The sheer volume of production in the Later Bronze Age would seem to support this.

Social and economic factors

While the technical aspects of Bronze Age metal production are relatively well understood, the economic and social aspects are not. We know, for example, that in the Earlier Bronze Age, axes that were cast in the same mould were distributed widely throughout Ireland; the odd fact is that in the instances where the actual mould has survived (for example, at Ballyglisheen, County Carlow, Doonour, County Cork, or Lough Guile, County Antrim), there appear to be no examples of its products in the immediate vicinity of the find-place of the mould. We know too that axes from the same mould occur in different hoards of axes of the same type, with a marked concentration in the 'home' area of the axe type,

and we can even infer that the presence of copper cakes in a hoard seems to underline the 'home' area of that type of axe. What we do not know is how the axes were distributed through the country. The glib answer of course is 'by trade', but in a Bronze Age context what does that mean?

The estimates of the amount of labour required in the production of copper or bronze axes may not be completely accurate, but they are reasonable guesses. If we add up the labour and express it in terms of work-days, we find that to produce forty axes of Lough Ravel type requires over 700 work-days, not including the mining; if we increase this to 800 work-days to allow for the mining labour, we end up with a situation where each 500g (17½oz) axe of Lough Ravel type has cost twenty days of labour. That is twenty days during which one man has devoted all his energies to the manufacture of a single axe and, presumably, has had to be supported and victualled by others during that period. It has been assumed that 'natural resources', that is, one tonne of copper ore and 102 mature forest oaks are there for the taking, free of charge. Nor has the tin been costed, which, if imported from Cornwall, would inevitably have meant a considerable additional cost in terms of work-days for its transport. In modern terms we could express the cost of a single Lough Ravel axe as an average wage for twenty days — ostensibly in the region of £800. What we don't know is how, in the Earlier Bronze Age, this outlay was recouped, or what was the medium of exchange in the glibly postulated trade or barter system.

One possibility is a form of 'tribal' patronage, under which the metal-workers and their associates (for example, the foresters) were supported by the community in which they lived, and trade, accordingly, was between community and community rather than between individual and individual; thereby, the cost of the finished axes was offset by flocks, herds or the like. The metal industry of the Bronze Age could be viewed as sharing part, at least, of the roles of several modern government departments: energy, agriculture, labour, transport and education (the skills and knowledge had to be passed on), and possibly, environment and economic development.

Bronze Age goldwork

Mary Cahill

As the technological processes which led to the manufacture of copper and bronze were being developed and refined, a new source was discovered from which artifacts of a totally different nature and purpose could be produced. This material was gold, and from it a variety of ornamental objects were manufactured which would be prized and traded throughout the Bronze Age.

Earlier Bronze Age goldwork

At first the gold-working techniques were limited in application and scope. Objects were simply produced by hammering small ingots or nuggets into sheets which were cut and trimmed to various shapes. Some of these sheet-gold objects were plain, others were decorated. The range of artifacts produced was also very restricted. Two examples of plain cylindrical-shaped earrings, called basket earrings, and about twenty of the decorated circular objects known as 'sun-discs' are known. These sun discs were usually decorated by the *repoussé* technique (decoration in relief, worked from the back of the object). The designs consist of simple cruciform shapes, radial lines and circles arranged in groups. Each disc has two small central perforations which, it is thought, may have been used to attach it to an organic backing. The lack of finds associated with burials means that we can only speculate as to their function, but racquet-headed pins in copper, with very similar decoration, are known from Bohemia and Slovakia, and the discs may represent a local variant.

Earlier Bronze Age gold-working seems to have concentrated mainly on the production of crescent-shaped sheet-gold collars known as lunulae. There are over one hundred finds of lunulae from Western Europe, eighty-one of which are from Ireland. As many as four have been found together, but they are usually found singly. Studies have shown that three different types were made: classical, unaccomplished and provincial. The examples which have been found on the continent include Irish exports of the classical and unaccomplished types, and provincial examples which seem to be copies of the Irish forms. The classical type was the most skilfully fabricated and most expertly decorated. These are the largest lunulae, made with very thinly beaten sheet-gold. The unaccomplished type reflects less competent gold-working technique, and in some cases the ornamentation is uneven and careless.

Decoration consists mostly of groups of lines, zig-zags and hatched triangles arranged in panels. These motifs are grouped together in a zone covering about one-third of the lunula, on the narrowest surface at either side. The inner and outer edges are also decorated. The design is produced by incising the surface with a sharp tool, such as a graver. Jet and amber necklaces of similar shape and decoration have been found in graves in Scotland and England.

The most striking feature of this early period of gold-working in Ireland is the restricted nature of the output, which was confined to the production of these simple, flat shapes. This probably reflected both the level of gold-working techniques and the restricted availability of the raw material.

Later Bronze Age goldwork

We do not know precisely when the production of lunulae ended or when the new types of gold ornament which feature so prominently in the next phase of the Bronze Age were introduced. The change, however, could hardly be more dramatic. The goldsmiths around 1200 BC seem to have turned their skills to the development of new metal-working techniques and to the production of ornaments which required large quantities of metal. The manufacture of twisted ornaments, known as torcs, may have been due to influences from east Mediterranean Europe, but once introduced, the concept of twisting strips and bars of gold was developed to a very high level, as is evidenced by the fine example from Tipper, County Kildare. Ribbon torcs were made from plain strips of gold and bar torcs from bars of varying cross-sections — circular, square and triangular examples are known. A further variant was introduced by the use of flanged bars, that is, by hammering up the angles on a bar of square or triangular cross-section. By varying the size and shape of the bar and by twisting to a greater or lesser extent, an infinite variety of torcs could be made. Further elaboration was introduced by the addition of highly ornate terminals with spiral or knobbed attachments, as

(opposite)
Drawing of a
double cist, from
Glenacurna,
County
Tipperary.

with the torcs from Tara, County Meath. Earrings, neck, waist and arm ornaments were all produced in this way.

While most of the smiths' production during this early phase of the Later Bronze Age was devoted to twisted ornaments, some objects of sheet-work were also produced, but it was a much more massive production than the earlier works. Good examples of this technique can be seen in the armlets from Derrinboy, County Offaly. This phase of gold-working seems to have petered out at around 1000 BC.

The period from about 800 BC marks an upsurge in the production of all metal types. Many hoards are known from this period, several exclusively of gold. Others are a combination of bronze tools and weapons, together with gold ornaments and amber beads, including some complete necklaces. The Mountrivers hoard in County Cork is a very good example of this type of association, as it contains two socketed bronze axeheads, two particularly well made dress-fasteners, and eleven amber beads. Dress-fasteners, sleeve-fasteners and bracelets are especially well represented during this period. One of the best known discoveries is the hoard from Mooghaun, County Clare, which contained at least 137 bracelets, six gold collars, several neck-rings and other objects. Unfortunately only twenty-nine objects have survived — the rest were melted down. Dress-fasteners such as those from Mountrivers consist of a 'handle' or 'bow' with two terminals, which are usually hollowed or dished. The terminals are sometimes decorated with hatched triangles and zig-zags. They seem to be an Irish adaptation of a Scandinavian fibula (brooch) which functioned with the aid of a pin. There are no Irish examples with pins; they appear to have been used with the aid of loops or double buttonholes. The heaviest example is the highly decorated one from Clones, County Monaghan, which weighs over one kilogram.

One of the most remarkable finds of this period is the hoard from Gorteenreagh, County Clare, discovered in 1948 by a farmer shifting stones. It is unusual in that it seems to have formed a suite of jewellery for a single individual. It contains a gold collar, two hair ornaments called lock-rings, two bracelets and a small dress- or sleeve-fastener. The decorated terminals had been forcibly removed from the collar to which they had been stitched, but even the gold wire has survived. Of the twenty or so lock-rings that are known, the pair from Gorteenreagh are undoubtedly the finest. They are made from very fine, coiled gold wires, soldered or fused together, and held by C-shaped binding strips. Eight collars like these survive and most of them have come from the area bordering the lower Shannon — Counties Clare, Limerick and Tipperary. Perhaps the best known and best preserved was found at Gleninsheen, County Clare. These collars are noted for the extremely high quality of their manufacture. They are distinguished by the raised bands which alternate with rows of cable-like ornament or punched dots. The terminals feature the conical bosses and concentric circles which are also used to decorate gold boxes and sunflower pins of this period. North European prototypes in the form of triple and multi-ribbed neck ornaments have been cited as possible models for the development of these uniquely Irish massive gold collars.

The goldwork of the Later Bronze Age is remarkable for its immense quantity, variety and quality. It represents a pinnacle of achievement developed over a period of fifteen hundred years, starting from very simple and unsophisticated origins. While many outside factors influenced these developments, we can say that Irish goldwork of the Bronze Age achieved a standard unequalled by our European neighbours.

Death in the Earlier Bronze Age

John Waddell

The graves of the Earlier Bronze Age provide a wealth of detail about the burial rites and funerary pottery of the time. New fashions in burial custom demanded not only formal and durable graves, but also the frequent inclusion of one or more of a whole range of pottery vessels. The result is the survival of hundreds of complete pots and sometimes, other objects of bronze, stone or bone. The graves themselves reveal a lot about the different rituals involved, and sheer variety of custom is one of the most outstanding and indeed puzzling features of this body of evidence. Unfortunately, many of these graves have been chance discoveries, often by people engaged in some

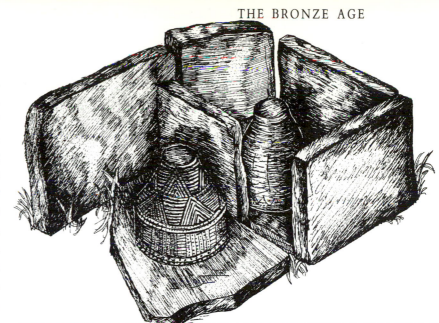

agricultural activity like ploughing or land-clearance. Inevitably some damage is done in these circumstances. What survives offers a fascinating insight into many facets of life and death some four thousand years ago. For instance, the skeletal material can tell us something about ancient diseases, and quite a number of skeletons display some indication of such ailments as arthritis or tooth abscesses. In one unusual case, traces of a serious mastoid infection have been identified, and it has been suggested that the rarity of this ear condition in prehistoric skeletons may mean that common modern disorders such as flu and measles, which can cause this sort of ear trouble, may have been relatively uncommon.

One unfortunate man, found in a grave at Ballybrew, near Enniskerry, County Wicklow, had broken his leg quite some time before he died, and the break had never healed. When he did die, his body was bound in a crouched position and placed on its back in a cist grave, which also contained the skull and some bones of another burial, that of a child. A pottery bowl had been placed beside the man's head. This cist, a short rectangular slab-built box with a roof slab, is a typical example of one of the commonest forms of grave, and like so many others, had been placed in a pit in the ground; it was found quite by chance in the course of digging for gravel. Whole cemeteries of graves are sometimes casually discovered in this manner.

Burial customs

Both unburnt burial and cremation were popular ways of disposing of the dead, and while many graves contain the remains of just one individual, it is not uncommon to find the bones of more than one person. Corpses were often placed in a crouched position, though more often than not lying on their sides. This was a common burial posture in prehistoric Europe at the time, and it may have been widely adopted because it conveniently allowed some economising in grave size and conformed to some magico-religious imperative. Indeed it is possible that a crouched or squatting position with arms raised had some special ceremonial significance in life as well. Some crouched burials were not placed in cists but deposited in simple pits in the ground, and it is probable that the provision of a carefully constructed cist, particularly one laboriously made of large stones, was meant as a mark of special status. This may be true as well of those graves covered by a stone cairn or a mound of earth, or

Encrusted urn found with a food vessel in a pit burial at Nevinstown, County Meath.

Cist grave with skeleton and food vessel, Glassamuckey, County Dublin.

Food vessel from Aghnahily, County Laois.
(see p213)

distinguished by some other evidence of a more complex burial ritual. For example, a low oval mound with a kerb of boulders at Loughfad, near Naran, County Donegal, was found to cover a rectangular cist which had been divided in two by an upright slab. Each compartment, less than 30cm (12in) wide, contained the disarticulated or mixed-up bones of an adult: the long bones lay on the floor and the smaller bones and the skulls lay on top. Obviously no intact corpse had been stuffed into these small compartments; instead, the bodies had been stored elsewhere for a period of time and only given final burial when the bones were thoroughly defleshed. Perhaps the flesh had been allowed to decay naturally but it is conceivable that this process was hastened by exposure to the elements or to carrion birds. Indeed, in one burial of this general period in England, the discovery of a regurgitated food pellet of a bird of prey inside the skull of a partly disarticulated individual is rare confirmation of this practice of exposure.

The cremation of corpses on a funeral pyre was also a common custom but it is not at all clear why some people were treated in this way and others buried unburnt. In time, however, cremation seems to have become the general fashion. Again the deposits of burnt human bone were often placed in cists or in pits, either below ground-level and unmarked, or in burial mounds. Sometimes a small pottery vessel accompanied the bones in the grave, but frequently the small pieces of burnt bone themselves were placed in a large pottery urn which was then put into the pit or cist. These bones often represent just part of the cremated skeleton of one, two, or more persons.

The cases of multiple cremation raise many questions. For example, the burnt bones in a very small cist in Beau townland, near Lusk, County Dublin, represented four adults and two children, and while they were all seemingly buried simultaneously, whether they all died at the same time is an unanswered question. Again it is possible that some corpses were kept someplace apart until a propitious moment for a collective cremation or burial ceremony. There are other less pleasant possibilities too: for some, life in the Bronze Age may have been nasty, brutish and short. Though there is no certain evidence for human sacrifice, in a small number of cases deposits of cremated human bone have been found carefully placed on top of crouched unburnt burials and such a disagreeable ritual is one conceivable explanation.

Grave pottery

Many graves contain no offerings or grave-goods, but of those that do, a pottery vessel is by far the commonest find. All the pottery was hand-made by building up coils of clay and by firing the result in a simple oven. Different shapes and sizes of vessel have been found, and on the basis of these and other stylistic variations, four major pottery groups or traditions can be identified. It is tempting to think that each of these separate traditions represents a distinct population group, but without detailed knowledge of the contemporary settlements and their domestic pottery, it is impossible to be sure of this. Pottery from ritual contexts is not a sure guide, and the differences here in a funerary context could reflect religious or social distinctions of some description, or even just changes in pottery fashions through time.

The Bowl Tradition

Some of the most highly decorated pottery belongs to a major group named the Bowl Tradition, in which different forms of small bowls, usually about 10 to 15cm (4 to 6in) high, have been profusely ornamented, usually with dots and triangles impressed in the soft clay before firing. Quite a number of these little vessels have star-shaped or cross-shaped designs impressed on their bases, as if this part of the pot was meant to be seen as well. The impressed dot (or so-called comb) ornament is the same sort of decoration as that found on Beaker pottery in Ireland and elsewhere, and these bowls, and whatever rites they were part of, were at least partly inspired by Beaker fashions. These pots have sometimes been called 'food vessels' because, since they often stood mouth upwards beside a crouched skeleton or even beside a pile of burnt bones, it was generally believed that they once contained an offering of food for the deceased. No trace of food has yet been found in any of them so it is possible that some once held a form of drink, perhaps a mead-like substance, as in contemporary grave offerings elsewhere. However, this is certainly not true of a number of bowls which were deposited mouth downwards in the grave. Neither can it be true of a bowl found in a cist at Dungate, near Cookstown, County Tyrone, which had been carefully placed with its mouth against the top of the skull of an adult male. Could it be that this pot at least had been intended as a temporary resting place for the dead man's spirit? This grave also contained fragments of a second bowl and a few bones of the skeleton of a three-year-old child which may have been taken from some place else (and recall the child's bones in the Ballybrew grave).

Unburnt burial and cremation were equally popular in the Bowl Tradition, but it is not at all clear why one or other rite was adopted.

The Vase Tradition

The pottery makers of the second major group, the Vase Tradition, by and large favoured fire as a ritual agent and cremated their dead, but they nonetheless had a whole series of different ways of disposing of the bones. They made small vases, often decorated with incised ornament, to accompany or even contain some of the burnt remains, and they produced larger pots, vase urns or encrusted urns (with characteristic applied strips of clay as decoration) to contain and protect most or all of the cremation deposit. The urns are frequently placed in small pits or polygonal cists, just large enough to take them, and while a few are placed mouth upwards, a majority are inverted.

The cordoned and collared urn traditions

The two other pottery traditions are numerically less significant, and both seem to be expressions of close contacts with Scotland and northern England, where similar pots are particularly well known. Cordoned urns, so called because they have two or more narrow horizontal cordons or ribs on their exteriors, are often found inverted in pits. The same is true of collared urns, named after their distinctive collar between mouth and neck.

Social implications

With all of these urn burials the destructive rite of cremation presents problems: it is sometimes difficult to age and sex the dead accurately, particularly because prehistoric funeral pyres occasionally attained a high level of efficiency, distorting and shattering the bones. Nonetheless, scientific analysis at least demonstrates that adult males, females and children were all accorded the privilege of combustion by each of these groups of pottery makers. Since the same is true of the unburnt burials, elaborate mortuary treatment was obviously not confined to adult males; thus it is possible that a woman's

status in life was broadly similar to a man's, and children were recognised as members of the community. Of course, it is also possible that some graves are no indication of the status of the deceased, but more an attempt by one of the living to enhance their own standing in the community with a lavish funeral for a relative. The evidence is not always easy to interpret. Multiple burials, of children and male adults for instance, as at Ballybrew and Dungate, might at first seem to support the notion of a measure of equality between the sexes and between the different age groups. But perhaps for some, status was only acquired by being formally buried along with a particular individual, even if this meant a period of temporary storage for one of them. If the social significance of the different rituals and of the various pottery types is imperfectly understood, the same is undoubtedly true of the social implications of the grave goods that occur now and then. Flint knives and flint scrapers or flakes are the commonest of these other finds, and bone pins or other bone objects are found occasionally. Boar's tusks, beads of various substances, axeheads of polished stone, and bronze items such as axes, daggers or knives are fairly rare. The scarcity of objects which we might consider prestigious or valuable may be less than helpful to the modern archaeologist but it does not imply a low level of material wealth.

Cemeteries

The variety of methods of burial, the range of pottery types and other grave offerings, and the questions they all raise, are well illustrated in the cemeteries of the period. Just as some isolated burials were in unmarked or flat graves, or covered by a burial mound, so too both flat cemeteries and cemetery mounds occur. Flat cemeteries were not marked in any monumental way, and all the graves were below ground-level. Originally, the position of individual burials was probably marked in some way, perhaps by a pottery vessel, a pile of earth or stones, or even some animal bones. The cemetery at Edmondstown, County Dublin, provides an indication of some sequence in the deposition of graves, but how long the cemetery was in use is difficult to say. At Edmondstown, about eighteen burials were found. The core of the cemetery seems to have been two cists (nos. I and II) containing crouched skeletons of teenagers, each with a bowl by the head. A third cist (III) to the west contained the cremated bones of a youth, also with a bowl, and a small fourth cist with the cremated bones of an adult had no pottery. The other burials, mainly to the south of the cists, were all cremations, some scattered deposits (two of them partly covering the capstones of cists I and II), others placed in urns. The urns included collared urns and encrusted urns. Other grave goods were for the most part unremarkable: they included two miniature pottery cups, a flint knife, a small tubular bone object, and several stone beads. One burial (cremation no. 12), an encrusted urn placed mouth upwards in a pit, was protected by a few stones, some of which may have been taken from cist IV. A much smaller group of burials comes from a different, enclosed cemetery at Urbalreagh, near Portrush, County Antrim, where a very shallow ditch, with an entrance on the east, enclosed a circular area just under 6m (19½ft) across. At the centre was a cluster of three burials: a very fine cordoned urn (burial 1) was inverted in a pit; immediately to the west, a second, plain urn (burial 2) had been placed mouth upwards in another pit; and a short distance away a pit contained a cremation and a burnt flint flake (burial 3). The cremations were those of an adult male, a child and a juvenile respectively. In this instance the adult male clearly had the better urn, and the circular ditch demarcated the sacred burial area.

There are different sorts of cemetery mounds too: in some instances Neolithic mounds were re-used or even added to, but in others mounds were built expressly to contain several burials. Some of these may even have been built in stages, with one or more burials coinciding with each phase, and the final period of use perhaps consisting of burials actually inserted into the finished monument. A broad, flat-topped mound on top of a conspicuous hill named Knockast, near Moate, County Westmeath proved, on excavation, to be one of the largest cemetery mounds so far recorded. It contained thirty-nine cremated and four unburnt burials, one of which was an extended skeleton about 50cm (19½in) below the surface of the 95cm (37in) high mound, and thought to be more recent than the Bronze Age. Of the remaining three unburnt burials, one was crouched (and accompanied by a pig's tusk), and the other two had been disturbed by the insertion of subsequent cremations. A few of the cremations were placed in cists, some in urns, including cordoned urn and encrusted urn, and some

simply placed in holes made for them in the cairn. A study of the unburnt and burnt remains revealed the sobering fact that almost two-thirds of the population of the cemetery died before their early thirties. Given that the remains of children were clearly under-represented, and numbered less than half a dozen — possibly because their bones would not always survive the heat of the pyre or because they were simply disposed of in another way — it seems fair to suggest that the people of Knockast broadly conformed to the grim prehistoric norm of an average life expectancy of twenty to twenty-five years. The eleven or so adults who survived into their forties or fifties must have been venerable members of the community.

The large number of individuals buried at Knockast is unusual, it is matched only at the 'Mound of the Hostages' at Tara which also contained some forty burials. Here the burials had been inserted into a Neolithic mound covering a small passage tomb. All but one were cremated. The unburnt burial was exceptional: the skeleton of a youth, with legs flexed, lay on its back, and in the region of the neck were the remains of an unusual necklace of bronze tubing, jet, amber and a synthetic glass-like substance called faience. The cremations included collared urn and encrusted urn burials.

Most Irish cemeteries are surprisingly small: the majority contained less than a dozen graves and over half had as few as two or three. It does look as if these small cemeteries could only have served a fraction of a community, so perhaps formal burial was an honour accorded only to a few. It is also possible that we are wrong to call these smaller burial groups 'cemeteries' because they may have had some other role in society. Rather than being places specifically for the disposal of the dead, they may have been places where token burials were made by several communities to placate spirits or to strengthen a social or political alliance. If some sites had such a special purpose, then a mixture of pottery types might be anticipated.

It is worth remembering that these graves, which to our eyes mark the final rite of passage, quite possibly signified a new beginning to our Bronze Age forefathers for, as likely as not, their dead were honoured in this way not because they were defunct, but because they were about to have a new role in society and become revered ancestors.

Stone circles, stone rows, boulder-burials and standing stones

Seán Ó Nualláin

The Bronze Age in Ireland saw the appearance of new forms of megalithic monuments. The wedge tomb continued the custom of communal burial for a time but the dead were now often buried individually in pits or small stone boxes (cists), sometimes grouped together in or under mounds of earth or of stone (cairns). Megalithic tombs were no longer built, but the knowledge and skills of the tomb-builders seem to have survived and are embodied in the monuments we know as stone circles, stone rows and standing stones (or monoliths). These terms immediately indicate what such monuments look like but give no idea of their purpose. Even the experts cannot be sure why these monuments were erected, but as many of those investigated were found to be associated with burial, in one form or another, it has been concluded that they were ritual or ceremonial monuments associated with a cult of the dead. The new types of megalithic monument were not incorporated in cairns. They were composed of stones, set apart rather than contiguously, to form free-standing circles and rows (sometimes called alignments) or set singly as monoliths. Individual stones became important in their own right, and the size and shape of the stones and the precise number employed in certain classes of monument clearly had some special significance.

Free-standing megalithic structures of different classes are often found in the same regions, and sometimes occur together in closely-knit complexes. There are two major concentrations in Ireland, a south Munster series occupying large areas of Cork and part of south-west Kerry, and a mid-Ulster series, and between these are

Stone circle near Castletownbeare, County Cork.

a few small isolated groups. In Britain stone circles and rows occur mainly in western districts, from Devon and Cornwall to Cumbria and south-west Scotland, and also in Aberdeenshire, where there is a notable concentration of circles which share some of the characteristics of the south Munster series. The best known British circle is,

Boulder burial, Kenmare, County Kerry.

Stone row, Gleninagh, Connemara, County Galway.

Stone circle with outlying monolith, at Ardgroom, County Cork.

of course, Stonehenge, on Salisbury Plain in the south of England. This world-famous monument differs in many respects from all the other British and Irish stone circles, and indeed the great lintels which cap its outer circle and the paired stones of the U-shaped setting within are unique. Few stone circles are known in Brittany but stone rows and monoliths occur there in profusion. Most notable are the stone rows at Kermario, in Carnac, where seven major lines of huge stones, set parallel, extend for a distance of over 1km. Sub-rectangular megalithic enclosures and semi-circular settings of stones which occur there are sometimes attached to stone rows and may be akin to the Irish and British stone circles.

The south Munster group

The principal components of this group are stone circles, stone rows, monoliths and simple structures called boulder-burials. The circles consist of uneven numbers of spaced stones which vary from five to seventeen and enclose areas ranging from 2.5m (8ft) to about 17m (55½ft) in diameter. The stones are symmetrically arranged, with the entrance towards the north-east, and directly opposite this is the lowest stone on the perimeter, known as the axial stone. Over one hundred such circles are known, about half of which are of the small five-stone variety. These smaller rings tend to be D-shaped while the larger rings are more circular in outline. In three instances the circle is surrounded by an earthen bank or a bank and ditch. About a fifth of the larger circles contain a monolith and about the same proportion enclose one or more boulder-burials.

Boulder-burials consist of a cover stone, up to 2m (6½ft) in maximum dimension and 1m thick, set resting above low supporting stones. Over seventy boulder-burials are known in south Munster, and apart from a single example in County Sligo, none are known elsewhere. One excavated example was found to stand above a pit containing a cremation burial, and it may be that these structures are memorials set above burials rather than formal chambers intended as receptacles for burial deposits. Some of the circles are accompanied by outlying rows of up to four stones or by monoliths, while others have small, low cairns nearby.

Six of the south Munster circles have been excavated but few datable artifacts were recovered. Pits with cremated bone were located in four examples, and one of these, in the circle at Drombeg, near Glandore, County Cork, held the remains of a youth, contained in an inverted pottery vessel. Finds from Cashelkeelty, County Kerry, where a five-stone circle and a stone row stood close together, included two flint arrowheads, one leaf-shaped, the other barbed and tanged, which would be in keeping with the general Late Neolithic or Early Bronze Age dating for stone circles in these islands. However, radiocarbon determinations from the site, said to relate to the construction period of the circle, indicated a date of c.1000 BC and would seem to be in conflict with the archaeological evidence.

Over one hundred and seventy stone rows are known in Cork and Kerry, and single examples of similar type are found in six adjoining or nearby counties. Over half of these consist of no more than two stones. The number of stones in the larger rows varies from three to six. The stones are set with their long axes roughly in line and can extend over distances ranging from 2m (6½ft) to 13m (42½ft). In most instances the stones are graded in height, with the tallest stone at one end, more often than not at the south-west. Individual stones in the rows range from less than 1m (3ft) to about 4m (13ft) in height. Some of the taller rows are amongst the more impressive monuments of the region, and especially striking examples are to be seen at Castlenalacht near Bandon and Gurranes near Castletownsend, both in County Cork.

The rows are aligned along a general north-east/south-west axis and thus share a common custom of orientation with the stone circles of the region. This indicates an alignment of the monuments on the sectors of the heavens in which the sun rises and sets, and both series tend to cluster in a sector indicating a winter rather than a summer position for the sun. There is reason to believe that many of the six hundred or so slab-like monoliths recorded for the region may be found to display a similar orientation pattern in plan and, if so, this would link that series with the stone circles and rows of the region.

The stone circles, rows and monoliths of Cork and Kerry, like the wedge tombs of the region, frequently occupy upland areas of well-drained soils, and it may be that the builders of these monuments were also interested in raising cattle. Cereal cultivation is likely to have formed part of their economy, and direct evidence for this was provided by the recovery of cereal pollen from peat samples considered to be contemporary with the erection of the stone row and circle at Cashelkeelty, County Kerry. Circles, rows and monoliths are all represented in the copper-bearing coastal regions of the south-west, as are the boulder-burials, and again, like the wedge tomb builders, it is possible that some if not all of the groups represented by these monuments had an interest in the copper ores.

The mid-Ulster group

Many of the stone circles and rows of Tyrone, Derry and east Fermanagh are enveloped in bog, and the full extent of the monuments is often difficult to define. The precise number of monuments in the province is not known but there would seem to be about a hundred circles and perhaps as many rows. The rows and circles are very different from the south Munster examples. In Ulster they are normally set in clusters, which may also include cairns, cists and monoliths. Most of the Ulster rows, like the circles they accompany, are composed of numerous small stones set close together and seldom exceeding 1m (3ft) in height. The rows are usually set tangentially to the circles and can run to 30m (98½ft) or more in length. Occasionally, short rows of tall stones reminiscent of those in Munster accompany the circles or occur in isolation. The circles are irregular in outline and are seldom more than 15m (49ft) in diameter. The best known assemblage of monuments is at Beaghmore in County Tyrone, where excavation of the bog has so far uncovered a complex consisting of seven stone circles, ten rows and over a dozen small cairns extending over an area of two hectares (c. 5 acres). These monuments were built above an Early Neolithic site, and while a few artifacts from the earlier occupation were recovered, finds from the circles, rows and cists were few. Most of the cists were empty, but one contained a polished stone axehead. Two cremated burials were found in one of the cairns but it would seem that soil conditions were unfavourable to the survival of burial deposits. Studies of the pollen record recovered from the site suggest that the Neolithic activity there began about the fourth millennium BC and that the main period of the rows, circles, cairns and cists was the late second and early first millennia BC.

Little can yet be said of the lives of the monument builders. The monuments themselves indicate well-organised groups of people devoted to unknown ritual practices related to the dead. Despite their differing

The Long Stone: standing stone at Punchestown, County Kildare.

Aerial view of the Beaghmore stone circles and rows, County Tyrone.

characteristics and the considerable distance separating them, the occurrence of circles, rows, cairns, monoliths and small burial chambers in both the Ulster and south Munster groups suggests the presence of an underlying unity of tradition.

Smaller groups of circles and rows

Small though notable groups of stone circles occur at three locations, Lough Gur, County Limerick, Cong, County Mayo, and the west Wicklow/Kildare region. The circles in these groups do not share characteristic features and few display affinities with the circles of the two major groups. However, they do seem to be linked by the occurrence in each group of monuments where stone rings and earthen banks or ditches are brought together to form composite monuments. The best known example is the circle at Grange, beside Lough Gur, where the great earthen bank is lined internally by contiguous stones. There is a somewhat similar monument at Castleruddery in County Wicklow, and this is also

surrounded by two concentric ditches. One of the Cong group, in County Mayo, though consisting of spaced stones, is surrounded by a bank. Such monuments are sometimes taken to indicate a convergence of the traditions of stone circle builders and those of the groups who built the so-called henge monuments found in the east of the country. However, present knowledge would suggest that these small though important groups of stone circles are best considered as representing localised but important episodes in the prehistory of Late Neolithic/Early Bronze Age Ireland.

Recent fieldwork has identified a group of five stone rows and seven pairs of stones in the Clifden region of north-west County Galway. These are rather similar to the Munster series though most are aligned in a contrasting north-south direction. However, the presence of a probable five-stone circle near one of the rows — at Derryinver — does suggest strong links with the builders of the south Munster monuments.

TIME CHART

From earliest times to the first century

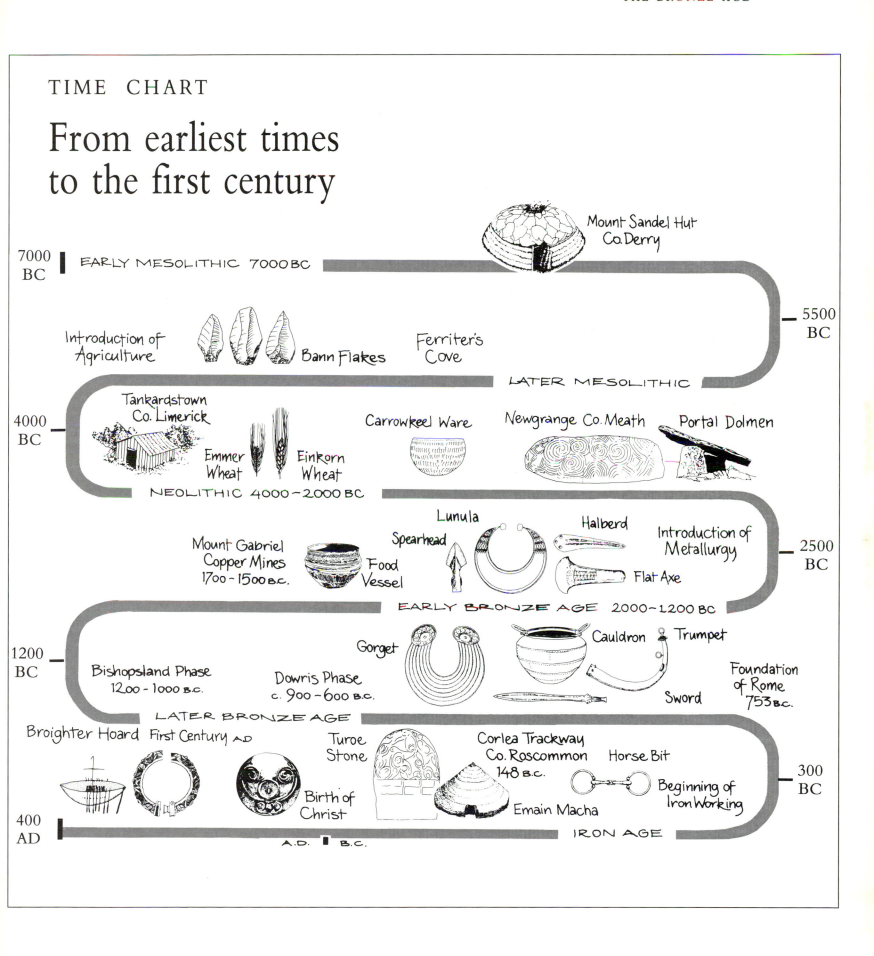

7000 BC — EARLY MESOLITHIC 7000 BC

Mount Sandel Hut Co. Derry

5500 BC

Introduction of Agriculture — Bann Flakes — Ferriter's Cove

LATER MESOLITHIC

4000 BC — Tankardstown Co. Limerick — Emmer Wheat — Einkorn Wheat — Carrowkeel Ware — Newgrange Co. Meath — Portal Dolmen

NEOLITHIC 4000–2000 BC

Mount Gabriel Copper Mines 1700–1500 B.C. — Food Vessel — Spearhead — Lunula — Halberd — Flat Axe — Introduction of Metallurgy

2500 BC

EARLY BRONZE AGE 2000–1200 BC

1200 BC — Bishopsland Phase 1200–1000 B.C. — Dowris Phase c. 900–600 B.C. — Gorget — Cauldron — Trumpet — Sword — Foundation of Rome 753 B.C.

LATER BRONZE AGE

Broighter Hoard — First Century AD — Turoe Stone — Corlea Trackway Co. Roscommon 148 B.C. — Horse Bit — Birth of Christ — Emain Macha — Beginning of Iron Working

300 BC

400 AD

A.D. ▮ B.C.

IRON AGE

93

The Later Bronze Age

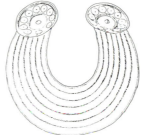

Great changes took place in Europe in the thirteenth century BC. Long-established, apparently stable cultures underwent rapid and dramatic changes of the sort which suggest large-scale disruption of political groupings. The excavation of city sites in the Mediterranean shows that here, too, there was a period of great confusion. Ireland was no exception, with changes in bronze technology, in imported gold-working techniques, and in the resumption of the practice of concealing hoards of weapons, tools and ornaments. Is this to be explained as a kind of knock-on effect, by perhaps the arrival of new people displaced from elsewhere, who may have taken a dominant position? If so, are we to attribute this to a major, if transient, climatic deterioration? Can we speak in these terms at all? For the opening phase of the Later Bronze Age, only one habitation site and no burials are so far known. Our knowledge as yet comes almost exclusively from a study of metal objects found in hoards and evidence in pollen studies of continued and perhaps even increased agriculture.

The metalwork suggests a continuing progression in the period between the thirteenth and the eighth century BC, but little in the archaeology of those centuries prepares us for the astonishing flowering of metal-working of the highest quality in the eighth and seventh centuries. New techniques appear, like sheet-bronze working, sophisticated casting of complex objects, and a greatly increased variety of artifacts, many copied or adapted from foreign models. Influences from the Mediterranean as well as the Scandinavian regions are identifiable. The distribution of objects — many important hoards of gold ornaments were found in the Lower Shannon area — suggests that regional power groupings had emerged; this impression is reinforced by the appearance of defended hilltop sites at this time, some of which remained important into and throughout the Iron Age. Objects found in a lake at Dowris in County Offaly, after which this final period of the Bronze Age is named, included variants fashionable either in the extreme north-east or south-west; this has suggested to some that it was a votive deposit, of significance to the whole island. (In early Irish place-lore, Birr, nearby, was the navel of Ireland.) The final phase of the Later Bronze Age is known not only through its hoards, which are numerous, but also through the lake dwellings of the period as well as production centres where many clay moulds for casting objects have been excavated. Burials in the form of simple cremations in pits, sometimes under round mounds, are once more identifiable.

The Later Bronze Age was a period of great economic advance and, probably, social reorganisation, when much of what was to follow in the Iron Age was foreshadowed. Can we say that this society collapsed, or did it gradually change over the centuries, adapting to influences from outside? In the Iron Age we can see in the objects which survived and their style of decoration, the influence of people who, in late prehistoric Europe, are identified as the Celts of history. The end of Later Bronze Age culture is bound up with the vexed question of when Ireland became 'Celtic', of whether we are dealing with an event — say an invasion — or a process whereby Ireland simply continued to share in the gradual developments — material, social and linguistic — of the peoples of those parts of Europe with which there had long been contact.

The deposition of hoards, such as the small group of implements in the foreground, found in a wooden box in a bog at Bootown, County Antrim, is typical of the later stages of the Bronze Age.
(see p213)

Daily life in the Later Bronze Age

George Eogan

A hoard of axeheads, rings and disc-headed pins of a type known as 'sunflower' pins from Ballytegan, County Laois: found in a pit in a gravel ridge.

The thirteenth century BC was a time of great turmoil and change in Europe. The great Mycenaean culture of Greece collapsed — just one of the many changes which took place amongst the civilisations of the eastern Mediterranean. Towards the end of the century the Nile Delta was raided by the mysterious 'peoples of the sea', and the mighty Hittite kingdom, centred on what is now Anatolia in Turkey, was put under pressure by people from the north. What triggered these events is unknown, and without a historical record we can only say that Europe north of the Alps underwent dramatic changes at the same time — burial rituals changed, industry became more organised, with large-scale exploitation of metal resources. The archaeological record shows that new types of equipment were adopted, including, probably for the first time, waggons with spoked wheels. The cumulative impression of all this in the archaeological evidence is that Europe was changing rapidly in its social and economic order, its settlement patterns and its developing technology. These changes, in what may now be called the barbarian world, must have owed a great deal to external stimuli, and they reflect what we know from the records of the higher civilisations of the south. Ireland was not immune, and the same period saw the beginnings of technological and probably other change, which altered the pattern of Earlier Bronze Age life irreversibly.

Land, settlement and subsistence

It is difficult to establish how the climate differed from today's, but there is some evidence for short periods of climatic deterioration. The countryside would have been more heavily forested, wild animals and fish would have been more plentiful and, due to lack of drainage, marshes would have been more common. There is also evidence for the expansion of bogs during this period. Lakes would have been larger, and intensive flooding after rain a regular feature. In many parts of the midlands there would have been a significant deterioration in communications.

Little is known about domestic houses during the early stages of the Later Bronze Age but, between the ninth and the seventh centuries BC, there is clear evidence for the existence of individual farmsteads with a dwelling house, usually circular in plan. In some instances there were small associated structures, such as open-air hearths or rubbish pits, while some sites were built in lakes or on lakeshores and therefore were protected by water; the dryland sites had only limited protection, such as a shallow ditch or a palisade.

No evidence for house furnishings has come to light, and apart from pottery — coarse, flat-based vessels — and a couple of wooden dishes from Ballinderry, County Offaly, neither is there evidence for household utensils. Bronze knives probably had many uses — domestic, woodwork, butchering and the like. The discovery of Later Bronze Age habitations has been largely a matter of chance, and we do not have sufficient information to build up a reliable picture of the pattern of settlement of the period. This we have to guess at from the distribution of chance finds of artifacts. Domestic animals raised included cattle, sheep, goats, horses and dogs. Grain crops, barley and wheat in particular, were grown. Bronze sickles were used for reaping; initially a non-socketed type was used but later, socketed ones were manufactured. Grain was ground in saddle querns.

Towards the end of the Bronze Age the harnessed horse appears, and this must have improved transport and communications. Horses may have been used for drawing carts, although clear evidence for vehicles is not yet available; however, wooden block-wheels from Doogarymore, County Roscommon, and Timahoe East, County Kildare, might date from the period. Boats must have been used by those who dwelt on lake sites, but the evidence is sparse: perhaps the dug-out canoes from Lough Eskragh, County Tyrone, may be of the Later Bronze Age. Wooden trackways across bogs, such as those from Corlea, County Longford, were a response to the disimproving communications brought about by the expansion of the great raised bogs.

Manufacture and industry

The Later Bronze Age is characterised by an intensification of production in different materials. With the exception of amber, Ireland was fortunate in having substantial native supplies of other raw materials. Woodworking and pottery manufacture have been mentioned. The hoard from Cromaghs, Armoy, County Antrim, gives us a unique insight into textiles of the period. A large leather shield from a bog at Clonbrin, County Longford, provides the best evidence for leather-working and clearly shows that the technique of moulding leather had been mastered. A small number of chisel-like tools with broad crescentic blades may have been leather knives.

Wood was the most widely used material, as is clearly shown by the abundance of wood-working tools, the classic type being the socketed axe of which nearly two thousand examples survive. At the beginning of the Later

A hoard of two gold dress-fasteners, a bronze bracelet, eleven amber beads and two axeheads, from Mountrivers, Coachford, County Cork.

Bronze Age, palstaves and related axes were standard, but they were being replaced by the socketed axe, which proved to be very versatile for heavy and light wood-working. There were also specialised tools, like the socketed gouge, but tanged and socketed chisels could also have been part of the carpenter's kit. Of the half a dozen or so hoards of the period that consist of tools only, all could have belonged to a wood-worker. From the remains of a large square structure (12m x 12m; 39ft x 39ft) at Ballinderry Crannog, No. 2, the scale of the timbers of some of the bog trackways indicates that massive work was well within the competence of the craftsmen. The moulds used in the manufacture of leather shields — of which a few survive — show that large trees, at least 50cm (19½in) in diameter, were cut up and worked. The shield moulds, the small dish from Ballinderry, and a little box made to contain gold ornaments, from Killymoon, County Tyrone, demonstrate that fine wood-working was appreciated. Indeed, the craftsman/carpenter was probably a valued member of society, the use of wooden objects being essential to the entire community.

Metal-workers had a pivotal role to play in serving society, as the thousands of metal artifacts which survive from the period demonstrate. The Later Bronze Age saw not only a change in the types of object being produced, but also a change in methods of manufacture. The stone mould which had been favoured in Ireland from the beginning of the Bronze Age was replaced by the sophisticated clay mould. We have direct evidence for manufacturing centres such as Sites D and F, Knockadoon, Lough Gur, County Limerick and Rathgall, County Wicklow. At Knockadoon, Site F, there was a rectangular building, slightly over 8m x 6m (26ft x 19½ft). The walls had a stone foundation, with perishable material, possibly sods, above. The Site D building was much smaller, somewhat oval in shape and measuring about 5m x 3m (16½ft x 10ft). Its construction seems to have been similar to that of Site F. The Knockadoon smiths cast a variety of objects, notably rapiers, looped spearheads and palstaves. At Rathgall there was a wooden building of indeterminate shape and size. The presence of four thousand fragments of clay moulds and other debris indicates the intensity of production, probably the permanent workshop of a smith. Other sites produced mould fragments but the numbers were small. Dalkey Island, County Dublin, for

instance, yielded about one hundred and forty mould fragments and forty pieces of crucible, so perhaps there were also itinerant metal-workers serving the needs of homesteads.

The changes in the organisation of metal-working and the increase in the range of tool types are mirrored in the changes in technology. The working of bar-gold is added to the repertoire of the goldsmith, while sheet-gold ornaments are often decorated with motifs in strong relief. The most remarkable objects of the beginning of the period are the magnificent flange-twisted bar torcs.

During the final stage of the Later Bronze Age, sheet- and bar-gold (although not twisted) were in use, but techniques became more elaborate. One of these was the manufacturing of the face plates of lock-rings by soldering tiny wires parallel to each other, to create the effect of a milled or ground plate. Another was the placing of a gold sheet over a bronze backing, as is sometimes found on the heads of disc-headed pins. Certain important objects were made in sheet-bronze. This is best seen in the metal shields and the splendid buckets and cauldrons of the time. Superb examples of craftsmanship, the vessels were made of riveted sheets. To carry out this work a wider range of tools was available. Some of these may have been shared with the carpenter — socketed hammers for example — but anvils were probably made specifically for the smith.

Warfare

In the earlier part of the Later Bronze Age the two main weapons in use, the looped spear and the rapier, both represent an older native tradition. But during the course of the Later Bronze Age, Irish weapons took on a more international flavour with the introduction of the leaf-shaped slashing sword and the plain leaf-shaped spearhead. Round shields, in both sheet-bronze and leather, were part of this paraphernalia. By the end of the Later Bronze Age, a number of hilltop sites had been enclosed, probably for defence. It may be that the wealth of the period reflects the emergence of rival power elites.

The people

The scarcity of skeletal remains makes it difficult to assess what people looked like — we lack information from burials which could shed light on stature, nutrition, prevalence of certain diseases and the like. We can, however, make certain educated guesses from artifactual evidence about fashions in appearance. Small, double-edged tanged blades with fine edges, which could have served as razors, suggest that men were probably clean-shaven, while bronze tweezers may have been used by both men and women. We have no evidence for foot or head gear, but the find from Cromaghs, County Antrim, clearly shows that a cloak made from woven wool was worn. The find also included the remains of a horse-hair belt with elegant, tablet-woven tassels. Such cloaks could have been fastened by dress-fasteners or by disc-headed pins with straight or bent stems. It is tempting to think of the Cromaghs' material as throwing light on the life of a travelling carpenter at the end of the Bronze Age, going about his work with his tools (socketed axehead and socketed gouge, his razor in a leather case), wearing a woollen cloak fastened by a disc-headed pin with bent stem, and a woven horse-hair belt around his waist.

A number of hoards in which different types of ornament are found together show how important lavish ornaments were to some people. Bar torcs were worn as neck ornaments in the early part of the period. These might be coupled with two bracelets, either plain or twisted, and two tress-rings, perhaps intended to gather the hair at the sides. Spiral finger rings were also worn.

During the final stage the number and variety of ornaments increased, as did the range of material used in their manufacture. Apart from pins, few were made from bronze; gold predominated, but other materials, especially amber and jet (or lignite) were sometimes used. In Munster, the gorget — the most elaborate ornament from prehistoric Ireland — enjoyed a vogue. Another important neck ornament of the time is the amber necklace, especially the multiple-stranded variety, a striking example of which was found in a bog at Derrybrien, County Galway, with six strings of graded beads, numbering about five hundred in all. A few ornaments combining gold and amber survive, such as the necklace from Croghtenclough, County Kilkenny.

Objects that could have been worn as hair ornaments, to gather the hair on each side, are the finely made gold penannular objects of triangular cross-section, the lock-rings, and small penannular rings called hair-rings. Penannular bracelets increased in popularity, but now the terminals were expanded evenly, yet there were detailed differences. In some examples they are solid; in others hollowed. Again, hoards suggest that more than one bracelet, including different forms, could have been worn by the same person. Other ornaments could have had a practical function. The dress-fastener could have been used for fastening a cloak across the chest while the sleeve-fastener may have had a related function, indeed to fasten a sleeve or even a light cloak in the manner of the dress-fastener. Pins could also have been used for fastening garments, which were most likely to have been cloaks.

Ritual and ceremony

In contrast to the Earlier Bronze Age there is practically no evidence for ritual in burial. Rathgall, which consists of a complex within a circular area delimited by a ditch 16m (52½ft) in internal diameter and 75 to 80cm (29½in to 31½in) wide, provides the best evidence there is. In the centre there was a cremation burial in a pit, with another in a coarse pottery vessel nearby. But there are other features and trappings that may have been associated with ritual activities, perhaps some of the ornaments already described. Some of the gold objects may have had a purely amuletic function, more appropriate to ceremonial occasions. Other objects, for example the metal vessels, especially the great buckets and cauldrons, may also have had a ceremonial purpose. It is easy to envisage such elaborate objects being used at a funeral or other festival rather than domestically. Double-hooked bronze objects, the flesh forks, could have been used for removing the joints of meat from the pot. Bronze horns might also have been used at such gatherings. As a number of individual objects and also hoards were found in places where retrieval would have been difficult, such as swamps or bogs, their deposition may have been part of a ritual act. We do not have enough evidence to indicate if these were special ceremonial centres, but the great hoards, of over a hundred objects, from the Bog of Cullen, County Tipperary, Mooghaun, County Clare and Dowris, County Offaly, may suggest that there were sacred lakes to which objects were finally committed. It is also possible that ritual centres were constructed, and perhaps one such monument was the King's Stables, near Emain Macha, County Armagh. This is a sunken, water-filled circular area, 25m (82ft) in diameter, surrounded by a bank; it might have been a ritual pool into which objects were deposited on special occasions.

Bronze spearhead found near Roscrea, County Tipperary. (see p213)

(opposite) Leaf-shaped sword of bronze. (see p213)

(opposite)
Hypothetical reconstruction of a Later Bronze Age habitation site based on a variety of sources.

Framework of a house of Curraghatoor (County Tipperary) type based on a number of sources.

Overview of the period

The Later Bronze Age was a time of considerable economic development and ritual change. A contributing factor was Ireland's natural wealth, good farmland and woodland, and native supplies of metal. But society was versatile, adaptive and creative. It absorbed new ideas and types from diverse areas, ranging from the Mediterranean in the south to the west Baltic in the north. These influences contributed to the build-up of a lively industry that was also an exporter, as is clear from finds not only in Britain but also on the continent of Europe, such as the gold bracelet of Irish type from Gahlstorf, near Bremen, Germany.

The farmer and the craftsman constituted the basis of society, but it is difficult to comprehend its nature fully. The large, wooden, circular building indicates that Rathgall was a place of importance, a high status site. This is supported by the fact that its inhabitants had exotic objects such as glass and amber beads, a composite bead of gold and glass and a small number of gold objects. Furthermore, it was a bronze-manufacturing centre. It may have been the occupation site of a wealthy and important family. Could its head have been the local chief? It is possible that society was highly stratified and the imposing ornaments could have been the regalia of those of high status. But one should not over-emphasise the material side. Communal ceremonies involving ritual also appear to have been a feature. Gold ornaments, sheet-bronze vessels and bronze horns probably played an important role on such occasions, perhaps at ritual centres such as the 'golden' bog of Cullen, the King's Stables or Dowris, County Offaly. The Later Bronze Age seems to have been a time of social stability and material wealth, but it was also a society that had a deep religious foundation.

Despite this, the culture of the Later Bronze Age did not survive long into the changed European world that was emerging during the seventh century BC. Whatever about the settlement pattern it is at least clear that demand for the rich products in bronze declined, and this might reflect the introduction of corruptible iron. However, there may be more to it than that. Some new metal types, still in bronze, and principally warrior equipment such as swords and chapes (the metal guards of scabbard tips), but also novel socketed axeheads, appeared during the seventh century. The Earlier Iron Age cultures of middle Europe provided the ultimate prototypes of these new

objects. These people were technologically advanced in their use of iron and their well-harnessed horses for travel and transport. The major question is unfortunately unanswered: Did Ireland witness an arrival of foreigners during the seventh century, and if so, were they the major factor that led to the end of the local Bronze Age civilisation, or did the native culture simply and almost imperceptibly change under the influence of a new Europe?

Bronze Age settlements

Martin G Doody

Tassel of tablet-woven horsehair.
(see p213)

The settlement sites of the Bronze Age are rare. The recovery of metal artifacts and the distribution of burial sites show that the country was extensively occupied throughout the period. The graves, which were probably located near the settlements, show widespread occupation of the north and east of the country. In parts of Munster the burial evidence is slight, but this is possibly due to present land use, which makes the discovery of unmarked graves difficult.

Most prehistoric settlement sites do not show on the surface because the timbers used in their construction, once dacayed, leave no visible features above ground and are usually only found when topsoil is removed during industrial or agricultural activities. The thousand or more burials of the period have almost all been recorded during rescue excavations, and so there has rarely been an opportunity to look for areas of possible associated settlement.

The scarcity of the evidence makes it difficult to generalise about the nature of the settlement sites. It is likely that permanent farmsteads of one or more families, with houses, storage facilities, livestock enclosures and field systems, existed. This was so in Britain, where stockaded farmsteads were a familiar feature of the landscape.

In Ireland it has rarely been possible to get an insight

into the broader settlement pattern. Bronze Age houses seem to have been largely round or curvilinear in plan. A Later Bronze Age site at Curraghatoor, County Tipperary, provides evidence for houses of this type. Excavation has so far revealed the remains of at least twelve structures, including huts and possible fence lines. Although the full picture is not yet known, Curraghatoor is likely to have been a substantial settlement. Evidence for cereal production was found, which indicates that this was a settled agricultural community. Differing construction techniques were used on the site. A circular house consisted of upright posts set in the ground. Cross beams may have been fitted on top of these, upon which rafters of a low-pitched roof were mounted. The walls were probably made of an interwoven arrangement of wattles, which formed a framework for a plaster of mud and straw. The roofing material is likely to have been thatch. Such house design was common throughout the Bronze Age, and examples are known from sites at Lough Gur and Aughinish Island, County Limerick, Downpatrick, County Down, and Cullyhanna, County Armagh, to name but a few. Evidence for internal furnishings is quite rare, but occasionally the remains of a roasting spit around a hearth are found.

Other huts at Curraghatoor were much smaller and of different construction, and may not have been used as domestic buildings. In these examples, a shallow foundation-trench was dug. This served as a footing for the framework of the hut. The huts might be reconstructed in the form of an upturned basket. The internal floorspace in one was little more than 3m (10ft) across, which would make it rather cramped as living quarters, and it may be that it was used for storage. Other examples of this construction technique include those at an Earlier Bronze Age site at Downpatrick, County Down, a Later Bronze Age site at Rathgall, County Wicklow, and a rectangular building close to the stone circle at Bohonagh, County Cork.

It is likely that most settlements were enclosed, perhaps in the manner of Cullyhanna. An oval, stone-built house,

Reconstruction of a Curraghatoor type house.

Reconstruction drawing of the lakeside habitation of Cullyhanna, County Armagh. (see p213)

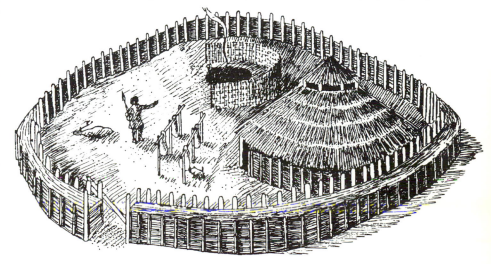

dating to approximately 1100 BC, was excavated at Carrigillihy, County Cork. This house was surrounded by a yard and enclosed by a stone wall. Two sites of similar nature and date were found at Aughinish Island. A disturbed site at Ballyveelish, County Tipperary, revealed, on excavation, a rectangular occupation area enclosed by a ditch, but no evidence of houses was found. Finds from the ditch, however, were of a domestic nature, and indicated that cattle, sheep and pigs were kept, and that cereals such as barley were cultivated.

Several lakeside sites are known from the Later Bronze Age. Lake levels have altered considerably since then and it is difficult to establish if the dwellings were built on artificially constructed islands or on old shores. At Ballinderry 2, County Offaly, a rectangular building constructed of parallel oak planks was built by the side of the lake. There was evidence that cattle, sheep, pig and goat were kept by the occupants. At Lough Eskragh, County Tyrone, four sites were recorded along the eastern lake shore. Three of them may have been constructed on the lake using a foundation of wooden piles, while a fourth appears to have been a lakeside platform.

Evidence from excavated sites supports a view that areas close to rivers were favoured settlement sites. At Sheepland, County Down, a rock-cut stair which descended from a habitation area on a slope to a stream in the valley bottom conjures up an image of a site from which expeditions were mounted to fish and fowl. Other sites of similar location include Downpatrick and Ballyrennan, County Down, where there was evidence of settlement on both sides of a stream.

Undoubtedly hunting and fowling played a part in the Bronze Age economy. An Earlier Bronze Age site at Cullyhanna Lough, County Armagh, indicates that some sites served as hunting camps for at least part of the year. The site consisted of a round house, with evidence of hearths and drying racks. It was surrounded by a stockade, perhaps to protect the carcasses of game from predators.

In the Later Bronze Age, prominent hilltop locations were being chosen as settlement sites. At Navan Fort, County Armagh, prior to the construction of the large mound, a round house of Bronze Age date was built next to a circular stockade. The house appears to have been reconstructed several times on the same spot. The site continued in use in the Iron Age, when it became an important ritual centre.

Excavation at Rathgall, County Wicklow, showed that it was a major settlement site and an industrial centre. The excavation revealed a large house on the hilltop, standing within an enclosure. The house was approximately 15m (49ft) in diameter. Extensive Bronze Age activity was found across the hill, showing that Rathgall was at least a substantial, permanently occupied Later Bronze Age industrial and settlement site.

The most numerous monuments of the period are the *fulachtaí fia* or cooking places, often referred to as burnt mounds. These sites are often found in waterlogged areas. Water was boiled in a stone or wood-lined trough by immersing hot stones in it. The used stones were raked out and cast aside to build up the characteristic kidney-shaped or oval mounds which surround the site of the trough. Because of the lack of permanent structures associated with the *fulachtaí fia* they have often been described as temporary hunting camps. Other theories suggest that they were used for bathing or as sweat houses. Despite their apparent lack of association with settlement sites, the frequency of these monuments suggests that they may have been an integral but specialised aspect of the settled community.

Smiths' workshops have been found on several settlement sites. Lough Gur, County Limerick, which was an important centre throughout the Bronze Age, is the location of at least two such sites. Excavation of a house at Site D, of stone foundation, revealed associated crucibles and moulds for the production of bronze artifacts. The house at Site F was sub-rectangular, with three sides of stone while the fourth incorporated the natural rock-face. This was also a centre of artifact production. Later Bronze Age metal smiths established themselves at Rathgall, County Wicklow and at Lough Eskragh, County Tyrone. The large number of moulds for characteristic Later Bronze Age artifacts at Rathgall is evidence that metal-working was carried out on a commercial scale.

Bronze Age settlements in Ireland display great diversity in terms of site location and materials used, reflecting the varying needs and requirements of different communities.

DISTRIBUTION OF HOARDS

*Final period of the Later
Bronze Age
(Dowris Phase)*

8th-9th Century B.C.

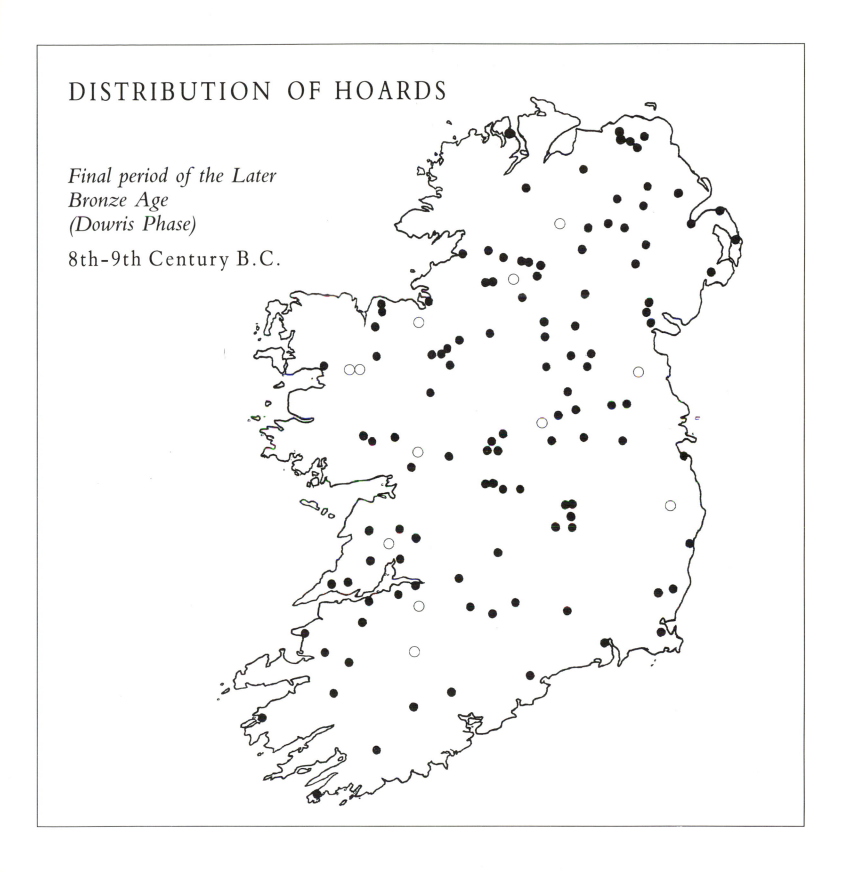

IV
The Iron Age

There is a commonly-held view that the appearance of iron-working in Ireland coincided with the arrival of groups of people speaking a Celtic language. These newcomers, it is often said, gave to the island the language, placenames, social organisation and ethos that formed its character for almost two thousand years. Their arrival — and hence the 'beginning' of the Iron Age — was put in the third century BC. There is, however, very little to support these conjectures. By definition, archaeology in the prehistoric period has little of significance to say about language, and the evidence available does nothing to support the notion of a major invasion during the period in question. If anything, there is strong evidence for continuity at some of the major sites of the final Bronze Age — Emain Macha (Navan Fort), County Armagh, for example. The question of when a Celtic language was first spoken in Ireland remains open.

What we do know is that an art style, the La Tène style, which was practised by the Celtic peoples of Europe, was established in Ireland at about this time. Hilltop enclosures, similar to but smaller than those of Celtic Europe were in use, and some of them became the focus of cycles of saga and myth which themselves illuminate the Celtic world. In the first century AD, refugees and traders from Roman Britain were established in the east of Ireland, and by the fourth century, the Irish, known as Scotti to the Romans, were raiding the island of Britain. As Ireland emerged into history, it is clear that a Celtic language — ancestor of modern Irish — was spoken throughout the island, and that powerful kingdoms had emerged, the fortunes of which form the framework of subsequent history for hundreds of years. Sagas set in the Later Iron Age were written down much later by Christian monks, but how far these were fresh literary compositions and how far they embodied more ancient traditions is debatable. Their vivid picture of a chariot-driving warrior aristocracy engaged in cattle-raiding and warfare, and their otherworldly atmosphere, are irresistible and may well broadly reflect the reality of earlier times, even if the detail is more appropriate to the ninth or tenth century AD. It used to be thought that these sagas and the ancient laws of Ireland embodied the ethos and social structure of the Later Iron Age in a fossilised form, but we are increasingly becoming aware that what has come down to us passed through the filter of the Medieval world and is heavily influenced by Christian thought. Archaeology has the potential to add to our knowledge, but the scientific excavation of Iron Age sites is only beginning and much remains to be done.

Weapons, horse gear and personal ornaments of bronze form part of the striking equipment of the Early Iron Age.

The geology and raw materials of the Iron Age

John Jackson

Iron

Iron melts at 1540°C, a temperature quite outside the technical ability of the Iron Age metallurgist — and one which was not achieved in furnaces until much later. It can however be produced in the solid state (a 'bloom') at about 1200°C. At 1150° to 1170°C the slag entrapped in the ore melts and drains away, leaving a solid iron sponge. Iron Age peoples could, and sometimes accidentally did, produce cast iron, but it is brittle and, not being malleable, is incapable of being forged; the metallurgist of those times did not possess the technology to convert it to wrought iron and thereby make it workable. When the solid porous sponge of iron, the bloom, was taken from the furnace, it was hammer-forged, thus mechanically removing most of the residual slag and at the same time shaping the iron by alternately heating and hammering into any desired shape.

Iron, unlike copper, is widespread, whether as clay-ironstone nodules in the Millstone Grit and the Coal Measures, as iron-rich beds in the very old Lower Palaeozoic rocks of the midlands, or in the Old Red Sandstone of the south, as interbasaltic lateritic iron ores of County Antrim, and as bog iron ore of the raised bogs of the midlands and the blanket bogs of the west. The Iron Age peoples could, therefore, set up their smelters close to the ore source almost anywhere in Ireland. Evidence of smelting in Ireland is abundant; furnaces and slags are known from many Early Medieval ring-forts, for example.

Most of the iron used is assumed to be bog iron ore (limonite, hydrated iron oxide), clay ironstone nodules (siderite, iron carbonate) from the Millstone Grit and the Coal Measures; and possibly haematite (iron oxide) of the Old Red Sandstone of the south, but this ore, although very rich, is also very difficult to smelt because of its denseness. The extraction of bog iron ore and of clay ironstone nodules would leave little or no trace, for the bog would quickly close over the extraction site, and clay ironstone nodules could be picked up loose from stream beds into which they would have rolled, eroded from the adjacent cliff of enclosing shales. Thus the locations of Iron Age mine sites are to a large extent conjectural. A bog iron ore site, possibly exploited in the Iron Age, was revealed during turf-cutting operations near Clonaslee, County Laois, in 1871. Here some 90,000 cubic metres (117,715 cubic feet) of surviving bog iron ore were exposed which, when dried, would represent some 5000 tonnes (4921 tons) of iron. Several extremely long wooden shovels, or dredges, were found abandoned in the deposit, presumably the implements used for extracting the ore. Some 1.8m (6ft) to 2.4m (8ft) of peat had accumulated over the abandoned shovels, suggesting that they were ancient.

Clay ironstone nodules

Clay ironstone nodules have attracted attention since Neolithic times. They are sideritic ironstone nodules and are chemically the carbonate of iron. During the Iron Age, in Medieval times and later, they formed a major part of the ore used for smelting iron. The last iron furnace in Ireland using native ore was extinguished at Creevalea in County Leitrim about the end of the last century. In the seventeenth century Boate, in his *Natural History of Ireland* (1652), describes in detail how clay ironstone nodules were used together with bog iron ore (limonite) to produce iron. It is interesting to note that

Iron shears from Garryduff, County Cork. (see p213)

Small iron anvil, seventh/eighth century AD, from a metal workshop at Garryduff, County Cork.

the mixture of clay ironstone nodules and bog iron ore was a blend of ores still used by Irish ironmasters in the seventeenth and eighteenth centuries AD. The clay ironstone had first to be roasted, thus releasing carbon dioxide, as happens with calcined limestone, and the resultant ore was an oxide of iron which could be haematite and which could be smelted with ease. Bog iron ore was raised in Derrygreenagh Bog, County Offaly, as late as the 1950s, but then only for export for gas-scrubbing (town gas purification) and for paint pigment (ochre). During the recent excavation of the great passage tomb at Knowth, County Meath, a new linear arrangement of these nodules was revealed flanking the western entrance to the tumulus, and this is assumed to have had religious, magical or ritual significance.

Clay ironstone nodules are characteristic of the Millstone Grit and the Coal Measures and so are common in those parts of Ireland in which these formations are developed: Castlecomer, County Kilkenny, Slieveardagh, County Tipperary, Arigna, County Leitrim, Kanturk coalfield, County Cork, Coalisland, County Derry, Ballycastle coalfield, County Antrim. They are often thought to be artifacts and are collected as such, but they are, in fact, natural.

The Early Iron Age

Barry Raftery

Sporadic experimentation in iron-working has a long antiquity in Europe, stretching back into the early second millennium BC; in Asia Minor, by the fourteenth century BC, a fully developed iron industry was already in existence. A comparable industry did not emerge in Europe north of the Alps, however, until the last decades of the eighth century BC. This earliest European Iron Age is named the Hallstatt Culture, after an important Austrian cemetery, and it is among the people of this culture that the ancestors of the Celts may be sought.

From 700 BC onwards, the Hallstatt culture spread rapidly across Europe. During the sixth century BC, rich and powerful ruling dynasties emerged in certain areas, their wealth derived from control of trade with the Mediterranean. By the fifth century, however, the Hallstatt world had collapsed and for a time there was social and economic decline.

Around the middle of the fifth century BC a new culture — now emphatically Celtic — appeared in Europe, one which extended a Celtic Iron Age civilisation from the Atlantic to the Black Sea. This is the La Tène culture, so called after the site of a significant votive deposit on Lake Neuchâtel in Switzerland. It is the culture which may be equated with that of the *Galli* or *Galatae*, as described so vividly by Poseidonius, Caesar and other classical commentators.

For several centuries the La Tène Celts were the dominant people in Europe, and for a time, in the fourth century BC, they shook the very foundations of Mediterranean civilisation. By the end of the millennium, however, they had succumbed to the organised military might of imperial Rome. England and Wales were soon incorporated into the Empire, but a Celtic way of life survived for many centuries in parts of Scotland and in Ireland.

Archaeology and the written sources combine to give us a vivid picture of the continental Celts, emphasising above all their warlike character, their love of personal adornment, and their complex religious beliefs and practices. Among their many achievements was the creation of the first, major, non-classical art of Europe, a curvilinear art, derived ultimately from the plant designs of the Mediterranean, but utterly changed and metamorphosed into flowing, abstract compositions, of great power and originality. It is this La Tène art style which is, perhaps, the clearest and most lasting physical manifestation of Celtic cultural unity in Europe.

The Irish Iron Age

Ireland, as far as we can tell, was scarcely touched by the spread of the Hallstatt Iron Age across Europe. A small number of bronze swords and other items of Hallstatt type are recorded, but they hardly point to the presence in the land of Hallstatt immigrants. A few objects of forged iron, which may reflect older traditions of Bronze Age manufacture, suggest that iron-working was acquired gradually and peacefully by indigenous groups, without any significant change in the population structure of the country. The period is, however, poorly

The great gold collar from Broighter, County Derry, found in a hoard with a small gold boat, a bowl and other ornaments. (see p213)

generally devoid of archaeological context. The quantity of surviving material is small and of a decidedly insular character, so that it is not clear to what extent, if at all, it is representative of a movement of Celtic peoples into the country. If, indeed, such did take place, it must have been on a relatively minor scale, with rapid subsequent absorption by indigenous cultural elements.

It should also be noted that La Tène objects are not found in all areas of the country. They are concentrated in two principal regions, in eastern Ulster on the one hand, and in a broad discontinuous band from Meath to Galway on the other. There is an almost total absence of La Tène artifacts from southern areas of the country, and we have no clear idea as to the nature of southern Irish society in the late prehistoric period.

The scattered La Tène artifacts thus represent but one strand of a complex multifaceted Irish Iron Age. From them we can, however, get some information about the character of Irish Iron Age culture, but the resultant picture is seriously gapped and incomplete. Many of the ordinary, mundane aspects of everyday life are absent from the surviving archaeological record, which is to a large extent dominated by high-quality, prestige items, doubtless the trappings of an elite stratum of society. There is thus a danger that our attempted reconstruction of Irish La Tène culture is biased in favour of an unrepresentative social group.

We can assume that the bulk of the population were mixed farmers, living in dispersed rural homesteads. Everyday life can have been little different from that portrayed in the literature of the early historic period, with cattle-rearing a dominant preoccupation of the

represented in the Irish archaeological record and the centuries which saw the demise of the Bronze Age and the emergence of incipient iron-working industries are often referred to as a Dark Age in Irish archaeology.

Equally difficult is the question of the introduction in the third century BC of La Tène cultural influences into Ireland. The great inhumation cemeteries and the massive fortified settlements — clear testimony to the spread of the La Tène Celts across the continent — are absent in Ireland, and our picture of La Tène civilisation here is based to a very large extent on scattered artifacts,

Some of a group of Iron Age objects said to have been found in a bog at Lisnacrogher, County Antrim, during the nineteenth century.

masses. There were kings and petty kings, and numerous grades of nobles, to whom the peasantry owed allegiance. The different classes of druids and seers held important positions in society, and the skilled artificers, especially the blacksmiths, were particularly regarded.

We know little in detail about the ordinary people. We can say virtually nothing of the houses in which they lived or the tools they used in the course of their everyday activities. They were, however, the first in Ireland to use rotary quern-stones for the grinding of corn, and this was an undoubted advance on the cumbersome saddle-querns of earlier times. For some inexplicable reason, however, they abandoned the use of pottery vessels and presumably relied in the main on wood for the manufacture of domestic containers.

Metal-working

It is the craft of the metal-worker which is most clearly evident in the archaeological record. Iron, doubtless because of its poor preservative qualities, does not often survive, but what there is, mainly swords and spearheads, displays considerable technical competence. Gold is also rare in Iron Age Ireland, in sharp contrast to the situation in the Later Bronze Age, but where native manufacture can be established the quality of the workmanship is outstanding.

Bronzes, however, predominate. In casting and in sheet metal-working, the Irish bronzesmiths were the equal of any in Europe. They were adept at using the lost wax process to create fine, three-dimensional castings, such as the splendidly naturalistic bird's head cup-handle from Keshcarrigan, County Leitrim. Raised decoration was also produced by hammering sheet-metal, and elaborate designs in two-dimensional form were created both by freehand engraving and by the skilled use of a compass. Open-work ornament was also popular, and the gleaming, gold-coloured bronze was often enhanced by the application of blood-red enamel, either as studs or in molten form.

The Irish La Tène craftsmen also applied the techniques of metal ornamentation to the decoration of stone and bone. A series of polished ribs from Lough Crew in County Meath are magnificent examples of Celtic virtuosity with the compass, and the famous standing stone from Turoe, County Galway, a lavishly ornate granite monolith, shows an exceptional skill in stone-working.

This expanded drawing of the ornament of the Turoe Stone shows that although the motifs have a continuous rhythm, the pattern is carefully planned to have four 'sides'.

Carved monolith, Turoe, County Galway.

La Tène artifacts

Weapons, horse-trappings, ornaments and a range of decorative bronzes, many of uncertain function, are the principal artifacts of La Tène type from Ireland. Spears and swords were probably in widespread use, the latter short-bladed for combat at close quarters. They were carried in scabbards of sheet-bronze which were often decorated along their length with engraved, curvilinear ornament. The finest examples have been found in a bog

Drawing of one of two block-wheels found in a bog at Doogarymore, County Roscommon.
(see p213)

Reconstruction drawing of a wooden trackway at Corlea Bog, County Longford.
(see p213)

deposit at Lisnacrogher, County Antrim, and in the River Bann. Shields were simple but effective rectangular implements of wood and leather. One leather shield from Clonoura, County Tipperary, still retains the scars of battle on its outer surface.

Pins and brooches were used as dress-fasteners, and a variety of bracelets of bronze or glass were worn. Glass beads were also in fashion, and it is possible that some of these were made locally. Of the colourful and elaborately woven garments which were doubtless worn in Ireland at this time, no trace remains.

Among the more spectacular items of personal decoration are two gold buffer torcs. The older, dating to about 300 BC, comes from a bog at Clonmacnoise, County Offaly, while the second, perhaps two centuries younger, was found with other items of gold, at Broighter, County Derry. Both are outstanding pieces and, while the former may well be an import from the European mainland, there can be little doubt that the lavish ornament on the County Derry collar was produced in a native workshop.

Among the finest examples of Irish La Tène bronze-working are the trumpets, four complete or fragmentary examples of which survive. These are elegantly curving tubes of hammered sheet-bronze, measuring up to 1.42m (4½ft) from tip to tip. Exceptional skill was involved in their manufacture, not only in the formation of the

tubes, but also in the way in which they were sealed by means of a narrow strip of bronze riveted on the inside of the tubes, along the junction of their folded edges. On the finest specimen, from Ardbrin, County Down, no fewer than 1094 rivets were used, and to this day the tube is airtight and can be blown.

Transport

Numerous bridle-bits from the country, almost all of bronze, testify to the importance of the horse in La Tène Ireland. The fact that most are isolated finds suggests that horse-riding may have been widespread, but they are occasionally found in matching pairs, thereby implying use in paired draught. This could, perhaps, be taken as evidence for the use of the chariot in Iron Age Ireland, but positive proof of this remains elusive.

The importance of wheeled transport is, however, clearly demonstrated by the great wooden roadway recently uncovered in a bog at Corlea in County Longford. This was a massive construction, extending for almost 2km (1¼ miles), which was made of huge oak planks 3.5m to 4m (11½ft to 13ft) in length. These were laid down edge to edge on supporting pairs of longitudinal runners, to provide a broad, level routeway across the ancient surface of the bog.

The Corlea roadway has been precisely dated by dendrochronology to 148 BC. It is one of the largest of its type in western Europe, and there can be little doubt that it was built for the passage of wheeled vehicles. Its imposing dimensions, which required the felling and splitting of hundreds of oak trees, underlines the highly organised nature of contemporary society. We do not know, however, if the Corlea roadway was of purely local significance or whether it was part of a wider network of communications.

Earthworks and royal sites

The Corlea road is but one of a series of great monumental works which were being constructed in the second and early first centuries BC. Recent evidence indicates that it was at this time that spectacular linear earthworks, such as the Black Pig's Dyke (in Counties Armagh, Monaghan and Donegal) were being built. These earthworks are lines of banks and ditches which stretch discontinuously for kilometres across northern parts of the country. Like the building of the Corlea road, their construction clearly required the efforts of a whole community. What their purpose was, however, remains uncertain. They might have served as routeway protections, as attempts to hinder large-scale cattle rustling or, in combination with natural obstacles, to delimit tribal areas.

One of the most substantial of these earthworks, that known as the Dorsey in south Armagh, incorporated, in one phase of its construction, timbers which had been felled in 94 BC. The date is significant, for it coincides exactly with that of the felling of timbers used in the building of the large wooden structure, often interpreted as a temple, which once stood on the summit of Navan Fort, County Armagh. The site has been reliably identified as Emain Macha, the capital of the ancient Celtic province of Ulster.

The latter half of the second century BC appears thus to have been a critical period in Irish Iron Age cultural developments. It was a period which saw the creation of large-scale works of ostentation, signalling, perhaps, the emergence of new kingdoms or the expansion and consolidation of older dynasties. It may well be that there is a link between this phase of activity and the spread of La Tène influences across the country.

Navan Fort is not the only identified royal site of the Celtic Iron Age in Ireland. There is also Tara in County Meath, Dún Ailinne, the former capital of ancient Leinster, in County Kildare, and west of the Shannon, in Roscommon, is Cruachain, the focus of Celtic Connacht. Today these sites are marked by earthworks of varying types. Cruachain consists of a series of mounds, enclosures and linear earthworks spread over a wide expanse of rolling countryside. The character of the earthwork complex is well in keeping with the deep-seated, archaic traditions which emphasise that this was a major focus of cult and ceremony. Navan Fort, Tara and Dún Ailinne, however, are all hilltop enclosures, each distinguished by the possession of a deep ditch upslope from the surrounding rampart. This defensively illogical feature strengthens further the probability that these were centres of assembly and of ceremonial activities rather than formal habitations.

Hill-forts

Such royal sites were obviously exceptional in contemporary Ireland. Despite their hilltop situations and imposing dimensions, they cannot be viewed as defensive hill-forts. Hill-forts of more conventional type do occur, and some of these may have been defended settlements during the Iron Age. Their roots lie, however, in the Later Bronze Age, so that close dating of unexcavated examples is not possible. Similarly, we know little of the dating of coastal promontory forts in Ireland, but some of these too could belong to the Iron Age.

The distribution of hill-forts in Ireland is, however, significant, for the great majority of examples occur in those very southern areas of the country which are devoid of La Tène remains. The hill-forts are therefore likely to have been built by a people distinct from those responsible for the production of La Tène metalwork. The southern Irish hill-forts might thus be the centres of the non-La Tène Iron Age cultural groupings, which are otherwise so elusive in the archaeological record.

Some of our hill-forts, even in their modern ruinous state, are impressive field monuments. Mooghaun in Clare, for example, covers 12.5 hectares (31 acres) and is defended by three massive concentric walls of limestone rubble. Two great ramparts defend the ten-hectare hill-fort of Rathcoran, high up on the summit of Baltinglass Hill in County Wicklow. Inland promontory forts in Antrim and Kerry are also imposing defensive sites. Two in Kerry, in particular, stand out. Both are more than 600m (1968ft) above sea-level and in each case, vertically sided spurs of land are defended by stone walls which cut across the promontory from cliff edge to cliff edge. One of these sites, Benagh, on Mount Brandon, lies on a towering mountain ridge no less than 762m (2500ft) above sea-level, and is thus the highest fortification in the country.

The purpose of the great fort of Dún Aengus on Inishmore in the Aran Islands, prodigiously defended by three walls, a band of limestone spikes and the vertical sea cliffs, remains obscure. Never precisely dated, it is likely to belong to the Iron Age, but the bare limestone will doubtless forever retain the secrets of its function and origin.

Burial customs

Our knowledge concerning the disposal of the dead in Iron Age Ireland is little better than our information about the habitations of the living. There were no great cairns or burial mounds such as those erected in Neolithic or Earlier Bronze Age times. Iron Age burials in Ireland were simple and unpretentious. In earlier phases of the period the dead were burned and placed in simple pits which were sometimes inserted into pre-existing tumuli, or sometimes placed in low, freshly built mounds with surrounding ditch and external bank, known as ringbarrows. Later, perhaps through Roman influence, inhumation gradually replaced cremation as the normal burial rite. Grave goods were never spectacular. When such were present, they usually consisted of a few items of adornment, such as brooches, beads or bracelets.

Roman contacts in the early centuries AD influenced, but did not radically alter, the character of Irish Iron Age society. Unconquered by Rome and untouched by the folk-movements which followed the collapse of the Empire, Ireland preserved an archaic Iron Age culture for centuries after it had ceased to exist elsewhere. And it was the skills and traditions of pagan Iron Age craftsmanship which laid the foundations for the golden age of Irish art in the seventh and eighth centuries after Christ.

The earliest history of Ireland

Richard Warner

The Irish Early Iron Age is strictly prehistoric in that, as far as we know, there is no written record of Irish history or society before the sixth century AD. On the other hand the contemporary Mediterranean (classical) cultures of Greece and Rome were literate, and their enquiring writers wrote not just of their own civilisations but also of the distant world of the 'barbarians'. Ireland was on the edge of history, recorded through the often ill-informed and unsympathetic eyes of others.

Archaeological evidence demonstrates contact between the Mediterranean and Ireland during our Early Iron Age. For instance, the Barbary ape that died in the settlement at Navan, County Armagh, travelled on a boat from north Africa during the second century BC. Slightly later another boat brought a gold bracelet from Egypt that was buried in the Broighter hoard in County Derry. The occupants of such boats, be they merchants

or adventurers, took back to their home ports stories of Ireland. The Roman historian Tacitus wrote of Ireland at the end of the first century AD:

'the interior parts are little known, but through the commercial intercourse and the merchants there is better knowledge of the harbours and approaches'.

Tacitus' contemporary, the Greek historian Strabo, thought that Ireland was where 'the limits of the known world should be placed', adding that it was the extreme cold that made the people so savage. The first century BC Syrian historian Poseidonius seems to have been the first reporter, if not the originator, of the belief that 'the Britons who inhabit the region called Ireland...eat men'. Refinements of this were repeated (along with various accusations of a sexual nature) over the next five centuries. In the fourth century St Jerome wrote, shocked, that he had actually seen the 'Scots...feeding on human flesh'. We need neither accept nor deny these apparent calumnies, for the sobre Tacitus assures us, perhaps ambiguously, that 'the character and civilisation of the people do not differ much from Britain', and Strabo, after repeating the scandals, adds 'we relate these things, perhaps, without having trustworthy authority'.

While Early Iron Age Ireland was certainly on the edge of history geographically, it was also on the edge of history chronologically. With its end the great flowering of Irish written learning of the Early Medieval period began. It has been claimed that the heroic tales recorded at this later time have their roots in, and describe, the preceding pagan Iron Age society. These stories are clearly non-Christian and therefore, one may argue, pre-Christian. Several of the political groups who were dominant after the fifth century AD are not included in the tales. Finally, many of the heroic themes can be paralleled in remarkable detail in the classical descriptions of the continental Celts. For example, the Roman author Athenaeus wrote of the Celts:

'when the hindquarters of the roast boar were served up (at a banquet) the bravest took the thigh-bone, and if anyone challenged this the two arose and fought a duel to the death.'

We may compare this with the description of a banquet in the Irish tale 'The story of the pig of Mac Datho' :

'How shall the pig be divided, Conchobar?' asked Ailill. 'How would you divide indeed' said Bricriu mac Carbaid from his couch, 'where the men of Ireland are, but by contest of arms, and let each of you therefore give a blow on the other's nose'.

Then follows a series of verbal duals between the contenders for the 'champion's portion', with the threat of violence always present. Many other striking similarities between the classical and Irish sources may be found, leading to a widespread belief that the Irish hero tales give us a 'window on the Iron Age'. Although most modern scholarship has little sympathy for this view, there is evidence of the survival of some ancient information, as we shall see.

Diodorus of Sicily, in the late first century BC, wrote of a fertile northern island 'beyond the land of the Celts...and inhabited by the Hyperboreans' in which were 'a magnificent sacred precinct of Apollo and a notable temple which is adorned with many votive offerings and is spherical in shape.'

We cannot prove that Diodorus was referring to Ireland, but we do know that Ireland possessed at least one sacred place whose remains match this description — the ritual monument at Navan, County Armagh. This was visited already in the second century BC, as we have seen, by a Greek or Phoenician traveller. This traveller, with his gift of an ape, would have seen the 6 hectare (15 acre) circular enclosure, with its massive internally ditched earthen bank ('magnificent sacred precinct'?). Inside this he would have seen, among other things, a circular wooden building with a larger annexe, one of a series of almost identical buildings on the same spot.

Our traveller may well have witnessed the ritual immersion into the adjacent Loughnashade of human and animal sacrifices, and of the four great bronze trumpets that were discovered with the bones two centuries ago. But he would not have seen, for it was not yet built, the great circular wooden structure for which Navan is now famous. In exactly 94 BC, one of the most precisely dated buildings in barbarian Europe was erected, with 275 oak posts in concentric rings and a huge central post. The building was roofed and measured 40m (131ft) in diameter. If this was the 'spherical temple' of Diodorus, dedicated to Appollo, it was visited soon after its construction by his informant, for we know that it was quickly enclosed in a great mound and burned. In fact we do not need to suppose this, for similar structures

Aerial view of Navan Fort, the ancient Emain Macha, County Armagh. (see p213)

Decorated gold strip from a cemetery of the first century AD, on Lambay Island, County Dublin.

The skull of a Barbary ape from Navan Fort. (see p213)

certainly existed in Ireland.

Two great sites parallel Navan closely — Tara, County Meath, and Knockaulin, County Kildare. Each contains a great circular internally ditched enclosure, that at Knockaulin covering an enormous 16 hectares (39½ acres). Excavations here showed that a circular wooden structure exactly the same size as that at Navan existed within the enclosure. It is of further interest that all three sites find a place within the heroic literature as centres of power in pre-Christian times — Emhain Macha (Navan), Temhair (Tara) and Dún Ailinne (Knockaulin).

We have already seen the range of Irish Early Iron Age material, both objects and sites, and it was stressed that these changed only slightly during the two centuries before Christ and the three or four after. Yet the social and material changes in adjacent parts of Europe were profound. The Gaulish (Celtic) peoples were conquered by the ambitious, expanding Romans during the first century BC. Britain followed in the first century AD and by the end of that century was firmly in the Roman Empire. Much of this success can be attributed to General Gnaeus Julius Agricola, father-in-law (and biographical subject) of the author Tacitus.

Agricola, Tacitus tells us, had with him in southern Scotland in about AD 82:

'an Irish petty king, expelled in a local struggle, and, under the guise of friendship, retained him to be made use of should the opportunity offer.'

That opportunity was the invasion and conquest of Ireland which Agricola believed could be undertaken 'with one legion and a moderate number of auxiliaries'. He saw the advantage to the Empire 'if Roman arms were to be seen on every side and liberty vanished off the map'. His plan was surprisingly reminiscent of Strongbow's use of Diarmait MacMurrough a thousand years later. There is no documentary evidence that Agricola actually invaded Ireland, and it is indeed certain that Ireland remained always outside the Roman Empire (as did Scotland for most of the life of the Empire in the west). However, there are hints that Irish campaigns were undertaken, witness for instance the claim by Roman satyrist Juvenal in the early second century AD that 'we have extended our arms beyond the shores of Ireland'.

In the mid-second century AD an Alexandrian geographer, Claudius Ptolemaius, published an extraordinarily accurate atlas of the then known world. Only the tables (in Greek) of places and peoples, with their coordinates of latitude and longitude, survive, but with these we are able to reconstruct his maps. The shape of Ireland is easily recognisable, and many tribes, river mouths, headlands and 'cities' are marked. A small number of these are identifiable today, such as the rivers Buvinda (Boyne) and Senos (Shannon). Some survived without question into Early Medieval literature, such as the people called the Iverni (Érainn), and the Auteini (Uaithne). For some others we can make educated guesses, for instance that the 'city' Raiba should be on Lough Ree, and that the River Dabrona is probably a scribal error for Sabrona, the River Lee. But most of the names are quite lost to us, and will probably defy all attempts at interpretation. Most interesting is the fact that the tribes of the south-east, for instance Manapii and Brigantes, have names that are paralleled in Britain and Gaul.

The word 'Roman' should be understood to include Romano-British throughout this chapter. The influence of Rome spread to parts of Europe outside the Empire, through traders, adventurers, refugees, soldiers and marines. Material originating in the Roman dominated world has been found in Ireland, though less than one would have expected.

The native material, particularly the fine metalwork, is uneven in its geographical distribution. In some areas of the country, such as the north-east and the midlands, it is common. In others, such as the south and the north-west it is virtually absent. Significantly some of the gaps, such as the north-western one, are filled by numerous corn-grinding querns of the 'beehive' type, which are virtually absent in the 'metalwork' areas. It is an inescapable conclusion that two populations, differing at least in their economies (rich ranchers and poor ploughmen), are represented here.

The southern native-metalwork desert is partly filled in the south-east by material of Roman origin. This is, of course, the area most adjacent to the province of Britannia and intercourse would be expected here. But the almost complete absence of native material here, and the nature and contexts of the intrusive material, require a more complex explanation than trade alone — gold coins in the southern outskirts of Dublin; Roman brooches at the ceremonial site of Knockaulin; the tag from a military uniform and evidence of iron-working in the abandoned hill-fort at Rathgall, County Wicklow; inhumation graves with coins at Bray; a cremation in a glass urn at the crossing of the Nore at Stonyford, County Kilkenny; a brooch on the rock of Cashel (the name itself a borrowing of Roman *Castellum*), and the stamp for marking the eye-ointment required by campaigning soldiers taken from a field of bones at Golden, County Tipperary.

Most of these south-eastern finds belong to the first

and second centuries AD, and this concentration coincides almost exactly with the distribution of the intrusive tribal names mentioned by Ptolemaius. Can we really escape the conclusion that at least the aristocracy of the south-east were Romanised Britons and Gauls, and is there even reason to suspect a military campaign in the area?

The island of Lambay lies just north-west of Dublin Bay, and we might be forgiven for calling this the northern limit of Roman influence. In the late first century AD, warriors with northern British grave-goods were buried here. It is tempting to see these as the graves of refugees from the Roman advance or from the consequences of one of the numerous British anti-Roman or factional wars. There is growing evidence that these people, who also settled on the adjacent Irish mainland and on the Isle of Man, were actually an influential element in Irish culture.

We now believe that a major trading post was located on the coast north of Dublin. We might imagine that the trade was in bronze and gold in return for cattle and slaves. A large bronze ingot from Damastown, County Dublin, may well have been one of the commodities imported, and we know that the numerous gold ornaments of the Irish Early Iron Age were made from imported gold. Roman gold ornaments found at the passage tomb of Newgrange in the Boyne valley, along with silver and bronze coins and brooches, attest to an attempt to appease a god at this major shrine. That the appeasers included Latin speakers is demonstrated by the fragment of a far older Irish gold torc, bearing Roman script, plundered from some Bronze Age ritual deposit. Gold was clearly important to the depositors. As to the importance of Irish cattle, we need only quote the first century AD Pomponius Mela:

'...so luxuriant is the herbage, in quality both nutritious and savoury, that the cattle eat their fill in a small part of the day...'

These traders were probably responsible for the bronze ladle found at Bohermeen, County Meath. Less easy to assess is who deposited a perfectly good Roman-style boat in Lough Lene, County Westmeath. According to the third-century Solinus 'The natives sail in boats of wickerwork covered with the hides of oxen', and in such boats they crossed the Irish sea. The multi-oared and masted boat model in the Broighter hoard, however,

indicates that rather more splendid craft were available to the Irish. The natives' purposes in crossing hither and thither were loot and settlement, and they became known to the Romans as the 'Scotti', a name they later adopted. The products of their looting, silver plate and ingots, have beeen found in Counties Derry and Limerick. But it was as settlers, in the north and west of Britain, that they had the most long-lasting effect.

These settlers were numerous and aristocratic. A tradition survived as late as the ninth century that:

'at that time [the second or third century AD] great was the power of the Gaels over the Britons... And the Gael used to dwell to the east of the sea no less than in Ireland.'

It is quite clear that these expatriate Irish returned in a very Romanised form, with British companions and especially British women. This may explain the strong influx of late Roman influences in the third and fourth centuries, including many showing a fusion with Irish traditions that must have occurred in Britain. Borrowed Latin words; Roman dress (the tunic and cloak); the Latin-grammar-based script known as ogham, and the idea of patronymic memorials; pins and penannular brooches developed in Britain; the rite of inhumation

Map of Ireland reconstructed from coordinates given by the second-century geographer, Claudius Ptolemaius (Ptolemy).

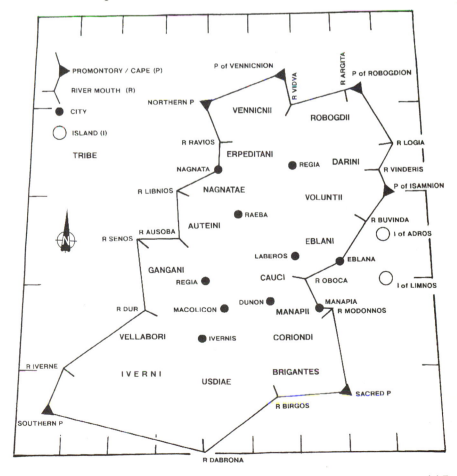

Bronze disc, just under 10.5cm (4in) in diameter, dredged from the River Bann at Loughan Island, County Derry. First/second century AD.

While iron became the principal material for weapons and tools of the Iron Age, bronze remained important for decorative work and for accessories. (see p213)

burial; a sword type based on the Roman short-sword, and even a new religion — Christianity. All these and other artifacts and ideas arrived during the last couple of centuries of the Roman occupation of Britain. They had spread here by the end of the fourth century, that is before the traditional event that brought in 'early Christian' Ireland — the coming of Patrick.

It seems likely from the distribution of these influxes (for instance, a concentration of ornaments in the Boyne valley) that the agents of change entered on the east coast — the area already heavily Romanised a century or two earlier. The material and influences can then be followed, developing westwards into the midlands and south-westwards into Munster. The introduction of Christian missions into the same areas, from Gaul and from Britain, was simply part of the process.

So profound and widespread are these intrusions that we are obliged to ask whether the picture we have reconstructed from archaeology and the classical authors is in any way reflected in the mythology preserved in Irish Early Medieval literature. Surprisingly, and despite my earlier unencouraging description of the status of this literature, we find that it is.

We have an indication of one influx of great importance in the legends of Tuathal Techtmar, and his conquest of Ireland, which the Medieval historians would date to around AD 100. Two places with which he is associated have produced early Roman material of just that date — Clogher, County Tyrone, and the Six-Mile Water valley, County Antrim. Another possible literary echo relates to our postulated Dublin Bay trader-settlers. They may be represented by the person of Forgall Monach, eponymous ancestor of the Monaig who were descendants of the Menapii, located in the south-east by Ptolemaius. He is described as a trader in gold and his settlement, judging by placename evidence, was at Loughshinny, County Dublin.

For the later influxes we find that the archaeological evidence is paralleled in extraordinary detail by the legends and early history of the Uí Néill and the Eoganachta. These Goidelic peoples, quite unknown in any sources before the fifth century, appear as the major power groups as soon as history begins. Their own origin legends stress their British connections (including the British origin of the population name 'Goidel') and several sites associated with these people at an early date have produced Roman material.

A further example illustrates this later development particularly well. At Clogher, County Tyrone, in the sixth century AD, a factory producing penannular brooches — a Romano-British invention of the fourth century — was using as its scrap bronze a fourth-century Romano-British bracelet, a family heirloom? The tribe, or at least the dynasty, who founded this place were closely allied to the Uí Néill and had an origin legend in which their ancestors came from Britain in the fourth century.

Two conclusions must be drawn. Although Ireland was not formally part of the Roman Empire it was greatly influenced by that powerful neighbour. The Irish Early Iron Age La Tène-based culture continued alongside, rather than completely fusing with, the Roman. Until, that is, the Goidelic intruders, with Roman arms, ornaments and manners returned with their own external fusion of those cultures. A fusion that had happened while the Irish were settlers within the Empire. This was the true origin of the Early Medieval period — an inexorable process of Romanisation over several centuries, both within and without.

V
The Early Medieval period

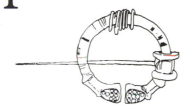

When the Romans invaded Britain they established a sophisticated colony with cities, towns, roads and organised commerce. They set up a regular system of government and a permanent garrison to keep order. Ireland, however, remained a backwater with a rural, tribal society. Historical references to Ireland by classical authors are few and do little more than record some places and tribal names which we can recognise from later sources. There is evidence of trade with the Empire: Roman coins are fairly common in Ireland and Roman trinkets were found at the great passage tomb of Newgrange. By the end of the third century, the Irish had joined with the Picts from what is now Scotland to raid the Roman colony of Britain. The raiding intensified in the fourth century as the Irish and Picts were joined by Germanic raiders from the east. The Empire was also suffering internal dissensions and its ability to defend Britain was in decline. The legions withdrew in AD 406, and in 410 the Emperor, in response to a plea for help from Britain, told the province to look to its own defence. The Irish began to establish colonies in north and south Wales inside the Roman province. They also took control of what is now Argyll in western Scotland, in a region that emerged as the powerful Medieval kingdom of Dál Ríada.

It is likely that the circumstances of raiding Britain and the control of trade favoured the emergence of a new political leadership in Ireland. Later evidence shows that in the fifth century an ancient political order was breaking up and new and aggressive dynasties were expanding at the expense of older tribal kingdoms. In the midlands and the north-west, the Uí Néill came to dominate. They were a federation of dynasties descended from their semi-legendary ancestor, Niall of the Nine Hostages. Their premier king took his title from the ancient site of Tara, to which their foes of Leinster maintained an ancient claim. The expansion of the Uí Néill in Ulster initiated the retreat of the Ulaid from their ancient centre of Emain Macha (Navan Fort in County Armagh) until their power was effectively confined to the east of the River Bann. Munster came to be dominated by the Eoghanachta, another group of dynasties claiming descent from a common ancestor. Their premier king took his title from Cashel, on which there must have stood an imposing fort — the placename derives from the Latin word castellum, meaning a fort.

The society in which these events were unfolding was townless, coinless and, with the exception of the awkward ogham script used for short inscriptions, illiterate. But there is clear evidence that Ireland was already receiving Christian converts. In AD 431 Pope Celestine sent Palladius as bishop to the Irish believing in Christ. Palladius was followed by other missionaries, of whom the best remembered was Patrick. He had first arrived in Ireland as the booty of pirates who had carried him off from his well-to-do home in Britain to be sold into slavery.

Carved pillar representing two back-to-back figures, from Boa Island, County Fermanagh. (see p213)

Decorative sieve from Moylarg Crannog, County Antrim. Eighth century AD.
(see p213)

The crannog of Cro-Inis, Lough Ennel, County Westmeath.
(see p213)

Crannogs

Eamonn P Kelly

Crannogs are habitations constructed on artificial islands in lakes or, less commonly, in rivers and in the sea. The name is derived from the Irish word *crann*, meaning a tree. Originally the term may have been applied to the timber palisades which surrounded such sites, the timber buildings within them or the timber foundations on which they were erected; nowadays it refers to the entire structure. The same name is used in Scotland, where similar sites occur. In Ireland crannogs are concentrated mainly in the north midlands and south Ulster, along the drainage systems of the rivers Shannon and Erne and in the isolated lakes of the drumlin zone. Their distribution is largely determined by the availability of suitable locations in which to build them.

Crannogs may have developed partly from a habit of living on small natural islands, either as a means of exploiting the fish and wild fowl of lakes or for providing security in times of danger. It is often difficult to distinguish small natural islands from true crannogs on the basis of a superficial examination. The identification and systematic study of crannogs began in the nineteenth century when drainage operations exposed the structure and contents of many examples. While the majority of finds recovered then were of Medieval date, objects of every period from the Mesolithic through to modern times were found. It was therefore assumed that crannogs were being constructed throughout this period. Research this century has clarified the picture. In prehistoric times, platforms were erected at lake edges, or in shallow water or marshy ground. In the main, these appear to have been associated with hunting and fishing or with industrial pursuits, rather than with long-term habitation. True crannogs, that is, artificial or substantially artificial islands, containing a dwelling and surrounded by one or more palisades, were being constructed in the Early Medieval period and these may be regarded as the wetlands' equivalent of contemporary ring-forts. Dendrochronology suggests that there was a major phase of building during the sixth and seventh centuries AD.

These points are well illustrated by the crannog in **Moynagh Lough, County Meath**. The excavator noted that the earliest activity on the site dated to the Mesolithic period. At that remote time, two low knolls, which were above the lake surface, were added to by throwing down stones, pebbles, twigs and brushwood. This resulted in the formation of a small platform on which flint and chert implements were made, an activity which probably related to the exploitation of the lake's food resources. On two separate occasions during the Earlier and Later Bronze Age, further layers of stones were laid down to consolidate the site, and the implements uncovered during excavation were consistent with its use as a temporary hunting camp. A dendrochronology date for a palisade timber from the site indicates that around the year AD 748, or slightly later, a true crannog was constructed. This was a large artificial island, up to 50m (164ft) long, which was built by laying down layers of stone, peat, gravel and brushwood. Enclosed by a palisade, which was later added to, it contained a large round house 11m (36ft) wide. Evidence of metal-working was found as well as domestic refuse, animal bones and an assortment of tools, weapons and personal ornaments. The site does not appear to have been inhabited beyond the ninth century AD, but finds of pot-sherds dating to the thirteenth or fourteenth century, and a ninteenth-century pipe, show that it was visited occasionally.

There is also evidence from a number of other sites for the construction, in pre-Medieval times, of platforms and other structures along lake margins and in shallow water, the exact functions of which are uncertain. The bulk of those excavated appears to date to the Later Bronze Age. One example was found underlying a crannog of Early Medieval date at **Ballinderry, County Offaly** (Ballinderry No. 2). Although a layer of brushwood had been laid down over part of the site, it was not an artificial island during the Bronze Age. It contained the remains of what appears to have been a large rectangular house and ten small wicker structures of unknown function.

At **Lough Eskragh, County Tyrone**, four areas of Later Bronze Age piling were investigated in 1959 and 1973. Two of them — sites B and C — appear to have been natural rises in the lake bed which were consolidated by piling or by laying down layers of stones. The precise nature of site C was not determined, but it was clear that site B was a workshop associated with metal-working. Site D, a linear group of piles covering an area of 15m x 5m (49ft x 16½ft), was of uncertain function, but it may have supported a platform standing clear of the water. A larger, linear area of piles at Site A, measuring 38m x 7m (124½ft x 33ft), might be similarly interpreted. This was located to one side of a small platform 10.5m (34½ft) in diameter and constructed of brushwood, horizontal timbers and piles. Later Bronze Age habitational debris, including pottery and implements, was recovered from its surface.

At **Rathtinaun, Lough Gara, County Sligo**, a structure was found which had been occupied and abandoned on three occasions. The site consisted of a platform of brushwood and peat laid down in shallow water and surrounded by wooden piles. During the earliest phase it appears to have been a metal-working site. Clay moulds for casting bronze and characteristic Later Bronze Age objects were found associated with this phase. The second phase appears to represent a

Two plough-coulters, one from Ballinderry Crannog No. 1, County Westmeath, the other from Bellair, County Westmeath. (see p213)

Bone pin with carved animal head from Lagore Crannog, County Meath.

Pottery vessel from Ballydoolough Crannog, County Fermanagh.

transitional period, as bronze and iron implements of both Later Bronze Age and Early Iron Age types were found together. The final phase produced a range of objects similar to those found on sites of the Early Medieval period, but which in this case the excavator believed to date to the Early Iron Age.

A group of important Iron Age objects was found during the last century at Lisnacrogher, County Antrim, apparently close to large quantities of stakes, timber and wickerwork. The function of the structure is unknown and the association between it and the objects is unproven.

All the crannogs excavated to date have been situated in locations which had been drained earlier. Underwater

Reconstruction drawing of a crannog in its setting. (see p213)

The crannog of Ballinderry, County Offaly, in the course of excavation. (see p213)

There is evidence for the refortification of Cro-Inis and a crannog in Lough Kinale, County Longford, during the first quarter of the twelfth century, which may relate to warfare between the king of Meath and Turlough O'Connor, king of Connacht. This, however, appears to have been the final period of importance for the midland crannogs, as the invasion of the area by the Normans later that century resulted in a change in settlement patterns and the abandonment of most of the sites. Cro-Inis, perhaps because of its former royal associations, appears to have been exceptional in this respect.

In south Ulster the use of crannogs continued. Dendrochronology has been of particular help in identifying such sites. Dates in the late fifteenth/early sixteenth century have been obtained for crannog timbers from **Mill Lough**, **Lough Eyes**, **Corban Lough** and **Carrick Lough**, all in County Fermanagh. It has been suggested that refortification of these crannogs may be related to warring between the O'Rourkes of Breffni and the Maguires of Fermanagh. At the end of the sixteenth century, crannogs were used by Hugh O'Neill as supply depots and as strongholds in the war against the English. At one stage, during 1600, his headquarters was the crannog of **Lough Lurcan, County Armagh**.

A crannog at **Deredis Upper, Lough Inchin, County Cavan,** proved to have been erected on an earlier, though similar, structure. The finds from the earlier crannog were not particularly diagnostic, but are probably of the Early Medieval period. A prick-spur found on the later site suggests that it was constructed in the fourteenth or fifteenth century, but pottery finds hint that it may have been occupied up to the early eighteenth century.

Social and economic implications

Results obtained from the excavation of crannogs convey the impression that they were inhabited by prosperous families whose economies were based on agriculture and who were also, to some extent, engaged in or controlling manufacturing and trade. Excavations at three major sites document this in detail: **Lagore Crannog, County Meath, Ballinderry No.1, County Westmeath,** and the nearby **Ballinderry No. 2,** just over the county boundary in County Offaly. On all three sites a number of phases of Early Medieval occupation were discovered, and all were enclosed by palisades. Lagore produced evidence of three phases of use between the seventh and

survey is beginning to identify rocky mounds erected on foundations either of timber frames or large radial timbers. These are enclosed near the waterline by palisades of oak planks. Erected in the deeper water around them are horseshoe-shaped arrangements of birch posts, which are open and facing the lakeshore. They may have been defensive, or perhaps supported docking platforms. In the west of Ireland, where timber was scarce, crannogs built entirely of stone are common.

Stone buildings of unknown date can be found in a number of midland crannogs. The remains of a tower-house of the Later Medieval period, which was the residence of the chief of the O'Coffeys, can be seen on **Cro-Inis in Lough Ennel**. This was probably the building in which Domhnall O'Coffey and his sons were murdered in 1446. The area around it was roughly paved and three paths or slipways led down to the water's edge. A similar tower-house was erected on a crannog at **Island McHugh, County Tyrone**, probably during the fourteenth century. Cro-Inis was a royal site and it was here that Maelsechnaill II died in AD 1022, the last of the Southern Uí Néill to acheive a dominant kingship. The O'Coffey family, who resided there in the fifteenth century, were formerly poets to the kings of Meath.

A feature of many souterrains are changes of level, which oblige the person entering to crawl, while those further in can stand comfortably. (see p213)

The stone cashel of Leacanabuaile, County Kerry. The drystone wall enclosed a round and a rectangular house.

early eleventh centuries AD; Ballinderry No.1 had two main periods of occupation during the tenth and eleventh centuries AD, while the Early Medieval activity seems to have occurred between the sixth and eighth centuries at Ballinderry No. 2. At both Lagore and Ballinderry No. 2, evidence of fine metal-working and other industrial activities was uncovered, together with a range of tools, weapons and personal ornaments of a high quality. Among the more important objects was a bronze penannular brooch, decorated with enamel and millefiori, from Ballinderry No. 2, and a hinged collar, with an attached chain for a prisoner, from Lagore. The finds included objects of organic material, such as leather and wood, which do not normally survive on archaeological sites; a remarkable wooden gaming board was discovered at Ballinderry No. 1. Lagore crannog is identified as a royal site, associated with the Kings of Southern Brega, which accounts for the high-quality material found there.

A crannog unearthed during reclamation at **Newtownlow, County Westmeath**, was partially excavated, and revealed a habitation area 20m (66½ft) in width, erected on a platform of timber and brushwood, and enclosed by a palisade of oak planks. Two hearths and a D-shaped structure built of oak stakes, measuring 14m x 5m (46ft x 16½ft), were uncovered. A number of artifacts were found, including tools, personal ornaments and coins, as well as up to 40,000 animal bones, representing both domestic and wild species. A central date of about AD 1000 was proposed for the occupation of the site.

Pottery known as E Ware, imported probably from south-western France during the seventh and eighth centuries AD, and fragments of continental glass vessels of the same period found at Ballinderry No. 2 and Lagore, suggest the wide-ranging nature of trade at that time. The later levels at Lagore, Ballinderry No. 2 and the site of Newtownlow all produced finds which were

heavily influenced by Scandinavian styles, and were probably influenced by contact with Dublin. A Viking sword from Ballinderry No. 1 and a hoard of Anglo-Saxon coins from Newtownlow may suggest contacts further afield. The quality of the finds recovered from such sites, as well as the amount of labour involved in their construction, would appear to indicate that they were mainly aristocratic dwellings.

Although the construction of true crannogs appears to have been restricted mainly to the period between the sixth and the seventeenth centuries AD, crannog-like structures were being built in Ireland throughout most of its habitational history. Investigation of these provides important insights into the lives of the communities who constructed and used them. Excellent preservation of organic remains allows for close dating of the sites, a comprehensive interpretation of their function and a detailed knowledge of the lives of their inhabitants.

The hill-fort of Tara, County Meath. (see p214)

Dunbeg promontory fort, County Kerry. (see p214)

Ancient cooking site of the type called fulacht fia. (see p214)

Hand-made pottery known as 'Souterrain Ware'. (see p214)

Staigue Fort in County Kerry. (see p214)

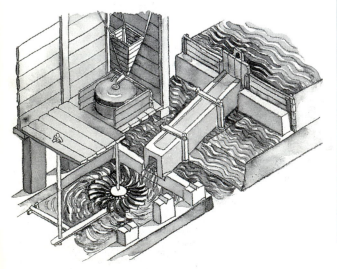

St Patrick to the Vikings

Michael Ryan

The introduction of Christianity began a process of accelerated change in Ireland. But progress was slow at first and we have no reason to believe that the Irish were converted overnight. There is some evidence of tension between Christians and non-Christians well into the sixth century, but the process of change is largely unknown to us. Apart from two texts attributed to St Patrick, we have no solid documentation before the seventh century. We must base our understanding of the period from about AD 450 to about AD 650 largely on later records of what we believe may be authentic early traditions.

Monasticism was known in St Patrick's time, as it is mentioned in his writings, but it was in the sixth century that most of the famous monastic houses were founded: Bangor, Clonfert, Clonard, Clonmacnoise, Durrow, Derry and, perhaps most famous of all, Iona, established in AD 563 by St Columba or Colmcille on an island off the coast of Scotland. The very idea of monasticism was oriental, but the immediate origins of Irish monasteries lay in the west: there is no evidence of the influence of the Coptic church in Ireland despite much writing to this effect. Monasticism proved very popular in Ireland and by the eighth century many of the early foundations had become prosperous enterprises, playing an important role in secular affairs.

The collapse of the Roman Empire in the west in the fifth century marked a great historical divide between the ancient and the Medieval world. New kingdoms emerged: the Franks in what had been Gaul, the Visigoths in northern Spain, the Langobards (Lombards) in northern Italy, and so on. These kingdoms gradually developed away from the organisation of barbarian warbands towards a more institutional form of monarchy, often based on the remnants of Roman government. Gradually the new forms of administration spread outwards from the Germanic kingdoms to the tribes which lay outside the former Empire, reaching Anglo-Saxon England and Scandinavia. We cannot be certain of this, but echoes of the newer pattern of kingship may

also be detected in Ireland. It has long been thought that Irish society in the Early Medieval period preserved a very primitive form of law and a tribal kingship with priestly undertones. Indeed the air of mystery which pervades the ancient sagas encourages this view. These are, however, late literary compositions which reflect the prejudices or political realities of the writer's own day. If we look at the *record* of early Ireland, we see kings behaving as real powerbrokers and we see laws which have adopted many of the concepts of the Roman world. This may be reflected in the appearance of the true crannog, a form of defended settlement, the building of which called for a huge outlay of effort. Substantial ring-forts are sometimes associated with royal dynasties. Like some crannogs, they show evidence of foreign trade in luxury items and of high quality metal-working on site. It has been suggested that the construction of enclosed sites for defence, for residence and for the concentration of trade and craftworking, goes hand in hand with the development of kingship.

Society was tribal and there were many petty kingdoms. Some of these may have had a recognisable territory, others may have been more diffuse. Some kingdoms were thought to be ethnically distinct, but attempts to confirm this have been unsuccessful. Many of these groups were subordinate kingdoms in Early Medieval times and their alleged ethnic status may have been propaganda, reflecting their current position rather than a genuine ancient tradition. A similar problem arises when we come to consider the question of the ancient divisions of Ireland — the fifths or provinces. These were

(opposite, bottom left)
A reconstruction of a horizontal mill.
(see p214)

A hoard of Roman hacksilver (cut-up pieces) and 1506 coins, found at Ballinrees, near Coleraine, County Derry, deposited about AD 420.
(see p214)

The Early Medieval period has left the greatest legacy of surviving monuments—the mainly earthen ring-fort and its equivalent, the stone cashel. It has been estimated that at one time there were 30 000 of them, but counting those which are now only visible as crop-marks, there may have been many more. It seems that the majority were built in the period between AD 500 and AD 1000. When excavated, most reveal traces of the dwellings of an agricultural society and of craft-working. Research is beginning to reveal a hierarchy of ring-forts and to suggest that some may have formed clusters of dependent dwellings, others may have been associated with monasteries, while still others were sited with defence in mind or were intended to impress. The Irish words associated with them, rath, lios (of ring-forts), and caher and caiseal (of stone forts), are enshrined in placenames throughout Ireland.

adjusted constantly as power changed hands and they cannot be taken to reflect a truly ancient dispensation.

The aggressive Uí Néill dynasties harried their foes, the Ulaid, constantly, and the exaction of tribute from Leinster is a constant theme of the history of the period. In the sixth and seventh centuries they allied with the kingdom of Dál Ríada, located in both Antrim and Argyll, to put pressure on their enemies, and this alliance, facilitated by the monastery of Iona, an Uí Néill church, brought them into contact with the Angles of Northumbria and the Picts and Britons of what is now Scotland.

By the early eighth century the two great dynasties, the Uí Néill of the midlands and the Eoghanachta of Munster, had come into direct conflict in the midlands, and a rivalry which was to last for over four centuries was initiated. It has been suggested that this clash began because the great belt of bog in the midlands, which had once separated them, had become much less a barrier by the eighth century; many monasteries had been founded in these wilderness areas, making them more accessible. This situation spawned a new theory, that ancient Ireland had been divided into two halves, northern and southern, Conn's and Mogh's. The historians of the day were entirely in the service of the politicians.

What is certain is that when Ireland emerged fully into the light of history, the ancestor of modern Irish was the uniform language of the population, settlement was entirely rural, society was tribally organised, and the economy comprised a mixture of stock-raising and agriculture. Communities were dependent on craft-working for the majority of their domestic needs, but there was some long-distance trade for luxury goods such as wine. Monasteries were an important part of the economic and political system, and they were probably responsible for many new ideas which were being adopted in all walks of life. Kings, in theory, acted as war leaders and gave judgement. But their powers and functions were increasing, while the law was preserved by a hereditary class of jurists, the brehons. An academic class inherited some of the mystique of the pagan druids, but their role seems to have been that of the poet, genealogist and preserver of historical lore of all kinds. Society was aristocratic, and lawyers had developed elaborate status schemes into which the clergy were ingeniously slotted.

Early Medieval houses

Chris Lynn

Documentary sources and excavations have taught us much about the way of life in the Early Medieval period. The sites of about two hundred and fifty houses have been examined in excavations over the last fifty years, and it is now possible to identify a few well-defined house-types. The majority of houses have been found inside ring-forts and related types of settlement, including stone forts, ecclesiastical enclosures and crannogs. The information, therefore, only becomes really plentiful from the seventh century onwards, and practically nothing is known about Irish houses and settlements of the first five hundred years AD.

At the beginning of the Early Medieval period the normal house was circular in outline, a diameter of about 6 or 7m (16½ to 23ft) was most common, and it was made of woven hazel rods, except for the door frame. Houses of this type have been exposed in excavation in the form of arcs of post-holes, as well as secondary features normally associated with this method of construction, such as well-slots, drainage gullies, arcs of boulders and circular burnt areas.

Sometimes houses were combined in pairs to give a figure-of-eight plan. One of these was the *cuile*, a backhouse or kitchen, which was usually the smaller element of the pair, and it could be entered only from the main house. There is no evidence that these structures were further subdivided into separate rooms, but bedding and sitting areas against the walls (of the larger structure in the case of a pair) were defined by rows of small post-holes. The woven superstructures indicated by the post-holes would have retained bedding material such as straw to a height of about 30cm (12in) above floor level and, carried higher at the ends, helped to screen the bed from the rest of the room.

The doors of the houses nearly always faced east or south, and this preferred orientation seems to have influenced the layout and siting of the ring-forts in which the houses are often found. The eastern or southern aspect would have sheltered the doorway from most of the bad weather. Drainage and run-off were arranged to avoid seepage into the house, so the ground frequently slopes away from the doorway to the east. Since the easiest way to get rid of water was to let it drain through the ring-fort entrance and since the occupants appear to have preferred to see the ring-fort entrance from the house, the entrances to the ring-forts themselves should tend to face southwards most commonly and, where there is a choice, to lie on land sloping gently in the same direction. This hypothesis is supported by recent surveys of ring-forts in areas of clayey subsoils.

Drystone circular houses do not appear to have been built from the very beginning of the period. They are common, however, in the stone forts and ecclesiastical enclosures in south-west Ireland, but in several excavated sites the stone houses were preceded by a phase of Early Medieval wooden or wicker houses. The best excavated example of such a site is the ecclesiastical enclosure at Reask, County Kerry, where the drystone-walled houses reflect features of wicker houses known from elsewhere. The round, stone-walled houses may have been developed from wicker houses after the first Early Medieval settlements were established in this relatively windy and stony environment.

In the course of the Early Medieval period the form of the normal dwelling house changed from round to rectangular, so that by the twelfth century, round houses were probably unknown. Why, how and when exactly this important change came about are still matters for speculation, but cultural pressures for change must have been strong, as Ireland seems to have been the last area in Europe to use round houses. The round form may have been perceived as socially inappropriate, despite its structural and aerodynamic efficiency. Rectangular houses were more commonly built using stone in their walls than their round predecessors, but we have little evidence for the materials and construction of the upper walls and roofs of most excavated examples.

Although information derived from excavation about the layout of Early Medieval settlements is relatively plentiful, it is also difficult to interpret because it represents only a fraction of activities and structures at the sites. Apart from a few excavations on crannogs, such as Lagore, County Meath, and Ballinderry No. 2, County Offaly, all of the excavated sites have been on dry land, where remains of wooden structures and organic layers have decomposed, leaving little or no evidence for their existence and scale. Only at sites where most of the buildings were of stone can we expect traces

Entrance to house, Deer Park Farms. Mid-seventh century AD.

Model of house, showing cavity walling.

General view of Deer Park Farms excavation.

of a significant proportion of the buildings to survive. On the other hand, at most sites with predominantly wooden buildings, only a few of the structures which might have existed may have left traces detectable in excavation. This makes it difficult, if not impossible, to study the architecture and social arrangement of the sites, and to relate them to the documentary sources.

The Deer Park Farms settlement

At one rural site, through a freak combination of factors, evidence of unique quality for houses and the activities of their occupants has been preserved. A group of five contemporary wicker houses, dating from around AD 700, was found at one level in the rescue excavation of a ring-fort at Deer Park Farms, Glenarm, County Antrim. The site had so much material dumped in it during its occupation that it had built up into a large, flat-topped mound. The wickerwork of the lower walls of the houses, their floors, bedding material and external midden layers were so perfectly preserved that it looked, at one level in the mound, as if the site had been abandoned only a few months previously. This was

Full-size reconstruction of Deer Park Farms house.

because the occupants of the primary midden-filled ring-fort decided to heighten it, an operation which was carried out in stages, possibly over a number of years. One at a time the houses were emptied of possessions, stripped of re-usable materials, such as door-frames, and abandoned. Their lower walls were either encased in the build-up material (clean, gravelly soil obtained by deepening the ditch around the ring-fort), or were pushed over and pinned down under it. The water-table rose in step with the rising level of the mound, with the result that large areas of the walls of these houses were still preserved when exposed in rescue excavations in 1986-7. The gradual process of rebuilding only one house at a time minimised disruption of the settlement and spread demand for the necessarily large quantities of hazel rods over a longer period.

At this level, the ring-fort was entered through an unusual inturned entrance-way or antechamber, at the west end of which was the east-facing door of the main house. This had a stone-kerbed hearth at the centre, with a bed on either side against the wall. The bed was a platform of rough branches and twigs, covered with finer vegetable litter, much like a large bird's nest. One of the beds had woven wattle screens across its ends, fixed into holes drilled into oak beams on the ground. Joined onto the back of this main house, which was about 7m (23ft) in diameter, was a smaller building some 5m (16½ft) across. This was presumably the 'backhouse' mentioned in Early Medieval written sources — and it could be entered only through the main dwelling. It also had a central hearth, but there was no sign of a bedding or

sitting area.

On either side of the main house there were two other wicker houses, each approached by a stone path leading from the end of the entrance-way. On the north there was another double building, the western element of which had stood on its own for a number of years before a larger structure was added to its front, converting the original dwelling into a backhouse. On the south of the enclosure there was a single structure, 4.2m (13½ft) in diameter, with a central hearth. The position of a bedding area against the north wall was indicated by lines of small post-holes. Indeed, in all cases where it could be identified, the principal bedding area was against the north wall.

As a result of the almost miraculous preservation of wickerwork at this dryland site, it was possible to work out, for the first time, exactly how the lower walls of an ancient circular house were constructed. Previously such houses were known, at best, from circles of stake-holes, and it is important to note that at Deer Park Farms the houses were built using more efficient techniques than could have been suggested from post-hole evidence alone.

All of the houses with preserved upright stakes were double-walled, and ranged in internal diameter from about 4m to 7m (13½ to 23ft). They were made almost entirely of hazel, although other species, such as alder and oak, were occasionally used as uprights. The outer walls of the houses ran about 40cm (15½in) outside the inner, and were of relatively light construction, designed mainly to hold a 'cavity wall insulation' of grassy packing between the walls. The upright stakes were driven into the ground about 20cm (8in) apart, but they were less than a 1m (3ft) high. When the horizontal weaving reached this height, the ends of new short uprights were driven down into the wall beside the original stakes. The wall weaving was then carried up for 70 or 80cm (27½ to 31½in) to their tops, and another set of uprights was added and so on. The horizontal rods, each of which was about 2m (6½ft) long, were woven in spiralling sets using a basket-weaving technique. This was far superior to the simple in-and-out weave, using a single rod at a time, generally presumed to have been used in ancient wattle structures. The uprights were solidly encased in twisted hazel rods on both sides, and the exposed surfaces of the walls were smooth, as the weaving technique ensured that the sharp cut ends of the rods were hidden in the cavity. The maximum height of pushed-over walling which survived was more than 2.5m (8ft), and no change in the weaving technique, which would indicate well-defined eaves or the start of the roof, was noted. Either the vertical walls of these early eighth-century houses were taller than we have assumed, or else there was no sharp distinction between the walls and the roof. The weaving technique would have allowed the inner wall to be gradually curved in to become a conical or dome-shaped roof structure. This in turn could have been covered by a reed or heather thatch.

The most remarkable single discovery was a complete door frame, the lintel of which had been crushed down between the jambs. There were holes in the threshold and lintel for a door to pivot, and the lintel had been fixed to the uprights using pegged mortice-and-tenon joints. The jambs were carefully squared oak branches, each with a deep slot in one side to receive the wattles of the wall. The timbers were incompletely trimmed below ground-level, and preservation of bark on both examples enabled tree-ring dating to show that both were felled in AD 648. The door aperture was only about 1m (3ft) high, and it was clear from a row of holes in the top of the lintel that woven work, either vertical wall or sloping roof, continued above the lintel to complete a rigid cylinder or cone. This was necessary for stability of the integrated structure which was interrupted by the door.

The huts uncovered at Deer Park Farms were simple and unsophisticated structures, but they were better constructed than could have been suggested without seeing the preserved walling. About 8km (5 miles) of hazel rods, each 2m (6½ft) long, would be required to build one of these houses. The recognition here in Glenarm of the double-walling and the basket-weaving technique recalls the fact that no firm evidence for the use of daub (mud plaster, often assumed to be used with wickerwork) has come from an Early Medieval site in Ireland. Evidence for the lighter outer wall, which to an extent seems to have substituted for daub, could easily disappear from the record. Double-walling, therefore, may have been more widespread than the surviving evidence suggests. The largest Early Medieval wicker house known, from the Moynagh Lough crannog, County Meath, was also double-walled. We can assume that the simple but very effective wattle-weaving

Small copper alloy brooch and glass beads from Deer Park Farms, County Antrim.

technique, recognised for the first time at Deer Park Farms, was used more widely. Indeed, we may be seeing in these circular huts the end of a prehistoric tradition of house building which was once more widespread in Ireland and perhaps also in parts of Britain.

The outlines of thirty houses were found in the upper levels of the mound at Deer Park Farms. As in the lower waterlogged levels, three or four houses, sometimes joined together, appear to have stood at the same time; these were replaced singly, not as a group, except on one occasion when all of the structures appear to have burned down together. In these undisturbed but dried-out upper levels, nothing organic was preserved. House walls, which were presumably similar to those actually seen in deeper levels, were represented by a variety of features such as post-hole arcs, burnt layers, arcs of boulders, and by curved upstanding ridges of rubbery clay. The ridges of clay were plastered against the bases of the inner walls on the outside before the outer wall was built, and were probably intended to form damp-proof courses. These features occured in combination and in isolation, but the sites of doorways were usually indicated by pairs of post-holes on the east side, and there were central stone-kerbed hearths.

The layout of the site, the design of the house in it, and the types of artifact used, conform in detail with the material attributes of the lower grades of landowners listed in the seventh-century law tract called the *Crith Gabhlach*. The *óg-aire* (young or lower noble), for example, should have had a house measuring 5½m (19ft) and a 'backhouse' measuring 4m (13ft). The house was to be interwoven to the 'lintel', with an oak board between every bed. He had a share in a kiln, a barn and a mill. Significantly, the most remarkable wooden finds from the midden layer in the ring-fort were the discarded hub and a paddle from a horizontal watermill.

Plan of excavation at Deer Park Farms.

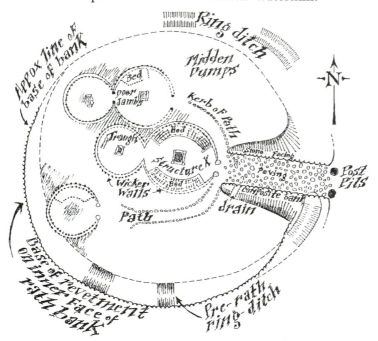

Other details of the buildings described in the law-tract can be understood properly for the first time as a result of the evidence of the Deer Park Farms excavation. For example, the requirement that the *óg aire's* house should be 'smooth and free of projections' is explained by the technique of hiding the sharp, cut ends of the wattle rods of both inner and outer walls in the cavity. The statement that his house should have 'two doors, a door in one and a hurdle in the other', has been interpreted as indicating the existence of two doorways to the exterior. In fact, the doorway with the hurdle would have communicated with the backhouse and there was only one door to the outside. It is now clear that the writer of *Crith Gabhlach*, regarded the figure-of-eight unit of conjoined round structures as the standard form of dwelling for a family of any status.

Artifacts and other finds

Most of the metal finds from the excavation were fragments of familiar objects such as knives, nails and pins, but a good many were of unusual interest. These included three-pronged flesh-forks, a bill-hook, a pruning-hook, shears, a wooden axe, a plough-sock, a drill-bit and candleholders. Coming from excellent contexts, these helped to fill out the picture of subsistence crafts and everyday life on the site. One good example of active craft work was the discovery of staples (used for fastening hoops on wooden vessels) tucked in the wicker of an interior wall. Several unfinished staves and tub components were found on the floor. Small items of personal adornment were often lost in bedding areas; a bronze brooch was found in one bed and another contained a bronze pin and seven glass beads of various types. More than eighty glass beads were recovered as separate finds in all levels of the mound.

The waterlogged levels of the ring-fort in Deer Park Farms preserved a range of organic finds not normally seen on dryland sites. These include parts of wooden vessels, discarded off-cuts of leather and identifiable parts of shoes, and scraps of textiles. A carved oak trough, abandoned or forgotten on the floor of one of the filled-in houses, contained a neatly carved wooden shoe-last. These were most common in upper levels of the mound. Environmental evidence was perfectly preserved in the deeper waterlogged layers. Dumped vegetable and other organic material did not rot, and a mass of compressed plant remains, woody fragments, animal bones, insects, food refuse and discarded bedding was preserved. Studies of samples from this material have scarcely begun, but unusual remains already noted include fins of fish, animal hair, woad pods and puff-balls. Against expectations, there was no obvious evidence of agricultural activity, such as threshing, winnowing or grain storage, inside the ring-fort enclosure, although laboratory examination may alter this impression. It seems likely, however, that farm animals were not normally kept in the ring-fort.

The results of this excavation will revolutionise studies of Early Medieval settlement, as no other site has preserved evidence of this type in such a clear-cut form. There must have been variation in many aspects of settlement sites of the seventh and eighth centuries, and no one excavated example can be regarded as typical of them all. But the evidence from Deer Park Farms already allows us to reinterpret earlier excavations and understand better some hitherto mysterious features. Similarly, some dramatic parallels can be drawn between the houses, the equipment and the layout of the site at Deer Park Farms and the details of status specified in ancient Irish laws dating from around the same period. These aspects of the archaeology of Early Medieval Ireland form an intriguing case-study, because we have a house form, settlement type and culture which are in some respects prehistoric compared with the the rest of Western Europe, and have encouraged some scholars to use the term 'Later Iron Age' for the period in question. These prehistoric traits can be understood to an extent through written sources, the legacy of the new learning, and can be described in some detail, and interpreted, from excavations on sites such as this mound in Glenarm, County Antrim.

Early Irish Christianity

Dáibhí Ó Cróinín

In AD 431 Palladius was sent by Pope Celestine I 'to the Irish believing in Christ'. This bare statement, from a contemporary continental chronicle, answers some of our most basic questions about the first century of Christianity in Ireland, but it also leaves a great number unanswered. Who were these 'Irish believing in Christ'? How many were there, and where were they to be found? How did they acquire their faith, and why had they no bishop of their own? These and a myriad of other questions have been asked by historians over the years, but most of our problems remain unsolved. The most famous conundrum of all, the 'Problem of Saint Patrick', has generated a literature all of its own.

There are, however, a number of things that can be presumed about the earliest Irish Christianity, even if the evidence is insufficient to allow us to state them as definite facts. The first Christian missionaries came, probably, from Britain, when it was still or had only recently ceased to be a Roman province, with its own church. The man we know as Saint Patrick undoubtedly came from this background, and the influence of British missionaries on the fledgling Irish Christian communities was to be a lasting one. Patrick had said that 'many thousands of others' were taken into captivity along with himself, so even if we were to confine ourselves to that statement, the number of British Christians in Ireland must have been substantial. The history of Christianity in other countries, however, teaches us that the process of conversion is always slow and unspectacular. The heroic conversion of the Irish people, almost single-handed, by Patrick is the stuff of legend, not of history. The usual process is one of steady infiltration, sometimes by returning soldiers who might have acquired the faith during their service in the Roman legions, sometimes through the contacts that always exist between exiles and their homeland. There were Irish colonies in Britain during the fourth and fifth centuries (to which the bilingual Irish—Latin ogham stones still bear silent witness), and there are Irish names among the clergy of the late Roman church in Britain. By these means (and others, yet to be discovered) Christianity must have gained a foothold in Ireland.

Our earliest datable reference to Christianity in Ireland, however, is that statement about Palladius. The source, a chronicle written by Prosper, an Aquitanian cleric resident in Rome, is unimpeachable. Furthermore, the same chronicle has another reference to Palladius under the year AD 429, where he is mentioned in relation to a mission by Bishop Germanus of Auxerre to Britain. This link with Germanus, the most influential prelate of the Gallican church in his day, and the connection with Auxerre, the most important Gallican church of the early fifth century, provide evidence of another strand in the missionary thread, besides the British one. This second, continental strain in the earliest Irish Christianity must also have left its mark.

Organisation and script

Two things stand out at first glance as distinguishing features of the early Irish church: its organisation and its script. Neither feature has yet been adequately explained. The first Irish churches were presumably

The colophon or entry ascribing authorship in the copy of Adomnán's Life of Columba, written before AD 713 by the Iona bishop Dorbbéne.
(see p214)

Pillarstone with ogham inscription, Coolmagort, Dunloe, County Kerry.

The Book of Ballymote.
(see p214)

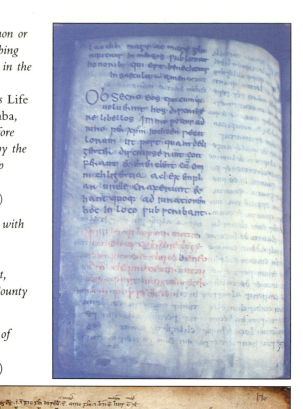

established along British and continental lines, with small communities ruled over by their own bishop, in a diocesan pattern much like that which still obtains in modern Christian churches. During the sixth century, if not earlier, a gradual shift seems to have taken place towards a system of monastic 'federations' (*paruchiae*), which linked far flung foundations to a mother-house. By the seventh century, when our information first becomes plentiful, this monastic system had gained the upper hand, and was eventually to replace the diocesan system almost entirely. The result was a church organisation markedly different from that of its neighbours in that the Irish churches gave primacy of authority to the abbot, not to the bishop, and the territorial diocese gave way to a mixture of tribal bishoprics and monastic federations. Bishops still retained their dignity of orders, of course, but the administration of the church was now in the hands of abbots. This feature, and some others of a liturgical or ritual nature, were to cause problems when the Irish took to the missions.

Christianity is a religion of the book, and the Irish, like every other Christian community, had to learn to read and write the Scripture which formed the basis of their beliefs. The earliest continental and British missionaries would have brought with them books written in the standard scripts of the fourth and fifth centuries, 'uncial' for important books, and 'cursive' or everyday script for general use. The curious feature about our earliest Irish manuscripts, however, is that none is written in these continental hands. The most famous Irish manuscripts of all, the Books of Durrow and Kells, are written in 'half-uncial', a development of the older script, as the term implies, but not the pure uncial hand. Irish manuscripts, from the time when we first encounter them (*c*. AD 600), are invariably written in the 'Irish hand'. In its majuscule (half-uncial) and minuscule (cursive) forms, the Irish hand attained a perfection and beauty which still dazzle the eye. It was also one of our most successful exports ever, for the Irish hand was taken by Irish missionaries to England and Scotland in the sixth and early seventh centuries, where it became the 'national' script of those countries.

Pilgrims of the early Irish church

By the end of the sixth century the Irish church had taken on most of the features that historians describe as 'Celtic'.

Whatever the influences of the Gallican and British churches may have been in the formative period, the Irish church now had the air of an autonomous and self-confident institution. Indeed, **Columbanus**, our first missionary to the continent, wrote a letter *c*. AD 600 to no less a person than Pope Gregory the Great, in which he severely chastised the pope for views which did not accord with those of the Irish!

When Columbanus arrived in Burgundy he encountered a church which differed in some significant respects from his own. Although official Christianity had come to Ireland from Gaul, changes in the Irish churches meant that Columbanus and his followers experienced difficulties, particularly with the local bishops. The result was a series of episcopal synods at which the Irish and their ways were loudly condemned. They were criticised for their peculiar methods of calculating the date of Easter, for their liturgical and ritual practices, and for their resistance to local episcopal control. Columbanus — a fiery spirit — wisely stayed away from these occasions, but he has left us an account of his troubles in a series of five letters.

Columbanus eventually moved on from Burgandy to Switzerland, where one of his followers, **St Gall**, founded the monastery of that name, and from there to Italy, where he ended his days at Bobbio, perhaps the most famous of all Irish foundations on the continent. More than any other Irish missionary to Europe, Columbanus left a genuinely lasting impression. A forceful and charismatic personality, his effect on the church in Gaul was little short of revolutionary. The amalgam of Irish and Frankish customs, termed 'Iro-Frankish' monasticism by historians, combined the distinctive traits of Irish practices and those more appropriate to local conditions. The result was a striking growth in the number of Frankish monastic houses founded either by Columbanus's disciples or by native Franks who had come under their influence. The monks of Columbanus's Burgundian foundations, at Luxeuil, Fontaine, and Annagray, eventually abandoned the Irish Easter, but other Irish practices proved more lasting.

Closer to home, off the west coast of Scotland, the monastery of Iona was founded by **Colum Cille (Columba)** in AD 563. This, the first Irish missionary effort abroad of which we have any detailed knowledge, was to have an impact in Britain equal to if not greater than that which Columbanus and his followers had on

The manuscript known as the Cathach of St Columba, a psalter or book of the Psalms. (see p214)

the continent. Iona became the centre of a far-flung community that included monasteries at Durrow, County Offaly, and Derry, County Derry, and other lesser houses scattered throughout Ireland, England, and Scotland. It is probably nothing more than coincidence that the most famous illuminated gospel-books of our period, the Book of Durrow and the Book of Kells, were produced for Columban centres, but it is a fact that Colum Cille and his successors nurtured a 'love of learning and desire for God' that produced some of the most notable achievements of early Irish ecclesiastical literature.

Almost everything we know about Colum Cille derives from a biography of the saint written by the ninth abbot of Iona, Adomnán (†AD 704). This *Vita Columbae* is preserved in a manuscript at Schaffhausen (Switzerland), which is one of the oldest (and finest) Irish manuscripts to survive, dating to within a few years of the author's lifetime. It was written on Iona, in the distinctive Irish script, by a bishop of the community, and bears witness to the scribal skills of the monks, skills which were inherited from the saint's own day. The Royal Irish Academy houses a manuscript of the Psalms, called the Cathach (Battler), which tradition ascribes to the hand of Colum Cille himself. Modern scholarship, usually sceptical of such claims, has found no reason to doubt that the handwriting could indeed be as old as the late sixth century.

By the mid-seventh century, Iona had risen to a position of power and prestige, rivalled only by Armagh. Besides the contacts which it maintained with daughter-houses in Ireland and Scotland, the monastery also attracted visitors from the continent. One such traveller was Arculf, a Frankish bishop, who journeyed to Iona and recounted to Adomnán his experiences in the Holy Land, where he had been for well over a year. The bishop's account was carefully recorded by Iona scribes on wax tablets, and an edited version was then published by Adomnán, with the title *De locis sanctis* (Concerning the Holy Places). It is one of the earliest descriptions we have of the Holy Land, and makes fascinating reading. A later Iona writer, Dicuil, author of a cosmographical treatise, also preserved details of the Near East, this time from an Irish traveller. He records the experiences of another Iona monk, **Fidelis**, who, amongst other things, had sailed down the Nile to the point where, it was believed, the Jews had crossed the Red Sea. He was apparently disappointed when the local boatmen ignored his request to stop at the spot so that he could examine the ruts left by Pharoah's chariots! He did, however, observe the pyramids — which he called Joseph's barns, and which he took the trouble to measure exactly — and many more interesting historical sites.

Iona is principally remembered, however, for its role in the evangelisation of Northumbria. The monks of Iona who, from AD 635 onwards, carried Christianity to the English, did so from their base on the island of Lindisfarne (now Holy Island), and the result was that the north of England, in the words of one eminent English scholar, became a 'cultural province' of Ireland. The script which was hitherto distinctive of Irish penmanship now became the adoptive hand of the English as well, and the general cultural exchange that took place between the two peoples (and the Picts of Scotland) led to a century or more of artistic creativity in metalwork, manuscript illumination, and stone carving, which produced some of the finest treasures of western civilisation.

Some Iona monks sailed northwards and were halted only by the barrier of Arctic pack-ice; others established hermitages on the smaller North Sea islands and perhaps also in Iceland. The dramatic adventures which they experienced are occasionally recorded in Adomnán's *Vita Columbae*, and such tales may well have provided the inspiration for the *Navigatio Brendani* (The Voyage of Brendan), which became an international 'best seller' in its time. The Irish became such a frequent sight on the continent that one ninth-century German scholar described pilgrimage as being second nature to them. They brought their books with them, and that is why some of the oldest and most valuable Irish manuscripts are preserved in continental libraries. Würzburg in Bavaria, St Gallen in Switzerland, Milan in Italy, and countless other places where the Irish stayed or visited, still house the 'books written in the Irish script' (*libri Scottice scripti*), referred to in a ninth-century library catalogue of St Gallen.

Some of these Irish pilgrims have left us a glimpse of their world in their letters that have survived. One group of scholars, travelling through Wales on their way to the continent, had a curious experience: they were confronted at the Welsh king's palace with a text written in secret script, and were challenged to decipher it. Nothing daunted, they consulted their books and announced triumphantly that they had broken the code. Their account of the episode is still preserved in a manuscript in Bamberg, Germany, and the evidence of other Irish books on the continent enables us to follow their travels through France and Germany. The Irishman who penned the poem about his cat, Pangur, into another manuscript, now in Austria, must have travelled a similar route, for Pangur is a Welsh name.

Not all of them were scholars of the first rank, of course, though many of them certainly were. So widespread was the belief that every passing Irishman must be a scholar that one poor pilgrim, returning from Rome via Liège in Belgium, had to apologise to the local bishop for the fact that he was not a grammarian, nor learned in Latin. Another, travelling in the opposite direction, finds the journey too arduous for one of his years and is hindered by the soreness of his feet, while a third writes with the startled indignation of the professional bookman who finds that he cannot survive on scholarship alone: 'I cannot live in such squalor', he protests, 'with nothing to eat or drink except dry bread and awful beer'. Despite everything that has been said and written to the contrary, the Irish were not great beer-drinkers; they preferred wine. **Sedulius of Liège** sang its praises and the great **John Scottus** is supposed to have drunk the emperor Charles the Bald under the table, though not before he had delivered himself of a withering *bon mot*: 'What is there between a sot and a Scot?', asked the emperor, to which John replied, 'The table'.

Sedulius and John Scottus were only the best-known of a remarkable stream of Irishmen who took themselves to the continent in the ninth century. Irish scholars had made a name for themselves in the Carolingian age; men like Clemens at the palace school in Aachen, or Bishop Dungal in Pavia. But in John Scottus, Ireland produced not only the most formidable intellect of his time, but a man who was to shape the destiny of western thought for centuries to follow. He alone of his contemporaries had mastered Greek philosophy, and when he applied it to theology the effect was electric. First summoned to the limelight in order to defend the church against the heresies of Gottschalk, John found that his ideas were too much for the conservative bishops, and he himself was promptly condemned. He departed as mysteriously as he arrived: nothing is known either of his place of origin or of where he went.

The Irish abroad were not always appreciated, however, and sometimes with reason. Even in the eighth century English and continental councils were urging caution in the case of these wandering clerics, bishops without a diocese. The Englishman Boniface, Apostle of Germany, had no great love for his Irish neighbours and complained bitterly about several of them, including one **Clemens** who showed more clemency than tact in his theory that Christ's descent into hell had freed all the souls there, righteous and unrighteous. Boniface also complained to Rome about **Virgil of Salzburg**, whom he accused of believing that 'there are another world and other men under the earth, and another sun and moon' — the so-called theory of the antipodes.

But after John the Scot the Irish star was on the wane, and none of his calibre was to be seen again in Europe. Pilgrims there were still, some of them kings, though not all of them were enamoured of the journey: 'To go to Rome — great labour, little profit' wrote one of them, and the Céli Dé ascetics back home made a virtue of his scepticism. Others were attracted by the imperial court, like **Israel Scottus**, who became tutor and later confidant of archbishop Bruno of Cologne, brother of the emperor

Otto the Great († AD 973). **Marianus Scottus**, a century later, compiled a history of the world while walled up in Fulda and later in Mainz, where he died in AD 1082 at the age of fifty-four. Marianus's *Chronicle* was very highly regarded, and spawned a whole genre of literature, in Europe and England. But by then the schools of Chartres and Paris were beginning to make their mark, and the kind of traditional learning which had characterised Irish scholars was giving way to the more speculative and exciting theories of the scholastic philosophers. Some of these new doctrines did make their way back to Ireland: the gospel commentary written into the so-called Gospels of Máelbrigte at Armagh in AD 1138 seems to derive from the lectures of **Peter the Lombard**, who was teaching in Paris 1139—40; and in an Oxford manuscript written at Glendalough in the twelfth century is preserved a copy of **Bernard of Chartres**'s *Glosses on Plato*. The Annals of Ulster record the death in AD 1174 of **Flann Ua Gormáin**, head of the schools at Armagh for twenty years before his death and who, before that again, had been 'a year and twenty learning among the Franks and the Saxons'. There were doubtless other Irish 'travelling students' whose names have not come down to us, and they must have been instrumental in channelling the new learning of the continental schools back to Ireland.

The overall impression given by the surviving Irish manuscripts of the later Middle Ages, however, is of a conservative, antiquarian learning. Although Irishmen still travelled through Europe in those centuries, the steady advance of the Normans at home seems to have driven native scholarship slowly westwards. The gradual disintegration of traditional Irish society, and the consequent decline of patronage for the men of learning, led inevitably to the point where few native scholars could even read the old Latin books. By the time of the Franciscan Four Masters and John Colgan in the seventeenth century, and the Jesuits Brendan O'Connor, Stephen White, and Patrick Fleming, historical research was almost solely reliant on the manuscripts unearthed by these Irish workers on the continent. And it was a strange irony of fate that the 'rediscovery' of Old Irish was to be the work chiefly of German and Swiss scholars, led by the great and pioneering Johann Casper Zeuss (1806—56). The wheel of history had come full circle, and the debt which Europe owed to Irish 'saints and scholars' was repaid in full.

(top left)
Beehive hut on the monastery of Skellig Michael, County Kerry.
(see p214)

(top right)
Drystone church at Gallarus, County Kerry.
(see p214)

(above)
Monastic site of Templeoran, County Westmeath.

Early Irish monasteries

Michael Ryan

By the close of the eighth century, the Irish monastery had developed a more or less standardised form. The principal characteristic was the enclosing bank or *vallum*, which was often a double enclosure, the inner one enclosing the church and cemetery and the outer one defining an area where domestic and craft activities were carried on. Normally they were circular in plan, but there were variants dictated by local conditions. The buildings inside were predominantly of wood. A misleading impression is created by the well-preserved, stone-built hermitages of the west, such as Skellig Michael. Wooden churches seem to have remained the norm until the twelfth century. The first reference to a stone church in Ireland is to an oratory at Armagh in AD 789. Stone churches were an uncommon occurrence and the surviving remains probably date to the eleventh and twelfth centuries.

Early Irish stone churches were simple in plan, rectangular in shape, and sometimes with features borrowed from wooden constructions. A distinctive native development was the stone roof, which in its ultimate form was propped up by a barrel-vault. Doorways had simple lintels and sometimes a carved architrave enriched their appearance. Doubtless, many stone churches were roofed by shingling or thatch. The boat-shaped, corbelled oratories, like that of Gallarus, County Kerry, are likely to date from the twelfth century. There is little surviving physical evidence of wooden churches, but texts speak of them as richly decorated, and we know that they were sometimes floored with boards.

The round tower is a striking feature of many monasteries. Referred to as *cloigtech* (belfry) in Irish texts, the round tower was tall and tapering, with a conical cap on the corbelling principal. There were usually four windows at the top. The towers may have had additional functions such as storage of valuables or refuge in times of stress. The fact that many are provided with doorways raised high above the ground supports this theory. Internally they had wooden floors reached by a ladder. They were not equipped with hanging bells, which seem to have been unknown in Ireland before the twelfth century. The towers were probably an imported idea adapted to native techniques of stone-building, but they are far from simple structures. They possess the feature of *entasis*, an invention of classical architecture whereby the line of the side of a column is slightly convex to counter the optical illusion of concavity which an observer would get if the sides were straight. Doorways range from simple lintelled forms to elaborate arches. Later towers tend to have better quality masonry than earlier ones and incorporate decorative features, such as Romanesque traits. Present evidence suggests that they were being built in the period from the ninth to the twelfth century. The majority are to be found on sites in the midlands, but there are also a number in coastal locations. The popular idea that they were a response to the Viking invasions is unconvincing. They are much more likely to have been a reflection of the increasing wealth and sophistication of monasteries and a statement of their status.

The monastic enclosure of Moyne, near Shrule, County Mayo. A small graveyard can be seen just off centre.

This aerial view of Lusk, County Dublin, shows how property boundaries and street lines partly preserve the line of the ancient monastic enclosure.
(see p214)

Early monastic sites

D Leo Swan

The earliest documentation concerning the Irish church shows that it was established on conventional hierarchical lines, with the bishop pre-eminent in his own diocese (*paruchia*). In the sixth century the church had to adjust to a largely pagan society, but by the seventh century things had begun to change and earlier foundations had developed into great monastic federations. These were often under the control of an abbot (*comarba*) who was the heir of the founding saint, and succession within the family, often from father to son, was common. Many such abbots were laymen or in minor orders. The federations were sometimes referred to as *paruchiae*, the word which had originally designated a diocese. The monastic community was known as the *familia* (family) of the founding saint. The more significant *paruchiae* included those of Columba (Colmcille), Patrick of Armagh, Brigit of Kildare, Ciaran of Clonmacnoise, Finian of Clonard, Brendan of Clonfert, Comgall of Bangor, Maedoc of Ferns and Enda of Aran. Bishops enjoyed a high status because of their

(opposite, centre) Teampull Finghín, Clonmacnoise, County Offaly. (see p214)

(bottom right) Aerial view of the monastery of Devenish, Lough Erne, County Fermanagh. (see p214)

(bottom left) A cross-inscribed pillar, Glencolumbkille, County Donegal. (see p214)

ecclesiastical functions, but they seem to have had a limited administrative role. Territorial bishops did exist, however, and the notion that the Irish church was completely monastic does not fit the surviving evidence fully. A range of smaller church sites, lacking many of the characteristics of the monasteries, have now been identified throughout the country. These may well have provided the pastoral care of the wider community and may have had a relationship with the larger monastic establishments, but this is undefined.

Monasteries were a significant source of labour and this was used to further their economic well-being. Many of their members were laypeople; the term *manach*, a monk, was used by the eighth century to signify a monastic tenant. While monasteries became large economic enterprises, they also maintained their religious functions. Many were renowned for their support of scholarship. The abbots of leading monasteries had a high social standing and might be compared to the prince-bishops of Medieval Europe. The scale of the monasteries as well as the abbots' connections with secular rulers brought them increasingly into politics and, like their continental contemporaries, some foundations were taking part in war by the end of the eighth century.

Characteristic features

The study of monasteries has been complicated by a tendency in the past to concentrate on a few well-documented examples. These have suffered by being the focus of continuous burial, by having their churches rebuilt over the centuries, or by being absorbed into later settlements. As a result, only fragments of the original sites may be detectable today. The attention given to the well-preserved monastic sites of the Atlantic seaboard has created a false impression of what is typical. Their stone buildings are often inaccurately dated and the degree to which they resemble the great houses of the midlands, with their predominantly timber structures and large communities, is questionable. On those sites which have escaped significant later interference, a number of distinctive remains occur consistently: churches, cross-inscribed slabs or pillars, bullaun stones (stones with hollows ground in their surface, presumably from use as communal mortars), and occasionally souterrains. A cemetery is always present and there is sometimes a special grave or tomb shrine, traditionally that of the founding saint. There was, if not a plan, at least a general

pattern, almost universally accepted, to which the layout of our early monastic sites conformed. Similar features and arrangements are common in areas of Irish missionary activity in Britain, for example, Iona and Whithorn in Scotland, and Jurby and many other *keeil* (church) sites on the Isle of Man.

Early Irish monastic sites were usually enclosed within oval or circular embankments. Larger sites often contained two concentric embankments, with the area of greatest sanctity at the centre. The outer space was the 'suburbana' of early literature, where everyday work took place — the industrial, commercial and domestic activity essential to the well-being, prosperity and advancement of the community. Most excavations of monastic sites have yielded evidence of food-production, metal-working, trade and so forth. The enclosure or enclosures are invariably focused on the church site, which is normally located within the cemetery. On larger sites the principal church is normally in the centre, while on smaller sites the south-east quadrant is favoured. On island sites the church is located in the south-east.

The mid-seventh century description of the monastic city in Cogitosus's *Life* of St Brigit of Kildare describes it as a 'vast and metropolitan city. . .with its suburbs, which Brigit had marked out with a definite boundary'. Surprisingly it was not surrounded by an enclosing wall, which must then have been standard practice elsewhere. There was an inner enclosure because the author speaks of the 'ornate cashel which surrounds the church where many people congregate'. The church is described as having a 'spacious site' and being of 'awesome height'. The author calls it a 'cathedral church' and says that it was divided internally into three. To the right and left of the altar were the tombs of Brigit and Bishop Conleth 'adorned with a refined profusion of gold, silver, gems and precious stones'.

The entrance to a monastery was often marked by a cross. When round towers were first built in the tenth century, they were normally located to the west of the churches, with their doorways facing those of the church. The cemetery was usually to the south. This may have originated as an open area (the *platea*) whose focal point was a cross-slab or a founder's tomb. The abbot's house may have had its own sub-enclosure. The *tech mór* or great house, referred to in texts but, like the abbot's house, not yet identified by excavation, may have been the chief domestic building of the community. Wells are consistently associated with monastic sites, although they are seldom within the enclosures and may be some distance away. Most of these wells are now regarded as holy.

Aerial photography

Aerial photography has done much to clarify the layout of monastic sites. Where monasteries lie within the heart of modern towns and villages, this technique can reveal in the line of the streets and property boundaries, as at Duleek, County Meath, or in actual surviving portions of bank, as at Killeigh, County Offaly, the clear outlines of the ancient monastic enclosures. Tírechán, in his seventh-century *Life* of St Patrick, describes him laying out his monastery in two concentric enclosures. The present-day city of Armagh shows this pattern clearly. The ancient core of the site is represented by the Church of Ireland cathedral and its cemetery, and the older part of the town with its circular street pattern can be seen to be focused on this. Lusk and Clondalkin, County Dublin, and Kells, County Meath, show similar patterns. Lusk and Clondalkin both have round towers, while Kells still boasts an impressive group of early ecclesiastical remains, including a round tower, high crosses and a church.

In the countryside there are many important monasteries which never developed into towns but which were used extensively for burial and even some building in Medieval times. Here, too, aerial photography has helped in identifying the original enclosure, as at Monasterboice, County Louth, Durrow and Clonmacnoise, County Offaly, Ardpatrick, County Limerick and Glendalough, County Wicklow. Yet there are far more undocumented examples throughout the country, whose existence may only be known by a traditional name or dedication, by the presence of a holy well, some carved stones or perhaps just the continued use of the site for burial. Sometimes the burial ground may contain the remains of a Late Medieval church. Aerial photography will often recover the evidence of an early enclosure, if only as a crop- or soil-mark. There are many sites which have only been identified from the air. Added to the better-known examples they help build a more comprehensive picture of ecclesiastical settlements in Ireland. Reliable estimates suggest that as many as 2000 early ecclesiastical sites of various kinds may have existed in Ireland.

Elements of manuscript production in the Middle Ages

Bernard Meehan

When the historian Giraldus Cambrensis visited Kildare in 1185, he was shown a gospel book of such artistic quality as to make him wonder, in a celebrated phrase, whether he was looking at the work of angels rather than of men. The scribes and artists whose skills could attract this praise were drawing on long traditions of craftsmanship and innovation applied to written forms.

Writing materials

In different periods and cultures, many diverse materials have been used for writing: **stone**, **clay**, **sherds of pottery** (ostraca), **bark**, **bones**, **wood**, **palm leaves** and **papyrus** among others. Papyrus and waxed wooden writing tablets continued to be used well into the Medieval period, but gave way in popularity to **parchment**, a generic term for the prepared skin of almost any animal, but principally sheep. In Medieval Ireland, with its cattle-based economy, calf skin — otherwise known as **vellum** (from the Latin *vitulus* = calf) — was predominant. The advantage of skin over papyrus was that it provided a smooth yet tough and,

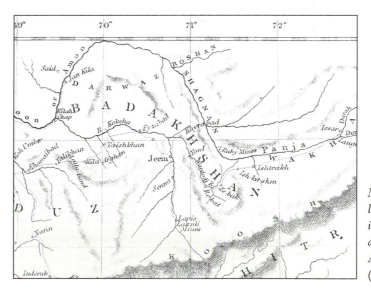

Map showing lapis lazuli mines in the Badakshan district of Afghanistan. (see p214)

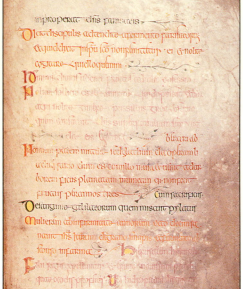

(above left) Book of Kells (c. AD 800) fol 22r. Breves Causae of Luke. Mottling of the skin is caused by bacterial decay in the course of production. (see p214)

(above right) Corpus Christi College Cambridge, MS 4, fol 241v: detail of artist holding brush in one hand and inkpot in the other. (see p214)

The production of a book (caption opposite)

sheets of papyrus, perhaps originally folded in concertina fashion. The preparation of parchment is complex and varies a little in time and place, but the essential features in the Middle Ages were that the skin was first placed for several days in a bath of lime or excrement in order to loosen the hairs. The length of time this process was allowed was crucial, since over-long immersion left the skin susceptible to bacterial attack, a process which seems to have affected some leaves of the Book of Kells. Thrown over a beam, the pelt was worked with a blunt knife to remove the animal's hair, the epidermal and hypodermal layers and perhaps any fat left behind after flaying. Drying followed, the skin tensioned on a frame, attached by cords running from the frame to small stones pressed into the skin. A *luna* knife (of half-moon shape) was used to remove residual hair and hypodermal debris, care being taken to avoid puncturing it; then re-wetted, abraded with pumice to give a nap, finally re-wetted and left to dry. The process of drying under tension stretches the dermal fibre-network and leaves the skin with a stiff consistency, suitable for writing. The best and smoothest skins are made from young animals with a low fat content, since ridges of fat are difficult and time-consuming to remove, and leave patches of transparency not suitable for writing.

Writing tools

The scribes and artists of the manuscripts are depicted using **pens** which they made from the tail feathers of the goose or swan (Latin *penna/pinna* = feather); **brushes** of no doubt varying fineness, the most fine perhaps made from marten fur; and **knives** to scrape away mistakes. For the decorated pages, stiff **wooden instruments**, **compasses**, **rulers** and **templates** were also employed. **Cow horns** served as ink-wells, the sharp end stuck in the ground, as St John's seems to be in the Book of Kells. To this day, scribes in Ethiopia follow the same practice. St Colum Cille (died AD 597), an assiduous scribe and founder of the monastic *familia* of which Kells became head, may not have planted his ink-horn with sufficient firmness in the ground on the occasion when, according to his biographer Adomnán, a clumsy visitor knocked it over with the hem of his cloak.

Inks and pigments

An **iron-gall ink** was most commonly used, made by combining iron sulphate and crushed oak apples in a

under the correct atmospheric conditions, durable writing surface that could without risk of damage be sewn both into the form of rolls and of codices (in other words, what we think of now as books). While the roll coexisted with the codex for a considerable time, the latter was less cumbersome and could more readily be consulted. The codex was pre-eminently a form suited to the promulgation of the Christian message. The pages of large gospel books, written in a bold script which could easily be read aloud to a congregation, could be turned to display, at a distance, key images and phrases. The codex developed, in ways still not fully agreed by scholars, both from the tradition of thonging together wooden tablets, and from the sewing together of cut

(opposite page) Bamberg, Staatsbibliothek Msc Patr 5, fol 1v. The roundels illustrate the production of a book, in a twelfth-century manuscript from the Benedictine abbey of Michelsberg in Bamberg, Germany.
1. Cutting the pen.
2. Rough draft on wax tablets.
3. Preparing the vellum.
4. Cutting the wooden boards to size.
5. Folding into quires (? or correcting).
6. Sewing the quires together.
7. Trimming the leaves.
8. Making clasps and studs.
9. The finished book.
10 Showing it to students.

Book of Kells (c. AD 800) fol 291v. Portrait of St John. (see p214) binding medium of gum, in a solution of water, wine or vinegar. The iron sulphate caused the ink to etch into the parchment, though gall inks were liable to fade in light. Black **carbon inks**, used along with reds and purples by one of the scribes of the Book of Kells for decorative effect, were of great antiquity, being known to Pliny in the first century AD. They could be produced simply, by burning animal fats or wood. Carbon inks did not fade, but they had a tendency to flake off the page. Prepared inks were poured into small bags made from animal skin and hung in the sun to dry.

The use of pigments represents a further stage of elaboration. An orange red, derived from **red lead**, was used in the first Irish manuscripts, such as the early seventh-century gospel book, Usserianus Primus. To produce a red lead, prepared white lead was heated, pulverised by grinding, washed, returned to the oven and stirred over a period of two or three days.

In addition to red lead, the Book of Durrow, late in the seventh century, used yellow from **orpiment**; green from **verdigris**; and yellow, discolouring to brown, from **oxgall**, a substance readily available in Ireland. Orpiment (yellow arsenic sulphide) was a non-native pigment, found in Italy, Hungary, Macedonia, Asia Minor and parts of Central Asia. Occurrences in Ireland have occasionally been reported, but it is unlikely that deposits were ever of sufficient size to be exploited. As its name suggests (in the Roman world it was known as *auripigmentum* or 'gold pigment'), its vibrant yellow was prized as a substitute for gold, but it was difficult to use, being toxic and noxious smelling. Care had to be taken not to use it next to lead and copper-based colours, with which it was chemically reactive, leading to areas of oxidation and darkening. The Book of Durrow has suffered badly from the unstable nature of verdigris ('green of Greece'), another pigment known since ancient times, which has in places first darkened, then eaten through the vellum. Verdigris was formed by the action of acetic acid and heat on copper. The method of preparation described in a treatise by the twelfth-century German craftsman Theophilus was that thin sheets of copper were placed inside a hollowed section of oak, and smeared with honey and ground salt. The oak, having been capped with a piece of wood, vinegar or hot urine, was poured in, and the oak was piled over with dung for four weeks. At intervals thereafter the pigment could be scraped off the copper plates.

The palette of the Book of Kells a century or so later was more extensive. In addition to the Durrow pigments, the artists of Kells had access to blues from the oriental plant **indigo** (*Indigofera*) or the north European plant **woad** (*Isatis tinctoria*) which are often hard to differentiate from each other; reds from **kermes** and from **vermilion**; purples and plum reds from **folium**; **white lead**, formed by lead roasted and suspended above vinegar (despite its toxicity, employed a great deal both on its own and as a base for overpainting, since it was not susceptible to cracking); and most exotically, several shades of a most durable mineral blue made from **lapis lazuli**.

Kermes red, known since the time of Moses, was produced from the bodies and eggs of the female of the *kermococcus vermilio*, a Mediterranean insect of the shield-louse family which lives in clusters on the leaves of the prickly kermes oak. Like other organic pigments, the colour was extracted in ammonia (urine) and fixed onto an insoluble mineral salt (aluminium hydroxide). Vermilion (red mercuric sulphide), otherwise known as cinnabar, was probably obtained from Spain. Pliny knew it as 'minium', a name which came later to apply to the red of red lead and whence the term 'miniature' derives. The Roman source of vermilion was 'Sisapo', now Almadén, about sixty miles from Cordoba in southern Spain. Folium (*Crozophora tinctoria*) grew in marshy areas around the Mediterranean. It seems often to have been used for the dying of garments, and, like most imported organic pigments, may have come to Ireland in the form of small rags of dyed cloth.

Lapis lazuli, a mineral of the sodalite group, was known in modern times as ultramarine (beyond the seas) and remained the most expensive artists' pigment well into the eighteenth century. In the Middle Ages its only known source was deep in the mountains of the Hindu Kush, in the Kokcha valley of Badakshan in north-east Afghanistan, an area rich in precious stones. Access was slow and hazardous. This was true as late as December 1837, when the Scottish geographer John Wood of the East India Company's Navy visited the mines in weather so bleak as to make him yearn for the relative comforts of a Scottish winter. He reported that stone of the deepest blue — that most valued by artists — was found in the darkest rock nearest to the river. The stone could be dislodged with crowbars only when the rock surrounding it had been sufficiently softened with fire.

Lapis came to the Mediterranean over the caravan routes and reached Ireland after passing through the hands of many intermediaries. It is possible that some of it came in a refined or partly refined state, though the artist was able to determine for himself the depth of colour by the coarseness or fineness of the grinding, and presumably preferred to make his own.

Binding materials

The binding media used for the pigments were most commonly the white of egg (glair) and the yolk; natural gums; and animal gelatine.

Bejewelled treasure bindings of a type popular from late antiquity do not survive in Ireland. The closest to this tradition found in an Irish context is the lower board of the Lindau Gospels, associated with the monastery of St Gall and dating from c. AD 800. Irish manuscripts seem more often to have been bound in a style similar to the nine volumes of the Bible which are shown behind the scribe Ezra in the Codex Amiatinus (written in England c. AD 716), or to the volumes shown in the Book of Kells, such as that held by St John. The original boards of the Book of Armagh are covered with red morocco (goatskin), retaining its delicate pink on the inside covers, decorated with blind tooling. Coptic manuscripts were probably an influence. The binding of Chester Beatty Library MS 815, for example, a sixth-century manuscript found at a site near Sakkara and containing portions of the Psalms and St Matthew's Gospel, has parallels in its cross and interlace decoration with such early manuscripts as the Book of Durrow.

Satchels and shrines

Manuscripts were often transported or stored in leather satchels, hung on pegs in monastic cells. Satchels form another remarkable parallel with the Coptic church. The half-ruined Coptic monastery of Souriani, which Robert Curzon visited in search of manuscripts in 1837, was situated in the region of the Natron lakes north-west of Cairo, in an area of great monastic antiquity, where practices had probably not greatly changed from the Middle Ages. The community there had given refuge to a number of Abyssinian monks, whose library Curzon illustrated, the satchels reminding him of soldiers' knapsacks and cartridge boxes. While satchels were probably manufactured individually for the most important manuscripts, they could also be designed to

Engraving of the library used by Abyssinian monks at the Coptic monastery of Souriani, near Cairo, in 1837. Several book satchels are hung on pegs around the room.
(see p214)

hold more than one book. This is made clear by the size of the Late Medieval satchel associated with the Book of Armagh, which is too large for that volume and may have originally been made for a different manuscript (or more than one), and by St Colum Cille's biographer Adomnán, who recounted the miraculous tale of a man, many years after Colum Cille's death, falling from his horse and drowning in the river Boyne. The satchel of books he was carrying fell in with him. When the body was brought to land, it was discovered that everything in the satchel had rotted, with the exception of a page written by Colum Cille. Adomnán went on to describe a hymnal in Colum Cille's hand which had been dropped by a Pictish priest, Iogenan, and had lain submerged in a river from Christmas until Easter. When it was recovered and brought back to Iogenan it was found to be clean and dry. Adomnán drew the common hagiographical inference that it was their association with the saint which had caused these volumes to be unharmed by water. In each case he added the comparison that the books had the appearance of having been kept not in the water but in a shrine ('*in scriniolo*' / '*in scrinio*'). A manuscript was placed in a shrine if it was regarded as the relic of a saint, but it did not, despite Adomnán, normally survive well there, since it was usually loose fitting and subject to impact damage, of a type suffered by the Book of Durrow, the Cathach, traditionally attributed to St Colum Cille, and Usserianus Primus. What Adomnán perhaps meant was that a book kept in a shrine was less likely to experience adventures because it was looked after more carefully and because, once enshrined, it was no longer available for consultation as a text, the shrine having been constructed so as not to allow ready access.

(top left)
Bone motif- or trial-piece from an occupation site in the sand-hills of Dooey, County Donegal.
(see p214)

(top right)
Cross carpet page which precedes the Gospel of St Matthew in the Book of Lindisfarne.
(see p214)

(below)
The Ardagh Chalice, made of beaten, lathe-polished silver and decorated

with gold filigree, stamped copper, knitted silver and copper wire, engraving, enamel, amber, malachite.
(see p214)

(bottom right)
Penannular brooch of bronze, with enamel and millefiori decoration, from Arthurstown, County Kildare. An elaborate example of the type, it dates to the sixth or seventh century AD.

Cover of a book-reliquary from Lough Kinale, County Longford.
(see p214)

(opposite page)
The Tara Brooch, County Meath.
(see p215)

Hooked implement, County Kilkenny. (see p214)

Page from Stowe Missal (see p215)

Early Medieval art

Michael Ryan

Animal-head handle with its escutcheon plate and frame in the style of the Tara Brooch and Book of Lindisfarne. Donore, County Meath.
(see p215)

(opposite) Detail of animal ornament from The Book of Durrow. Later seventh century AD.

To many people, the art of the Early Medieval period is its best-known legacy. It is an art which has frequently been imitated in modern times, so much so that aspects of it have become hackneyed by over-exposure on tea towels, chocolate boxes and table mats. For all that, it is as misunderstood as it is frequently reproduced.

The local version of the La Tène style of abstract ornament on metalwork, based on curves and fleshy scrollwork and occasional use of red enamel, seems to have survived in Ireland into the Early Medieval period. We cannot document this in detail because of the problems of dating objects and the difficulty of locating sites of the time. A related style was practised amongst the Celtic peoples of Britain, both outside and within the Roman province. When the legions withdrew in AD

406, there was a resurgence of native peoples, and rulers in the Celtic tradition emerged. Some of these originated north of the Roman frontier, but urban life on the Roman pattern was maintained well into the late fifth century over much of what is now England. The Irish, too, were active, and Irish colonies were established in western Scotland, Wales and, probably, Cornwall.

The native metal-working traditions enjoyed a new vogue, but in a modified form. Work in bronze embellished with red enamel continued, but new motifs also appeared, some influenced by provincial Roman style. The penannular brooch — a form adopted earlier from the Romans — became the high-status garment fastener *par excellence*. The terminals of its ring became the field for the display of ornament of scrollwork and sometimes Christian symbols. Another product of the period is the so-called hanging-bowl — small bronze, or occasionally silver, bowls equipped with hooks to suspend them. Early examples have simple openwork escutcheons attached to the hooks or fine, simple, engraved scrollwork filled with enamel. Later bowls carry much more elaborate schemes of enamelling; new colours appear and very complex patterns are built up of combinations of curves and trumpet scrolls. Penannular brooches are found widely in Britain and Ireland. The hanging bowls are found mainly in pagan Anglo-Saxon graves of the sixth and seventh centuries. Why?

To understand this, we must look at how southern Britain came to be dominated by the Germanic tribes known in later times as the Anglo-Saxons. When the Roman Empire came under pressure in Europe north of the Alps, and in Britain, its rulers often adopted the strategy of forming alliances with barbarian kings and war leaders, and recruiting large numbers of their followers into their service, often settling them in frontier lands to act as a buffer against more hostile peoples beyond. This process had been going on in Britain in the fourth century, and Germanic mercenaries were evidently being stationed in the south and east as a protection against Saxon raiders, themselves Germanic in origin. After the legions left, local rulers seem to have adopted the same practice, and so it is thought likely that the conquest of England was a slow process and, in some areas, a comparatively bloodless one, as the growth of mercenary power gradually outweighed that of the employers, the native rulers. In such a scenario, the

continuation of Celtic metal-working styles in southern Britain is very likely, and much material of that nature could have found its way into Germanic hands legitimately and, in its turn, influenced their craftsmen. It is unnecessary to argue that all the hanging bowls, for example, represent booty taken by the pagan invaders from the Celtic lands of western Britain.

The Germanic tribes brought with them an interesting and vigorous art. This was itself based, in part, on the style of military buckles and other accoutrements of the late Roman world. In particular, in Scandinavia and north Germany, a lively animal art developed which took elements of Roman design and elaborated them to produce a remarkable group of styles which appeared everywhere Germanic peoples overwhelmed the Empire and settled. Rich casting in silver and bronze was especially characteristic of the finest work. The technique was designed to imitate deeply faceted engraving. Motifs included strange beasts, men, animal heads in relief, and a limited range of scrolls and angular patterns. Some of the animal motifs got broken up and elements only are detectable in an almost meaningless pattern. Later, in the sixth century, the idea of interlace — borrowed probably from Italy — was married to animal patterns to produce a new style which was later to have dramatic effects in Ireland.

It is likely that cross-fertilisation of the Germanic and Celtic traditions took place in Britain, but it would be unwise to conclude that this was exclusively so. Although trade declined with the Roman Empire, it did not die out completely. Trade amongst the Germanic peoples is documented, and this network extended to include the Celtic lands — an Irish-style hand-pin was discovered on a site in the Netherlands. Trade was, however, much more widespread — there is good archaeological evidence for trade in wine and oil between Ireland and western Britain and the eastern Mediterranean in the fifth century — whether it was direct or not is uncertain. Later, pottery evidence shows trade with south-western Gaul, which is supported by our earliest texts and other linguistic evidence. These continuing contacts would have refreshed the Irish craftsman's knowledge of the arts of the Mediterranean world, in particular of craftsmanship in the service of the church. It would have added to the stock of Christian traditions introduced at the time of the conversion. These contacts were renewed and intensified by the burst of missionary activity begun in Britain and Europe by Irish monks from the late sixth century onwards.

The Irish art of the period from the seventh to the early tenth century is woven from a number of major strands — the La Tène tradition as it survived and was modified in Britain and Ireland; the Germanic animal art style, and other Roman influences transmitted and modified through it; Mediterranean Christian artistic traditions as they were introduced at the time of the conversion (although we can only guess at these), and continuing continental influences through trade and travel. Documenting this is very difficult; often we must guess at the process from elements of later or entirely undated objects.

If we were to take stock of what we know about Irish fine craftsmanship at about the year AD 600, we would be able to say that it had changed quite considerably from what it was in Later Iron Age times. It had changed technically under new influences: tinning and silvering were practised; solid silver objects had begun to appear; enamel was more freely used, and the new technique of millefiori glass had been adopted. New types of object had come into fashion: penannular brooches decorated with spiral scrolls and enamels; hand-pins, sometimes enamelled or decorated with millefiori; and probably also hanging bowls (but no complete example of the time has yet been found in Ireland). We know, too, of workshops where fine objects were made, for example, at Garranes ring-fort in County Cork and Ballinderry Crannog No. 2, County Offaly, and also, significantly, at the monastic site of Armagh.

While we know most about metalwork, we do have some knowledge of other areas: simple pillars and slabs with crosses and other symbols were erected at this time, although they are difficult to date; churches of wood were being built and occasionally also, perhaps, ones of stone. Writing, the churchly art *par excellence*, had developed its own distinctively Irish style by the time our earliest manuscript, the Cathach, came to be written. The scene was set for the emergence of the great art of the following period.

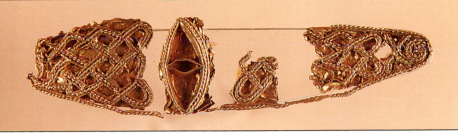

Seventh century

At the opening of the century, Irish art is known mostly from metalwork, but one manuscript, the Cathach of St Columba, with simply decorated initials and a characteristic Irish script already fully formed, survives from the late sixth or very early seventh century. The craftsman's repertoire of techniques was added to as the century progressed — gold filigree was apparently introduced during this period. It was mostly of Anglo-Saxon type, but making deductions from later objects, it is likely that Frankish and even Byzantine influences were affecting goldsmithing at this time. Trade, pilgrimage, foreign students and churchmen kept Ireland in touch with developments in Europe and Britain — a process which was intensified, but not begun, by the missionary activities of Irish monks from the sixth century onwards. Through Iona, there was close contact with the Irish, Picts and Britons of what is now Scotland. From Iona, Aidan went in the 630s to complete the conversion of Northumbria. Foundations such as Lindisfarne became great centres of artistic production, where Irish traditions of decoration were subjected to the renewed influence of Anglo-Saxon style, to produce a new hybrid art, best represented in manuscripts such as the Book of Durrow (possibly mid-seventh century) and the Book of Lindisfarne (late seventh century) which show the style at its mature stage. The evidence of

(opposite)
The Derrynaflan Hoard, County Tipperary. Found in 1980 on the monastic site of that name. (see p215)

(above)
A small piece of experimental gold filigree from the earliest, seventh century, occupation of Lagore Crannog, County Meath. (see p215)

(bottom left)
The hook and escutcheon of the largest of three hanging bowls from the Anglo-Saxon princely ship-burial of Sutton Hoo, Suffolk, England. (see p215)

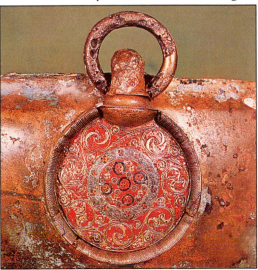

Human-headed mount of bronze, a binding strip from a composite object such as a saddle. Found in the River Shannon near Athlone during drainage works in the nineteenth century.

Bronze disc-headed pin from Treanmanagh, County Limerick. (see p215)

metalwork at the end of the seventh century and the beginning of the eighth makes it clear that the developed style was common to Ireland, Scotland and northern England at the same time. We have to imagine the style developing in both islands, with cross-fertilisation taking place at every stage — a view which fits the historical evidence well.

The golden age

The early eighth century saw the perfection of Irish art. The appearance of pieces such as the Tara Brooch, with a dazzling array of ornaments and techniques, is startling, but the suddenness may be more apparent than real. We depend on surviving objects for our evidence, and these may be rare and unrepresentative pieces, preserved because of their very exceptional nature. The Tara Brooch shows that the Irish craftsmen had become inventive with gold filigree and were thoroughly familiar with the style also shown in the Lindisfarne Gospels. The Donore door-furniture from County Meath is in the same style as the brooch and makes clear that classical models were being adopted by the bronzesmiths.

Excavation has revealed that ambitious metalwork was carried on at secular sites, such as the ring-fort at Garryduff, County Cork, and crannogs such as Lagore and Moynagh Lough, County Meath. Monastic workshops were also probably active, although the archaeological evidence which we have from Armagh and Nendrum, County Down, may relate more to the end of the eighth and the ninth century. The Derrynaflan Paten, one of the finest expressions of the Irish art, was assembled according to a lettered code, which might suggest that a literate artificer (a cleric?) was involved in its design. The paten and the closely related Ardagh Chalice show an astonishing range of techniques — filigree, enamelling, casting, engraving, stamping of foil and knitting of wire mesh — and an elaborate scheme of animal ornament which owes a good deal to the Anglo-Saxon version of the vine-scroll with beasts among its tendrils. They were both probably made in the middle or later eighth century.

The important monasteries devoted a great deal of effort to enshrining the relics of their founding saints and other holy men. The commonest reliquary was the house-shaped shrine — small, gabled, wooden caskets, inlaid or plated with metal, occasionally entirely of metal,

and carried by means of a leather strap around the neck. They are found in Ireland and Scotland. Three which were anciently exported are preserved in Italy (one of them still contains bones), and others, including many fragments, were taken by the Vikings to Norway in the ninth century. A unique belt-reliquary was found at Moylough in County Sligo by a man digging turf in 1944. It still contains the leather strap of a belt. It has a false buckle which, although made in the eighth century, copies the form of Frankish buckles of about AD 600. Despite damage by the acids of the bog, its inlaid studs, stamped silver ornaments, angular panels of enamel and millefiori glass, make it one of the great pieces of the period.

Manuscript painting in Ireland is not so well understood. Small gospel books were produced and embellished with simple illuminations. Larger books must have existed, as the Lough Kinale book-shrine shows. The greatest manuscript of the period, the Book of Kells, was painted probably towards the end of the eighth century in a Columban monastery (most likely Iona). This remarkable work of art brings together in uniquely complex and ingenious ways all the traditions of animal ornament, interlace, trumpet scrollwork, and combines them with narrative scenes of great power and dignity. There are strong links with Pictish sculpture in its ornament, which strengthen the case for its composition in Iona. The Book of Armagh, written and illustrated by Ferdomnach in the early ninth century, has a series of elegant and restrained pen-and-ink drawings, which shows the other side of artistic activity from the exuberance of Kells. Also in the ninth century Macregol, Abbot of Birr, found the time to illuminate a fine gospel which deserves to be better known.

Throughout the eighth century the rich and powerful, both lay and cleric, could command magnificent ring-brooches on the pattern of the Tara Brooch (in Pictland, similar decoration occurs on penannular brooches), and these continued to be made in the ninth century with simpler decoration, less enamel and impoverished filigree — or even crude attempts to imitate the effect of filigree by stamped foil. Nevertheless, in the early ninth century patrons could commission ambitious objects for the church, such as the Derrynaflan Chalice, despite the Viking raids.

TIME CHART

From Early Medieval to Later Medieval times

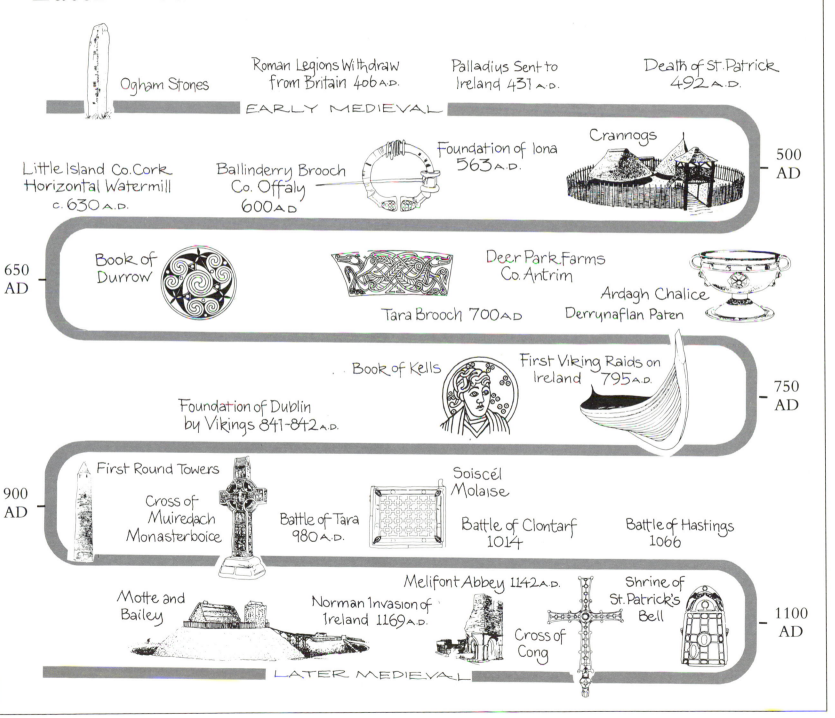

Ogham Stones

Roman Legions Withdraw from Britain 406 A.D.

Palladius Sent to Ireland 431 A.D.

Death of St. Patrick 492 A.D.

EARLY MEDIEVAL

Little Island Co. Cork Horizontal Watermill c. 630 A.D.

Ballinderry Brooch Co. Offaly 600 AD

Foundation of Iona 563 A.D.

Crannogs

500 AD

Book of Durrow

Deer Park Farms Co. Antrim

Ardagh Chalice

Tara Brooch 700 AD

Derrynaflan Paten

650 AD

Book of Kells

First Viking Raids on Ireland 795 A.D.

Foundation of Dublin by Vikings 841-842 A.D.

750 AD

First Round Towers

Cross of Muiredach Monasterboice

Battle of Tara 980 A.D.

Soiscél Molaise

Battle of Clontarf 1014

Battle of Hastings 1066

900 AD

Motte and Bailey

Norman Invasion of Ireland 1169 A.D.

Melifont Abbey 1142 A.D.

Cross of Cong

Shrine of St. Patrick's Bell

LATER MEDIEVAL

1100 AD

The Vikings

Few topics in ancient Irish history have excited more argument than the Vikings. At first historians were content to take their cue from the monastic annalists whose monasteries were the chief targets of these Scandinavian pirates, who exploited their wealth, captured potential slaves and took their precious materials. In this scheme of things, the Vikings were an unredeemed disaster, Irish society became more violent and there was a decline in religious practices. A revision of the traditionalist view has since taken place, but it has probably gone too far in trying to persuade us of the positive value of the Viking contact. While we must attribute some credit to the Vikings for our first towns, the increased expertise in shipbuilding, expansion of foreign trade, coinage and so on, the story is a great deal more complex than this.

We still do not know what caused the sudden eruption of piratical raids from Scandinavia at the end of the eighth century: perhaps a great increase in population put pressure on the available land. Shipbuilding technology had dramatically improved, enabling the adventurous to range much further than was previously possible. The Vikings had travelled as far west as north America, into the Mediterranean and down the rivers of eastern Europe to trade with the Byzantine Empire. They established powerful colonies in the west — their impact on England, as evidenced in placenames and in the language, was profound. In Ireland their status is more equivocal.

A raid on the Hebrides and the north of Ireland in AD 617 may have been an early manifestation of the Viking phenomenon, but the first definite onslaught is recorded for the year AD 795, when Inishmurray, Inishbofin and Rechru (either Rathlin Island or Lambay Island) were attacked. Iona was raided in 795, 802 and 804 when sixty-eight people were killed. In 807 the community of Iona settled in Kells. In the first forty years of the ninth century the brunt of the raids fell on the northern half of the island, mainly on the coast. Armagh was plundered three times in 832.

Despite their ferocity the raids seem to have had little impact on Irish society. The repeated attacks on certain monasteries show their economic resilience. But in the 830s more concerted raids by larger fleets began. In 840/1 the first encampment for overwintering was established on Lough Neagh. The following year defended ship harbours were built there and in Dublin. The raids intensified in the 840s, but gradually the Irish began to fight back in a more organised manner. Slowly but surely, the Viking enclaves at Dublin, Arklow, Wicklow, Wexford, Waterford, Cork and Limerick, and others less enduring, became part of Irish life and of a system which was characterised by numerous tribal kingdoms.

In 902 the Vikings of Dublin were expelled and their fortress destroyed. The inhabitants seem to have migrated in large numbers to north-west England. They returned in force in 917 to re-establish their settlement. An important series of silver hoards from both Ireland and England reflects the turmoil of this time. The early tenth century saw a renewal of Viking raids and extensive inland campaigning. But Dublin was also on the receiving end — it was burnt in 936 and 941. In 980 the Vikings were heavily defeated by King Maelsechnaill at the battle of Tara, and were never again to pose a serious threat. Their economic activity remained significant however. It is noteworthy that Irish kings never sought to eliminate the Viking enclaves, but to milk them for tribute. The archaeological evidence of this is impressive. Silver hoards of the Viking Age have been found in areas of Irish settlement. The evidence for Viking settlement outside towns is principally that of placenames and some hints preserved in later documents. A substantial area around Dublin, embracing parts of north County Dublin, north-east County Kildare and north Wicklow, may have been settled by the Vikings, and these areas possibly retained something of their distinctive character until the arrival of the Anglo-Normans. The great battle of Clontarf, fought in 1014 beneath the fortifications of Dublin, was not the climactic clash between the Irish and the Scandinavians but an episode in long-running dynastic rivalries in which the foreigners were just one factor. By then Scandinavians had been active participants in Irish politics for well over a century and a half.

The Vikings in Ireland initially enjoyed a considerable advantage in combat, wielding large well-made swords with hardened blades which were superior to those of the Irish.

(see p215)

Irish art during the Viking invasions

Michael Ryan

The impact of the Vikings on Irish art in the ninth century is difficult to assess. Although the Viking graves of Norway are rich in objects manufactured in Ireland, Scotland and England, it is a mistake to think of it all as booty. Some pieces were reliquary fragments, and it is unlikely that reliquaries were traded to the pagan Norse. The fact that some of these were adapted for use as brooches makes their occurrence all the more suspect. There are many objects, brooches, harness mounts and other pieces which could have been bought by the Norse, especially after they began to establish permanent settlements in the 840s. Similar material has been found in the Viking cemetery of Kilmainham—Islandbridge in Dublin.

As the ninth century advanced, changes in Irish metal-working styles took place. The enamels which gave colour to eighth-century objects were largely abandoned. There appears to have been a greater use of silver and solid metal ornaments to substitute for the elaborate effects of the earlier style. Large brooches of this period tend to have simple filigree decorations, or none at all, and the complex animal ornaments give way to simplified beasts, often placed along the margins. Open-work frills become fashionable. The increasing use of silver may be attributed to the Vikings, who had access to ready supplies from their trading links with the Orient. The logical outcome of these developments is represented by a series of penannular brooches of silver, with engraved animal patterns and prominent bosses which were current in both Ireland and Britain. Their ornament has a strong Anglo-Saxon flavour. These brooches are occasionally found in coin-dated hoards of the early tenth century, so it is likely that they had developed in the later ninth century. Another type, the thistle brooch, belongs to the same period, and variants of it are found in the Scandinavian homeland.

We cannot be sure that the impact of the Viking raids was uniform throughout the country. If the Derrynaflan Chalice was made in the ninth century, as seems probable, then it is unlikely that the workshops of Munster were seriously disrupted in the earlier ninth century. Other ambitious pieces were made for the church in the period after about AD 900, and included elaborate crosiers. Although ninth- and tenth-century metalwork is overshadowed by the spectacular pieces of the eighth century, production continued. We cannot therefore claim that the production of fine metalwork was extinguished by the Vikings.

Sculpture

Although manuscript painting was in decline, it now seems clear that stone sculpture enjoyed an extraordinary flowering. Research is beginning to show that the Irish schools of high cross carving were born in the ninth century. Whether the great crosses were developed here or whether the stimulus came from northern Britain is disputed. So far all efforts to identify a single line of development have been unconvincing. Differences between crosses may reflect local preferences in ornament and choice of didactic scene. Crosses may have been erected for a variety of purposes — commemorative, teaching, to define sanctuary and so on. What is clear from the evidence of inscriptions is that crosses which emphasise ornament seem to precede those with complex arrangements of scriptural scenes, as well as allegorical themes and ornament.

It used to be said that Irish patrons of the arts turned to sculpture in the Viking Age because the great crosses could not be carried off as spoil in the same way as precious jewellery or reliquaries might. This is wholly unconvincing. The crosses embody a complex of influences from overseas; they are also expressions of confidence and wealth, not the reverse. They are monuments designed to commemorate the power and

A large sarcophagus, now preserved in Cormac's Chapel, Cashel. (see p215)

prestige of the great monastic houses whose development had moved a long way from the simple communities of earlier times. We can see in the sculpture the influences of Italy, the Carolingian Empire, the Anglo-Saxons and perhaps the Picts of Scotland. The same cosmopolitanism can be glimpsed in the metalwork. Scandinavian influence is negligible — the principal impact of Viking art styles was not felt outside the coastal towns until the eleventh century, when the Viking Age proper had passed.

Viking Age art influences

Raghnall Ó Floinn

Before the Viking invasions, Irish and Scandinavian art had developed independently of one another, yet both practised a sophisticated animal art derived from the pagan Germanic tribes, an inheritance also shared by the Anglo-Saxons of Britain. Because of this, it is difficult to establish clearly the influence each had on the other, especially in the Viking Age. The settlements founded by the Vikings in Ireland and Britain during this period acted as centres for the exchange of new ideas through trade in imported goods and in the movement of craftsmen from one area to another. The large numbers of carved-bone motif pieces from the Dublin excavations show that the craftsmen there were experimenting with Irish and Viking motifs. Despite these borrowings from the Scandinavian and Anglo-Saxon world, the art of the period remained distinctively Irish and is easily recognisable from that of its neighbours.

It is clear from the large number of Irish objects found in Norwegian graves of the ninth and tenth centuries that the Vikings were familiar with and appreciated Irish metalwork. The Norse settlers in Ireland do not seem to have been greatly influenced by these works, and much of their jewellery continued to be imported from their Scandinavian homelands. Irish brooch types were copied to a limited extent there, especially in Norway, although they were decorated in a purely local style.

Silver and gold

The Vikings, through their vast trading networks which extended as far as the rich silver mining areas of the Middle East, were responsible for introducing silver on a massive scale to Europe, including Ireland. This consisted of silver bullion in the form of Arabic and other coins, and cut-up pieces of ornament, known as 'hack-silver'. This was often converted into jewellery by local craftsmen, and Ireland was no exception. The silver-bossed penannular and thistle brooches are examples of the later ninth and tenth centuries. The use of twisted

Ingot in mould, Moylarg Crannog, County Antrim. (see p215)

rods of gold and silver to make a variety of ornaments — collars, bracelets and finger rings, reminiscent of much earlier Irish Bronze Age jewellery — seems to be of Scandinavian inspiration, as does a series of armlets made of plain bands of silver, decorated with geometric designs stamped on with punches of various shapes. Whether these were made by the Irish or by the Vikings in Ireland we do not know, but they were certainly used by both. Few Viking motifs found their way into the repertoire of the Irish craftsman before the eleventh century. An exception is the ring-chain motif — a pattern of interlocking Y-shapes resembling a series of vertebrae — which is found on metalwork and carvings in stone, bone and wood.

Animal ornament

The later Viking art styles had a more profound effect on Irish artists. The *Ringerike style* — named after an area rich in stone carvings in Norway — dating to the early

Silver kite brooch, said to have been found in County Kilkenny. (see p215)

(opposite) The Roscrea Brooch, County Tipperary. (see p215)

(below right) The Cross of Muiredach at Monasterboice, County Louth. (see p215)

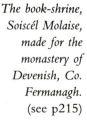

The south cross at Ahenny, County Tipperary. (see p215)

The book-shrine, Soiscél Molaise, made for the monastery of Devenish, Co. Fermanagh. (see p215)

(opposite page) Group of Viking Age finds from Fishamble Street and Christchurch Place, Dublin.

eleventh century, and the succeeding *Urnes style* — named after a decorated Norwegian wooden church — were widely adapted by Irish craftsmen, especially in metalwork. Ringerike compositions consist typically of an axial arrangement of interlaced animals, usually a large beast through which is threaded one or more smaller snake-like animals. The limbs of these animals degenerate into clusters of plant tendrils, the forward-pointing eye being the most prominent feature in an otherwise tangled mesh. The Irish version of this style is generally more disciplined, the animals being easier to identify, in keeping with the traditions of Irish animal ornament. It is quite common on metalwork and has more recently been found on a series of highly carved wooden objects from the Dublin excavations. The Ringerike style is rarely found on Irish sculpture.

The high point of Viking influence on Irish art comes at the end of the eleventh century with the Urnes style. The 'great beast' is still present, but now the design is more fluid, the animals' bodies stretched out in graceful figure-of-eight curves. The animals have recognisable limbs, and the organised arrangement of the design —

compared to the more ragged quality of the Ringerike animals — is probably what the Irish artist found most attractive. The final flowering of the Urnes style took place in Ireland, and there is a strong possibility that Irish artists played a part in the development of the style. Whatever the case, it was widely used in metalwork, sculpture and manuscript painting.

One of the most elegant expressions of the style is found on the Shrine of St Patrick's Bell. The side panels are covered with a rigidly geometric mesh of ribbon-like animals and snakes, their bodies elongated in a graceful arrangement of curved lines. This symmetrical repetition of motifs is unknown in Scandinavian art of the period and is an example of how elements of the foreign art style were adapted to local taste. Unlike the Ringerike style, Urnes decoration is rare in England, and this argues for a more direct link between Ireland and Scandinavia for this period.

The complete assimilation of the style is found in the west of Ireland and in north Munster, where it persisted well after it had gone out of fashion in its homeland. On objects like the Cross of Cong, the Shrine of St Manchan and the little plaque from a casket found at Holycross, County Tipperary, the surface is covered with an arrangement of paired beasts and snakes which fill the available space. In stone sculpture only the sacrophagus from Cashel compares in the quality of its workmanship with the best of Irish Urnes metalwork.

By the time the sculptor of the Cashel tomb was engaged in his work, sometime about the middle of the twelfth century, the fashion for an abstract art based on animal ornament had long since gone out of vogue over much of Europe. The impact of the new Romanesque art, introduced to Ireland by the reforming orders, especially the Cistercians, was already gaining favour, and by the turn of the century had overtaken it, bringing to an end one of the most vibrant animal art styles in Early Medieval Europe, which had lasted over half a millennium.

Fishamble Street, Dublin: Reconstructed view of a typical three-aisled house.

Reconstruction of house excavated at Fishamble Street, Dublin. (see p215)

Dublin in the Viking Age

Patrick F Wallace

Scandinavian evidence suggests that the Viking Age had deep roots and was the product of many technological developments, not least the perfection of the clinker-built boat and the use of carburised steel edges on long swords. Its origins in these islands, however, may be said to date from the last years of the eighth century, when records of Viking raids on the monastic settlements off our coasts were first chronicled. By the 840s the raiders had begun to over-winter and they established *longphorts* (shipping ports) at Dublin and Anagassan, County Louth. These earliest settlements were probably organised on Scandinavian lines and only lasted for a couple of generations.

In 902 the Dublin Vikings were banished, largely to northern Britain. On their return in 917 they appear to have established a real town at Dublin, based on their English experiences but tailored to local requirements. Limerick, Waterford and possibly Wexford and Cork also date from about this time. While Scandinavian and British evidence puts the end of the Viking Age at about the middle of the eleventh century (no later than the Battle of Hastings), Irish scholars usually extend it to the coming of the Normans to Ireland almost a century later. There is now very good evidence to suggest that the Viking Age in Ireland ended in the 1050s or thereabouts.

Viking legacies

The impact of the Vikings on Dublin and indeed on Ireland, was much greater than their numbers would suggest. Their greatest legacy is perhaps the fact that they established our first real towns and introduced to Ireland the concept of property-owning town dwellers. Their urban settlements were established primarily for commerce and exchange rather than for devotion, as was the case with the great monastic enclosures. Dublin and the other towns were part of an international trade network, extending from the Russian rivers and the Middle East to Scandinavia and the Atlantic. The large number of words for ships and parts of ships in the Irish language are borrowed from Old Norse. Evidence of Viking coastal settlements is also seen in the number of Norse placenames, family names and personal names in these areas. The Vikings introduced our earliest coinage in 997 and popularised and made available the use of silver in the tenth century. They helped promote new art styles which fused with native schools to produce the rich Dublin version of international Ringerike and later, Urnes. They popularised the use of the single-sided, multi-piece comb, and probably the wearing of trousers. They introduced new types of weapons and greatly influenced weapon manufacture and sword-smithing. Their commercial and later ecclesiastical links with England probably paved the way for the Norman invasion, which may be the greatest of all the Viking legacies.

Houses and settlements

In the twenty years following Breandán Ó Ríordáin's first excavations in Dublin's High Street in 1961, the National Museum of Ireland conducted what was probably Europe's largest series of urban archaeological excavations. Thanks to the scale of these excavations and to the 'open area' system adopted at Wood Quay/Fishamble Street, we now have an excellent idea of what Dublin looked like in the Viking period. More than a dozen tenements, yards or plots were traced at different levels in Fishamble Street, and the often intact foundation remains of over one hundred and fifty houses were unearthed. The plot or yard divisions consisted of post and wattle fences running at right angles from the street, creating rectangular or trapezoidal plots. Each of these had its own pathway leading from the street to a main house. The houses were located towards the street side of the plot, but set back from the street edge. In most cases the house straddled the widths of the plots, so that access to the backs of the plots and to the often smaller buildings which were located in them had to be through the main houses. There is also evidence of pits and paths, and of continuity of plot boundaries on the same locations. The influence of Viking Age town layout continued up to relatively modern times.

Five types of Viking house have been identified. In the most common type the floors were divided in a tripartite fashion consisting of a wide central strip running between doorways in the end walls, and raised, built-in bedding areas along each side wall. Often a stone-carved or paved hearth was located in the centre of the floor. The corners of the buildings were further subdivided by lower walls and were floored for different functions. The average floor area was about 36 sq m (387½ sq ft). The walls were low skirts comprising a single, or less often a double, line of post and wattle. Although evidence of daub was scarce, even in burnt layers, it is thought that some of the walls must have been smeared in dung. The thatched roof was supported on four main uprights set well in from the walls. These were arranged in transversely related pairs, each of which appears to have supported a truss on which the purlins and rafters were constructed. A layer of sod was inserted underneath the thatch. The doors often had very strong, squared jambs, presumably to support a wide lintel, to which the weight of the hip roof was transferred.

Two of the house types were smaller buildings. The first seemed to emphasise comfort, with the floors usually sunken and covered in woven wattle mats. A single entrance was common in one of the side walls. The second type was a slimmed down version of the most common building described earlier. The final type were small huts which possibly served a variety of functions,

View of the Fishamble Street/Wood Quay excavation in Dublin.

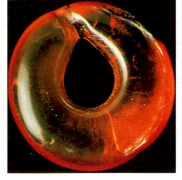

Amber bead found in the excavations at Christchurch Place, Dublin, in an eleventh century deposit. (see p215)

One of two gold bracelets found under the threshold of a house in the excavations at High Street, Dublin. (see p215)

Waterford in the Late Viking Age

Maurice Hurley, with Claire Walsh and Orla Scully

There are few extant documents relating to the Vikings in Waterford, but the foundation of the city by Sitricus, a Norwegian, is generally dated to AD 853. A more secure historical date, however, is the year AD 914, for in that year it is recorded in the *Fragmentary Annals of Ireland* that 'a great fleet of Norwegians landed at Port Lairge and they plundered northern Osraige and brought spoils and many cows and livestock to their ships'. There are several other gaps in the historical record, but many of these are now being filled by evidence from recent archaeological excavations.

Between 1987 and 1990 in excess of 6000 sq m (64,580 sq ft), or about 20 per cent of the total Viking area of the city, was archaeologically excavated. We know now that this area was densely settled by the mid-eleventh century. It was surrounded by a defensive ditch and bank, and streets fronted by houses had been laid out. The town may have had its origins in a defended ship harbour or *longphort* from whence, in the eleventh century, an unenclosed settlement began to expand along the ridge to the south and west. The construction of the defences was a necessary response to the increasing prosperity of the town's inhabitants.

A 35m (115ft) length of town defences was excavated to the eastern side of Bakehouse Lane. These consisted of a ditch up to 2.5m (8ft) deep, more than 8m (26ft) wide in places, and an earthen bank, formed from the upcast from the ditch, on the inside. A substantial stone wall, built against the outside of the bank, formed a revetment. The ramparts may originally have stood to a height of 4m (13ft), and it is possible that the ditch was originally surmounted by a wooden palisade.

A wooden drainpipe recovered from beneath the bank in Arundel Square was dated by dendrochronology to AD 1088±9. The base of the ditch filled rapidly with silt and rubbish from within the city. Most of the objects recovered from the fill of the ditch were animal bones

including that of pig styes.

Defences appear to have consisted of a large earthen embankment running right around the town, with a post and wattle palisade along its crest. This was gradually enlarged and by the end of the eleventh century a stone wall, possibly constructed as a revetment, was built as a defence. Dock-side accommodation was constructed along the edge of the tidal river. This stone defence would have greeted the Normans on their arrival in the twelfth century.

Thanks to the quality of the preservation, considerable light has been thrown on the diet preferences, butchery practices and general environment of Viking Dublin. This same preservation has yielded an abundance of artifacts from which craft districts can now be inferred and items and tools of various kinds identified. The crafts of the blacksmith, copper alloy workers, comb makers, shoe makers and ship builders are very well evidenced. So too are the decorative artifacts, especially in wood, which were produced to such a high standard in the Ringerike style. Finally, there is good evidence for trade and commerce, especially the finds of amber, walrus ivory and soapstone.

St Peter's Church, Waterford, from the east, showing the twelfth-century nave, chancel and apse.

(food refuse) and sawn pieces of red deer antler. The latter represent waste from comb-makers' workshops. A decorated leather scabbard was also found. Pottery imported from the Ham Green kilns in Bristol and from North Wiltshire shows that the people of Waterford had close trading contacts with the people of Bristol long before the arrival of the Norman armies.

Much of the archaeological evidence supports our sketchy historical references. Stone walls, for example, formed a significant part of the defences, and this corroborates Giraldus Cambrensis' description of the city as walled. The town fortifications were strong — it took Raymond Le Gros and Strongbow's forces three assaults to capture the city. Reginald's Tower, which is in a thirteenth-century Anglo-Norman style, may indeed have been built on the site of an earlier Viking tower or bastion, or may even incorporate parts of an earlier structure, for it is recorded that Ragnall, Prince of the Danes of Waterford, and Malachy O'Faelain, Prince of Decies, were imprisoned there by the Normans in AD 1171. The building of substantial stone towers was well within the capacity of the people who built the twelfth-century stone ramparts.

We know that the pre-Norman city of Waterford contained a number of churches. St Olaf's and St Peter's were close to the cathedral. These were probably in existence as places of worship by the early twelfth century, as the Viking inhabitants of Waterford had become Christians in the previous century. In AD 1096 the people of Waterford city established their own diocese and Malchus was consecrated Bishop of Waterford at Canterbury.

St Peter's church and graveyard lie immediately inside the ramparts. The earliest building may have been of wood, as several post-holes occurred in association with a group of burials in simple earth-cut graves, and two burials covered with charcoal. Charcoal-filled graves are commonly found in English Saxon contexts, but these are the first recorded examples from Ireland. By the early twelfth century the first stone building of St Peter's had begun.

Burials in stone-lined graves were placed around the church. The cemetery to the south of the church was delineated by a wooden fence. Shortly afterwards (c. early to mid-twelfth century) a stone apse was added to the eastern end of the church, simultaneously with, or slightly later than, the addition of the stone nave.

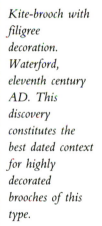

Gold ring-brooch, probably English, with filigree and glass decoration. Thirteenth century AD.

Kite-brooch with filigree decoration. Waterford, eleventh century AD. This discovery constitutes the best dated context for highly decorated brooches of this type.

Motif- or trial-piece found in the aisle of a wattle house in Waterford.

The semicircular apse is the only one of its kind associated with a parish church in Ireland — the Irish of this period never adopted this Roman-inspired architectural feature, preferring simple rectangular churches. Apses occur in Saxon contexts in Britain, and frequently on late eleventh or early twelfth-century Norman English churches. It is noteworthy that several apses dated to the tenth century were discovered at Winchester, where Malchus, the first bishop of Waterford, had been a Benedictine monk.

The occurrence of the apse and earlier charcoal burials emphasises the close connections which must have existed between Waterford and England during the eleventh and twelfth centuries — a point emphasised by their domestic architecture which, particularly in houses with floors sunk below ground-level, follows a style current in eleventh-century England.

The majority of the Late Viking Age houses were, however, rectangular, wattle-walled, three-aisled structures, very similar to those found at Fishamble Street in Dublin. The development of houses and streets was influenced by the topography. Two main streets ran parallel along the crest of the hill, where their modern counterparts, Peter Street and High Street, still follow roughly the same routes.

Houses fronted the streets, but not in a regular contiguous line as street fronts are today. A considerable variation in the placement and angle of the houses occurs from period to period, and not every available street front property was constantly occupied by a house. Several

houses also occurred in areas away from the streets, to which no access by path or laneway was apparent. Behind the street-front houses, several smaller houses may have provided additional sleeping accommodation.

A 16m (52½ft) length of the original surface of Peter Street was uncovered. The earliest paved surface was of late eleventh century date and was made from closely set small stones and gravel. The street, at least 2.6m (8½ft) in width, led to a gateway in the City Wall. Here the wall terminated in ashlar blocks, giving an opening of 1.7m (5½ft) wide, with no apparent additional defensive features.

The artifacts recovered from the recent excavations cover a period from the tenth to the seventeenth century. Objects of the twelfth to the fourteenth century are by far the most numerous — amongst these is a gold brooch of thirteenth-century date. Objects from the Viking Age are comparatively few, mostly plain bronze dress pins and pottery, but in one pit a spectacular kite-shaped brooch of the eleventh century was found. On one house floor a decorated bone was discovered, with a motif which was carved possibly prior to working the design in precious metals.

The Vikings of Waterford may, however, have looked to England and north-west France for their fashions in clothing, the same sources from which they obtained most of their pottery in the eleventh and early twelfth centuries.

We are gradually building up a picture of a city which expanded from the Late Viking Age (c. AD 1000) onwards. The search for the earliest settlements must await excavations in other areas. For now, we know that Waterford was densely populated, well defended, Christianised and prosperous. Most of the trade and economic contacts were with England and north-west France, whence the cultural and architectural inspirations were derived.

House types

Six semi-underground houses or 'sunken featured structures' have been excavated in Waterford, two of which were represented by entrances. All the structures are dug into the gravel to a depth of over 1m (3ft) and the upcast spread to form a low bank around them. They are characterised by impressive stone-built entrances, leading down a corridor into a rectangular chamber.

Reconstruction drawing of a sunken-featured house.

House 1 on Peter Street is the best preserved example. The walls are of radially split ash staves set vertically. The use of this floor as a dwelling is unlikely, as there is no hearth. The thickness of the wall staves and the large number of substantial wooden 'roof supports' suggest that the structure may have carried an upper storey. This may have been a dwelling above ground, possibly entered from the street, with a cellar partly below ground, with access from the back yard.

Two similar buildings adjacent to Olaf Street were entered from a common yard. Both buildings had the scant remains of very decayed timber walls, and both had hearths in the centre of the floor. House 2 had an entrance down a flight of stone steps. A slot set in the floor at the south-west corner may have been the base for a loom. All the structures of this type had been infilled with gravel from the low banks which encircled them, sometime in the mid-twelfth century. Similar buildings have been excavated in many English towns, including York and London, and occur widely throughout Europe. One possible example has been found in Dublin. Two or three found in Limerick probably date to the late eleventh century, and were backfilled in the twelfth century.

The most abundant form of habitation remains were clay floored, wattle-walled houses. These were excellently preserved and consisted mostly of the three-aisled type also found in Dublin. Stratigraphic sequences of these consisted of up to seven houses superimposed, with bracken bedding still in situ. They date from the eleventh century to the mid-twelfth century. The subsequent houses were predominantly of timber. Strong beams were laid horizontally as base plates, and upright planks slotted into a central groove in the beam formed the walls. Such timber houses have been dated to the twelfth century by dendrochronology, although current evidence points towards an overlap of the two styles throughout the twelfth century. An unusual structure was a rectangular stone edifice which had contemporary wooden beams inserted around the perimeter, presumably to support a wooden superstructure. Historical references seem to indicate that this could be the remains of the Hospital of St John, first referred to in historical records in AD 1212. (The dendrochronological dates complement this suggestion, producing a date of AD 1160 ± 9.)

The 11th-12th century Renaissance in metalwork

Raghnall Ó Floinn

Great artistic achievements can rarely be sustained over a long period, and inevitably fall into decline. This occurred in Ireland in the eighth/ninth century, and in the succeeding century only the high crosses compare in quality with earlier work. In the eleventh and twelfth centuries, that is, between the Battle of Clontarf and the coming of the Normans, a great revival in craftsmanship took place. The building of great churches in stone was perhaps the most dramatic expression of this change, but masterpieces such as the Cross of Cong were also produced which rival those of earlier centuries.

The reasons for this revival are to be found in the political and ecclesiastical history of the period. By a series of political alliances and military conquests, Brian Boru claimed, in the year 1005, to be King of Ireland (Imperator Scottorum). While this was not strictly true, he did initiate a process of gradual centralisation of power among a small number of provincial dynasties, who contended for control of the whole country over the next two centuries. At the same time, teaching and intellectual activity had revived in the monasteries after the raids of the tenth century. These, too, flowered in a few important establishments such as Armagh, Clonmacnoise, Kildare and Lismore, which could attract the support of powerful royal patrons. The movement to establish in Ireland a system of centralised church organisation, based on territorial dioceses, in line with the rest of the Christian world, was actively encouraged by Irish kings such as the O'Briens, who saw the opportunity to gain prestige and influence by granting lands to the church and by endowing the new ecclesiastical centres with buildings and rich furnishings.

Almost all of the highly decorated metalwork which survives from the period belonged to the church, and consists of shrines or reliquaries associated with early Irish saints. Some of these contained the bones of saints

(top left)
The Shrine of St
Patrick's Bell.
(see p215)

(top right)
Reverse of the
crest of the
Shrine of St
Patrick's Bell,
showing a
stylised version of
the ancient
Christian symbol
of two peacocks
flanking a vine.

(above)
Detail of one of
the ornamental
plates on the
twelfth-century
shrine, the Breac
Moedóic, from
Drumlane,
County Cavan.

(bottom left)
Bell shrine from
Glankeen,
County
Tipperary.
(see p215)

(bottom right)
Bronze crosier,
found in Lismore
Castle, County
Waterford, in
1814.
(see p215)

(near left)
The Shrine of St
Lachtin's Arm.
(see p215)

(opposite page)
The Cross of
Cong.
(see p215)

but, more commonly, objects associated with them, such as books or bells. Crosiers used by abbots and bishops were in later centuries venerated as relics. These objects, because of their associations, were spared from being melted down, and many were entrusted to a particular family of hereditary keepers and passed from generation to generation down to modern times. Many others, such as the famous *Bachall Íosa* or 'Staff of Jesus' — a crosier associated with St Patrick — were destroyed during the Reformation.

Secular metalwork lacked such saintly associations and was inevitably consigned to the crucible. Recent archaeological excavations in the towns founded by the Vikings in the tenth century are gradually providing information on the craft workshops and the ornaments and other possessions of wealthy lay people of the period. An example of this is the silver kite-brooch decorated with gold filigree and glass studs recently found in excavations at Waterford.

We know quite a lot about how such fine craftsmanship in metal was organised from historical

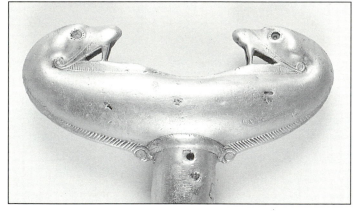

A crosier of tau-form from County Kilkenny, the only surviving example of its kind from ancient Ireland. Later eleventh or twelfth century.

sources, archaeological excavations and from inscriptions on the objects themselves. Most of the workshops were located in the great monasteries, although many of the craftsmen were lay people. Work was commissioned directly from these workshops. For example, in the year 1090 the relics of St Colum Cille were sent by the kings of Tirconnell along with 120 ounces of silver to the monastery of Kells, County Meath, to be enshrined. The work may well have been undertaken by the craftsman Sitric, whose name is found on the book-shrine known as the Cathach, made to enclose a manuscript also associated with St Colum Cille. The craft of the goldsmith was an hereditary one, as was the case with other professions in Ireland. The delicate work on the

Shrine of St Patrick's Bell was carried out by two generations of the same family, whose names are recorded on the backplate of the shrine.

The designs used to decorate these objects seem to have been largely inspired by earlier work. The book-shrine known as the *Soiscél Molaise*, re-made about AD 1000, seems to derive the layout of its cover from a manuscript of earlier date, while its use of gold filigree work and coloured stones against a silver background is reminiscent of the multi-coloured effect seen on earlier work, such as the Ardagh Chalice.

All the complete crosiers which have survived date from this period. The characteristic form of curved crook and short staff decorated with bosses or knops goes back to the eighth century, but new metal-working techniques are employed. The Clonmacnoise Crosier, for example, is decorated with inlaid strips of silver and niello (a black paste-like substance) which highlights the pattern of curving animals against the plain bronze surface. Also new is the use of twists of silver and copper wire, and of silver wires against a dark niello background, seen on the bell-shrine from Glankeen, County Tipperary.

New forms of object directly inspired by continental models were also being made. The shrine of St Lachtin's arm is one of the earliest dated examples of a type common throughout Medieval Europe. Made of plates of bronze inlaid with silver and niello interlaced animals, it takes the form of a clenched forearm which originally contained the saint's bones in a hollow in its wooden core. The magnificent shrine of St Manchan, the largest and most impressive of our surviving reliquaries, is comparable in size and decoration with many of the great continental tomb-shrines of the Romanesque period. The cast panels of interlaced animals and the bright yellow enamels found on this shrine are so similar to those on the Cross of Cong that both were probably made in the same workshop, which was located at a monastery west of the Shannon, perhaps at Roscommon or Tuam. The Cross of Cong was made under the patronage of Turlough O'Connor, king of Connacht, to enshrine a portion of the True Cross given to him as a gift from the pope.

The scale and technical brilliance of pieces such as the Cross of Cong and St Manchan's shrine indicate the level of prestige which royal patronage of the arts had reached in Ireland in the twelfth century, an achievement which was never to be surpassed in later centuries.

Cormac's Chapel, Cashel, County Tipperary. (see p215)

The Romanesque style in Ireland

Roger Stalley

Romanesque art became established in Ireland with the building of Cormac's Chapel on the rock of Cashel, County Tipperary, between 1127 and 1134. Erected under the patronage of the king of Munster, this small but prestigious oratory reflected the new, outward-looking approach of the Irish Church. Among the craftsmen who came to Cashel were at least some foreigners, including both masons and painters from England. A grandiose consecration ceremony held in 1134 underlined what an exceptional monument this was — the first time that Romanesque had been seen in Ireland in its full glory. Over the next few decades the techniques employed at Cashel were gradually absorbed into the repertoire of local masons, producing that unique blend of Romanesque which is distinctive to Ireland.

In Europe, Romanesque architecture is associated with the clear definition of the various parts of a building, the enlivening of walls with arcades and attached columns, and the accentuation of architectural forms by sculptured ornament — all features clearly illustrated at Cashel. The use of well-cut stone or 'ashlar' is another important facet of the style. Indeed, one way of distinguishing the twelfth-century round towers of Ireland from those built in earlier centuries is through the excellent quality of their masonry. Wherever possible, sandstone was preferred to the more widespread carboniferous limestones, as the latter are so much tougher to shape and carve.

Where Hiberno-Romanesque differs most markedly from the European approach is in the tiny scale of the churches, reflecting a long established antipathy on the part of Irish churchmen to the monumental architecture found abroad. 'We are Irish, not Gauls' cried one critic when St Malachy tried to build something more imposing at Bangor, County Down, in 1140. It was left to foreign monastic orders, particularly the Cistercians, to build on a grander scale, as at Baltinglass in County Wicklow, Boyle in County Roscommon, and Jerpoint, County Kilkenny. While the austere Cistercians built their plain but monumental churches, the ancient monasteries of Ireland constructed small but exquisitely decorated chapels, furnished with ornate doorways and chancel arches, as at Clonmacnoise in County Offaly, Tuam in County Galway, or Killaloe, County Clare. In addition, the older monasteries revived the concept of the free-standing high cross, though altering its form to suit the preoccupations of the twelfth century.

In place of the traditional Irish doorway, surmounted by a flat lintel stone, the typical Hiberno-Romanesque portal consists of several orders of sculptured arches supported on shafts or pilasters, a structured approach introduced from abroad. The use of semicircular tympana filling the space immediately under the arch is rare and, as in western France, this gives more prominence to the arches above. In the southern half of Ireland there are seven doorways which were surmounted by gables,

The high cross of Dysert O'Dea, County Clare, one of several twelfth-century crosses depicting Christ crucified together with an ecclesiastic.

The stones of the portal at Clonfert are densely engraved with patterns, some native, others foreign in origin.

A panel of two affronted beasts enmeshed in interlace, from the cross at Dysert O'Dea.

that at Clonfert in County Galway being notoriously steep and bizarre. A study of the techniques used by the sculptors reveals some interesting contrasts. Deeply cut forms are often found alongside subtle surface relief, as if the masons were merely drawing on the stone. The latter technique, which is very obvious at Killeshin, County Laois, and Tuam (market cross), County Galway, suggests that the chief task of the masons was to provide a guide for the painters. The importance of colour in Romanesque art is now hard to imagine, but the restoration of the wall paintings in Cormac's Chapel at Cashel is a reminder of how closely the arts were integrated in the Romanesque era. This includes metalwork, for several motifs favoured by the sculptors — biting heads and animal interlace for example — seem to have been inspired by the art of the goldsmith. The market cross at Tuam was, in effect, an attempt to reproduce the Cross of Cong on a gigantic scale in stone.

Given the sophisticated religious subjects found on the earlier high crosses, it is a surprise that figure sculpture played only a secondary role in Hiberno-Romanesque. Christian scenes can be found at Ardmore, County Waterford, Kilteel, County Dublin, and elsewhere, but there are no extensive programmes of iconography such as those found in France or Italy. On the high crosses of the twelfth century, attention was focussed on two large images depicting the crucified Christ and a bishop, the latter apparently chosen to assert episcopal authority at a time when new diocesan structures were being implemented.

The state of research

The sources exploited by the Irish masons were diverse and many buildings, in addition to Cormac's Chapel, reveal knowledge of foreign techniques. English Romanesque certainly had a major impact, as seen in the popularity of chevron or zig zag ornament, but French, German and Italian sources have also been suggested. Ideas from abroad were blended with indigenous motifs to produce a splendid if rather heterogeneous mix. On occasions there are hints of designs found in illuminated manuscripts, such as the Book of Kells, and the Irish version of the Urnes style, so prominent in metalwork, was frequently exploited by the sculptors. The delineation of human figures also reveals a well-established Irish pedigree.

Ongoing discoveries

Several aspects of Hiberno-Romanesque are still poorly understood. The routes by which foreign influences entered the country remain unclear, and so too do the relationships between the sculptors and other artists. It is not obvious where the major workshops were located or the extent to which regional 'schools' can be defined. Many important monuments have been lost, not least an outstanding portal built at Derry in 1155 by Flathbertach Ó Brolcháin. Indeed the well-preserved carvings in the chancel at Tuam were only saved when the Gothic rebuilding of the cathedral ground to a halt in the fourteenth century. A number of extant doorways have been reconstructed in more recent times and careful observation is needed to establish their original form. Even tiny fragments of Romanesque carving can sometimes be important. Quite recently, a piece of chevron was found at Inch Abbey, County Down, which confirmed the existence of an earlier Romanesque church on the site before the Cistercian monks arrived. No doubt, more Romanesque carving will come to light in the future, like the superb sculptures found at Devenish in County Fermanagh a few years ago when a graveyard wall was dismantled. In cases like this, careful measurement and calculation can go some way towards reconstructing the form of lost doorways and arches.

It is a fallacy to imagine that Romanesque was suddenly brought to a halt by the Anglo-Norman invasion of 1169—70. West of the Shannon Romanesque traditions continued until well into the thirteenth century, and carvings by one outstanding master at Boyle and Ballintober in County Roscommon can be dated between 1215 and 1225. Even the 'baroque' doorways of Killaloe, County Clare, and Clonfert, County Galway, are now thought to have been carved long after the invasion. In Leinster the Anglo-Norman settlers brought craftsmen of their own, and the English style carvings of Christ Church Cathedral in Dublin make a telling comparison with some of the soft, shallowly incised sculpture at Tuam or Ballintober. Hiberno-Romanesque art is thus full of contrasts and, with its diverse origins and varied expression, it represents one of the most delightful episodes in the history of Irish art.

The Romanesque portal of Clonfert Cathedral, County Galway, is one of seven Irish doorways with a gable above.

Boyle Abbey, County Roscommon. (see p215)

VI
The Later Medieval period

The Viking Age effectively came to an end in the early eleventh century when trade became the main focus of activity for the mixed Scandinavian townspeople. The links which had been established between colonies in the age of freebooters remained strong, and relations between England and towns such as Dublin and Waterford were especially close — this can be seen in their coinage, trade goods, art styles and also in political and ecclesiastical relationships. The towns were, however, dominated politically by native Irish kings, whose puppet kings or new-style officials controlled the settlements. Some Irish kings began to modernise, to issue charters and to develop an embryonic administration along the lines of mainstream European monarchy, a process which cut across ancient tribal and dynastic rivalries. One such king was Diarmait MacMorrough, King of Leinster, who was forced to flee his kingdom in 1166. He sought support from Henry II of England to restore his fortunes. Henry permitted some of his subjects to help, and in 1169 an advance party of Anglo-Normans arrived from south Wales, with followers drawn from England, France and Flanders. These were followed a year later by a stronger force under Richard de Clare (Strongbow), Earl of Pembroke. Thus began a process of conquest which saw the Anglo-Norman colony dominate most of the island. The initial success of the conquerors alarmed the king and Ireland was designated a lordship. Henry assigned it to his youngest son, John, and the outlines of a royal administration were developed.

The dynamic of the conquest was the need to find more and more land to reward followers. Security from attacks by the natives was of paramount importance, and castles were both the chief weapon of conquest and the best guarantee of long-term defence. For the Irish with their fragmented political system of rival kingdoms, a unified response was virtually unthinkable, and historians have failed to identify a convincing revival which was any more than local and short-term. The Anglo-Norman magnates ruled huge areas of territory and leading Irish kings frequently submitted to them. In areas of intensive colonisation the Irish were marginalised, but they clearly survived in large numbers, although little is known of their settlements. Elsewhere they survived with their social order more or less intact until the Tudor conquest. Native landholding practices may have influenced the way the new lords ruled their lands, but their need for settlers led them to charter new towns and to encourage immigrants from England. These newcomers were offered the privileges of burgesses — an early experiment in plantation. Archaeology is beginning to reveal the extent of this kind of settlement. Despite the considerable plantation of settlers, by the fourteenth century the Irish parliament felt the need to legislate against the colonists who were adopting native practices. By the sixteenth century many great Anglo-Norman lords were behaving very much like Irish chieftains.

The history of the Later Medieval period is complex, with changing economic and political fortunes, calamities such as the Black Death, climatic deterioration leading to a contraction of usable land, and constant warfare. The castles, abbeys and churches of the time are visible reminders of the changes wrought by the invasion. But there are more subtle influences, such as the basis of our legal system. Indeed many of the traditions and practices of government can be traced to the culture of the Anglo-Normans.

The lavabo (wash house) of Mellifont Abbey, County Louth.
(see p215)

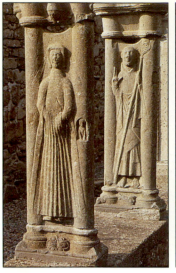

Jerpoint Abbey, County Kilkenny. (see p215)

The 'cadaver' effigy at Beaulieu, County Louth, with the skeleton infested by vermin, provides a stark reminder of the fleeting nature of earthly existence.

Late Medieval armour, as seen on the tomb of Pierce FitzOge Butler, who died in 1526, at Kilcooley Abbey, County Tipperary. (see p215)

The face of Piers Butler, eighth earl of Ormond, from his tomb in St Canice's Cathedral, Kilkenny, c. 1539. (see p215)

Gothic art and architecture

Roger Stalley

The settlement of large parts of Ireland by Anglo-Norman colonists led inevitably to the spread of English Gothic art and architecture. Among the hundreds of craftsmen who found their way to Ireland after 1170, were many stonemasons trained in English workshops. As a result, during the thirteenth century Irish Gothic design was almost indistinguishable from that in England. This was a boom period in Irish building, as new cathedrals, monasteries and parish churches were constructed in an optimistic economic climate. While Irish churches rarely attained the monumental scale of their English counterparts, except in Dublin, there are many buildings which were well abreast of English fashion. This situation continued for as long as people crossed the Irish sea with regularity.

As the end of the thirteenth century approached, the flow of immigrant masons diminished, and knowledge of English techniques became increasingly distant and remote. The lack of investment in building in the fourteenth century, due to economic decline, war, famine and pestilence, encouraged a more introspective approach to design. When things improved in the fifteenth century, there seems to have been little direct contact with England, at least outside the Pale. Whereas Ireland wholeheartedly adopted Early English Gothic in the thirteenth century, it largely ignored Perpendicular, the English Late Gothic style of the fifteenth century. Instead, Irish masons produced their own eclectic version of Gothic, an amalgam of past and present, described by one authority as an 'Irish national style'. This is a rather grandiose description, but there is no denying that Irish Late Gothic has a distinctive character of its own. Gothic art in Ireland thus falls into two distinct eras, separated by the social and economic traumas of the mid-fourteenth century.

Monasteries

There is no agreement about which building deserves to be regarded as the first Gothic design in Ireland, but

172

Rosserk Friary, County Mayo. (see p216)

one monument with a strong claim is the Cistercian abbey of Grey in County Down. Founded in 1193 by the wife of John de Courcy, the conqueror of Ulster, Grey is a good illustration of the wave of new building that took place after the Anglo-Norman invasion. By international standards its design reveals a relatively muted form of Gothic: there are no ribbed vaults — the stone roofs reinforced by thin ribs, which are such a striking feature of Gothic architecture abroad — and the plan of the church is very simple. But unmistakably Gothic is the character of the tall pointed windows which fill the east wall of the chancel. Grey was colonised from Holm Cultram in Cumbria, and its design is linked with Early Gothic architecture in the north of England.

Throughout Ireland, the abbeys of monasteries with English affiliations were built in the 'Early English' style, some on a more sophisticated scale than Grey Abbey. The monks at Graiguenamanagh, County Kilkenny, erected a huge church, with an elegant rib-vaulted chancel, and the stark and cavernous abbey church at Dunbrody in County Wexford is almost as large. In all these buildings it is easy to spot the vocabulary of English Gothic — the use of dog-tooth ornament around doors and arches, the regular employment of stylised leaf carvings, and the delight in detached circular shafts fitted to doors and windows. The foundation of a Cistercian monastery was an expensive undertaking, since the monks required substantial estates which they could farm themselves. Equally popular with Anglo-Norman lords were Augustinian houses, which often had smaller communities and did not necessarily require heavy investment. Such was Kells, County Kilkenny, one of the few Medieval monasteries to have been thoroughly excavated in recent years. It started in a small way when Geoffrey de Marisco brought four canons from Bodmin in Cornwall in 1193 but, as the excavations made clear, it eventually expanded into a very substantial monastery.

Tombs

One advantage to men like Geoffrey de Marisco in founding a monastery was that they acquired a secure and dignified place of burial, where prayers would be said for their souls long after death. In many cases the benefactors and their descendants commissioned costly tombs, a few of which have survived relatively unscathed. One of the best is the Cantwell effigy at Kilfane, County Kilkenny, the largest of its kind in Ireland and Britain. The Cantwells came to Ireland from Suffolk in the late twelfth century, and acquired a number of estates in Kilkenny and Tipperary. Although it is not clear which member of the family is commemorated by the great cross-legged effigy, it was carved in a mid-thirteenth-century style by a sculptor trained in an English west country workshop. Its design is similar to the famous tomb in Salisbury Cathedral belonging to Longespee, Earl of Salisbury, who died in 1225. There is another outstanding cross-legged effigy, dating from *c.* 1300, at Graiguenamanagh, this time carved in higher relief, with a greater sense of energy. The tomb chests of these early effigies rarely survive, but from Athassel Abbey in County Tipperary comes a marvellous tomb frontal (now moved to Cashel), carved with miniature knights, arranged in delicate and vivacious poses. Interestingly, the stone employed came from Dundry, near Bristol, and it is possible that the work was imported to Ireland ready carved.

Dundry stone

Dundry stone was employed extensively along the south

The well-preserved cloisters at Muckross, County Kerry. (see p216)

and east coasts of Ireland and, although it may seem odd to import heavy quantities of stone from England, it made economic sense. The quarries at Dundry supplied a good yellow limestone, easy to work, and as long as the building sites were close to the sea or a river, it was not too expensive to transport. In 1251 a consignment awaiting shipment to St Thomas's Abbey in Dublin was purloined by the sheriff of Bristol. Dundry stone was employed only for details and not wasted on plain walls. Both of the Dublin cathedrals made extensive use of it, along with polished shafts of 'marble', which may also have been imported from the Bristol Channel area.

Dublin's Gothic cathedrals

The two Dublin cathedrals are the high point of Gothic architecture in Ireland, and their designs are intriguing to compare. The nave of Christ Church (c. 1215–35) is contemporary with the start of St Patrick's, where construction was under way by 1225. Both cathedrals employed ribbed vaults over the main spans of the buildings, supported in the English fashion without flying buttresses (all the flyers there today have been added). In the later Middle Ages the fabric of both buildings was neglected, and catastrophic collapses occurred in the sixteenth century. The heavy restorations required in the nineteenth century have meant that the architecture of neither building has been taken as seriously as it deserves. Both designs incorporated three-storey elevations, with passages running along the wall in both the upper storeys, and there is an abundance of intricate mouldings and stiff leaf capitals. At Christ Church, the carving of heads amidst the capitals of the main supporting piers provide vital clues about the origin of the masons, for exactly the same hand can be tracked down in the village church at Overbury in Worcestershire. The master mason responsible for the nave of Christ Church was a gifted designer. The proportions of the building are carefully calculated and the upper storeys are neatly integrated together, in a fashion reminiscent of some French monuments. With its wall passages, ornate mouldings, deeply cut capitals and polished shafts, the Christ Church nave was a rich and characteristic example of Early English Gothic.

Other church buildings

Neither Christ Church nor St Patrick's exerted much influence elsewhere in Ireland, for they were too complex to help in the design of more humble buildings. Most Irish Medieval cathedrals were small, especially when compared with their French or English counterparts. One reason for this is that there were simply too many dioceses for the wealth available, a situation which resulted from the political fragmentation that existed when the diocesan structure was first established.

One cathedral church that did attempt something more ambitious was Tuam, County Galway, head of the archdiocese that covered Connacht. Around 1300, a new Gothic building was begun well to the east of the small Romanesque church. A new chancel was finished, complete with geometrical tracery patterns in the windows, and foundations for the transepts were prepared. But at this point work came to a halt, and the old Romanesque chancel sits where the Gothic crossing should have been. What caused the abandonment of Tuam cathedral is not known, but it must have had something to do with the economic difficulties of the fourteenth century. In 1312 the canons of the cathedral were searching, rather desperately, for financial aid, to help finish their church. Although a certain amount of building was carried out at this time, particularly by the friars, there were no major projects to compare with the Dublin cathedrals. Indeed many monasteries found it difficult to maintain their existing buildings. At Inch Abbey, County Down, the tower apparently collapsed at some point in the later Middle Ages, and instead of rebuilding it, the monks were content to abandon most of the church, fitting up the chancel and crossing area as a small chapel. The abbreviation of large unwanted buildings was not unique to Inch and there are plenty of examples in Ireland, Scotland and the north of England. The most dramatic case is at Athassel, the huge thirteenth-century abbey near Cashel, where the spacious early Gothic nave was also abandoned at some point after 1300.

The outstanding piece of Late Gothic architecture in Ireland is Holycross Abbey, County Tipperary, where the Cistercian monks were able to fund an extensive remodelling of their abbey on the proceeds of the pilgrimage to its precious relics. The relics were almost certainly displayed in the tomb-like structure in the south transept, an exquisite piece of architecture, furnished with spiral columns and a miniature vault. Parts of the church were covered by heavy ribbed vaults, of a type found elsewhere in the Tipperary/Kilkenny region. The windows were filled with a perplexing variety of tracery, most of it curvilinear in design. These flowing patterns had been all the rage in England a hundred years before, and it is puzzling that they took so long to become fashionable in Ireland. Scottish architecture reveals a similar preference for curvilinear patterns at this time, as if both countries were keen to reject the current Perpendicular style of England. There are in fact some quite specific links between Late Gothic architecture in Ireland and Scotland, not least the employment of tracery without cusps (the projecting points usually included in the tracery patterns), an approach which became fashionable in both countries in the sixteenth century.

Perhaps the most distinctive feature of Irish Late Gothic is the masonry itself. For the most part, builders were happy to use the hard native limestones, though chisels and axes must have required constant resharpening. Mouldings and sculptural details retain almost the same precision they had when they left the masons' bench. This is obvious on the polygonal corbels, habitually used to support the inner order of Late Gothic arches. Such corbels are found at Devenish, County Fermanagh, where the Augustinian canons rebuilt their tower about 1500 and added a finely moulded west door, complete with a carved head at the apex. All of this was executed in the hard blue-grey local limestone, which contrasts with the softer orange sandstone used slightly earlier in the church by the master mason Matthew Ó Dubigan.

Funerary monuments

Masons skilled at carving the hard limestones also produced a series of fine funerary monuments, of a distinctive Irish type. These consist of a tomb chest surrounded by figures of the apostles, an iconography which is not common elsewhere. Two workshops were active in the Kilkenny region about 1500, one of them led by the sculptor Rory O'Tunney. The other workshop, the so-called Ormond school, was responsible for a magnificent series of effigies of the earls of Ormond and their families. Like many Late Medieval Irish effigies, the style of the figures is puzzling, since the earls are shown in a type of armour which was outmoded in Europe at this time. The earls were well-travelled individuals, so they cannot have been ignorant of contemporary fashions abroad. Was the style deliberately retrospective, in order to stress the dynastic lineage of

The nave of Christ Church Cathedral, Dublin.
(see p215)

the earls, or was the continued wearing of such mail more suited to Irish warfare, as some authorities have suggested? Whatever the answer, the sculpture of the Ormond school is a delight to study, more neo-Romanesque than Gothic in style, with its smiling faces and clearly delineated features.

Friaries

The most active ecclesiastical builders of the later Middle Ages were the friars, particularly in the rural west. The two main orders of friars, the Dominicans and Franciscans, had been founded in the thirteenth century with the aim, in contrast to the older monastic orders, of ministering to the common people through preaching and pastoral care. In England, very little of their architecture survives, so the well-preserved Irish friaries at places like Muckross, County Kerry, Askeaton, County Limerick, Quin, County Clare, Kilconnell, County Galway, Rosserilly, Moyne and Rosserk, County Mayo, are of quite exceptional interest.

During the fifteenth century many new friaries were founded, especially within the Franciscan order, and donations, which in England might have been channelled into parish churches, went to the friars. Most memorable are the slender belfries, built on haunches between the

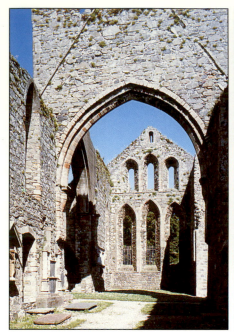

With its pointed lancet windows, the church at Grey Abbey, County Down, is one of the first Gothic buildings in Ireland.

Athassel Abbey, County Tipperary. (see p215)

(opposite, centre) St Canice's Cathedral, thirteenth century, with the round tower of the Early Medieval monastery on which the cathedral was built. The street plan in its vicinity should be compared with that of Lusk, County Dublin, and of Armagh.

chancel and nave. The laity were accommodated in the nave of the church, which was sometimes provided with an aisle, and often had a south transept, producing a lop-sided plan which is characteristic of friary architecture. The small cloisters, several of which survive beautifully intact, are usually placed to the north. At Rosserk in County Mayo, Bonamargy in County Antrim, and elsewhere, there are no signs of stone cloister arcades, which suggests that the cloister walks must have been timber structures. In such cases archaeological investigation would be of great value in establishing their original design.

Timber played a more important role in religious architecture than is commonly realised. Many of the outbuildings in monasteries and friaries were made of wood and, when a house was first founded, temporary timber churches may have been erected. In some Cistercian abbeys timber cloisters were probably not uncommon, and it was only in the fifteenth century, after two centuries of decay, that they were replaced in stone. This seems to be the explanation for the extensive amount of cloister construction carried out in the fifteenth century, particularly by the Cistercians.

The most ornate of all Irish cloisters is that at Jerpoint, County Kilkenny, where the dumb-bell piers supporting the arches were decorated with an array of human figures — apostles, ecclesiastics, knights and aristocratic ladies. It is a measure of the worldly atmosphere pervading the cloister that the Cistercian monks felt it appropriate to decorate the inner sanctum of their monastery in this way.

Another outstanding cloister was discovered by chance in Dublin in 1975, when a seventeenth-century wall was being demolished in Cook Street. It appears that stones from one of the city's monastic houses had been salvaged after the dissolution of the monasteries. When the fragmentary stones were reassembled, a beautiful arcade in the English Perpendicular style came to light. It is likely that it came from the wealthy Cistercian house of St Mary's, a monastery with English connections, where this type of design might be expected. St Mary's, which lay just to the west of Capel Street, was one of the most cosmopolitan of all Irish institutions, a point reflected in the fine wooden Madonna, which the monks purchased from a north German or Flemish workshop about 1500.

Recent archaeological discoveries

The Dublin cloister is a reminder of how important archaeology will be in the future if more is to be discovered about the evolution of Irish art and architecture. In many cases the plans of important buildings, not least the first Cistercian monastery at Mellifont, County Louth, are known only through excavation. Until relatively recently, however, archaeologists were concerned principally with establishing the lines of foundation walls and (to use a favourite phrase of around 1900) 'digging out the rubbish'. Much evidence about tiled floors, window glass, roof structure, the position of altars and screens, and so forth, may have been lost. Where loose stones are carefully recorded it is sometimes possible to reconstruct windows and arches, and two fine tracery windows at Clontuskert and Athenry, County Galway, have been reassembled in this way. Over the last twenty years the standards of excavation have been far more exacting, and many exciting discoveries have been made, including a delightful cloister arcade at Kells Priory, County Kilkenny. At Moor Abbey in County Tipperary, excavation has revealed what may have been the base of the scaffolding posts used by the Medieval builders, and at Corcomroe, County Clare, incised architectural drawings have been detected on the plaster walls. For religious sites, the biggest archaeological challenge of the future lies in Dublin, where remains of two of the most prestigious monasteries in Ireland, St Mary's and St Thomas's (behind the modern Thomas Street) still lie buried beneath the soil.

The Medieval walls of Fethard, County Tipperary. (see p216)

St Canice's Cathedral (caption opposite page)

Shee Almshouse, Kilkenny. (see p216)

The thirteenth-century barbican of St Laurence's Gate, Drogheda.

Anglo-Norman towns

John Bradley

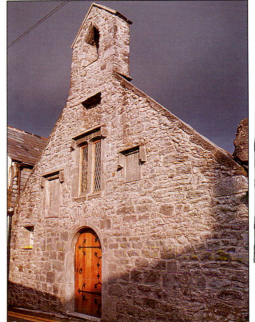

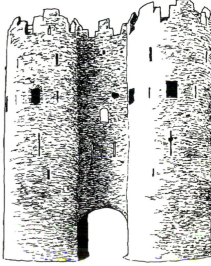

The Anglo-Normans established towns throughout those areas of Ireland which they colonised. The heaviest concentrations occur in the east and south, particularly in the counties of Louth, Meath, Kildare, Kilkenny, Tipperary and Limerick. In the north and west only a handful were established, and their distribution is much more scattered.

The earliest towns were established in the east, where the former Viking ports were expanded, and others were founded beside a number of pre-Norman ecclesiastical sites. The Hiberno-Scandinavian populations of Dublin, Waterford and Wexford were resettled in the early 1170s and their property was taken over by newcomers. By 1176 the important pre-Norman cathedral centres at Ferns, Kildare and Kilkenny had been selected as town sites, and by 1182 Cork began to expand outside the confines of the Viking settlement. Pre-existing settlements exerted a powerful influence on the location of the initial Anglo-Norman towns, but the foundation of new sites on virgin ground shows a clear desire to break away from the constraints of the older settlement pattern.

Drogheda, founded before 1186, is the earliest of the new towns. The original Drogheda (*droichead átha* 'ford of the bridge') was located at the crossing point known

(opposite)
Map of Medieval Kilkenny

Founded as a monastery in the seventh century, the curved alignment of Dean and Vicar Streets preserves the outline of the boundary of the Early Medieval monastic site. (see p216)

A. St Patrick's Church: an Early Medieval foundation.
B. Kilkenny Castle: twelfth and thirteenth century.
C. St Patrick's Tower: a circular thirteenth-century tower on the walls.
D. Magdalen Hospital, founded in the thirteenth century. Its fifteenth-century gatehouse survives.
E. Shee Almshouse, 1582.
F. Augustinian Priory of St John, founded between 1202 and 1211.
G. St Mary's, parish church of the Anglo-Norman town, founded 1202.

(contd. opposite)

today as Oldbridge, but a site 3km (2 miles) to the east was chosen for the new town because it contained a ford and was also much easier to defend; in addition, the site was accessible from the sea. The documents of the time refer to it as the 'new bridge of Drogheda' so as to distinguish it from the old bridge, but in time it came to be known simply as Drogheda. A few towns have retained their new-town status, however. New Ross, Newtown Trim and Newtownards still preserve the nomenclature of those thirteenth-century days when they were innovations in the landscape.

The Anglo-Norman penetration westwards into Tipperary and Limerick in the years after 1185 was followed by a wave of town development. This resulted in the expansion of the Viking port of Limerick and the foundation of towns at older centres, such as Cashel, but it also saw the formation of many new towns. Carrick-on-Suir, Clonmel, Fethard, Adare and Kilmallock were established in the closing years of the twelfth century. Penetration into Kerry in the years after 1215 was followed by the foundation of Tralee and Dingle, but it was not until after 1235 that the Anglo-Normans began to establish towns in Connacht. Galway was founded about 1238, and Sligo, the largest town in the north-west, was established in the early 1240s. Roscommon did not come into being as a town until about 1270, and its refoundation in 1283, after a particularly disastrous attack by the Gaelic Irish, effectively marks the end of Anglo-Norman town foundation in Ireland.

Characteristic features

The typical Anglo-Norman town was defended by walls and entered through gates, such as the magnificent example of St Laurence's in Drogheda. Within the walls there was often just one main street along which lanes and narrower streets were arranged at right angles. The main street generally functioned as the market place, and sometimes it might be expanded at one end, or in the centre, to accommodate the additional stalls and animals on market days.

A market cross set on a plinth was a frequent embellishment, and proclamations and public notices would be read from its foot.

Individual properties, known as burgage plots, were carefully arranged in strips along the streets of the town. These properties consisted of a house on the street

frontage, with outhouses, workshops and gardens behind, stretching back to the end of the plot.

The constraints of space often meant that it was the custom to build houses with their gables fronting onto the street. Access to the houses was gained by going down a lane beside the gable end, and this practice explains the many narrow laneways which are a characteristic feature of Anglo-Norman towns such as Clonmel, Drogheda and Kilkenny.

These towns usually had one parish church, in contrast to the older monastic centres and Viking towns where a multiplicity of churches tended to prevail. Religious houses, particularly friaries and hospitals, were generally located outside the wall, and occasionally suburbs developed in their vicinity.

The fourteenth century: a period of decline

The thirteenth century was the heyday of Anglo-Norman town development, when some fifty to sixty towns were established. By 1300, however, there were already indications of decline. The Gaelic Irish began to attack the towns of the west, particularly in counties Galway, Roscommon and Sligo, and monies to repair and defend them were becoming increasingly hard to find. The population started to migrate, and accounts begin to mention waste and abandoned burgage plots. It was the upheaval accompanying the Bruce invasions of 1315–17, however, together with the destabilising of the north and west which followed the assassination of the de Burgh earl of Ulster in 1333 — whose family had been dominant for some time — that led to the decline of the towns in the region, and in parts of central Ireland. Coleraine, Roscommon, Rindown, Athlone and Mullingar were abandoned, while towns like Carrickfergus and Athenry shrank considerably in size. Even in the more prosperous areas of the east and south, burgage plots were abandoned and properties became derelict.

Fifteenth-century renewal

The fifteenth century is by contrast a century of renewal. It is not marked by the foundation of new towns although there is some evidence to suggest that centres such as Athy and Castledermot were remodelled by Gearóid Mór, the great earl of Kildare, during the later half of the century. Nor is it marked by any suburban expansion outside the Anglo-Norman towns themselves.

Rather, this renewal takes the form of internal development. It is most apparent in the numbers of fortified town houses which were built, in the refortification of town defences, and in the building activities which were renewed in parish churches, friaries, and castles.

Fortified houses are a characteristic feature of Irish towns during this period. Built by merchants and wealthy landholders, both lay and clerical, they were inspired by the tower houses of the countryside. In many towns, such as Dalkey, they survived into the seventeenth and eighteenth centuries, when they were seen and recorded by travellers, and it is from this source that the common tradition of a town having 'seven castles' developed. Good examples still survive at Ardee, Dalkey and Fethard, while the attractive Gaelic Revival decoration on 'The Mint' at Carlingford shows that the fashion continued into the sixteenth century.

The fifteenth century also saw interesting developments within Gaelic Ireland. In particular, the foundation of a number of inland centres, such as Granard, which deflected trade away from the Anglo-Norman towns by setting up regular markets and fairs. In the north-west, largely because of the movement of the herring shoals and the opening up of the wine trade with Spain and Portugal, Sligo witnessed a revival of its fortunes under the patronage of the O'Connors.

End of an era

By the sixteenth century those towns which had survived the vicissitudes of the previous two hundred years were prosperous, and their endurance in relative isolation from the Crown had enabled some of them, like Waterford, Cork and Galway, to develop into virtually autonomous city states. The dissolution of the urban monasteries (1539—40) provided new land for building and development, which many towns were poised to take advantage of. The middle years of the sixteenth century are characterised in some of the towns of the east and south by the emergence of wealthy speculators, such as William Brabazon of Dublin, who made their fortune by developing the former monastic sites for private and commercial uses. The most striking feature of the sixteenth century, however, is the foundation of new towns in the midlands, west and south-west of the country, as part of the English government's policy of conquering Ireland. The earliest of these 'plantation towns' were established in 1556 at Maryborough (Portlaoise) and Phillipstown (Daingean), as part of the plantation of Laois and Offaly. With their formation and the introduction of Renaissance concepts of town layout and defence, the story of Medieval urbanisation in Ireland may be regarded as having drawn to a close.

Medieval Kilkenny

Founded as a church site in the seventh century, Kilkenny (*Cill Chainnigh* 'Canice's Church') expanded, and by the twelfth century it had become a cathedral town under the patronage of the MacGiolla Patraic kings of Ossory. The curving alignment of Dean Street and Vicar Street preserves the outline of the former ecclesiastical boundary of the ancient settlement. The Anglo-Normans established themselves here before 1176 and the town's development over the course of the succeeding century can be traced in a series of stages.

It was laid out along one main street, linking the Anglo-Norman castle with the cathedral, which is still known today by its Medieval name of High Street. The old cathedral town did not form part of the Anglo-

KILKENNY

(contd. from p178)
H. The Medieval marketplace, High Street. Its market cross stood here from 1335 to 1771.
I. A section of the town wall preserving a thirteenth/fourteenth-century arrow-loop.
J. Rothe House, a merchant's residence built in 1594.
K. Black Freren Gate. Only the arch of this gate-house, named after the nearby Dominican (Black Friars) Friary, survives.
L. Dominican Friary, founded about 1225.
M. Franciscan Friary, founded about 1225.
N. St Canice's Cathedral. The street plan in its vicinity should be compared with that of Lusk, County Dublin, and of Armagh.
O. The site of St Maul's Chapel, first mentioned in 1300 but perhaps commemorating an Early Medieval saint.

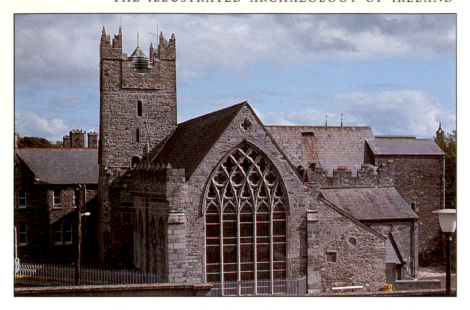

The Dominican Friary, Kilkenny, founded about 1225.
(see p216)

Norman town but it survived as a separate entity, known as Irishtown, with its own corporation until 1843. East of the Nore was the ward of St John's, which was formed around the Augustinian monastery of St John the Evangelist, established between 1202 and 1211. The town was the size shown here by the end of the thirteenth century, when much of the walls had been built. These walls were to define its limits for almost three hundred years, until the 1580s, when it began to expand along Maudlin Street, to the east, on land which had formerly belonged to the dissolved Augustinian monastery.

Rural settlements

Terry Barry

The Anglo-Norman invaders found a country dominated by dispersed rural settlements, apart from the beginnings of urban centres in the Hiberno-Norse ports such as Dublin and Waterford and at some of the larger monasteries like Clonmacnoise, County Offaly, and Kells, County Meath. In the eastern two-thirds of the country they established a network of *nucleated* rural settlements, where houses were located around a central focus. The form and geographical extent of these settlements has yet to be fully established, but in many areas of the Anglo-Norman lordship, especially in counties Kilkenny, Tipperary and Wexford in the south-east, the classic English lowland model of villages was established, with the tenants' houses grouped around a church and castle or manor house.

In Ireland the earthwork traces of deserted Medieval villages have been located, mainly with the help of aerial photography. They can be generally identified by the rectangular layout of the houses and associated plots of land, all focussed upon the remains of a Medieval church or churchyard, a castle or moated site, and a sunken roadway which carried the traffic of the settlement.

Many of these villages were granted charters of rights by their feudal lord, which were intended to attract settlers from the over-populated areas of England, Wales and beyond, in order to consolidate the Anglo-Norman conquest. The charters were nearly always modelled on the one granted to the small town of Breteuil in Normandy; they gave their inhabitants 'burgess status', which fixed their annual rental for their messuages (house and plot of land) at one shilling, allowed them their own court and the right to tax themselves. Thus these burgesses were free from most of the onerous duties required under the feudal system.

These settlements, which were primarily agricultural in function but which were also given borough status, have been called 'rural boroughs'. It is thought that they probably account for a majority of the three hundred or so Medieval boroughs that have been discovered in Ireland. More than fifty Medieval villages with a market have been identified.

Some suggest that the pre-existing townland (smallest administrative area in Ireland) system has meant that these villages or rural boroughs may not be found in all parts of the lordship. They argue that the centre of an Anglo-Norman manor (the smallest self-contained unit in the feudal lordship) was often only marked by the church and the defended house of the manorial lord, with the houses of the tenants scattered around the neighbouring townlands. This was possibly so in parts of County Dublin, in the earldom of Ulster and along the borders of the Anglo-Norman lordship, in areas such as County Westmeath.

However, this virtual plantation of eastern Ireland with manorial villages and rural boroughs is significant for the later settlement history of the country, as many of them are still successful settlements to this day. Their distribution pattern gives us some idea of the density of the Anglo-Norman population, and through a study of the surviving documents the socio-economic framework of these areas can be established. The names, number, and sometimes the trades carried on by the burgesses of the rural boroughs or the principal tenants of the villages can also be seen. Nevertheless, there are limitations, as these sources only list heads of households who own property, so that possible population sizes can only be guessed.

In the western third of the island, which remained under Irish control, it is very difficult to be sure of the pattern of rural settlement because of the lack of research to date. It is probable, however, that the dispersed defended farmsteads, the ring-forts, were still being occupied throughout the Medieval period, and it is arguable that some new ones were being constructed. Some monastic enclosures were occupied, and there were nucleated groups of farms and associated structures which lacked the identifiable service functions of the villages of the Anglo-Norman areas.

With a comparative dearth of contemporary documentary information on the majority of Medieval rural nucleated settlements, archaeology is important in identifying the chronology, layout and function of these villages. However, archaeological excavations on these sites have generally produced limited evidence, possibly because of the small number sampled.

Piperstown

The only identifiable deserted Medieval village in County Louth, at Piperstown, is a complex, seven acres (2.83 hectares) in extent, which is made up of four sub-rectangular platforms and several other irregular enclosures. There are also the remains of a sunken way, and a small motte castle is located on the settlement's eastern margins.

A limited excavation there revealed the very tenuous remains of a mud-walled structure, 8m (26ft) long, with a possible entrance-way in its south wall. Slight traces of burning were found within it, as well as a large drystone flagged drain. Over four hundred artifacts were recovered, most of them brown and black ware pottery of the early eighteenth century, although a number of locally made Medieval pottery sherds were also located. Among the artifacts was one thirteenth century hunting arrowhead. Although it would seem that this settlement was abandoned in the early eighteenth century, it obviously had its origins in the Medieval period.

Ballintotty Tower-House, County Tipperary

Tullahogue, County Tyrone — the inauguration site of the O'Neills of Clandeboye — from an early-

seventeenth-century map. Note the houses within the ring-fort still in use.

Aerial view of the deserted village of Piperstown, County Louth.

Reconstruction drawing of a moated house site. The rectangular earthworks of this type of settlement are very common in the south-eastern counties.

Newtown Jerpoint

Perhaps one of the most comprehensively documented nucleated rural settlements in Ireland is located at Newtown Jerpoint, County Kilkenny, beside the important Cistercian abbey. Its layout is shown on the first edition of the Ordnance Survey's 6-inch map of 1839, and we know from an entry in the Close Roll (copies of letters sent folded and sealed by the Crown) that it was probably founded in *c.* AD 1200 and deserted sometime in the seventeenth century. From a manorial extent of 1289 we know that there were twenty-two principal landowners there, and this corresponds almost exactly with the twenty-three houses shown on the OS map. We can also see that all the dwellings were long houses (their length being more than twice the dimension of their width), typical of deserted Medieval villages in lowland England, and we can trace the gardens associated with each of them. The only building of this settlement to remain above ground, apart from the foundations of a later tower, was the ruined Medieval parish church and the piers of the bridge across the River Nore. The tolls

Aerial view of the deserted Medieval village of Kiltinan, County Kilkenny.

and customs which were levied on commodities crossing the river at this point provided an important income to the burgesses.

From the manorial extent we know of the existence of a mill where the town's inhabitants were obliged to grind their corn, and that a small brew-house was located within the settlement. There is, however, no trace of a manor house or castle surviving at the settlement, although a possible Medieval grange (moated manor house) was excavated in 1973 some distance to the west of the town at Jerpoint Church.

Medieval granges

Unlike lowland England, Medieval granges are not usually found closely associated with nucleated settlements. Altogether seven hundred and fifty possible moated sites have been located cartographically in Ireland and this probably represents a minimum figure for the distribution of such earthworks. They are concentrated within the heartland of the Anglo-Norman lordship, in the south and east of the island, and are usually located more than 3.4km (6 miles) from the nearest known Medieval nucleated settlement. Indeed they are often located on the edges of the Anglo-Norman lordship, in isolation from each other, where their inhabitants would have required the water-filled moat and earthen banks topped with a wooden palisade for protection against external aggressors, be they Irish or Anglo-Norman.

Although only six moated sites have been excavated, they have all produced evidence of occupation in the thirteenth and early fourteenth centuries. At Rigsdale in County Cork, the site occupation was dated to this period both by coins and by polychrome pottery sherds imported from Saintonge in south-western France. All the other artifacts found during the excavation indicated that Rigsdale functioned as a defended farmstead until it was over-run during the Desmond rebellion in the 1320s.

Desertion of the rural settlements

It is not possible to be sure at what exact period the majority of these Anglo-Norman rural settlements were deserted. Despite contemporary accounts of the socio-economic disruption caused by the Great European Famine (1315—17) which coincided with the invasion of Ireland by Edward Bruce, and even more by the bubonic plague, the Black Death, (1348—50) which reduced the population by between a third and a quarter,

it is very difficult to prove the widespread desertion of villages in the fourteenth century. For instance, the only certain Black Death desertion was of the village of Kinsalebeg in County Waterford. But the plague and the succeeding famines and epidemics weakened many small settlements (as the majority of Irish examples were) to such an extent that they wasted away, until their final desertion in the later Middle Ages. It is probably true that the clearer the earthwork remains of a deserted rural settlement, the later the date of desertion. This can be seen at Buolick, County Tipperary, where the original burgage settlement and parish church moved to cluster around a nearby tower house in the Later Medieval period, and at Kiltinan, County Kilkenny, where there were fine earthworks until they were deep ploughed recently.

The full effects on these settlements of the Gaelic resurgence of the later thirteenth and fourteenth century, which coincided with a shift toward a more pastoral economy, has yet to be established. It is likely that dispersed settlements predominated again in the areas outside the English 'Pale' around Dublin, and this is given concrete expression in the construction of several thousand tower houses, in both Anglo-Irish and Gaelic areas of the country. These functioned like the ring-forts or moated sites of an earlier period, to protect the goods and chattels of that part of the population wealthy enough to have them constructed. In the areas of Gaelic control many people probably lived in impermanent clusters that do not leave an easily identifiable trace on the landscape, while in the Anglo-Irish 'Pale' retreat and retrenchment along with widespread decline in the size and number of boroughs and villages seems to have been the order of the day.

Anglo-Norman fortresses

David Sweetman

B y the time Prince John arrived in Ireland in 1185 the Anglo-Normans held the cities of Dublin, Waterford and Cork, along with their immediate hinterlands. Their rapid military successes must be attributed to their fighting skill, especially on horseback, their organisation, and their ability to build strongholds rapidly, in strategic positions in conquered lands. The most common form of early Norman fortification is the motte and bailey or motte castle. Less well known is the ringwork castle.

Reconstruction drawing of what a motte and bailey castle may have looked like.

Motte and bailey

The motte was a large artificial earthen mound, usually situated on a natural height, with a wooden stockade around its summit, enclosing a wooden tower. The bailey was a low platform, usually rectangular in shape and situated to one side of the motte, but separated from it by a fosse or ditch which fully surrounded both structures. The bailey was used mainly to shelter servants and animals. Some large mottes had two baileys on opposite sides of the mound. Very few mottes and baileys in Ireland have been excavated and fewer still have been published, so our knowledge of them is largely limited to historical references and field survey. However, at Lismahon, County Down, an almost square wooden house with a wooden tower attached to it was discovered

on top of a mound. Excavations at Lurgenkeel, County Louth, also produced traces of a wooden tower surrounded by a palisade. Another common feature found on the summits of mottes in Ireland are pits around the periphery which were used as emplacements for archers. Placenames which contain 'mote' or 'brittas' in them (from *breteche* = wooden castle) indicate the presence of such a fortification in the area.

Clough Castle, County Down, a motte and bailey which was erected around AD 1200, is situated close to the direct road from Downpatrick to Newry, a route which was probably followed by John de Courcy when he invaded Ulster in 1177. This route is also marked by the great motte and bailey known as the Crown Mound, near Newry, while Downpatrick has another strong motte castle, almost certainly built by de Courcy. In Drogheda, Hugh de Lacy built a large motte on Millmount about the time he established the town in 1186. Another de Lacy fortification dominates the area at Trim, County Meath. However, the earliest Norman fortification there was probably a ringwork rather than a motte, despite a reference in *The Song of Dermot and the Earl* to the building of a fortified house, and a later reference during the reign of King John to the demolition of a tower on the site.

At Trim Castle, the ringwork appears to have had its entrance-way defined by a large stone tower, while excavations at Clonard, also in County Meath, revealed the remains of a palisade associated with an embanked structure.

Artist's impression of a siege tower being used in an assault on a fortification. (see p216)

Cahir Castle, County Tipperary. (see p216)

Roscommon Castle, County Roscommon. (see p216)

Mottes are commoner in the eastern half of the country. They are concentrated in the areas controlled by the Anglo-Normans but, strangely, absent in some of the areas occupied by them, such as counties Cork and Limerick. Not every motte can be considered as the earliest Anglo-Norman fortress in a given area because in many instances they were also used at a secondary stage of colonisation, when the conquerors were consolidating their position. Native structures such as ring-forts were sometimes refashioned as military fortifications.

Few of the mottes of Ulster appear to have had a bailey, and where they did, it seems that they formed part of the main fortification for the soldiers, and not merely a protection for servants and animals. The owners of mottes in Ireland were not just from the upper social strata, some came from quite far down the hierarchical scale. Nor would all of them have been of Anglo-Norman stock; there are at least sixteen mottes west of the Bann, an area controlled by the native Irish, whose owners clearly had begun to imitate the newcomers. In some instances Irish mounds of this type may have preceded the conquest. At Big Glebe in County Derry, recent excavations produced evidence for this type of structure in the Early Medieval period, and in County Monaghan there are a number of similar sites.

Ringworks

While the motte castles are easily recognisable, the ringwork castle is more difficult to identify. At its most basic it consisted of an embanked enclosure with an external ditch and palisade around the top of the bank. It almost certainly had a strong timber gate-tower and a wooden tower in the interior; the ringwork castle depended on these for its main defences, whereas the motte's strength lay in its height. The only visible remains of a ringwork castle normally is an earthen bank.

Where mottes or ringworks were situated in newly established Anglo-Norman towns, they were often replaced by large stone-built fortresses such as those at Kilkenny, Trim and Athlone. This also happened to a lesser extent on rural sites such as Clough Castle. However, in most instances after their initial use mottes were allowed to fall into disrepair, and they do not appear to have been occupied in Ireland much into the second quarter of the thirteenth century.

Trim Castle, County Meath. The donjon is to the right.
(see p216)

Anglo-Norman castles

The great Anglo-Norman stone-built fortresses, without the clutter of modern development which now surrounds them, must have been awe-inspiring sights. The great period of castle building in Ireland was from about AD 1190 to 1310, with the main phases of activity being around the turn of the twelfth and thirteenth centuries. The size and layout of castles of this period varied considerably depending on the suitability of the site, finances, skilled labour and materials such as stone. The siting of castles, therefore, sometimes represents a compromise between strategic requirements, access to building materials and resources to pay for the work.

The largest and best known fortresses of the early period are to be found in the eastern half of Ireland, especially near the coast. Two of the greatest are Trim, County Meath, and Carrickfergus, County Antrim; one built by Walter de Lacy, the other by John de Courcy. Both reflect the power of those families in the early period of the conquest. These first stone castles were built to dominate and intimidate and, in the beginning, were not often used as permanent residences. A look in some detail at Trim Castle which has been partially excavated and its history correlated with the material evidence, gives a good insight into the building and fortification at this time.

Trim Castle

Hugh de Lacy chose the site for the fortification on high ground at the west side of the River Boyne. According to the heroic Norman-French poem of the conquest, *The Song of Dermot and the Earl*, of 1172, he fortified a house at Trim and threw a trench around it, and then enclosed it with a stockade. Excavation revealed that this early fortification was a type of ringwork rather than a motte. Hugh died in 1186 and was succeeded by his son Walter, who began building the massive stone castle which enclosed over three acres. Although most of the castle as seen today was completed by 1220, the work undoubtedly commenced about twenty years earlier.

Two distinct phases of building, which may be directly related to Walter de Lacy's political problems, can easily be seen in the structure. The first building phase was begun about AD 1200 when the massive central keep or *donjon*, the north-west gatehouse, the north angle tower and the other towers along the east curtain wall were built. The keep was built inside Hugh's ringwork, in the same way as the impressive one at Adare, County Limerick. Stone for the structure was quarried from a massive moat cut into the bedrock immediately below the curtain wall, and dressed into rough ashlar blocks. Because Walter was at loggerheads with King John he fled to France in 1210 and did not return to finish Trim until 1220. Then he completed the more sophisticated Dublin gateway with its barbican and drawbridge and the D-shaped towers of the south curtain. Trim was not used as a residence and was merely garrisoned until Geoffrey de Geneville, a French nobleman in the service of the king, married Matilda, granddaughter of Walter de Lacy, and made it his domain manor in 1254. At this time he raised the height of the keep and added a massive plinth to its base. Excavation around the plinth revealed traces of temporary habitation under the scaffolding. Ham Green pottery from Bristol was discovered, indicating perhaps that de Geneville brought artisans and such people with him from his home area in Wales.

Trim, like Adare, County Limerick, King John's, Carlingford, County Louth, Carrickfergus, County Antrim, and Greencastle, County Down, was built close to water for ease of access. At Adare, excavation revealed a mooring area close to the castle walls. In Medieval times, because of difficult river crossings, it was very often faster to travel by boat where possible.

Keeps and other features

Large castles did not always have a keep. Living quarters were often within the towers of the curtain walls as well as in wooden structures inside the bawn or enclosure. The so-called keepless castles were for the most part constructed in the second half of the thirteenth century, and were often sited on high ground where bedrock was close to the surface. However, the keepless castles of the cities of Dublin, Limerick and Kilkenny were built in the first half of the thirteenth century. Dublin Castle had a royal writ issued for its erection in 1205, but building was still in progress in 1248, which gives a good indication of the length of time it took to complete these undertakings. It is also, incidentally, one of the few castles in Ireland that really was built on the instructions of King John.

Most of the keeps of the early period are almost square in plan, but at Greencastle, County Down, and Carrickfergus, County Antrim, there are large rectangular ones. Circular keeps occur at Dundrum, County Down, Nenagh, County Tipperary, and other sites, while at Athlone, County Westmeath, and Castleknock, County Dublin, there are polygonal examples. For defensive reasons the keep was normally entered through a door at first floor level, and there was frequently a chapel on the second floor immediately above the entrance. The great hall, which was for the use of the lord and his family, was also situated at first floor level, while their private chambers were on the floor above. Most of the servants and the soldiers would have occupied buildings within the ward. At Trim Castle there is a separate hall with a vaulted area underneath for storing provisions, while at Adare there are two halls and two kitchens in the outer ward, as well as other buildings.

Ferns Castle, County Wexford, which was built by the Marshall family, is a large, impressive and prominently sited structure. It had a large rock-cut moat which provided the material for the building. When the

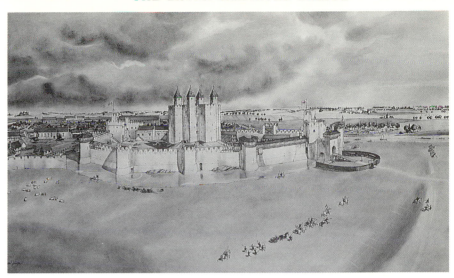

immediate source of the material ran out, other stone was used, and this change in the masonry is obvious. Ferns is one of a small group of castles which were substantial square or rectangular buildings with circular towers at the angles. Excavation at Ferns showed no evidence for internal stone structures, so they must have been made of wood. Traces of two drawbridges and outer defensive works were revealed, as well as evidence of a possible ringwork which may have pre-dated the building of the castle. There is a very fine chapel in the second floor of the south-east angle tower. It is lighted by two trefoil-pointed windows and is covered by a vault with six moulded ribs springing from corbels, which are in the form of capitals with truncated shafts. Ferns produced good evidence for an outer bailey and defensive outworks of a type still to be seen at another of these castles at Lea, County Laois.

Some of the most spectacular castles are situated on well-elevated rock sites, such as Roche, County Louth, Dunamase, County Laois, and Carlingford, County Louth. Dunamase sits high up on the rock commanding a pass through the hills which divide the Laois plain, and was previously a native Irish stronghold. Roche, built by the de Verdun family when they moved from Castletown near Dundalk, is sited on and encompasses a large rock outcrop which drops away dramatically on all but the east side. There, a ditch has been cut through the bedrock. The entrance to the castle is across this ditch and through an imposing entrance, flanked by half-round towers which are the remains of what was originally a massive gate building. The interior of the castle has a large rectangular hall in the south-eastern angle. The tops of the walls have crenellations with arrow slits and square holes below them, which were used to carry a wooden hourd or gallery. King John's Castle, Carlingford, is also situated on rock outcrop which juts out into the lough, and must have offered considerable protection to the Medieval town which lay just to its south.

Most of the later castles of the thirteenth century are keepless, and their most impressive feature is a massive gate building. This consisted of a pair of outwardly projecting half-round towers. Gate buildings of this type were often added to earlier castles, and good examples can be seen at King John's, Limerick, Lea, County Laois, and Castleroche, County Louth. Roscommon town has probably the finest example of this type of castle, and

Ballymote, County Sligo, is also impressive. Roscommon Castle had a narrow moat around it, with a barbican and drawbridge protecting the south gate. At the north side there is a massive gateway with a D-shaped tower each side of the passage-way, and with large towers at each angle. At Ballymote there were additional towers in the east and west walls, and excavation revealed the remains of the gate building which had been built with a double facing. This technique of double facing was used to make it more difficult to breach the walls. An odd feature at Ballymote is that archaeological excavations at the south of the castle demonstrated that there was no proper moat. Ballymote was built by de Burgh about 1300, but it soon fell into the hands of the Irish and remained so until 1584.

About 16km (10 miles) north-west of Roscommon is Ballintober Castle, probably the largest of these late thirteenth-century keepless castles. Its plan is similar to Ballymote and Roscommon, but its gateway is small and it had polygonal towers at the angles of the curtain wall.

The period at the end of the thirteenth century and the beginning of the fourteenth century marks the end of the building of large Anglo-Norman fortresses. The

Artist's impression of Trim Castle in its heyday.

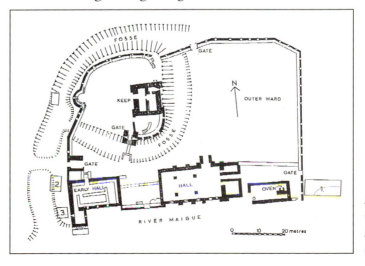

Plan of Adare Castle, County Limerick. (see p216)

A fine example of a tower-house at Burnchurch, County Kilkenny. (see p216)

The O'Doherty castle of Burt, Inishowen, County Donegal. (see p216)

The trussed timber roof of Dunsoghley Castle, County Dublin. (see p216)

lack of great castle building in the second half of the fourteenth and the first half of the fifteenth century, before the tower house appears on the landscape, can be accounted for by the Great European Famine, the Bruce invasion, and later by the Black Death which drastically reduced the population and hence the resources to build. Big castles were expensive — for instance, it cost just over £3,000 to build Roscommon Castle and to refurbish Rinndown in County Roscommon, and Athlone — and the English kings who mainly financed them had other preoccupations at home in the fourteenth century, and they were constantly short of cash. By the beginning of the fifteenth century, when castle building resumed on a large scale, the predominant form was the tower house, more a strong private residence than a military fortification.

Later Medieval castles

D Newman Johnson

Various factors in the fourteenth century combined to hinder building in stone. The upheaval of the Bruce invasion of 1315—17, which coincided with the Great European Famine, must have been destructive enough, but more disruptive was the bubonic plague — the Black Death — which arrived in Ireland in 1348. This recurred several times, and by the end of the century it has been estimated that the population, especially the Anglo-Irish who lived in the cities, may have been reduced by half. Even in relatively prosperous England there are signs of a pause in building activity, and Edward III constantly issued commissions of impressment to all masons and carpenters within reach, commanding them to attend at Windsor in order to keep major works there in progress. In Yorkshire they were even given distinctive red clothing lest they try to escape, since the king's stipend was not known for its generosity.

Although these troubles resulted in a contemporaneous sparse achievement in architecture in Ireland, there is some documentary evidence that castle building was carried out, but identification is difficult and further hindered by destruction and alteration. Towards the end of the fourteenth century a hill-top castle in County Tyrone is associated with Henry Aimreidh O'Neill, who died in 1392. Known as Harry Avery's Castle, its polygonal curtain walls have gone, but an imposing twin-towered gatehouse remains. This has surprising features, however, since entry leads not directly into the inner ward but into a vaulted ground floor from which a mural stair leads to a hall above. As a gatehouse it is a sham; it is really a disguised donjon or keep.

Castle types

Irish castles up to the early fourteenth century are of enceinte type, where an enclosing curtain wall with flanking towers provides the main line of defence, with the gatehouse or an extra large mural or freestanding tower acting as the owner's private quarters. This type, because of its size and complexity, was time-consuming and very costly to build — even Edward I did not complete some of his Welsh castles. In a reaction to this, the prominent castle type to re-emerge during the later fourteenth century was the 'magna turris' or great tower, although a few smaller castles of enclosure, the courtyard type, continued to be built. Economy in defenders as well as cost was another factor in favour of these towers, not to mention the status symbol of a strong high tower overshadowing the neighbourhood and serving as a strategic watchtower. The loss of the tactically superior defence systems of the larger castles was partially compensated for by surrounding the tower with a strong wall of some kind, in the better examples of stone, with battlements and towers, known as bawns in Ireland and barmkins in Scotland. These outer defences were overlooked by the tower.

Thus these later castles returned — like their fellows throughout Western Europe — to the same basic principles of defence as the Norman donjon and bailey, albeit with more sophisticated detailing for easier defence and more comfortable living. In Spain during the 'Reconquista', this type was generally used during the fifteenth century to consolidate areas captured from the Moors, while in France the strongest donjon remaining in the country, at Largoet-en-Elven, near Vannes, was erected towards 1394. Similarly Sir William ap Thomas,

Slade Castle, County Wexford. (see p216)

a Welsh knight who had fought at Agincourt, made the principal feature of his castle at Raglan on the Welsh marches a 'magna turris' — the hexagonal 'Yellow Tower of Gwent', constructed c. 1435–45.

In Ireland, as in Scotland, endemic civil strife and minor warfare necessitated the building of castles, and the revival of the concept of a strong high tower completely dominated castle architecture in both countries until the need for their existence faded out during the seventeenth century. The tower of this period has become known as a tower-house, a relatively modern term that perhaps over-emphasises the essential domestic element within the definition of a castle and which was also present in the Norman donjon. When the building was not a fortress-residence for kings, lords, landowners and wealthy merchants, and was garrisoned only by soldiers, then it comes under the category of a barracks or fort.

The proto-tower-houses

Vast numbers of tower-house castles were built in Ireland during the fifteenth and sixteenth centuries. Estimates of the total number of all castle types can only be approximate, and 3500 may be conservative, with the large majority of these of the tower-house type. The Anglo-Irish and Gaelic lords and landowners alike built and lived in tower-house castles. The tower-house, mostly in ruins, often with its defensive enclosure damaged or removed, is perhaps the most commonly seen Medieval building in the countryside. It is, as already indicated, of the same basic type as the Norman donjon and bailey castles, which were constructed in the early

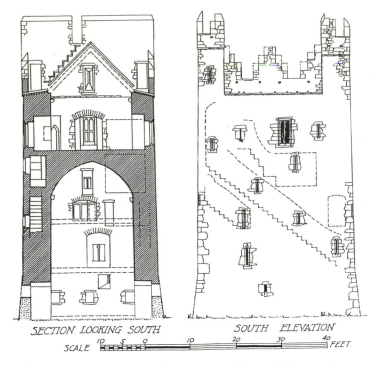

SECTION LOOKING SOUTH

SOUTH ELEVATION

SCALE 10 5 0 10 20 30 40 FEET

Drawing of the south elevation and cross-section of Burnchurch tower-house, County Kilkenny.

thirteenth century, and there could well have been continuity in tower development from the donjon to the tower-house. In support of this, some towers which seem to belong to the fourteenth century because of their architectural detailing, have features which later became common in the tower-house.

Three towers in the north of County Wicklow illustrate some of these features. The massive hall donjon at Kindlestown (the name comes from the reputed builder, Albert de Kenly, sheriff of Kildare in 1301) once had a tall slender gable-tower, and still has the remains of a barrel-vaulted ground floor and also a projecting garderobe or latrine tower. A tower which is also of transitional type is Kiltimon, with its verticality, double-splayed loops, primitive garderobes, and murder hole over the entrance. Fake battlements and other changes were made when this tower was turned into a folly in the early nineteenth century by Lord Rossmore, who also added a circular bawn. The interesting donjon at Threecastles has a thick full-height cross wall of Norman type, with stone vaults under its fourth floor and a projecting staircase and garderobe tower especially typical of later tower-houses. The large rectangular corner tower to the left of the gatehouse at Ballyloughan, and two frontal corner towers at Clonmore, both in County Carlow, are also indicators of the architectural development of towers in the early fourteenth century.

The misadventures of John Sely, Bishop of Down

from 1412 until he was deprived of his see in 1441, help to date an early group of towers. His downfall came after complaints of his living in 'castro de Kylcleth' with Lettice Thomas, a married woman. This dates Kilclief Castle to the early fifteenth century: it is tall, rising to four floors — the first tower-house barrel-vaulted in stone with corner cap-houses, and it has two projecting towers on the same face, forming a U-plan tower. One contains the entrance (in the re-entrant angle), together with the spiral stair, and the other the garderobes. They are joined at the top by an arch concealing a murder-hole or machicolation which protects the door, the total effect being not unlike a twin-towered gatehouse. Audley's Castle and Jordan's Castle are also in County Down and are so similar that they were likely to have been built by the same band of masons. All three possess an early feature — double-splayed loops at ground-floor level. These tower-houses, as Harry Avery's Castle, were influenced in their external appearance by the Edwardian gatehouse, though the internal planning was very different.

The Medieval tower-house

In 1429 King Henry VI gave a boost to the building of fortalices (as these castles are occasionally termed in contemporary documents) when he issued a statute which states: 'It is agreed and asserted that every liege man of our Lord the King, of the said counties [the Pale — Dublin, Meath, Kildare and Louth], who chooses to build a castle or tower sufficiently embattled or fortified, within the next ten years, to wit twenty feet in length, sixteen feet in width and forty feet in height or more, that the Commons of the said counties shall pay to the said person to build the said castle or tower ten pounds by way of subsidy.' As a tower-house might cost all of £100 in those days, the sum was not over-generous. This castle subsidy (pre-dating house subsidies!) was acted upon, however, for shortly afterwards another act prescribed minimum internal dimensions of fifteen feet (4½m) by twelve feet (3½m) for the castles of Meath, and in 1449 the numbers to be built were curtailed. Known as '£10 castles', a number of towers in the Pale correspond closely to the requirements of the statute. One known to most Dubliners is Corr Castle, on the Howth isthmus. Protecting the peninsula, it consists of a square tower, four storeys high, with a stone barrel-vault covering the first two floors. A square spiral-stair tower rising to a cap-house is situated at one corner, while there is evidence for an attached hall to the north, now removed. Carrigaphooca Castle, County Cork, seems an early tower, with a correspondingly simple plan; only two mural chambers and a garderobe, otherwise it has single rooms on each of the five storeys, reached by a straight stair becoming spiral at the third floor, with a vaulted fourth storey providing a stone floor for the top room. The surprising absence of fireplaces means that only the upper floor could have had a central fire, with a smoke vent in the roof, and lends credence to the tradition that it was built by Dermot Mór MacCarthy, a Gaelic chieftain, in 1436.

The enormous popularity of the tower-house is attested by an agent of Philip II of Spain, who reported: 'Every petty gentleman lives in a stone tower, where he gathers into his service all the rascals of the neighbourhood (and of these towers there is an infinite number).'

These late castles, unlike the early ones that were built in an international style, developed architectural characteristics that were essentially Irish, in a similar tradition to the Scottish towers, which were copied to create the Scottish baronial style popular in the nineteenth century. External Irish features include their essential verticality, the graceful batter of the walls, loop-holes in the corners of the tower, double or treble-stepped merlons or battlements, and corbelled, machicolated galleries at the corners, mostly at the wall-head but sometimes halfway up. Internally, the stone vaults, usually over the basement and under the upper floor for fire-proofing purposes, were built over woven wickerwork centering. The main room, the chieftain's hall, was on the upper floor, where slightly larger windows were allowed than the small loops provided lower down for defence. The stout oak door, protected with shot-holes and a box machicolation over an iron grille, led into an enclosed lobby defended by a further murder-hole overhead. The door in front led into the ground floor, the one on the right or left (usually the left) led to a straight or spiral stair, and the door opposite entered into the guard-room.

In the mature, late-fifteenth century tower-houses such as Clara, County Offaly, or Burnchurch, County Kilkenny, chambers and passages are tunnelled through the walls and vaults in profusion, producing complicated plans and providing all sorts of lesser accommodation, including secret chambers, oubliettes and garderobes, the latter having a rectangular shaft dropping down through the walls and discharging externally at ground-level. Designed to confuse intruders, the stairs could switch from one side to another. The basic plan was rectangular, but circular examples such as Ballynahow Castle, County Tipperary, are not uncommon, while Newtown Castle, County Clare, is unique in having a circular body resting on a square tapered base. Other plan types are the L-plan with one projecting tower, and the Z-plan with opposing towers. Often these attached towers contained a spiral stairs or garderobes, while at Burt Castle, County Donegal — a Z-plan tower — the opposing towers provide complete flanking fire as well. A stone hall was often attached, as at Slade Castle, County Wexford.

Some towers are large and complex, like Blarney Castle, County Cork, or Bunratty Castle, County Clare,

Derryhivenny Castle, County Galway, the latest tower-house to be built in Ireland. An inscription over the bawn gateway dates the construction to 1643.

which is square with square corner towers linked by an arch on opposing sides. Dunsoghly Castle, County Dublin, of similar plan, has its original trussed oak roof. Other towers are small and very compact, like Moygaddy Castle, County Meath. There are large numbers of towers in some western counties, especially Limerick and Galway, while concentrations of fortalices could defend frontiers like the Pale, or harbours such as Ardglass, County Down, or Dalkey, County Dublin. The bawn could be omitted in towers which were in

Blarney Castle, County Cork. (see p216)

harper begins to tune and singeth Irish rymes of auncient making ....'

The last castles

The desire for more luxurious living led to the lateral expansion of the tower-house in the closing years of the sixteenth century, and more complex towers became common, often still surrounded by a bawn with flankers attached for defence. Larger mullioned and transomed windows were introduced, together with higher ceilings, often richly plastered, and the stair was wider and of oak. The earliest and one of the most important is Rathfarnham Castle, Dublin, built *c.* 1589 by Archbishop Adam Loftus, which has a massive rectangular central block with large spear-shaped flankers, in the developing tradition of the bastioned star-fort. Often a new residence was attached to the tower-house, as at Loughmoe, County Tipperary, where a wing ending in a tower bigger than the original was built by the Purcell family.

Around this period Scottish planters in Ulster built castles in the exuberant native style, perhaps the finest being Monea Castle, County Fermanagh, built by Malcolm Hamilton, who became Archbishop of Cashel in 1623. The requirements of the Scots and English settlers were that those with 2000 acres (809 ha) built a castle and bawn, those with 1500 acres (607 ha) a stone house and bawn, and those with 1000 acres (405 ha) a bawn. The undefended house set within a defensive bawn, with spear-shaped flankers, such as Faugher, County Donegal, represents the last examples of the castle tradition in the country, although the tower-house tradition itself died hard after its long and diverse development. Some so-called 'castles' were only using the name, as a summary of a Scottish legal case of 1630 points out: 'this house was not a tower ... and had neither fosse nor barmkin-wall about it, nor battling, but was only an ordinary house....' This could apply also in Ireland, but some true fortalices were built here in a very late period, such as Derryhivenny Castle, County Galway, which has Jacobean details, such as the clustered stacks and orderly windows of its tower-house within its L-shaped bawn. This has opposing towers and encloses a hall, while the gate bears the date 1643. However, Castle ffrench, County Galway, was perhaps the last tower-house; unfortunately it has gone, but the gate-tower of the bawn bears the date 1673, which must make it among the last of the true castles to be built in Western Europe.

close proximity; it had no standard defensive pattern, but might incorporate a hall and utilised towers and machicolations as the site and importance of the owner dictated. There are surprisingly few artillery defences, due to the boggy nature and dense woods of the Medieval countryside, which made it very difficult to transport cannon. Castles reached by sea, river or mainland routes were occasionally provided with defence; Poulnalong Castle, dating from 1543, on the Bandon River, County Cork, has gunports at ground level, while Limerick Castle was provided with an artillery bastion in 1611.

In 1644 a Frenchman by the name of Boullaye le Gouz wrote of life in these castles: 'The castles or houses of the nobility consist of four walls extremely high, ... square towers without windows, or at least having such small apertures as to give no more light than a prison. They have little furniture ... put rushes a foot deep on their floors and on their windows, and many ornament their ceilings with branches.' The latter comment must refer to the wicker soffits of the vaults. Slightly more cheerful is another seventeenth century visitor, Luke Gernon: 'We are come to the castle already. The castles are built very strong with narow stayres, for security. The hall is in the uppermost room, lett us go up, you shall not come down agayne till tomorrow ... you shall be presented with all the drinks in the house ... you must not refuse it. The fyre is prepared in the middle of the hall where you may sollace yourselfe till supper time, you shall not want sacke (wine) and tobacco. By this time the table is spread and plentifully furnished with variety of meates ... they feast together with great jollyty and healths around; towards the middle of the supper the

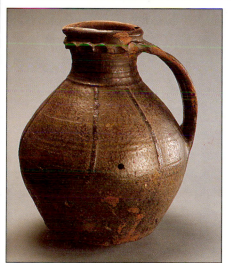

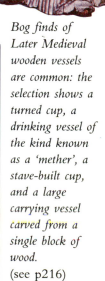

*Dunvegan Cup,
Isle of Skye.
(see p216)*

*A group of
weapons of the
Later Medieval
period.
(see p216)*

*Glazed jug,
13th century*

*Wooden
sculpture,
Fethard, County
Tipperary*

*Bog finds of
Later Medieval
wooden vessels
are common: the
selection shows a
turned cup, a
drinking vessel of
the kind known
as a 'mether', a
stave-built cup,
and a large
carrying vessel
carved from a
single block of
wood.
(see p216)*

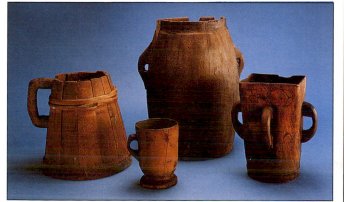

The Domhnach Airgid.

Later Medieval decorative arts

Raghnall Ó Floinn

The introduction of new communities of reformed orders such as the Cistercians in the early twelfth century, and the arrival of the Anglo-Norman settlers later in the century, were responsible for changes in patronage and artistic taste. The larger monasteries of pre-Norman times provided an environment in which craft skills could be developed over several generations, and which produced masterpieces such as the Ardagh Chalice and the Cross of Cong. These monastic workshops do not seem to have survived much beyond the thirteenth century. Their fate was sealed by the Council of Cashel in 1172 which decreed: 'thus in all parts of the Irish church all matters relating to religion are to be conducted hereafter on the pattern of Holy Church, and in line with the observances of the English church'.

Our knowledge of Irish craftsmen in the later Middle Ages suggests that they were based mainly in towns, working for wealthy lay and ecclesiastical patrons. Royal charters gave towns the right to set up guilds, and a guild organisation was already in existence in Dublin by the end of the twelfth century. In the larger towns it would appear that immigrant English craftsmen were employed; one Oliver de Nichol, goldsmith, was admitted to the Dublin Guild Merchant in 1226. A high proportion of valuables was imported, mostly from England, such as silver plate for the table and the altar, mass books, ecclesiastical vestments, jewellery and horse harness.

The decorative arts are poorly represented for a number of reasons. The effects of confiscations during the Reformation were devastating and many works of art were destroyed, including, in 1541, St Patrick's crozier or Bachall Íosa, the prized possession of Christ Church Cathedral and Ireland's most venerated relic, which was burned in public. Natural disasters contributed to the loss of other valuable items. In July 1461 the east window of Christ Church Cathedral was blown in by a storm and the falling stones broke chests containing jewels, relics, ornaments and altar vestments.

The wars of the sixteenth and seventeenth centuries caused such devastation that not a single example of pre-Reformation panel-painting, stained glass or church vestments of Irish origin survives.

A unique survivor from this era is the gilt silver crozier and jewelled mitre made in 1418 by the goldsmith Thomas O'Carryd for Connor O'Dea, bishop of Limerick. In the crook of the crozier is an Annunciation scene, and immediately below this is a pelican 'vulning' or wounding herself — a common Medieval analogy to Christ's sacrifice. The jewels that adorn the mitre are of little intrinsic value. They consist largely of rock crystal with a few amethysts and sapphires — stones which are also found on contemporary secular jewellery.

The most important Irish families employed their own craftsmen. In 1479 the Annals record the death of Matthew Ua Maelruanaigh, master craftsman and eminent goldsmith to the Maguires of Fermanagh. A decorated ceremonial goblet belonging to the Maguires and made by Matthew's successor is preserved today at Dunvegan Castle on the Isle of Skye. The only other secular piece of metalwork of note is also associated with a great Irish family. This is the Kavanagh 'Charter' horn, so called because it symbolised the owners' claim to be kings of Leinster. It consists of a carved tusk of elephant ivory held in a brass stand.

Much of the metalwork which survives consists of additions or repairs to earlier shrines associated with Irish saints, which were preserved in the hands of successive generations of 'keepers'. These hereditary keepers were often descended from the *airchennaigh* or erenaghs, who were the administrators of church property. One of the finest is a shrine known as the Domnach Airgid. This was made in *c.* AD 800 to contain relics associated with St Patrick which were kept at Clones, County Monaghan; it was completely remodelled around 1350 and is decorated with silver-gilt plaques bearing figures of saints and apostles. We do not know for certain where the craftsman John O'Barrdain made this piece, but a goldsmith of the same name is recorded in Drogheda.

The only wooden furnishings to have escaped destruction are the late fifteenth century oak choir stalls of St Mary's Cathedral, Limerick. Carved wooden figures, being portable, have fared somewhat better. The Madonna and Child from Kilcorban is one of a group of 'transitional' wooden sculptures from east Galway

which preserved Romanesque traits well into the thirteenth century. The few pieces of later wooden sculpture are less accomplished.

Manuscript illumination was perhaps the most conservative medium. In the twelfth century, manuscripts were written in Irish script and decoration was confined to evangelists' symbols (in the case of gospels) and elaborate initials which opened the main sections of the texts. This arrangement had hardly changed since the Book of Durrow, some five centuries earlier. The contrast with contemporary English illuminated manuscripts could hardly have been greater, in script, colour and decoration.

Two distinct manuscript traditions emerged as a result of the Anglo-Norman invasion and the church reforms of the twelfth century: one based on foreign, mainly English prototypes, and one which copied the arrangement and style of earlier Irish manuscripts. Most of the surviving manuscripts in the former category consist of cartularies and other administrative documents. The illuminations in these documents are not of very high quality but deserve further study. Other manuscripts such as missals and psalters are so close to their English models that it is hard to distinguish between the two. The manuscripts of the second tradition were written for Irish patrons and contain diverse material, such as genealogies, saints' lives, medical tracts, poems and mythology. Many of these compilations were copied from earlier works without knowledge of or training in the principles of interlaced ornament. Consequently, the work often appears ragged and roughly laid out, as in the case of the Book of Ballymote which was compiled in County Sligo around the year 1400.

Excavations, especially in the Medieval towns throughout the country, offer the best hope of increasing our understanding of where craft workshops were located and the kind of tools that were used. The results so far have been limited. Sherds of pottery are the most frequent finds from excavations of Later Medieval sites. The Anglo-Normans introduced the potter's wheel and the technique of glazing. Much of the pottery was imported, especially from western England and south-western France. Pottery kilns have been excavated at Downpatrick and Carrickfergus. Compared to similar kilns in England, the range of products uncovered was limited. However, we can tell from the shape of the jugs

The Kavanagh Charter Horn, twelfth century AD.
(see p216)

The Lislaghtin Cross.
(see p216)

and skillets found that the potters came originally from the Chester area. Pottery from the kilns was discovered on sites within 15km (9 miles) of the source, indicating a localised trade. Many of the artifact types, such as brooches, finger rings and horse harness, are very similar to those used in England and France and few come from excavated sites. Finds of small pieces of jewellery and other decorated metalwork from excavations not only increase the number of known examples, but also offer closer dating for older finds. Further study will enable us to establish which pieces were imported and which were manufactured in Ireland.

VII
The early modern period

A series of developments in the sixteenth century resulted in profound changes in Ireland, but we should avoid the temptation of nominating any one as marking the divide between the Medieval and the modern world. Those who lived through the period would have been as conscious of continuity as of change. The effect of dramatic events such as the dissolution of the monasteries was unevenly felt. Under the Tudors, royal power was asserted in a more organised way, and English administrators were appointed to rule in Ireland in place of Anglo-Norman magnates. Ireland was, however, a backwater, and could only be described as a second-hand participant in the ferment of the Renaissance and Reformation. The Irish for the most part remained Catholic, while the English followed the Reformation; this exacerbated relations already complicated by ethnic differences. The descendants of the old Anglo-Norman colonists often resented the new men sent from England. Many of them added the Catholic faith to an Irish identification already part-forged by ties of marraige, language and custom with the native Irish, whose fate they shared in the seventeenth century.

Rebellions by Irish chieftains in the mid-sixteenth century and later, resulted in a revival of the policy of 'planting' English settlers, which had already been tried by the Anglo-Norman conquerors. The defeat of the last Gaelic chieftains of Ulster in 1603 marked a great turning point, and their flight in 1607 enabled the Crown to plan the most successful plantation of all, that of Ulster. Brehon Law was officially abolished in 1603, but it along with many native traditional practices lingered on well into the seventeenth century, although their relevance became questionable as English customs spread. Contemporary Irish literature is full of lament for the passing of the old order. Native scholars began to rescue as much as they could of the history and traditions of the Irish, and a new diaspora of Irish churchmen ensured that much of this work was preserved in continental libraries. The wars of the 1640s facilitated a larger plantation scheme, and by the end of the seventeenth century the pattern of landholding had been radically altered.

Our limited knowledge of Irish archaeology for this period shows a conservative society. Tower-houses continued to be built until the mid-seventeenth century. Arms and armour were archaic in appearance, though well adapted to the guerrilla warfare of the forests and bogs. Some magnates began to experiment with a more gracious lifestyle. Carrick-on-Suir Castle and a panelled room in Malahide Castle are reminders of a luxurious life, but only fragments of the evidence survive. With very rare exceptions, house contents of the period failed to survive into modern times. Urban archaeology is only beginning to throw light on town life — in the past this period was normally ignored by archaeologists. However, other scholars have documented changes in the organisation of manufacture, in the widening of trade and the growth of capital. Rural archaeology has likewise been largely ignored, except for the study of the plantations. There is an enormous amount to be done to document settlement, change of land use, deforestation and mineral extraction.

Chimney piece, Donegal Castle, 1610. (see p216)

The archaeology of the Munster plantation

Denis Power

In the second half of the sixteenth century Queen Elizabeth I of England was attempting to wrest political control of Munster from its traditional feudal overlord, the earl of Desmond. The Desmonds were Geraldines (Fitzgeralds) of Norman origin and owned vast estates, mostly in County Limerick, but also in north Kerry, north and east Cork and west Waterford. Conflict soon erupted, and after a protracted struggle with Elizabeth's army the Desmond forces were defeated and the earl himself murdered in 1583.

Once declared a rebel, the earl was no longer entitled to hold land under English law. The queen was now free to dispose of some 300 000 acres (121 410 hectares) as she willed. Munster had long been perceived as a likely back door for a Spanish force to invade England, so it was decided to create a loyal and Protestant bulwark by planting the Desmond lands with English people.

The vast Desmond estate was divided into thirty-five units (seignories). Each seignory was granted to a single individual (undertaker) on condition that he settle the area according to a pre-determined plantation scheme. The undertaker was to finance the entire operation himself. In theory, each seignory was a block of 12 000 acres (4856 hectares), and a surviving diagram shows the intended plantation scheme, with the undertaker himself occupying 1000 acres (405 hectares) of demesne and his tenants leasing farms varying in size from 47 to 400 acres (19 to 162 hectares). A village of thirty-two cottagers, together with a church and a mill, was also to be built. In practice, the seignories varied in size from 1300 acres (526 hectares) up to 42 000 acres (16 997 hectares) — this enormous estate on the lower reaches of the Blackwater was given to the queen's then favourite, Walter Raleigh. Nor were the grants convenient blocks of land, but a patchwork of holdings scattered over five counties. Indeed, a number of undertakers had difficulty determining exactly what lands they were entitled to.

However, by the early 1590s the plantation was beginning to take shape and some 4000 newcomers had arrived. But the settlements were neither strongly defended nor accepted by the native population, and in October of that year the entire plantation was destroyed by an uprising in support of the rebel, Sugán Earl of Desmond.

What had been achieved before the uprising can be gauged from Ireland's oldest surviving estate map, showing lands leased by Henry Pyne from the undertaker Sir Walter Raleigh at Mogeely, County Cork, in 1598. Surrounded by remnants of the native woodlands are newly enclosed fields with English-sounding names like: 'the park close', 'the new close' and 'the warren close'. At the centre is the village itself, with its Protestant church. This enclosed landscape suggests that pastoral farming predominated amongst the immigrant farmers — a fact borne out by the greatly increased amounts of wool and cattle exported from Munster during this period.

After the Battle of Kinsale in 1601 and the end of the Nine Years War in 1603, the way was open to re-establish the plantation. In effect, it was up to the individual undertakers to reclaim their estates. A number never even returned to Ireland but sold out their interests, and the pattern which emerged was more the result of individual enterprise than of central-controlled planning. For example, the most powerful English landowner to emerge was Richard Boyle, later the earl of Cork, who was not even among the original undertakers but purchased the great Inchiquin seignory from Sir Walter Raleigh.

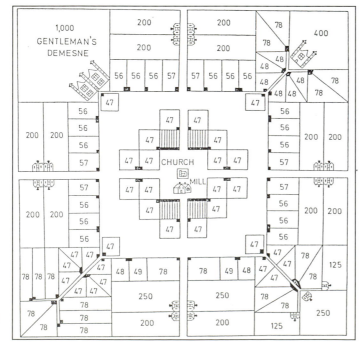

Proposed lay-out of a Munster seignory of 12 000 acres, 1586, showing roads, houses and farm boundaries.

The first four decades of the seventeenth century saw relative peace return to Munster, along with some degree of prosperity. The planted population had grown to about 5000 by 1610 and by 1620 had reached 14 000. The number of English settlers reached a peak of roughly 22 000 by 1640.

A survey was carried out in 1622 by a royal commission of James I. Its report reveals a plantation well underway, but of a very mixed nature and with some obvious weaknesses, notably the few undertakers who were permanently resident on their lands — about half the total. With the exception of the towns there is scant reference in the returns to the building of new 'English' houses, and most undertakers and chief tenants were content to live in the many, now renovated Desmond castles. One notable exception was at Mallow, where Sir Thomas Norreys built himself 'a goodly, strong and sumptuous house, built upon the ruins of the old castle, with a bawn to it, about 120 foot square and 18 foot in height and [with] many convenient houses of offices'.

But other great stone houses were being built in the south-west at the time of the plantation, by Gaelic and Old English (Norman) landowners. The remains of these houses can be seen at Kanturk (McCarthy), Coppinger's Court (Coppinger), Ightermurragh (Fitzgerald), Coolnalong (McCarthy), Monkstown (Archdeacon), Mountlong (Long), Kilmaclenine (Barry), Reenadysert (O'Sullivan), White Castle (Roche), Dromaneen (O'Callaghan) and Lisgriffin (Barry), all in County Cork. These houses are clearly distinguishable from sixteenth-century tower-houses but are also different from Mallow Castle. For example, the polygonal and pointed turrets at Mallow do not re-appear; instead, all the planning is at right angles, more in keeping with the tower-house tradition. These houses seem to represent the opening up of a traditional craft to new ideas rather than the introduction of a completely new architecture.

Whilst the commissioners of 1622 were bemoaning the lack of urban development in conjunction with the plantation, there was one significant success at Bandonbridge in County Cork. The commissioners described this as 'a large and beautiful town, consisting of about 250 houses — the inhabitants being all English'. Bandon has been described as 'the outstanding new town in Ireland in the generation before 1641'. Although it

was not founded by the earl of Cork, the town flourished in the 1620s and 1630s under his patronage. He underwrote the building of a wall around the town in the 1620s. Contemporary plans give us a good idea of what the town looked like in 1630. The houses are of 'English' type — two-storey, with slated roofs and stone or brick chimneys. By contemporary European standards the defences of Bandon were very archaic, but the town did survive the 1641 hostilities as a Protestant enclave. Today very little of seventeenth-century Bandon can be seen, apart from some fragments of the town wall and the older fabric of Kilbrogan church.

None of the other plantation towns can match Bandon in layout or size. Mallow had about 200 houses stretched along the main street, while Tallow, a town relying on the nearby ironworks for its prosperity, had some 150 houses. Many of the English settlements were abandoned after the 1641 debacle, like Lough Gur in County Limerick and Mogeely in County Cork. But we should not underestimate the influence of the plantation in the

Mallow Castle, County Cork. (see p216)

Reconstruction drawing of what an ironworks may have looked like.

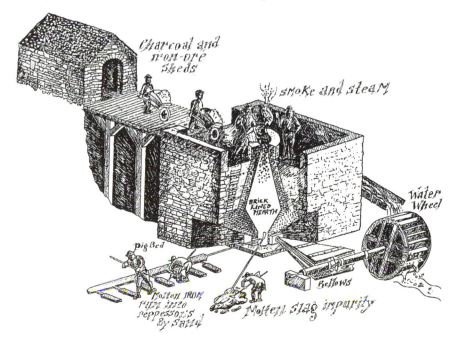

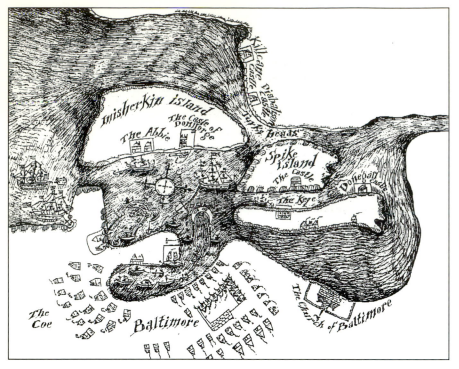

Baltimore,
County Cork.
(see p216)

development of urbanisation in Munster, where town building on this scale is only matched in the thirteenth-century heyday of Norman expansion. In County Limerick the lowland sectors of the planted lands were studded with new villages, a number of which later became successful towns, like Bruff and Hospital.

The increased trade which the plantation created boosted the economies of the old port towns in Munster, especially Youghal. Once again its prosperity owed much to the patronage of Richard Boyle, who built a house for himself there. He also erected an extraordinary memorial to himself in St Mary's Church, which is only matched by another great monument to his own memory in St Patrick's Cathedral in Dublin. A fine house of the period survives in the town at Myrtle Grove, with transverse gables and high stone chimney stacks. It contains some original interior fittings of the period, including a fine carved fireplace. Another building of this date stands on the main street of Youghal. This is the almshouse endowed by Boyle in 1634, which was much altered in the last century and again recently by Cork County Council — unfortunately without an accurate archaeological record of the structure being made.

After land, wood was the most important resource exploited by the Munster plantation. It was said that a squirrel could travel through the trees from Killarney to Cork, so densely was the countryside wooded, with stands of oak, ash and birch predominating. The wood was used by the settlers to build houses. It was also used

in ship-building and in the manufacture of barrel staves. Barrels were important as containers for the export of butter, meat, fish, tallow (fat), and the like. Oak bark was used in the tanning of leather.

However, the most insatiable consumers of wood were the ironworks. These required large quantities of charcoal — a fuel made by burning wood in a sealed kiln. Iron was in great demand by the ordnance industry for the manufacture of cannon and cannonballs. But most of the available woodland in England had been cleared by the seventeenth century and charcoal had become very expensive to produce. The great woods of Munster were the next to go.

Not all of the English settlement in Munster took place on the former Desmond lands. For example, the East India Company of London established a settlement of 300 people at Downdaniel near Bandon in County Cork. Here they set up a ship-building yard and an ironworks in 1612. The enterprise was the focus of much local hostility and failed to realise its full potential. It was abandoned before 1641. Some remains of a 'smelter pot as well as heaps of ash and spent material from the furnace hearth' have been identified in the vicinity of the fifteenth-century tower-house.

Fishing had developed little beyond a subsistence level on the south-west coast, but the new settlers were quick to realise its potential, especially the pilchard (a small sea-fish like a herring) which occurred in great numbers along the coast. Fisheries were developed from Ardmore in Waterford as far as Ballinskelligs in Kerry. Fish processing stations were set up in many places, and the remains of these can be seen today at Ardgroom, Sherkin Island, Baltimore and Crookhaven in County Cork (locally known as 'fish palaces'). The drawing shows how cured pilchards were pressed into wooden casks by levering a press beam down on the contents of the barrel. The fish oil (train oil) was thus extracted, to be used in a number of ways, including leather-working and as a lamp oil. The line of holes which housed the ends of these press beams can still be seen in the wall of the surviving 'fish palace' at Ardgroom, County Cork.

Also in this period, star-shaped forts were built by the English government at Haulbowline in Cork Harbour and at James Fort in Kinsale. These two great natural harbours were thought the most likely landings by a Spanish armada. The two forts were designed by the engineer Paul Ivy and have pointed bastions on which cannon were mounted. Very little of the Haulbowline fort survives, but James Fort is a spectacular ruin — now a national monument in state care. Recent work by Eric Klingelhofer (Mercer University, Georgia, USA) at Dunboy Castle near Castletownbere, County Cork, has shown that the fort built there in 1602 'may be the first (and only?) truly Renaissance fortification in Ireland that is not of English origin'. This work is part of a larger project 'to examine the archaeological evidence for Elizabethan colonising attempts in Munster, for comparison with other early colonies'.

In 1641 Munster was engulfed by war and the plantation was once again subject to destruction by Irish forces. The bloody end to both phases of plantation has left us few physical remains of this almost forgotten period in Munster's history.

The archaeology of the Ulster plantation

Brian Lacey

Formal plantations of English and Scottish settlers were made from 1609 onwards in the six counties of Armagh, Cavan, Coleraine (later Londonderry), Donegal, Fermanagh and Tyrone.

Simultaneously, informal colonisation took place in the three other Ulster counties, Antrim, Down and Monaghan. The people who came to Ulster in this way brought with them a whole new style of life, very different to that previously experienced by the native Irish. However, the Irish in turn influenced some of the methods of the settlers. Changes had already begun during the Nine Years War and its aftermath. As the English forces advanced against the Gaelic chieftains, overland into south Ulster in the 1590s, a series of campaign fortifications were built to secure those areas already captured. Although none of these forts has been excavated, several were beautifully illustrated on the contemporary picture maps made by Richard Bartlett, who accompanied the expedition. Likewise, drawings survive of the string of forts built at Derry and its vicinity by Sir Henry Docwra, who approached Ulster from the sea in 1600. More solid evidence of the English advance into Ulster at this time is provided by the remains of Moyry Castle near Newry. This three-storey defensive stone tower, with an adjoining bawn or walled courtyard, was built in 1601.

The plantation scheme

After the war, the 'flight of the earls' in 1607, and the rebellion of Sir Cahir O'Doherty of Inishowen in 1608, the government confiscated vast tracts of the Ulster countryside, with the intention of developing them along English lines and peopling them with British colonists. The plantation proper got under way in 1610. Estates

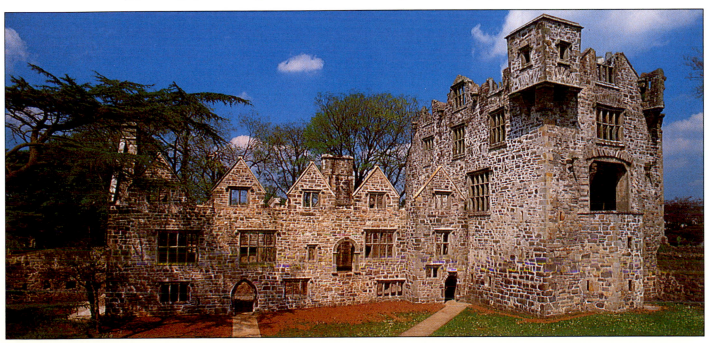

Donegal Castle, County Donegal. (see p216)

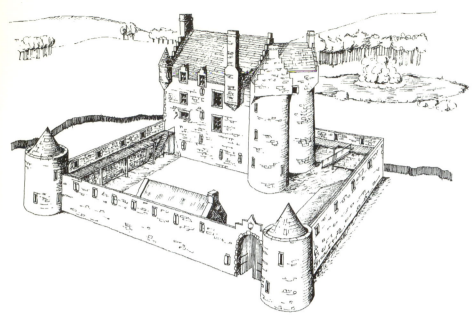

Monea Castle, County Fermanagh. (see p216)

a traditional Late Medieval Irish tower-house at Termonmagrath in south-east Donegal, which consisted of a five-storey rectangular stone house with a small circular tower for the stairs. The house had an attached bawn, with two circular flanking towers at its north-west and north-east corners. By the early seventeenth century this was an extremely old-fashioned type of building but, given the unsettled conditions of the country, the design chosen was probably appropriate. The archbishop's example was followed by others.

At Shannock in Fermanagh, the English settler Thomas Flowerdew built a timber-framed house in 1611 but, more sensibly, followed this in 1613 with an Irish-style stone tower. On the east side of the province, at Kirkistown on the Ards peninsula, the long-established Savages made a similar choice. Here a Medieval-type tower was built as late as 1622. This also had a bawn with rounded flanking towers similar to those at Termonmagrath. However, in the 1640s another member of this family built a very different kind of stone house a few miles away. Unlike the old-fashioned towers this was only one and a half storeys high, had large windows and was more typical of English contemporary domestic houses. However, it did have some protective features such as gun-loops and a bawn, which would have been unnecessary in England.

were granted to three kinds of recipient: 'servitors' who were being repaid in land for services already done for the crown; 'undertakers' who were required to meet certain conditions in return for a grant of land, and some native Irish who were considered safe or useful to the government. Depending on the amount received, specific requirements had to be met by the grantees. Undertakers who received a notional 2000 acres (809 hectares) had to 'build thereupon a castle, with a strong court or bawn about it'. Those who received the lesser grant of 1500 notional acres (607 hectares) were required to build a stone or brick house with a bawn, while the grantees who received the least amount of land were required only to build a bawn. These conditions were intended to ensure that a network of strong stone houses, or at least defensible courtyards, were available as refuges for the settlers in the event of any attack by the native Irish who, it was presumed, would be hostile. In the newly created county of Londonderry, the land was allotted to some of the 'companies' or ancient trades' guilds of the City of London, which were extremely influential in commercial and financial matters. The companies were treated as the equivalent of the undertakers in the other counties.

Unlike the English, who by the early seventeenth century were no longer used to building defended houses, the Scottish settlers were familiar with the construction of small castles of a type suitable for the unsettled conditions in the Ulster of their day. The remains of many of these survive in the areas colonised from Scotland. One of the finest examples is Monea Castle near Derrygonnelly in County Fermanagh, built about 1619. Like Termonmagrath, the main building forms the south-east boundary of the bawn enclosure, which was further defended by two smaller flanking towers. The castle has a number of features, however, which betray its Scottish origin. It is similar to Claypotts Castle near Dundee. The west side is dominated by two circular towers, each of which supports a square chamber carried on projecting corbels. The roof gables of these chambers are crow-stepped in typical Scottish fashion.

Fortified buildings

Remains of many plantation castles and bawns survive, reflecting in their design, detailing and building techniques the diverse English, Scottish and native Irish elements which went into the scheme. In about 1611, the native grantee, Archbishop Myler McGrath, built

A simpler Scottish-style defended house was erected about 1622 at Mongavlin in County Donegal. This consisted of a rectangular building with four corner turrets carried on moulded corbels. There were chimneys at each end, although only one fireplace, with an adjacent brick-lined oven, survives on the ground floor. There must have been at least one other fireplace at the opposite end of the house, probably at first-floor level. The building was divided into three storeys by timber floors and had timber stairs. The castle had a relatively large number of windows. One gun-loop survives near the main entrance, and it is likely that there were others. Another of the Scottish-type castles built during this period is Ballygalley on the Antrim coast.

The English involvement in the plantations was very considerable, not least in the area granted to the merchant companies of the City of London. Many of the castles built in this Londonderry colony reflect contemporary English Jacobean styles. At Brackfield Castle, on the Skinners' Company land, only the rectangular bawn with two diagonally opposite rounded flanking towers survives. A drawing, made in 1622, shows the original two-storey house along the south-western side of the enclosure. The picture was made by Thomas Raven, who drew all the plantation castles and bawns on the lands of the London companies. Although some original remains do survive at many of these sites, none of them have been excavated, except for the house built by Sir Edward Doddington in Dungiven.

Converted monasteries and castles

It used to be thought that Doddington's house had been located at the site of the present nineteenth-century Dungiven Castle. However, recent archaeological detective work, using Thomas Raven's 1622 drawing and other evidence, has shown that the actual site had been at the south-east corner of the nearby Augustinian Priory and beside the ruins of a Medieval tower-house of the O'Cahan family. An excavation was carried out there in 1982 and substantial evidence of the house was uncovered. Raven's drawing depicts a three-storey building. The excavation showed that the ground-floor was divided into two main rooms, each with a fireplace and timber floors. There was also a small lobby just inside the front door. A flagstone-floored room projecting from the rear of the house was interpreted as a scullery. Evidence of internal plaster on the stone walls was preserved, as was a quantity of coloured English and Dutch wall tiles, reflecting a touch of luxury in the decoration of the house. A collection of locks, keys,

handles and hinges for small doors was also found.

Another Medieval monastic building converted into a seventeenth-century dwelling house was the Carmelite Priory at Rathmullan in Donegal. In about 1618 the small nave and south transept were converted into an L-shaped dwelling house by Andrew Knox, Protestant bishop of Raphoe. A number of typically Scottish features, such as the two angle turrets supported by moulded corbels which can be paralleled on a large number of contemporary Ulster buildings, were added by Bishop Knox. A curious feature of the conversion was the construction of two elegant brick chimneys on the west gable. These must have been built as a purely decorative feature, as there is no sign of any fireplace or flue on this wall. Of more practical use were the pistol-loops added by the bishop. The chancel of the priory was used as a parish church. This was the fate of many of the other dissolved Medieval monastic houses. Buildings such as the naves of Dungiven Priory and Grey Abbey in County Down also show signs of seventeenth-century alteration for the worship of the new settlers.

Similarly several Medieval castles and tower-houses were adapted for use by the new colonists. Among the most elaborate of these conversions was that at Donegal Castle, where Sir Basil Brook added a wing in the style of a Jacobean manor to the existing Late Medieval tower-house of the O'Donnell family. Brook also inserted a number of large mullioned windows into the older tower-house and installed a very fine carved fireplace and overmantel in the main room of the building at first-floor level. Dunluce Castle in County Antrim and Dundrum Castle in County Down are among others which show changes and additions dating to this period. At Greencastle in County Donegal, two brick-lined ovens indicate renovations carried out there about 1611. Among the several innovations which the plantation introduced to Ulster was the skill of building in bricks.

Unfortified houses

The various sets of picture maps of the time illustrate the types of unfortified houses lived in by the ordinary people during the earliest phases of the plantation. Basically three distinct types are shown: English-style stone houses with slate roofs and brick chimneys; timber-framed houses and Irish-style thatched cottages. Frequently all three types are present in the one settlement. Although a number of houses are known in

Map of Mercers settlement in County Derry, during the plantation of Ulster, showing a stone house within a bawn, with corner towers, timber-framed buildings and small thatched houses.

View of Derry's walls.

Richard Barthelett's map of Armagh, c. 1603. (see p216)

Ulster from the end of the seventeenth century, buildings dating to the early plantation period have not been identified as easily. However, some later houses may mask details of earlier buildings. Excavation at Linenhall Street in Derry showed that the basements of later buildings had been formed from the ground floors of two houses dating to about 1630. Other similar remains may survive elsewhere.

The adjoining Linenhall Street houses measured approximately 5.5m x 9m (18ft x 30ft) in plan, and seem to have had at least one upper floor. They each had large stone fireplaces with attached brick-lined ovens. In one of the houses there was evidence for internal plastering, similar to that found at Doddington's house at Dungiven. Although Raven's map of 1622 seems to suggest that all the houses in Derry had slate roofs, quantities of red ceramic pantiles have been found all over the plantation city, including the Linenhall Street site. The two excavated houses had stone walls, as apparently did all the buildings in the city. Timber-framed houses were not erected in Derry itself, although they were built by the Londoners in their other settlements.

Development of towns

An essential part of the plantation scheme was the development of towns. Up until then there was very little urbanisation in Ulster. The new seventeenth-century towns were often built at locations which had some previous importance, perhaps as the site of a castle or monastery, or the seat of a bishopric. Excavation has taken place in some of the towns associated with the plantation, particularly in Coleraine and Derry. At Derry a small trading and garrison settlement, based on the ancient ecclesiastical ruins and the English Elizabethan fortifications, was incorporated as a city in 1604. This was destroyed by Sir Cahir O'Doherty in 1608, leaving a cleared site and paving the way for a bold new experiment in town planning.

Work began on the walled city of Londonderry in 1610. The defences consisted of a stone wall 2m (6ft) thick and averaging over 6m (20ft) high. Behind this an earthen rampart about 3.5m (12ft) thick was constructed; the material came mainly from a fosse or ditch about 9–10m (30ft) wide and 3m (10ft) deep, which ran on the outside of the wall for about half its length. There were originally four gates, two of which had drawbridges, while there was a portcullis at each of the others. The enclosed area was quite small, only 457m (500yds) long by 274m (300yds) at its widest. Internally, the streets were laid out in a grid pattern, leading to a central square. The design of the city, which was to be the jewel in the crown of the plantation, bears close resemblance to the new Renaissance town of Vitry-le-Francois in eastern France, finished about 1560 by King Francis II. American archaeologists and historians of town-planning have suggested that in turn the Londonderrry plan was the basis for the design of several settlements in the contemporary English colonies being established on the other side of the Atlantic.

There were several other similarities and parallels with the English colonisation of America. Many of the individuals active in the Ulster schemes were also involved in the American colonising projects, such as those promoted by the Virginia Company of London. Mention has already been made of the Flowerdew castle at Shannock in Fermanagh. There were close family associations between this and the Flowerdew Hundred settlement in Virginia, recently excavated, which was set up between 1619 and 1622. The excavator of the Martin's Hundred settlement near Williamsburg in Virginia has used evidence from the Merchant Tailors Company settlement at Macosquin in County Derry to interpret the remains of his American site which was occupied between 1619 and 1622.

Excavations on sites of this period in Derry and other locations have turned up many fragments of clay tobacco pipes, the first evidence of the newly introduced habit of smoking. These pipes are invaluable for archaeologists as they are frequently marked, and constant changes in bowl and stem shape and size help to date and identify the source of their manufacture. Different kinds of pottery have also been found. Most of the vessels were imported from the increasingly industrialised potteries in England. In Derry, sections through the town ditch outside the city walls have been exposed and several rubbish pits and garden areas of the plantation town have been uncovered. A number of stone-lined wells have been identified within the walls, which presumably were in use during the early seventeenth century. The most important plantation structure in the city, however, is St Columb's Church of Ireland cathedral. Constructed between 1628 and 1633, the design was already old-fashioned by that time. However, because many of its contemporaries were destroyed in the great fire of London, St Columb's remains one of the finest examples of Gothic survival buildings in these islands. Besides alterations to a number of existing Medieval buildings, several specially built churches were erected as part of the plantation for the new forms of Protestant worship then being introduced. Derryloran in County Tyrone and Derrygonnelly in County Fermanagh are among the most interesting of those surviving.

So far there have been few excavations carried out at plantation sites or studies made of the artifacts of the period. In the future, this kind of work by archaeologists, added to the documentary research of historians of the early seventeenth century, will give us a much clearer picture of the lifestyle of the early British colonists in Ulster and the effect this had on the native Irish.

Objects found in excavations at Derry.

TIME CHART
From Later Medieval to Early Modern times

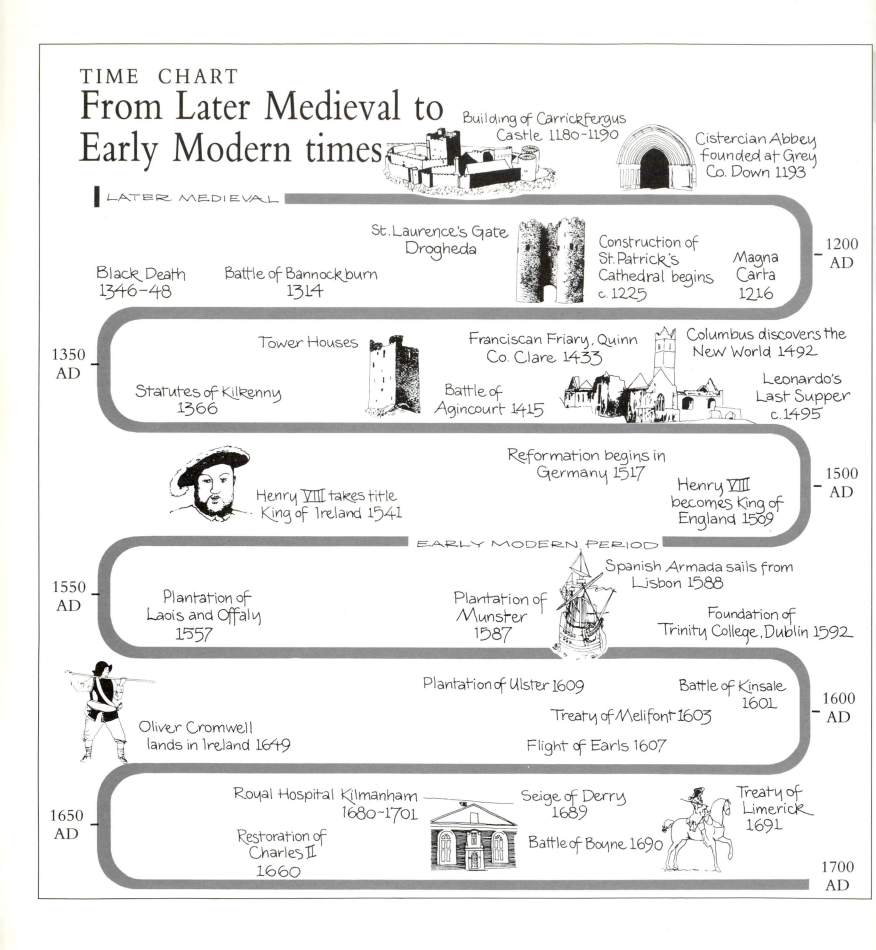

Building of Carrickfergus Castle 1180-1190

Cistercian Abbey founded at Grey Co. Down 1193

▮ LATER MEDIEVAL

St. Laurence's Gate Drogheda

Construction of St. Patrick's Cathedral begins c. 1225

Magna Carta 1216

1200 AD

Black Death 1346-48

Battle of Bannockburn 1314

1350 AD

Tower Houses

Franciscan Friary, Quinn Co. Clare 1433

Columbus discovers the New World 1492

Statutes of Kilkenny 1366

Battle of Agincourt 1415

Leonardo's Last Supper c. 1495

Reformation begins in Germany 1517

1500 AD

Henry VIII takes title King of Ireland 1541

Henry VIII becomes King of England 1509

EARLY MODERN PERIOD

Spanish Armada sails from Lisbon 1588

1550 AD

Plantation of Laois and Offaly 1557

Plantation of Munster 1587

Foundation of Trinity College, Dublin 1592

Plantation of Ulster 1609

Battle of Kinsale 1601

Treaty of Melifont 1603

1600 AD

Oliver Cromwell lands in Ireland 1649

Flight of Earls 1607

Royal Hospital Kilmanham 1680-1701

Seige of Derry 1689

Treaty of Limerick 1691

1650 AD

Restoration of Charles II 1660

Battle of Boyne 1690

1700 AD

Changes in living standards in the seventeenth century

Mairéad Dunlevy

War, plantations and political events in the sixteenth and early seventeenth century weakened Gaelic power and strengthened that of the 'New English' colonists. Parallel with this was a transition from a Medieval-style, self-sufficient society, to one with an embryonic industrialisation policy and a substantial agricultural surplus. Modernisation is seen in the enclosure of fields, the growth of towns, the increase in the number of fairs and markets, and the establishment of a regular postal service which, through ensuring the widening and improvement of roads to certain towns, opened up more of the land to direct influence from Dublin and London. Increased wealth gave rise also to theatres, music-halls, coffee-houses and the establishment of newspapers.

Growth of manors

The modernisation trend can be followed most clearly in the evolution of manors. Previously the gentry lived in tower-houses and robust, fortified homes. The new overlords, with confidence in control of the land and of eventual peace, used less fortified houses with large windows, some of which were surrounded with pleasure gardens and deer parks. These homes were divided within into a greater number of rooms so as to satisfy the increasing demand for personal privacy and for specialist use. The aim was to furnish them in the English manorial style, and so, after about 1660, English and Dutch portrait painters were given patronage and Irish artists emerged. Furniture in oak and walnut was made in styles akin to those in England and the Low Countries, and the other trappings of wealth, such as furnishings of damask and velvet, decorative ironwork and ceramics, were both imported and made here. Stucco-workers, stone-carvers, wood-carvers and gardeners were taught by craftsmen from England, France, Germany and the Low Countries — the countries which led the fashion of the time.

Cultural change

This cultural change was aided also through the large-scale immigration which took place in the seventeenth century. The newcomers were principally planters and artisans from England and Scotland, but there were religious refugees too, such as French Huguenots, German Palatines and Moravians, and Dutch and Flemish entrepreneurs and craftsmen. All adapted readily to their new land; indeed as early as 1623 they advocated a loyalty to Irish manufacture so as, they said, 'to help this poor country'. This loyalty was intended particularly for the industries which they had established, but also to discourage the 'wastage' of money out of Ireland in purchasing such exotica as Oriental porcelain, japanned furniture and Indian chintz from the East India Companies; tapestries from France, or items as cumbersome as the home of Gronix the linen-weaver, which, tradition claims, was transferred from Holland to Carrick-on-Suir.

Technological advances

The colonisation of much of the land allowed entrepreneurs to look on Ireland as on other 'remote' provinces of Britain and to introduce similar technological processes to it. In this way industrial iron-smelting and glass-manufacture were introduced. This increased the consumption of woodland, which suited the authorities. Deforestation was the official policy. The success of the earl of Cork's iron smelters is legendary

The plaster chimney-piece from Old Bawn House, Tallaght, County Dublin, built by Archdeacon Bulkeley in 1635. (see p216)

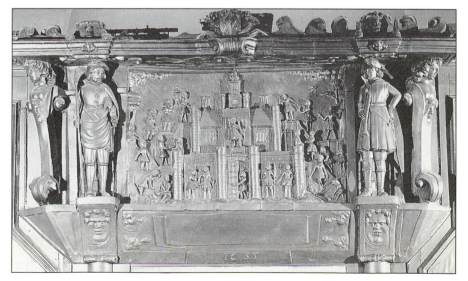

Costume of a reasonably well-to-do Irishman of the first half of the seventeenth century.
(see p216)

Glass bottle of Irish manufacture, from about 1690, found at Kenmare, County Kerry.
(see p216)

Imported French apothecary's wet drug pot, from about 1680. Found at Bride Street, Dublin.

Two sugar casters made by Richard Goble of Cork around 1690 for a member of the Sarsfield family.
(see p216)

example, meant that clay pipes were at first imported in bulk from Holland and England, but in the 1640s a specialised factory was set up in Waterford, followed soon afterwards by others in different parts of the country. Similarly, the demand for Oriental porcelain, as well as for the cheaper Dutch and London delft, led to the establishment of a delftware pottery in Belfast about 1698. This produced delft table and ornamental ware in imitation of, but less expensive than, Oriental porcelain, and also provided hygienic containers for apothecaries' shops.

All these new manufacturers were expected to produce items of uniform size and standard. The new industrial attitudes had their effect on the older craft industries: from 1637 gold and silver, and from 1697–8 pewter, had to be marked to guarantee a standard of fineness. The style of the precious metal products also changed because at this time demand for domestic plate was becoming greater than for ecclesiastical plate. The range of silver required then matched that of other sophisticated centres throughout Western Europe as beer bowls, caudle cups, spoons, basins, sugar-boxes, cans, porringers, candlesticks and trencher salts were assayed in Dublin in 1638.

Less wealthy new settlers also made an impact industrially. The importation at first of gravel-tempered and sgraffito-wares from North Devon and black-glazed red pottery from the East Midlands of England and North Wales gave rise to the establishment of small 'country' potteries which made similar ware here for local markets. Huguenots are credited with transforming the Irish silk industry, making it more commercial, introducing the broad loom, and weaving silk with Irish wool and linen, thus producing Irish poplins and tabinet. The Irish linen and woollen industries were also developed along more commercial lines.

The dichotomy in the Irish nation is obvious in that while these entrepreneurs, adventurers and planters were spearheading an early industrial revolution, change was slower in Gaelic Ireland, where many were reduced to a new poverty. But change was taking place. The adoption of English-style dress by many men, particularly from the 1640s, is a clear example. The goods carried on older traditional trade routes also emphasise this change: between Spain and the west coast of Ireland such new luxuries as sophisticated soft, pliable woollens, lustre ware and olive jars were shipped.

but, later, in an attempt to save the woodlands, the primitive glassworks were transferred from the interior to ports so that they could use imported coal. About the year 1675, glass factories in Dublin were making bottles and tableware. The quality of the latter was improved after George Ravenscroft invented a more reliable flint glass for the Glass Sellers' Company of England. When the Dublin factories discovered his recipe they quickly followed it and abandoned their manufacture of the fragile Venetian-style soda glass made elsewhere.

Demand for other foreign luxuries gave rise to factories at home: the growth in the addiction to American tobacco in the seventeenth century, for

LIST OF ILLUSTRATIONS

OPW = Office of Public Works
DOENI = Department of the
Environment, Northern Ireland
OSO = Ordnance Survey Office

ADDITIONAL INFORMATION ON THE ILLUSTRATIONS

THE LANDSCAPE OF IRELAND (Michael Ryan)

The Giant's Causeway, County Antrim. *Between 100 and 65 million years ago, molten basalt which had welled up through the chalk of the Antrim plateau, cooled to form this striking series of hexagonal columns.*

RESCUE ARCHAEOLOGY (Margaret Gowen)

Fishamble Street, Dublin. *A series of rescue excavations here and at adjacent sites between 1969 and 1982 revealed an astonishing wealth of material. Both structures and artifacts were recovered, shedding light on the growth of the Medieval town from the Viking Age to the Later Medieval period.*

In November 1983, archaeologists had a brief opportunity to investigate seventeenth-century Belfast. *They found that the earliest map of the town contained inaccurate details. Rescue excavation can take place throughout the year, regardless of the weather.*

Construction of the North Eastern Gas Pipeline. *Major projects such as this, or road-building, require careful archaeological monitoring lest important, hidden sites be destroyed.*

UNDERWATER ARCHAEOLOGY (Nessa O'Connor)

Finds from the Armada ship, the *Girona*, wrecked off Port na Spaniagh, near Bushmills on the Antrim coast. *The ship itself had disintegrated. The artifacts discovered included cannon, navigation instruments and this collection of jewellery, which includes a gold salamander pendant set with rubies.*

Artillery equipment, including shot-gauges, powder-scoop and ramrod, from the Spanish Armada ship *La Trinidad Valancera* which sank in Kinnegoe Bay, County Donegal in 1588. *The cannonballs are from the Girona. Recent underwater research has thrown new light on the organisation of the Armada and given fascinating insights into the deck cargoes of armaments intended for the invasion of England.*

A little gold boat. *This little model of a ship, complete with rowing benches, oars, mast, steering sweep and anchor, appears to be a votive object. It was the subject of a famous court action in London to establish whether it was Treasure Trove or not; it was argued strongly on one side that it was cast away as an offering to a god and on the other that it had been deliberately concealed and was therefore not abandoned property. The court found that it had been concealed and the find was thus deposited in the National Collections.*

A sixteenth-century sword. *Fords are important find-places of archaeological material, presumably because people often lost their possessions during the hazards of the crossing.*

WETLAND ARCHAEOLOGY (Ann Lynch)

Tawnamore, County Sligo. *His clothing consisted of a hat, coat, doublet, open breeches, knitted worsted stockings, felt garters and shoes of untanned leather.*

Hand-cutting of turf in a bog near Maam Cross, Connemara, County Galway. *Finds are more often made during hand-cutting of turf. The increasing mechanisation of peat exploitation, even on small, privately owned bogs, militates against discoveries or ensures that if finds are made they are often damaged and out of context.*

Woman's gown, of woollen twill, from Shinrone, County Tipperary. *Its style reflects international fashion in the decades around AD 1600, adapted to Irish traditions of tailoring.*

A gold dress-fastener of the Later Bronze Age found at Killymoon Demesne, County Tyrone, in the early nineteenth century. *It is one of a small number of precious objects of prehistoric times lost or deliberately deposited in bogs in carefully made wooden boxes.*

EARLY ENVIRONMENTS AND THE FIRST SETTLERS (Michael O'Connell)

Cross at Moone, County Kildare. *The panel shows the twelve apostles in a flat and simplified style. There is some dispute as to whether their appearance is the result of the carver's choice, or whether it is to some extent due to the difficulties of working the locally available stone.*

THE GEOLOGY AND RAW MATERIALS OF THE STONE AGE (John Jackson)

Three bracers (archer's wristguards) from County Antrim. *Objects of this kind were highly prized. Outside Ireland, they were frequently placed in burials, especially Beaker-burials.*

Whetstone, County Meath. *Whetstones of this type were used for sharpening tools and weapons. Whetstone amulets are known in Viking Age Scandinavia and very large examples occur in seventh-century Anglo-Saxon graves, where they may have been used as sceptres.*

FLINT AND STONE TOOLS (Elizabeth Anderson)

Modern Eskimo bow-drill with a flint bit, from Alaska. *The shaft is caused to rotate by means of the cord or thong looped around it, and moved backwards and forwards by a sawing action of the bow. Using a cylindrical bit without a tip, but with an abrasive powder such as fine sand, holes could be bored in hard stone. This required a great deal of effort, involving weeks of work.*

THE MESOLITHIC PERIOD (Peter Woodman)

Deposits excavated in 1935 at Curran Point, Larne, County Antrim. *Such deposits, containing Later Mesolithic artifacts, enabled Professor Hallam Movius to build up a convincing chronology of the Irish Mesolithic period before the advent of radiocarbon dating. He did this by relating the layers of material to the changes in sea-level following the warming effects of the post-glacial climate (often marked by changes in the molluscs preserved in the material).*

Excavations in progress at the Late Mesolithic site of Ferriter's Cove, County Kerry. *The evidence of a food-collecting community here shows that the Mesolithic inhabitants had extended their range to include the whole island of Ireland.*

THE NEOLITHIC ENVIRONMENT (Michael O'Connell)

Bark of an elm. *The spread of such a disease may well have caused the dramatic decline in elm pollen noted in Ireland, Britain and parts of mainland Europe around the time agriculture first appears in the archaeological record.*

Pollen diagram from Scragh Bog, near Lough Owel, County Westmeath. *There is a marked decline in the values for elm, coinciding with the increase in the values for grasses and ribwort plantain which occurred in the Early Neolithic period. A similar sequence of events took place in the Later Neolithic period.*

Twyford, County Westmeath. *A similar basket found at Aghintemple, County Longford, contained a polished stone axehead.*

The Early Neolithic site of Donegore Hill, County Antrim. *The darker curved bands are caused by the vegetation growing greener over the line of filled-in ancient ditches. Excavation has shown that the site was defended by two ditches and palisades and was occupied from about 4000 to about 2700 BC.*

THE FIRST FARMERS (Alison Sheridan)

Ritual stone object. *It has similarities with carved stone and bone objects, also interpreted as ritual, from passage tombs in Iberia. Neolithic period, about 3000 BC.*

A hoard of polished stone axeheads made of porcellanite, found at Malone, Belfast. *Porcellanite was the rock employed by the axe-factories of Tievebulliagh, County Antrim and Brockley on Rathlin Island. The polished stone axehead is perhaps the most characteristic tool of the Neolithic period.*

THE LATER NEOLITHIC PERIOD (Anna Brindley)

Ceremonial macehead. *The superb spiral and facetted decoration makes this one of the most imposing prestige objects from prehistoric Ireland. It has very close comparisons in Later Neolithic southern Britain and is arguably an import.*

Small dolmen. *In the distance is Queen Maeve's Cairn on Carrowmore Mountain. Passage tombs are regularly grouped in clusters, referred to as cemeteries, the largest of which are to be found in the Boyne Valley, at Lough Crew in County Meath and at Carrowkeel and Carrowmore in County Sligo.*

THE MEGALITHIC TOMB BUILDERS (Seán Ó Nualláin)

The burial chamber of the passage tomb of Fourknocks, County Meath. *This great chamber, measuring 5.5m (18ft) in maximum diameter, is almost twice the width of Newgrange. Its passage and three recesses contained the remains of upwards of sixty-five individuals, most of them cremated.*

Passage tomb at Newgrange. *Three recesses opening off the main chamber give this tomb the cruciform plan typical of many Irish passage tombs. The carvings visible on the stones are a feature of Irish passage tombs.*

Stone beads and pendants from the Carrowkeel cemetery. *With the exception of its coarse pottery (Carrowkeel Ware), the sophistication of the architecture of the tombs is mirrored in the finely made ornaments frequently found in the burial deposits.*

A well-preserved court tomb in its characteristic trapeze-shaped cairn, 18m (59ft) long, uncovered during land reclamation at Creggandevesky, County Tyrone. *The burial gallery was originally roofed by corbelling and contained the cremated remains of twenty-one individuals.*

NEOLITHIC SETTLEMENTS (Eoin Grogan)

Aerial view of the excavation of the central court tomb and rectangular Neolithic house of Ballyglass, County Mayo. *The Neolithic house was subsequently partly covered by the construction of the tomb. Had the tomb not been excavated, it is unlikely that the house would have come to light.*

THE ENVIRONMENT AND HUMAN ACTIVITY IN BRONZE AGE IRELAND (Michael O'Connell)

Schematic drawing of a section cut through a cultivation ridge at Carrownaglogh, County Mayo. *Pollen samples taken at the points indicated by bars gave a record of cultivation history in Bronze Age times. At A no pollen was preserved; at B cereal crops infested with weeds were grown, and the record at C suggests that arable farming continued in the locality as blanket-bog began to cover the site.*

THE EARLIER BRONZE AGE (John Waddell)

Inchnagree, County Cork. *Two halves of a mould for casting dirks, small blades, including a possible razor, and other implements. Second half of the Earlier Bronze Age. The evidence of moulds carrying matrices for more than one type of implement helps to establish what types were current at the same time.*

THE GEOLOGY AND RAW MATERIALS OF THE BRONZE AGE (John Jackson)

Bronze Age metalwork. *The history of the Bronze Age is encapsulated to a large extent in the history of metal-working. We can see in the development from the simple, flat copper axeheads cast in open moulds, an increasing sophistication in casting techniques. The socketed spearheads are cast in complex moulds, with a plug to form the socket, a technology introduced late in the Earlier Bronze Age. The rapiers and the leaf-shaped swords of the Later Bronze Age are masterpieces of casting. In the Later Bronze Age lead was sometimes added to bronze to improve its run in casting, demonstrating a sophisticated manipulation of raw materials. As the Bronze Age advanced, so too did the range of metal tools, from the simple axe forms and curved halberd blade of the early period to the similar but highly efficient sickle of the Later Bronze Age.*

COPPER MINING IN SOUTH-WEST IRELAND (William F O'Brien)

Wooden shovel and pick from mine 3, Mount Gabriel. *The waterlogged deposits in the mine preserved not only these artifacts but also wooden wedges, hammer handles, wooden chips for lighting, as well as the fuel used for setting fires.*

METAL PRODUCTION (Laurence Flanagan)

Massive gold dress-fastener, from Clones, County Monaghan. *At just over a kilogram in weight, it is one of the heaviest and largest of these typical Later Bronze Age ornaments. Dates to the eighth century BC.*

DEATH IN THE EARLIER BRONZE AGE (John Waddell)

Food vessel from Aghnahily, County Laois. *Specialised funerary pots such as this were made to accompany the dead in Earlier Bronze Age Ireland.*

THE LATER BRONZE AGE (INTRODUCTION)

The Later Bronze Age saw many changes in the Irish bronze industry. New techniques such as sheet bronze-working were mastered, and old technology was pushed to its limits to achieve more and more complex effects, as in the casting of the horns of the period. The deposition of hoards, such as the small group of implements in the foreground, found in a wooden box in a bog at Bootown, County Antrim, is typical of the later stages of the period.

DAILY LIFE IN THE LATER BRONZE AGE (George Eogan)

Leaf-shaped sword of bronze. *Weapons of this type are characteristic of the equipment of the warrior in the Later Bronze Age. Their handles would have been fitted with rivetted plates of bone, horn or wood. The shape of the blade ensures that the centre of gravity is near the point, and so it is well designed for slashing and stabbing, unlike the simpler rapiers of earlier times which seem to have been primarily thrusting weapons.*

Bronze spearhead found near Roscrea, County Tipperary. *While rapiers and, later, swords, were the prestige weapons in the Bronze Age, there is little doubt that the majority of fighting men were armed with spears. Tipping a wooden shaft with a metal head is a way of providing an efficient weapon for a relatively small outlay of metal, and in the Later Bronze Age small spearheads were common.*

Tassel of tablet-woven horsehair. *This may have been part of a belt found wrapped in a woollen cloth near the bottom of a bog at Cromaghs, near Armoy, County Antrim.*

BRONZE AGE SETTLEMENTS (Martin Doody)

Reconstruction drawing of the lakeside habitation of Cullyhanna, County Armagh. *It has been accurately dated by dendrochronology to the year 1526 BC and thus is firmly dated to the Earlier Bronze Age. Excavation failed to find evidence for intensive occupation and the site has been interpreted as a temporary hunting camp.*

THE GEOLOGY AND RAW MATERIALS OF THE IRON AGE (John Jackson)

Iron shears from Garryduff, County Cork. *There is evidence for the smelting of iron on many Early Medieval sites. Some simple iron-working must have been carried on to keep farm equipment in repair and perhaps to make the very simplest of tools. More complex tools and weapons would have called for the skills of the specialist smith, and ancient Irish law and legend combine to tell us that the master blacksmith enjoyed the highest status among craftworkers.*

THE EARLY IRON AGE (Barry Raftery)

The great gold collar from Broighter, County Derry, found in a hoard with a small gold boat, a bowl and other ornaments. *It was manufactured in the first century BC, and is one of the outstanding examples of craftsmanship in the La Tène style. It was old at the time of its concealment.*

Drawing of one of two block-wheels found in a bog at Doogarymore, County Roscommon. *The wheel was fitted with a sleeve for the axle. As the name implies, block-wheels were made of one or more solid pieces of timber. The Doogarymore wheels have been radiocarbon dated to about 400 BC.*

Reconstruction drawing of a wooden trackway at Corlea Bog, County Longford. *This road can be shown to have been built in 148 BC. Such roads may have been used to allow both pedestrians and vehicles to cross areas of bog between patches of valuable agricultural land.*

THE EARLIEST HISTORY OF IRELAND (Richard Warner)

Aerial view of Navan Fort, the ancient Emain Macha, County Armagh. *The great enclosure is 230m (754ft) in internal diameter and is defined by an internal ditch. The*

building may have been a shrine of some kind. Navan Fort is at the centre of a complex of monuments of the period from the end of the Bronze Age to the advanced Iron Age. Historically, it was the tribal centre of the kingdom of the Ulaidh and retained its importance into the fifth century, when the nearby church of Armagh was founded by St Patrick.

The skull of a Barbary ape from Navan Fort. *This exotic animal was presumably imported as a pet or sent as a gift to the potentate of Emain Macha in the second or third century BC.*

While iron became the principal material for weapons and tools of the Iron Age, bronze remained important for decorative work and for accessories. *The small swords characteristic of the time are the sort that the famous heroes of ancient Irish sagas, if they really had existed, would have wielded. Alas, for the sake of romance, the descriptions of weapons in epics such as the 'Táin Bó Cuailnge' (The Cattle Raid of Cooley), are those of the Viking Age, the time at which the sagas were composed.*

THE EARLY MEDIEVAL PERIOD (INTRODUCTION)

Carved pillar representing two back-to-back figures, from Boa Island, County Fermanagh. *This sculpture, fitted with a socket at the top, is one of a series of architectural carvings from Lough Erne. Often erroneously described as belonging to the pagan Iron Age, it was probably sculpted in the ninth or tenth century and could conceivably have been part of the decoration of a church, like the related figures from White Island, also on Lough Erne.*

CRANNOGS (Eamon P Kelly)

Decorative sieve from Moylarg Crannog, County Antrim. Eighth century AD. *Elaborate wine-strainers, with holes laid out in patterns, were common in the Roman world, and it is possible that the Moylarg sieve was used for the same purpose.*

The crannog of Cro-Inis, Lough Ennel, County Westmeath. *View from the ditch of the ring-fort of Dún na Sciath. Both the crannog and the ring-fort were occupied in the early eleventh century by Maelsechnaill, King of the Kingdom of Mide, and for a time premier king in Ireland until displaced by Brian Boru. The crannog is ringed by submerged piles and by a strong palisade of planks. The core of the artificial island consists of a massive mound of stones crowned by a small Later Medieval tower. The outlay of effort required in its construction could only have been commanded by a person of high status.*

Two plough-coulters, one from Ballinderry Crannog No. 1, County Westmeath, the other from Bellair, County Westmeath. *The Ballinderry coulter was found on the floor of a house of the earliest phase of occupation of the crannog and should date to the tenth century AD. It clearly signals the agricultural economy of the occupants. Coulters were large blades suspended from the beam of a plough, in front of the share, to cut the sod.*

Reconstruction drawing of a crannog in its setting, *published in 1886.*

The crannog of Ballinderry, County Offaly, in the course of excavation. *The typical build-up of wicker and dumped soil is evident, as is the logboat (dug-out canoe) sunk to form part of the foundation.*

SOUTERRAINS

Souterrains are underground structures consisting of a passage or passages leading to one or more chambers. The passages are normally lined with drystone and roofed with slabs, while chambers are often corbelled or roofed with a combination of corbelling and slabs. Chambers are usually round or rectangular. One wooden example has been found and there are some in the south-west which are partly or wholly tunnelled in firm subsoil without further support. They are frequently associated with ring-forts. Many examples are discovered during ploughing since there would now be no obvious monument in the vicinity; however, the former existence of one may often be suspected. The passage tomb mound of Knowth, occupied in Early Medieval times, is honeycombed with souterrains. They are extremely common in counties Antrim, Down, Louth, Meath, and in parts of Cork and Kerry, and are widely distributed elsewhere. There may well be as many as 3000 in Ireland.

A feature of many souterrains are changes of level, which oblige the person entering to crawl, while those further in can stand comfortably. This is clearly a defensive measure, so that an incoming attacker would be at a disadvantage. Souterrains would have been useful during small-scale warfare and raiding, where aggressors would not have had time to dig the occupants out. Souterrains would also have been useful as stores, and the very simple ones may have been built principally as cellars.

RING-FORTS

Dunbeg promontory fort, County Kerry. Running a rampart across the neck of a promontory is an economic way of building a defensive enclosure. The clochán at Dunbeg was occupied during the tenth and eleventh centuries AD.

Staigue Fort in County Kerry. An outstanding example of a cashel built of dry-stone walling. Cashels built in stony areas frequently have no ditch, Staigue is an exception.

The hill-fort of Tara, County Meath. The continuing importance of this Iron Age site in Early Medieval times is marked by the two conjoined ring-forts which occur inside its main enclosure. Just visible towards the top of the picture are the traces of the once impressive Rath of the Synods, a ring-fort which was occupied in the second century AD.

Ancient cooking site from the Earlier Bronze Age, of the type called fulacht fia. Cooking was carried out by heating the water in the central trough using stones heated in an adjacent hearth. The characteristic mounds of burnt stone are amongst the most common field monuments in Ireland.

Hand-made pottery known as 'Souterrain Ware'. With some minor exceptions, only in north-eastern Ireland was pottery made and used in Early Medieval times. This distinctive simple pottery was once thought to be a characteristic find in the souterrains of counties Antrim and Down. It is most often found on habitations such as ring-forts.

A reconstruction of a horizontal mill. Water from a chute strikes a wheel fitted with small paddle-like extensions, causing a vertical shaft to rotate and thus turning an upper millstone on a lower. Remains of horizontal mills are fairly commonly found in wetlands and a number have been dated by dendrochronology as early as the seventh and eighth centuries. The earliest occurrence of the water-powered mill in Ireland is uncertain, but by the time of writing of the earliest law tracts at about AD 700, they were an established part of the landscape.

ST PATRICK TO THE VIKINGS (Michael Ryan)

A hoard of Roman hacksilver (cut-up pieces) and 1506 coins, found at Ballinrees, near Coleraine, County Derry, deposited about AD 420. The character of the material suggests that it was booty taken from Britain shortly after the withdrawal of the legions.

EARLY IRISH CHRISTIANITY (Dáibhí Ó Cróinín)

From The Book of Ballymote. A manuscript compiled at Ballymote, County Sligo, in the fourteenth and fifteenth centuries, which gives the key to the ogham script. It is preserved in the library of the Royal Irish Academy, Dublin.

The colophon or entry ascribing authorship in the copy of Adomnán's Life of Columba, written before AD 713 by the Iona bishop Dorbbéne. It is now preserved in the Stadtbibliothek of Schaffhausen in Switzerland, having previously been in the library of the monastery of Reichenau.

The manuscript known as the Cathach of St Columba, a psalter or book of the Psalms. It is conceivable that this, the earliest surviving Irish manuscript, was written in the lifetime of the saint, if not as traditionally claimed by Columba himself. (Columba died in AD 597.) The decorative features which characterised the later magnificent manuscripts are already present in simple form in the Cathach.

EARLY IRISH MONASTERIES (Michael Ryan)

A corbelled beehive hut on the monastery of Skellig Michael, County Kerry. A monastery such as Skellig may have been largely penitential and have required the support of a mainland foundation. Recent research has revealed another monastery on the rock and at its pinnacle an artificial platform. While many monasteries were wealthy, cosmopolitan in their fashion and increasingly worldly, there was a strong and continuing tradition of prayer and penance in the early Irish church.

The small, drystone church at Gallarus, County Kerry. Often thought of as the earliest and simplest of Irish stone churches, yet there is good reason to believe that examples of this form may be as late in date as the twelfth century. A noteworthy feature of many Irish sites is the presence of a number of small churches.

Teampull Finghín, Clonmacnoise, County Offaly. A mid-twelfth-century church with a round tower incorporated in the design. Other churches incorporating a round tower, normally free-standing, are known, such as St Kevin's Kitchen at Glendalough.

Aerial view of the monastery of Devenish, Lough Erne, County Fermanagh. This monastery was founded by St Molaise. A pair of round towers formerly existed on the site. The surviving one bears Romanesque carvings.

A cross-inscribed pillar, Glencolumbkille, County Donegal. Monoliths carved with crosses may be amongst the earliest Christian sculptures to survive in Ireland, but examples are very difficult to date with confidence because of their simplicity. Pillars such as this one often became stations on pilgrimages in modern times.

The monastic enclosure of Moyne, near Shrule, County Mayo. A small graveyard can be seen just off centre.

This aerial view of Lusk, County Dublin, shows how property boundaries and street lines partly preserve the line of the ancient monastic enclosure. The nineteenth-century church is a replacement for a Later Medieval structure;

its bell tower, which was erected about AD 1500, preserves as one of its corner turrets the round tower of the Early Medieval monastery. Towns such as Armagh and Kells show a similar pattern.

ELEMENTS OF MANUSCRIPT PRODUCTION IN THE MIDDLE AGES (Bernard Meehan)

Map showing lapis lazuli mines in the Badakshan district of Afghanistan. From John Wood, A Personal Narrative of a Journey to the Source of the River Oxus (London, 1841).

Corpus Christi College Cambridge, MS 4, fol 241v: detail of artist holding brush in one hand and inkpot in the other, while an assistant grinds blue lump (? lapis lazuli) of pigment on a stone. Dover Bible, Christ Church Canterbury, c. 1150.

Book of Kells (c. AD 800) fol 22r. Breves Causae of Luke. Mottling of the skin is caused by bacterial decay in the course of production. The use of different inks may be noted: the purple is folium; the black is carbon ink; the yellow fillers are orpiment; the bright red probably vermilion. I owe the suggestion that vermilion was used in the Book of Kells to the kindness of Mr Anthony Cains.

Book of Kells (c. AD 800) fol 291v. Portrait of St John. The evengelist holds his gospel in one hand, his pen in the other. His ink-horn is at his right foot. The blues are made from lapis lazuli.

Engraving of the library used by Abyssinian monks at the Coptic monastery of Souriani, near Cairo, in 1837. Several book satchels are hung on pegs around the room. From Robert Curzon, Visits to Monasteries in the Levant (London, 1849).

EARLY MEDIEVAL ART (Michael Ryan)

Cover of a book-reliquary from Lough Kinale, County Longford. Early eighth century AD. This shrine would have been made for a large manuscript, probably a gospel-book.

Cross carpet page which precedes the Gospel of St Matthew in the Book of Lindisfarne, painted probably at Lindisfarne in the last decade or so of the seventh century 'for God and St Cuthbert', as a tenth-century note in it states. The same note attributes its writing to 'Eadfrith, Bishop of Lindisfarne Church'. (Eadfrith died in AD 721). The ornament consists of a complex interlacing of birds and beasts, constructed on a ruled grid with the aid of a compass and finished free-hand. The style of ornament was common to both North Britain and Ireland.

The Ardagh Chalice, made of beaten, lathe-polished silver and decorated with gold filigree, stamped copper, knitted silver and copper wire, engraving, enamel, amber, malachite. Made for dispensing the eucharistic wine at the Mass, it is one of the finest examples of the metal-worker's craft. Eighth century.

Bone motif- or trial-piece from an occupation site in the sand-hills of Dooey, County Donegal. Carved with motifs related to the ornament of sixth-/seventh-century metalwork, it is the earliest of a series of such horn and bone objects carved with patterns. These may have served as try-outs for designs, as pattern books or even in some cases as dyes for finished ornaments.

Hooked implement, Stoneyford, County Kilkenny. Decorated with spiral scrollwork, seen against a background of red enamel, this is a sumptuous example of a type of artifact found in Europe from Roman times until at least the eighth century. They are called 'toilet implements'.

Initial page from the Stowe Missal, a manuscript of the text of the Mass and a commentary on it, together with some prayers and spells. *It was written at either the monastery of Tallaght, County Dublin, or Terryglass, County Tipperary, towards the end of the eighth century, by a scribe called Moel Caich. It was bound with a text of St John's Gospel and preserved in a shrine made for it in the eleventh century.*

The Tara Brooch, found at Bettystown, County Meath, is made of cast silver, with gold filigree and amber ornaments on the front. *The filigree consists of combinations of wires and strips of gold soldered to foil backing. It is held in the panels provided by 'stitching' — small projections of metal are turned out from the sides of the panel to form hooks.*

Animal-head handle with its escutcheon plate and frame in the style of the Tara Brooch and Book of Lindisfarne. Donore, County Meath. *Early eighth century AD. The object is based on classical lion-head door pulls, but the treatment is wholly native in style.*

The Derrynaflan Hoard, County Tipperary. Found in 1980 on the monastic site of that name. *The hoard was probably concealed about the same time as the Ardagh treasure. It consists of a footed paten, a chalice, a liturgical sieve, and a basin which had covered the pieces when buried. The objects date to the eighth and ninth centuries.*

The hook and escutcheon of the largest of three hanging bowls from the Anglo-Saxon princely ship-burial of Sutton Hoo, Suffolk, England. *The enamelled scrollwork, ribbed mouldings and other features of this vessel are closely related to Irish metalwork of the later sixth/earlier seventh centuries AD.*

A small piece of experimental gold filigree from the earliest, seventh century, occupation of Lagore Crannog, County Meath. *This is perhaps the earliest identified filigree in Early Medieval Ireland. Its affinities with Anglo-Saxon work are clear.*

Disc-headed pin from Treanmanagh, County Limerick. *A small number of pins of this type were made in Ireland in the late seventh/early eighth century AD. They were dress pins, used to fasten cloaks.*

THE VIKINGS (INTRODUCTION)

The Vikings in Ireland initially enjoyed a considerable advantage in combat, wielding large well-made swords with hardened blades which were superior to those of the Irish. *Blades were often imported into Scandinavia from the accomplished forges of the Rhineland, where they were fitted with decorative hilts. Examples of these have been found in the graves of the ninth-century cemetery of Kilmainham/Islandbridge, Dublin. The picture shows the recently conserved magnificent twelfth-century sword-hilt from Lough Derg, County Tipperary, against a background of blades from the Viking cemetery of Dublin.*

IRISH ART DURING THE VIKING INVASIONS (Michael Ryan)

A large sarcophagus, now preserved in Cormac's Chapel, Cashel. *It was carved in the early twelfth century, and is a striking example of the Scandinavian Urnes style.*

VIKING AGE ART INFLUENCES (Raghnall Ó Floinn)

Ingot in mould, Moylarg Crannog, County Antrim. *This copper ingot is typical of the form favoured by the Irish. Ingots of this type have turned up in Viking Age silver hoards.*

The Roscrea Brooch, County Tipperary. *A silver brooch with simple gold filigree and amber, and simplified beasts along the margins, it is typical of the later brooches.*

Silver kite brooch, said to have been found with another in County Kilkenny in the last century. *Decorated with engraved interlace and fearsome animal heads. Its long pin, over 50cm (20in) would have made it particularly awkward to wear. The ostentatious use of silver is characteristic of personal ornaments of this period. Probably tenth century AD.*

The first major work of metal to show significant Scandinavian influence. The book-shrine, the *Soiscél Molaise*, made for the monastery of Devenish, County Fermanagh, in the first decade of the eleventh century by the craftsman Giolla Baith. *The symbols of the Evangelists on the front clearly signal that the reliquary preserved a gospel-book; the relatively plain reverse reflects the fact that the shrine was made, like many others, to be carried about, hung from the neck by a strap.*

The Cross of Muiredach at Monasterboice, County Louth. *Erected in the later ninth or early tenth century AD, this cross in its style, programme of scenes and superb carving is the stateliest and most magnificent of the Irish high crosses.*

The south cross at Ahenny, County Tipperary. *It is now clear that sculpture flowered in ninth- and tenth-century Ireland. Various styles of high cross were favoured in different regions; those at Ahenny are dominated by abstract ornament, strongly reminiscent of metal-working traditions; figure sculpture was confined to the base.*

DUBLIN IN THE VIKING AGE (Pat Wallace)

Reconstruction of house excavated at Fishamble Street, Dublin. *This tenth-century house is the most common type found in the pre-Anglo Norman levels in Dublin.*

One of two gold bracelets found under the threshold of a house in the excavations at High Street, Dublin. *Both were of Scandinavian style workmanship and had been partly distorted in order to make them fit into their place of concealment. In 988 AD, King Maelsechnaill exacted a tribute in precious metal from every house-plot in Dublin.*

Amber bead found in the excavations at Christchurch Place, Dublin, in an eleventh century deposit. *Amber was imported from the Scandinavian lands and workshops for producing beads and other items of adornment. Amber was known in Ireland in pre-Viking times — it occurs on the Tara Brooch and in Later Bronze Age hoards, but it became abundant as a result of Viking Age trade.*

THE 11th/12th CENTURY RENAISSANCE IN METALWORK (Raghnall Ó Floinn)

The Cross of Cong, made during the 1120s, probably at Roscommon, to enshrine a relic of the true cross. *The principal patron of the work was Turlough O'Connor, King of Connacht; the craftsman was Máel Isu Mac Bratdan Ua Echan. The cross is decorated with enamels which are revivals of aspects of the polychrome style of earlier times, and gilt-bronze openwork panels of Urnes-style animal ornament. The large rock-crystal surrounded by gold filigree would have served to protect and display the precious relic.*

Bronze crosier, found walled up in an ancient doorway together with an ancient manuscript in Lismore Castle, County Waterford, in 1814. *It was made by the craftsman Nechtan for Niall Mac Meic Aeducain, Bishop of Lismore 1090–1113.*

The Shrine of St Lachtin's Arm. *This was held by its hereditary custodians, the O'Healy family, at Donaghmore, County Cork, where there was a monastery traditionally founded by St Lachtin in the sixth century. Decorated with silver and niello inlaid plain and animal interlace. It was made during the first quarter of the twelfth century.*

Bell shrine from Glankeen, County Tipperary. *Said to have been found at the ancient church site of Kilcuilawn, St Cuilean's church. Decorated with silver and niello inlay, and twisted silver and copper wire in the Irish Urnes style. It dates to the earlier twelfth century AD.*

The Shrine of St Patrick's Bell, made at Armagh by Cudulig Ua hImainen and his sons between 1091 and 1105 AD at the behest of King Domhnall Ua Lochlainn. *The ornaments are amongst the finest of the Irish interpretation of the Urnes styles. Like many Irish shrines, it was preserved into modern times by hereditary custodians.*

THE ROMANESQUE STYLE IN IRELAND (Roger Stalley)

Cormac's Chapel, Cashel, County Tipperary. *This was built for the king of Munster between 1127 and 1134. With its wall arcading, decorative carving and fine masonry, the chapel introduced a new style of building to Ireland.*

Boyle Abbey, County Roscommon. *The Cistercians built on a grander scale than the monks of older Irish monasteries. The cylindrical piers, built in precisely cut stone, represent Romanesque at its most majestic.*

THE LATER MEDIEVAL PERIOD (INTRODUCTION)

The *lavabo* (wash house) of Mellifont Abbey, County Louth. *Dating from 1142, this Cistercian house was the first foundation of a regular continental monastic order in Ireland. The new orders were deliberately introduced to compete with the native monastic tradition, and were spectacularly successful. Their regular, integrated pattern of building, with church, cloister, monastic offices and domestic arrangements, contrasts sharply with the more diffuse plan of the native monasteries which comprised a multiplicity of separate structures. The Cistercians and other orders were heavily endowed by the lords of the Anglo-Norman conquest.*

GOTHIC ART AND ARCHITECTURE (Roger Stalley)

Late Medieval armour, as seen on the tomb of Pierce FitzOge Butler, who died in 1526, at Kilcooley Abbey, County Tipperary. *Much of the armour depicted on sixteenth-century effigies is peculiarly outdated by European standards.*

Jerpoint Abbey, County Kilkenny. *The sculptured figures carved in the cloister around 1400 include knights and aristocratic ladies, secular subjects which seem out of place in the seclusion of a Cistercian monastery.*

The face of Piers Butler, eighth earl of Ormond, from his tomb in St Canice's Cathedral, Kilkenny, c. 1539. *With its rounded modelling and innocent smile, this is a typical product of the Ormond 'school' of sculptors.*

The nave of Christ Church Cathedral, Dublin. *With the integration of the upper two stories, this is a sophisticated version of 'Early English' Gothic. The slight lean of the wall is a relic of the collapse of the stone vaults in 1562.*

Athassel Abbey, County Tipperary. *Following several disasters in the later Middle Ages, the church of this vast Augustinian abbey was dramatically reduced in scale. The door led to the choir of the canons and the arch above, now blocked, once held the rood or cross.*

Rosserk Friary, County Mayo. *Like many of the friaries in the west, Rosserk is almost intact, apart from the loss of its roofs. The elegant square tower is typical of friary design.*

The well-preserved cloisters at Muckross, County Kerry. *Built by the Franciscans, they underly the quality of Irish craftsmanship in the Later Middle Ages.*

ANGLO-NORMAN TOWNS (John Bradley)

The Medieval walls of Fethard, County Tipperary. *This is a typical example of a small Anglo-Norman market town. It has a single main street which expands at the east to form the marketplace. The tower of the fifteenth-century parish church of All Saints can be seen behind the wall.*

The Shee Almshouse, Kilkenny. *The dissolution of the monasteries deprived the destitute and poor of hostel and hospital facilities. Private individuals, often those who had made their fortunes from the dissolved monasteries, began to build almshouses to cater for the needy. Sir Robert Shee's Almshouse, built in 1582 to house six men and six women, is the oldest surviving example in Ireland.*

MAP OF MEDIEVAL KILKENNY

The Anglo-Norman town which developed from shortly before 1176, was laid out along one main street which linked the cathedral with the castle, known then and now as High Street. The settlement around the cathedral, Irishtown, remained a separate entity, with its own Corporation until 1843. The town had achieved the size shown here by the end of the thirteenth century, during which much of the walls were built. It did not expand again until the 1580s when the area along Maudlin Street was developed on land which had belonged to the dissolved Augustinian monastery.

The Dominican Friary, Kilkenny, founded about 1225. *Known locally as the 'Black Abbey' it is still maintained by the Dominican Order.*

ANGLO-NORMAN FORTRESSES (David Sweetman)

Cahir Castle, County Tipperary. *Built on the site of an ancient fortification, Cahir Castle dates from the fifteenth century and was restored in the nineteenth century. It is somewhat anomalous for its time as it harks back to the earlier tradition of castle-building.*

Artist's impression of a siege tower being used in an assault on a fortification. *The increasing sophistication of Medieval warfare abroad led to ever more sophisticated military architecture. The great castles of the period of the Anglo-Norman conquest of Ireland reflect those trends, but there is no evidence for extensive siege warfare in Ireland. Later, more simple fortifications proved adequate to local needs.*

Roscommon Castle, County Roscommon. *A keepless castle built in the late thirteenth century by the justiciar, Robert de Ufford. Its massive corner towers and gate defences are characteristic. Although at first a royal castle, it was for a time held by the O'Connors. It was secured for the crown in 1569, and in 1578 it was granted to Sir Nicholas Malbie.*

Trim Castle, County Meath. *One of the strongest castles to be built in Ireland, it served as a meeting place for the Medieval parliament and as a mint.*

Plan of Adare Castle, County Limerick. *This castle dates originally to the thirteenth century. It consists of an inner and an outer ward.*

LATER MEDIEVAL CASTLES (D Newman Johnson)

A fine example of a tower-house at Burnchurch, County Kilkenny. *It has corner loops, battered walls, stepped battlements and other characteristic features of the architecture of the type. Unusually, however, the two narrow sides are continued for a full storey above the long walls to create a pair of very wide turrets.*

The O'Doherty castle of Burt, Inishowen, County Donegal. *A sixteenth-century tower-house with diagonally opposed round corner turrets was placed within a bawn, with an external fosse and roofed corner bastions to provide flanking fire. It was captured for the Crown in 1601.*

The trussed timber roof of Dunsoghley Castle, County Dublin. *Surviving evidence of original Medieval timber roofs is extremely rare in Ireland and the fine preservation of that at Dunsoghley makes it unique. The castle was built in the fifteenth century by Thomas Plunkett, chief justice of the King's Bench.*

Slade Castle, County Wexford. *This castle was built in two stages, first the tall tower-house of the fifteenth and sixteenth centuries, to which was added a lower range in the later sixteenth or earlier seventeenth century.*

Blarney Castle, County Cork. *This tower, which shares the characteristics of the tower-houses, is the keep of a large McCarthy stronghold. It was built in two stages, the first a narrow tower of the mid-fifteenth century to which, at the end of the century, a larger tower was added so as partly to envelope the older structure. The tower stands 30m (85ft) high.*

LATER MEDIEVAL DECORATIVE ARTS (Raghnall Ó Floinn)

Dunvegan Cup, preserved by the MacLeod family at Dunvegan Castle on the Isle of Skye. *A four-sided drinking cup of wood covered with gilt silver mounts, some imitating Gothic tracery. It was originally made for Katherine O'Neill, wife of John Maguire, Lord of Fermanagh in 1493.*

Bog finds of Later Medieval wooden vessels. *Finds of groups of such vessels are not uncommon and occasionally examples will be found to contain butter ('bog butter').*

A group of weapons of the Later Medieval period. *The large thirteenth-century sword is from Charlemont, County Armagh, and the fifteenth- or eighteenth-century daggers are from Clogh, County Antrim and the River Barrow at Moore Abbey, County Kildare. The two silver-inlaid axeheads are of a type thought to have been used by the professional infantry of Irish chieftains, the galloglasses, who were recruited originally from the Hebrides.*

The Kavanagh Charter Horn, twelfth century AD. *A ceremonial drinking horn made of elephant ivory, dating originally from the twelfth century AD. The brass mountings are fifteenth-century additions. It was preserved for centuries by the McMurrough-Kavanagh family of Borris, County Carlow, and it symbolised their claim to the kingship of Leinster. This is the only surviving object which can be associated with Irish kings.*

The Lislaghtin Cross. *This processional cross of gilt silver was found in 1871 while ploughing reclaimed bogland. An inscription on the front records that it was made for John O'Connor, Lord of Kerry, in the year 1479.*

THE EARLY MODERN PERIOD (Michael Ryan)

Chimney piece, Donegal Castle, 1610. *Inserted into an earlier tower-house belonging to the O'Donnells. The carving includes the arms of Sir Basil Brooke and the strapwork and festoons popular in the ornament of the period.*

THE ARCHAEOLOGY OF THE MUNSTER PLANTATION (Denis Power)

Mallow Castle *is the only substantial rural remains of the Munster plantation. The castle consists of a rectangular block with pentagonal turrets at north-west and south-west corners, and projecting wings from the centre of the east and west walls. The house had three floors, with the entrance at ground-floor level and an attic under the main gabled roof.*

A contemporary plan of Baltimore *shows a prosperous fishing village, but the peace was rudely shattered in 1631 when Barbary pirates raided the town and carried away many of its inhabitants, to be sold as slaves.*

THE ARCHAEOLOGY OF THE ULSTER PLANTATION (Brian Lacey)

Donegal Castle, County Donegal. *The massive fifteenth-century O'Donnell tower-house was converted by Sir Basil Brooke during the second decade of the seventeenth century into a comfortable manor house in the Jacobean style by opening mullioned windows in the tower and reducing it in height.*

Monea Castle, County Fermanagh. *Built in the early seventeenth century by Malcolm Hamilton, Rector of Devenish. A plantation castle, built in a scottish style.*

Richard Barthelett's map of Armagh, c. 1603. *The map shows the outline of the Early Medieval monastic site with its high cross in position, together with the later cathedral and a contemporary artillery fort with bastions.*

CHANGES IN LIVING STANDARDS IN THE SEVENTEENTH CENTURY (Mairéad Dunlevy)

The plaster chimney-piece from Old Bawn House, Tallaght. *The scene depicts the building of the walls of Jerusalem under the protection of a constable and accompanied by music. The house at Old Bawn was unfortunately demolished at the turn of the century and only the chimney-piece and an important staircase were preserved.*

Costume of a reasonably well-to-do Irishman of the first half of the seventeenth century. *He wore an Irish coat, plaid fitted trews, a semicircular cloak (not shown), shoes and a conical sheepskin hat. He carried a bag made of untanned leather which contained a ball of worsted.*

Glass bottle, County Kerry. *A rare example of one of the new glass manufactures of the seventeenth century.*

Two sugar casters. *They remained in the possession of the Sarsfields until recently. Makers' marks first began to be stamped on silver in Dublin by order of the Corporation in 1605. The hallmarking of silver began in 1637.*

GLOSSARY

ADZE   An axe-like tool on which the head is mounted so that the cutting edge is at right angles to the line of the haft or handle.

APSE   The semicircular or polygonal end of the CHANCEL of a church. The altar was normally placed on the chord of the apse.

ARD   A simple form of plough which works by drawing a pointed beam through the soil to scratch but not turn it. It was often necessary to plough the field a second time at right angles to the first ploughing. Such cross-ploughing frequently resulted in the development of square fields. The ard originated in Mediterranean lands, where it is still in use today.

ARTIFACT   A man-made object.

AUGER   A hand-tool for boring holes in wood, consisting of a bit with a cutting edge at the end of a long shank. A horizontal handle, at right angles to the shank, is rotated to cause the bit to turn in the wood.

AUROCHS   Species of wild ox (*Bos primigenius*).

BAR TORC   See TORC.

BARBICAN   An outwork defending the gate of a castle or city.

BAROQUE   A seventeenth- and in some places eighteenth-century style of ornament and architecture characterised by exuberant decoration and frequently by extreme, often pompous grandeur.

BAWN   The walled courtyard of a tower house, sometimes provided with corner towers for improved defence.

BEAKER POTTERY   A beaker is a drinking vessel. In archaeology the term 'Beaker pottery' refers to highly ornamented, flat-bottomed vessels, with a sinuous profile. In Ireland Beaker pottery, wristguards and other associated objects are common, but the classic Beaker burial is absent.

BRIDLE-BIT   The metal portion of the bridle, which is placed in the horse's mouth and to which the reins are attached.

BTU   British Thermal Unit: the amount of heat required to raise one pound of water one degree Fahrenheit.

BUFFER TORC   Decorative Celtic Iron Age neck-ring, whose terminals are flat, circular expansions facing one another like railway buffers.

BULLAUN   A stone on which one or more round depressions have been worn by grinding.

CAIRN   A heap or mound of stones.

CAP-HOUSE   A small roofed superstructure to a stair leading to a parapet.

CAPITAL   The head or crown of a column.

CASTING   The process of producing an artifact by pouring liquid material into a mould. Pottery was frequently produced in this way in Roman times, but the technique was most commonly used in the making of metal objects; the metal was heated and poured into the mould in molten form. In the earliest metallurgy in Ireland, simple, open stone moulds were used, but later bi-valve or two-piece moulds of stone enabled artificers to fabricate more complex shapes. Clay moulds, also two-piece and made by pressing models into wet clay and then baking it, came into use during the Later Bronze Age and remained in widespread use throughout the Early Medieval period. There is evidence for the use of lost-wax casting in ancient Ireland: a wax model of the required shape was prepared, then invested in clay and baked so that the clay hardened and the wax melted away through vents left for that purpose. Molten metal was then poured in to take the shape of the wax model.

CATECHUMEN   In the early Christian church, the name given to a person undergoing instruction in preparation for baptism.

CAUDLE-CUP or porringer   A cup, often with a lid and one or two handles, from which gruel might be drunk. They were popular in Britain from the seventeenth to the nineteenth century, and were generally made of silver or pewter.

CENTERING   Wooden framework used in arch and vault construction. It is removed when the mortar has set and the structure has become self-supporting. In Irish tower-houses and related constructions, the centering is often faced with WICKERWORK matting and the impressions of the rods are to be seen in the mortar of their vaults.

CHANCEL   Originally the area of a church immediately around the altar, but now generally the whole section of the building east of the nave and transepts, separated from the rest of the church by a screen or a railing. The chancel is normally reserved for the clergy and choir.

CHEVRON   A term derived from heraldry, meaning a bent bar. Used in archaeology to denote essentially a V- or inverted V-shape.

CIST   Usually pronounced 'kist'. A rectangular or polygonal stone-lined grave constructed either in or on the surface of the ground. If the latter, they are usually covered by a mound or cairn.

CLINKER-BUILT   Of boats, made with external planks overlapping downwards and fastened with clenched copper nails.

COAL MEASURES   See MEASURES

CODEX   A manuscript bound in the form of a book.

COPTIC   Pertaining to the language and form of Christianity of Egypt. The Coptic language is essentially that of the ancient Egyptians, heavily influenced by Greek. It was widely spoken from about the third to the tenth century AD, when it was supplanted by Arabic. It is still the liturgical language of the Coptic church.

CORBELLING   The process of building a false dome by laying courses of stone one on top of the other and overlapping inwards so that the gap is eventually narrowed and capable of being bridged by a single slab. The technique was used in Ireland to construct the roofs of some passage tomb chambers, SOUTERRAINS, churches and clocháns.

CORBEL   A block projecting from a wall, used to support a beam.

COULTER   A large iron blade, suspended vertically in front of the ploughshare to cut the sod.

CRANNOG   From the Irish word *crann*, meaning a tree. A dwelling on an artificial, or artificially enlarged, island.

CRETACEOUS   From the Greek word *creta*, meaning chalk. The period of laying down of sedimentary rocks, especially chalk, which marks the end of the Mesozoic or period of 'middle life'. The Cretaceous period lasted for around seventy-two million years, from about 136 to 64 million years ago. The chalks of County Antrim were laid down during this period.

CROMLECH   A megalithic tomb, consisting now of a large capstone resting on upright stones. The Breton word 'Dolmen' is the more common name; however, if this name is used it must be qualified. Cromlech is archaic and dolmen is seldom used in Irish archaeological classification.

CURTAIN WALL   The outer defensive wall of a castle.

CURVE   Borrowed from mathematics and used to indicate the rise and fall of values on a graph.

DENDROCHRONOLOGY   Dating by means of tree-rings.

DIRK   A medium-sized, dagger-type weapon of Bronze Age origin; the larger examples are referred to as rapiers.

DOLMEN   See CROMLECH

DONJON   The principal tower of a castle, normally free-standing, with living quarters. Also known as a keep.

EARTHWORKS   A structure made mainly of heaped earth, usually banks, ditches and mounds. Often used in a specialised sense to denote defensive works.

ENAMEL   A vitreous or glassy material applied in powdered form to a metal surface and then fixed in place by heat fusion. Colours are produced by adding metal oxides.

ESCUTCHEON   A term derived from heraldry, used to denote a decorative applied plate. On hanging bowls, normally the plate from which the suspension hooks spring.

EXTENT   In Medieval times, a survey of the demesne lands of a lord and his tenants, including valuations.

FAMILIA   From Latin, meaning 'family'. Used to describe the community of associated monasteries claiming a common founder. See also PARUCHIA

FEN   A marsh or low land, partly or wholly covered by shallow water.

FILIGREE   Ornaments formed of soldered wires, usually of gold or silver.

FORTALICE   A small fortress.

FOSSE   A ditch.

FULACHT FIA   An ancient cooking-place, usually indicated by a mound of burnt stones at the site of a trough. Irish sources describe the cooking of meat by boiling it in the trough in water which has been heated by means of hot stones. The plural is *fulachtaí fia*. Archaeologists generally prefer to use the non-committal term 'burnt mounds'.

GARDEROBE   The privy or latrine of a castle. Usually a small chamber from which a shaft leads downwards through the wall to the outside.

GORGET   A large gold collar consisting of a crescentic plate and terminals of composite discs, dating to the Later Bronze Age. The term is borrowed from the crescentic gorgets worn as insignia of rank by military officers in eighteenth-century European armies.

GOTHIC   The architecture of the pointed arch, rib vault and flying buttress used in combination with other features to produce a distinctive style in which walls are reduced to a minimum. It first appears fully fledged in the mid-twelfth century at the Abbey of St Denis, Paris, and was to dominate European architecture in various regional styles throughout the later Middle Ages. The term is also applied to the decorative arts of the period.

HALBERD   In Medieval times, a military weapon used by infantry, consisting of a combination of spear and axe mounted on the end of a long wooden shaft. In archaeology it refers to a weapon or utensil with a blade mounted at right angles on a wooden shaft. Such weapons were especially common in the Earlier Bronze Age of Ireland and Central Europe.

HAND AXE   A large stone tool, usually oval or pear-shaped, from both faces of which flakes have been removed. They range in size from about 9cm (3½in) to about 25cm (10in), and are typical of some early Palaeolithic (Old Stone Age) cultures. Only modern imports exist in Ireland.

HENGE   A type of ritual monument confined to Britain and Ireland, consisting of a circular enclosure of bank and ditch, with one or two entrances. Henges rang in size from about 45m (197ft) to about 520m (1706ft).

HILT   The handle of a sword or dagger.

HORIZONTAL MILL   The simplest mechanised watermill which uses a wheel in the horizontal plane which does not necessitate gearing.

IGNEOUS ROCK   Rock deposited in molten form, either extruded onto the earth's surface or intruded into other rocks forming the crust. In the case of the latter, they will only appear on the surface after the overlying rocks have been eroded.

INGOT   A quantity of metal, usually in the form of a brick or bar.

ISOTOPE   A component of a chemical element, distinguished from other components of the same element by, amongst other things, its radioactivity.

JAPANNING European imitations of oriental lacquer using substitutes, such as shellac, for the true ingredients. The colours used are usually black, dark green and red.

KARST A limestone landscape of fissures, caves and swallow holes, where the rock has been extensively dissolved by rain water. The Burren of County Clare is a karstic landscape.

KEEP See DONJON.

KNEE SHAFT A right-angled wooden shaft, the shorter arm of which is split for the insertion of an axehead. Side flanges and a stop-ridge and bindings secure the axehead in position. The technique of hafting was in vogue in the Earlier Bronze Age and part of the succeeding period. The PALSTAVE was especially adapted to this form of hafting.

LA TÈNE The distinctive abstract art style of later Celtic Europe and of Ireland and Britain, named after a great votive deposit at La Tène on Lake Neuchâtel in Switzerland. Curvilinear patterns are especially characteristic. In its early phase it assimilated and adapted motifs of Greek and Etruscan origin. The name is also applied to the second phase of the European Iron Age, from the mid-fifth century BC until the Roman conquest. In Ireland elements of La Tène culture are traceable well into Early Medieval times.

LATHE A tool designed to spin wood or metal so that it can be carved (wood) into circular shapes, pressed into shape or polished. The lathe in early Ireland was probably muscle-powered, using a cord or belt to turn a spindle. This would have been attached to a flexible overhead beam which was made to spring up and down by means of a treadle.

LIGHTS The openings of a window: a window divided by one MULLION has two lights, by two mullions has three lights, and so on.

LOOP (Architectural) A narrow, usually unglazed window: hence arrow-loop.

LUNULA Literally 'little moon'. A crescentic ornament of sheet gold, probably for the neck, fashionable in Ireland and Scotland in the Earlier Bronze Age.

MACHICOLATION A small gallery projecting on brackets from the outside of a castle wall, with apertures in the floor through which rocks or hot liquids may be dropped on attackers.

MANOR The demesne of a lord, together with any other lands over which he has rights. It is often used to denote the house of the lord.

MEASURES Originally a mining term (now obsolete) referring to layers of sedimentary rocks which could be measured by drilling; loosely used to mean bed of rock, hence 'Coal Measures'.

METAMORPHIC ROCK Rock which has been altered especially by heat in the zone around an intrusive igneous rock.

MICROLITHS Very small artifacts, normally of flint or chert, designed to be mounted in grooves in wooden hafts or, occasionally, as points. They are particularly characteristic of Mesolithic cultures in Europe.

MILLEFIORI In Early Medieval Ireland, a type of ornament made from bundles of coloured glass straws fused together by heat, showing a pattern when viewed in cross-section. Millefiori rods were cut into platelets, which were then sunk in the enamel fields of ornaments or mounted directly on decorative metalwork.

MONOLITH A single block of stone, especially one shaped or simply set up undressed as a pillar.

MORAINE An accumulation of debris carried and deposited by a glacier.

MULLION A vertical post or stone dividing a window into two or more LIGHTS.

MURDER-HOLE See MACHICOLATION

NAPPER A flint-worker.

NAVE The main body of a church between the front and the CHANCEL, assigned to the laity.

OD Ordnance Datum: the letters are used to denote that the level given for a point is related to that from which the Ordnance Survey measures all levels in Ireland. Ordnance Datum proper is the level of low spring tide at Dublin Bar on 8 April 1837.

OLD RED SANDSTONE A type of sedimentary rock composed mainly of sand stained a reddish colour by oxide of iron and laid down in the Devonian period about 395 to 345 million years ago.

ORDNANCE Artillery.

OSSUARY A repository for bones. Frequently found in cemeteries where it was common practice to remove bones from graves after a period and place them in a specially constructed chamber.

OUBLIETTE A secret chamber reached from a trapdoor above.

OUTCROP The emergence of rock at the surface.

OUTWORK Any detached or advanced structure forming part of the defences of a place.

OXIDATION Combining chemically with oxygen. Rusting of iron, for example, is caused by oxidation, and rust itself is an oxide of iron. When pottery is fired in a kiln to which oxygen has access, it tends to turn a reddish colour.

PALAEOZOIC A geological period whose rocks contain fossils of the most ancient life forms.

PALE, THE The district comprising parts of the modern counties of Louth, eastern Meath, Dublin and parts of Kildare, over which the crown of England held effective control in the later Middle Ages. It was in part at least delimited by a double ditch and bank. The term was also applied to the English-controlled areas around Calais in France.

PALISADE A fence of stakes, especially a feature of defensive works.

PALSTAVE A form of bronze axehead with high side flanges and stop ridge, designed to be mounted in a split knee-shaft. Often equipped with a loop, sometimes two, for binding thongs to help secure the head more firmly. Palstaves were common in Ireland towards the end of the Earlier Bronze Age and the beginning of the Later Bronze Age. They were widespread in contemporary Europe.

PANTILE A pottery roofing tile.

PARUCHIA Of Irish monasticism, a term used to denote a loose federation of monasteries, usually with a common founder. It is not clear how paruchiae functioned, or if they had a corporate function. They cannot be regarded as the equivalent of regular religious orders. See also FAMILIA.

PENANNULAR An incomplete ring. Used especially to describe Early Medieval ring brooches in which there is a gap in the ring to enable a free-swivelling pin to pass through.

PERPENDICULAR STYLE An English version of the GOTHIC style, it emphasises vertical and horizontal lines and is restrained in its decoration. It was developed in the mid-fourteenth century and continued to influence building design until the earlier sixteenth century. Few examples of the style are known in Ireland.

PLINTH The lower square member of a column, often used to denote a platform on which a statue or other sculpture is placed.

POLING The stirring of molten metal or glass with a pole of green wood in order to reduce its oxygen content.

PORRINGER See CAUDLE-CUP.

PORTAL A door or doorway, gate or gateway of elaborate and imposing construction.

PORTCULLIS A gate of iron or (iron-reinforced) wooden bars made to slide up and down in grooves in the doorway of a castle.

POST-HOLE A hole dug in the ground to set a wooden post. These can be recognised in archaeological excavations by the different colour and texture of the soil within the ancient hole compared with that surrounding it.

POT QUERN See QUERN.

PURLIN Horizontal beam running along length of roof, resting on principals and supporting common rafters or boards.

PYROCLASTIC ROCK Igneous rock of a fragmented character formed by volcanic eruption, when it was explosively ejected either in a solid form or a liquid which cooled in the air.

QUERN A stone device for grinding corn by hand. *Saddle querns* are stones frequently worn to a convex shape by the action of rubbing cereal grains on them with a flattish stone in order to crush and grind them. The *rotary quern* operated by causing a circular upper stone to rotate on a fixed lower one and so grind corn poured through a central hole in the upper stone. Rotary querns remained in use in Ireland into modern times. *Pot querns* were small rotary querns, with a small upper stone which rotated within a dished lower stone with a pronounced lip.

RETAINERS Followers and dependants of a lord.

REVETMENT Retaining wall or facing.

RING BARROW A somewhat imprecise term, but essentially a circular burial structure in which a mound is enclosed by a bank and ditch or fosse ('barrow' is an old English term for a mound). In Ireland the term is frequently restricted to diminutive Iron Age burial monuments in which, by cutting a small ditch, the builders created a low platform of undisturbed ground in the middle. The spoil from the ditch was cast up outside to form a low outer bank. However, few of these have been excavated and published and the terminology is far from settled.

ROMANESQUE Essentially the architecture of the round arch. The style, which was widespread in Europe, preceded the GOTHIC.

ROTARY QUERN See QUERN.

SADDLE QUERN See QUERN.

SCRAPER Of flint, an implement interpreted as having been used for scraping, for example in the preparation of hides or in smoothing wood.

SEDIMENTARY ROCK Rock formed by the deposition of materials in water.

SHOT-HOLES Loops through which guns were fired.

SOFFIT The undersurface of a lintel, arch or vault.

SHERD Of pottery, a piece of broken pottery.

SOUTERRAIN An underground structure, normally consisting of one or more passages and chambers, often containing obstructions or traps for defence. Usually of drystone construction, but examples that are partly rock-cut, partly of timber, or wholly or partly tunnelled in unsupported clay are known. They were probably also used for storage. Common in Ireland in Early Medieval times, but also found in Scotland and Cornwall.

STOCKADE A defensive enclosure made of closely set stakes.

STRATUM Layer.

TOGHER A roadway across a bog.

TORC An ornament of twisted metal (from the Latin *torquere*, meaning to twist). Usually in the form of neck ornaments, armlets, finger-rings, earrings and girdles. *Ribbon torcs* are made of twisted strip gold; *bar torcs* comprise rods or bars of simple or complex cross-section. Torcs were common in Ireland in the first phase of the Later Bronze Age. Ribbon torcs were made at that time and also much later in the Iron Age.

TRACERY The ornamental intersecting of the stonework of the upper part of a window, panel or screen.

TRANSOM A horizontal bar of wood or stone across a window or panel.

TRENCHER SALT A small seventeenth- or eighteenth-century salt cellar in the form of a block of metal, usually silver, or pottery, with a hollow on its upper surface for the salt. Intended for the use of a single person.

TUMULUS Mound.

WATTLE Flexible stick used for interlacing with others to form walls, screens and the like.

WICKERWORK The weaving together of pliable twigs or sticks, especially of willow, to form baskets, mats, fencing, etc.

RECOMMENDED READING

The following recommendations for further reading are not intended to be exhaustive, but are aimed at giving a starting point from which the reader can go on to develop an interest in the subject as a whole or in a particular area. The publications listed all carry extensive bibliographies of more specialised and detailed works.

GENERAL

Barry, T. *The Archaeology of Medieval Ireland*, Routledge, London, 1987.

Bradley, J. (ed). *Settlement and Society in Medieval Ireland*, Boethius Press, Kilkenny, 1988.

Craig, M. *The Architecture of Ireland from the Earliest Times to 1880*, Batsford and Eason, London/Dublin, 1982.

De Paor, M. and L. *Early Christian Ireland*, Thames and Hudson, London, 1958.

Dunlevy, M. *Dress in Ireland*, Batsford, London, 1989.

Edwards, N. *The Archaeology of Early Medieval Ireland*, Batsford, London, 1990.

Flanagan, L. *Ulster*, Heinemann, London, 1970.

Flanagan, L. *A Dictionary of Irish Archaeology*, Gill and Macmillan, Dublin, 1992.

Harbison, P. *Pre-Christian Ireland*, Thames and Hudson, London, 1988.

Harbison, P. *A Guide to the National and Historic Monuments of Ireland*, Gill and Macmillan, Dublin, 1992.

Herity, M. *Irish Passage Graves*, Harper and Row, New York, 1975.

Herity, M. and Eogan, G. *Ireland in Prehistory*, Routledge and Kegan Paul, London, 1977.

Leask, H. *Irish Churches and Monastic Buildings*, 3 vols, Dun Dealgan Press, Dundalk, reprinted 1977–8.

MacNiocaill, G. and Wallace, P. (eds). *Keimelia Studies in Memory of Tom Delaney*, University Press, Galway, 1988.

Mallory, J. and McNeill, T. *The Archaeology of Ulster from Colonization to Plantation*, Queen's University, Belfast, 1991.

Mitchell, F. *The Shell Guide to Reading the Irish Landscape*, Country House, Dublin, 1986, 1990.

Mitchell, F. *et al. The Book of the Irish Countryside*, Blackstaff/Town House, Belfast and Dublin, 1987.

Ó Corráin, D. (ed). *Irish Antiquity: Essays and Studies presented to Professor M J O'Kelly*, Tower Books, Cork, 1981.

Ó Riordáin, S. P. *Antiquities of the Irish Countryside*, 5th edn, revised by Ruaidhrí De Valera, Methuen, London/New York, 1979.

O'Kelly, M. J. *Early Ireland*, University Press, Cambridge, 1989.

Ryan, M. (ed). *The Origins of Metallurgy in Atlantic Europe*, Stationery Office, Dublin, 1979.

Ryan, M. (ed). *Ireland and Insular Art AD 500–1200*, Royal Irish Academy, Dublin, 1987.

Ryan, M. (ed). *Treasures of Ireland: Irish Art 3000 BC–1500 AD*, Royal Irish Academy, Dublin, 1983.

Ryan, M. *Early Ireland: Culture and Treasures*, An Post, Dublin, 1991.

Rynne, C. *The Archaeology of Cork City and Harbour from the Earliest Times to Industrialisation*, Collins Press, Cork, 1993.

Rynne, E. (ed). *North Munster Studies*, Limerick, 1967.

Rynne, E. (ed). *Figures from the Past: Studies on Figurative Art in Christian Ireland in honour of Helen M Roe*, Glendale Press/Royal Society of Antiquaries of Ireland, Dublin, 1987.

Scarry, J./Office of Public Works. *Monuments in the Past: Photographs 1870–1936*, Stationery Office, Dublin, 1991.

Scott, B. (ed). *Studies on Early Ireland Essays in honour of Michael Duignan*, Association of Young Irish Archaeologists, Belfast, 1981.

Scott, B. G. *Early Irish Ironworking*, Ulster Museum, Belfast, 1991.

Spearman, R. M. and Higgitt, J. (eds). *The Age of Migrating Ideas: Early Medieval Art in North Britain and Ireland*, National Museum of Scotland, Edinburgh, 1993.

SPECIAL TOPICS

Prehistoric:

Brindley, A. *An Introduction to Prehistory in Ireland*, Country House/National Museum of Ireland, Dublin, 1994.

De Valera, R. and Ó Nualláin, S. *Survey of Megalithic Tombs of Ireland*, vols 1–, Ordnance Survey, Dublin, 1961 (continuing).

Eogan, G. *Hoards of the Irish Later Bronze Age*, University College, Dublin, 1983.

Eogan, G. *Knowth and the Passage Tombs of Ireland*, Thames and Hudson, London, 1986.

Kelly, E. *Early Celtic Art in Ireland*, Town House/National Museum, Dublin, 1993.

O'Kelly, M. J. *Newgrange*, Thames and Hudson, London, 1982.

O'Sullivan, M. and Scarry, J. *Megalithic Art in Ireland*, Country House, Dublin, 1993.

Raftery, B. *La Tène in Ireland: Problems of Origin and Chronology*, Vorgeschtliches Seminar, Marburg, 1984.

Raftery, B. *Trackways Through Time*, Headline, Rush, 1990.

Shee Twohig, E. *The Megalithic Art of Western Europe*, Clarendon Press, Oxford, 1981.

Waddell, J. *The Bronze Age Burials of Ireland*, University Press, Galway, 1990.

Early Medieval:

Alexander, J. *Insular Illuminated Manuscripts 6th to the 9th century*, Harvey Miller, London, 1978.

Bourke, C. *Patrick: the Archaeology of a Saint*, HMSO, Belfast, 1993.

Byrne, F. J. *Irish Kings and High-Kings*, London, 1973.

Hughes, K. and Hamlin, A. *The Modern Traveller to the Early Irish Church*, SPCK, London, 1977.

Harbison, P. *The High Crosses of Ireland*, Dr Rudolf Habelt GMBH, Bonn, 1992.

Henry, F. *Irish High Crosses*, Cultural Relations Committee, Dublin, 1964.

Henry, F. *Irish Art in the Early Christian Period to AD 800*, Methuen, London, 1964.

Henry, F. *Irish Art During the Viking Invasions 800–1020 AD*, Methuen, London, 1967.

Henry, F. *Irish Art in the Romanesque Period 1020–1170 AD*, Methuen, London, 1970.

Kelly, F. *A Guide to Early Irish Law*, Institute for Advanced Studies, Dublin, 1988.

MacNiocaill, G. *Ireland Before the Vikings*, Gill and Macmillan, Dublin, 1972.

Ó Corrain, D. *Ireland Before the Normans*, Gill and Macmillan, Dublin, 1972.

Ó Floinn, R. *Irish Shrines and Reliquaries of the Middle Ages*, Country House/National Museum of Ireland, Dublin, 1994.

O'Neill, T. P. *The Irish Hand*, Dolmen Press, Mountrath, 1984.

Ryan, M. *Early Irish Communion Vessels: Church Treasures of the Golden Age*, National Museum of Ireland, Dublin, 1985.

Ryan, M. (ed). *The Derrynaflan Hoard I: A Preliminary Account*, National Museum of Ireland, Dublin, 1983.

Ryan, M. *Metal Craftsmanship in Early Ireland*, Country House, Dublin, 1993.

Youngs, S. (ed). *The Work of Angels: Masterpieces of Celtic Metalwork, 6th to 9th centuries*, British Museum, London, 1989.

Stalley, R. *Irish High Crosses*, Eason, Dublin, 1991.

Later Medieval and Early Modern:

Barry, T. *Medieval Moated Sites of SE Ireland*, British Archaeological Reports 35, Oxford, 1977.

Canny, N. *From Reformation to Restoration 1534–1660*, Helicon, Dublin, 1987.

Cosgrove, A. (ed). *Medieval Ireland 1169–1534*, University Press, Oxford, 1993.

Ellis, S. *Tudor Ireland Crown, Community and the Conflict of Cultures 1470–1603*, Longman, London, 1985.

Hunt, J. *Irish Medieval Figure Sculpture*, Irish University Press/Sotheby Park Bernet, Dublin/London, 1974.

Johnson, D. *The Irish Castle*, Irish Heritage Series, Eason, Dublin, 1981.

Lydon, J. *Ireland in the Later Middle Ages*, Gill and Macmillan, Dublin, 1973.

MacCurtain, M. *Tudor and Stuart Ireland*, Gill and Macmillan, Dublin, 1972.

Nicholls, K. *Gaelic and Gaelicised Ireland in the Middle Ages*, Gill and Macmillan, Dublin, 1972.

Stalley, R. *Architecture and Sculpture in Ireland 1150–1350*, Dublin, 1971.

Stalley, R. *The Cistercian Monasteries of Ireland*, Yale University Press, New Haven, 1987.

Periodicals and Series:

The greater part of Irish archaeological work is published in the journals of various scholarly institutions and national and local societies. The societies welcome applications for membership and maintain active programmes of lectures and field trips. The principal periodicals for Irish archaeology are: *Proceedings of the Royal Irish Academy*, Section C, *Peritia (Journal of the Medieval Academy of Ireland)*, *The Journal of the Royal Society of Antiquaries of Ireland*, *The Journal of Irish Archaeology*, *The Ulster Journal of Archaeology*, *The Journal of the Cork Historical and Archaeological Society*, *The North Munster Antiquarian Journal*, and the *County Louth Archaeological Journal*. Internationally, the *Proceedings of the Prehistoric Society*, *Antiquity*, *Medieval Archaeology* and *The Antiquaries Journal* frequently publish material of Irish interest. Most good libraries will either have these journals or will be able to order them for you. The quarterly magazine *Archaeology Ireland* provides up-to-date articles on archaeological topics, news of recent developments, and reviews publications.

Important series are the volumes of the *Archaeological Survey* published by the Office of Public Works, Dublin; the *Transactions* of the Irish Archaeological Wetlands Unit published jointly by the Office of Public Works and University College, Dublin. The reports of the *Discovery Programme* are published by the Royal Irish Academy. The series *American Early Medieval Studies* (Oxford, Ohio) has published a substantial amount of Irish interest material in its first two volumes.

INDEX

Note: Archaeological periods are in bold. References to the illustrations are not included in the index. For these, please see the List of Illustrations.